☑ P9-EMB-866

WHOLE LANGUAGE:
GETTING STARTED . . .
MOVING FORWARD

by

Linda K. Crafton

RICHARD C. OWEN PUBLISHERS, INC.
KATONAH, NEW YORK

Library of Congress Cataloging-in-Publication Data

Crafton, Linda K.
    Whole language : getting started . . . moving forward / Linda K. Crafton.
        p.   cm.
    Includes bibliographical references and index.
    ISBN 0-913461-19-9
    1. Language experience approach in education.   2. Teacher-student
relationships.   I. Title.
    LB1576.C757   1991
    372.4—dc20   90-7977
                                                                  CIP

Photographs courtesy of Penny Silvers, Barbara Lindberg, Pat Miller, and Carol Porter. Photographs for back cover and Chapter Two by Karen Rodgers.

Richard C. Owen Publishers, Inc.
PO Box 585
Katonah, New York 10536

Book design by Kenneth J. Hawkey

Printed in the United States of America

9 8 7 6 5 4

**To Paul and Samantha
with love**

Foreword

Several years ago Dr. Linda Crafton asked if we would be keynote speakers at the first Chicago TAWL (Teachers Applying Whole Language) Conference. There was a catch. She could offer no honorarium as she was not sure how many teachers would show up and the Chicago TAWL group was new—and broke.

Having had a long personal relationship with Dr. Crafton, in that she did her advanced graduate work with us at Indiana University, we found her invitation impossible to turn down.

The day of the conference arrived. We were all anxious but we needn't have been. Over 500 teachers showed up! They all either knew or had heard of Dr. Crafton. They all wanted either to get started or to move forward.

Now, some five years later, Chicago's TAWL Conference is even larger and Dr. Linda Crafton's reputation as a whole language consultant has spread.

Whole Language: Getting Started . . . Moving Forward is designed for two audiences: The first, teachers who are just getting started; the second, teachers who have started but are now ready to move forward. Regardless of which group you are in, there are only two prerequisites for becoming a whole language teacher: curiosity and commitment. Curiosity begins the learning process. Commitment sustains it.

One of the underlying principles of whole language is that *no one becomes literate without becoming personally involved in literacy.* This is a far different hypothesis than one that suggests that we become literate by "phonicating" our way into literacy as was true of our old phonics programs, or one that suggests that we know what to teach, in what sequence, before we ever meet a child as is true of basal reader programs.

As teachers, the principle that everyone becomes literate through personal involvement in literacy means that we need to discover the ways children are already literate and support as well as extend what they are doing. This is at once obvious and yet a real basic in whole language. It's why whole language is a philosophy and not a method. If we, as educators, are to grow in literacy we, too, must get personally involved. If we don't our arguments about supporting literacy stagnate.

As a tenet *No one becomes literate without personally getting involved in literacy* captures the pulse of this book as well as of the whole language movement. Whole language is an attempt to get teachers and children in personal touch with the basic processes of reading and writing and teaching and learning. Whole language teachers take what they currently know to set up supportive language learning environments and then use this setting to learn more about children, language and how to support language use and learning. When seen from this perspective both the whole language movement and *Whole Language: Getting Started . . . Moving Forward* are about personal learning and personal curriculum or what Dr. Crafton calls "connected teaching" and "connected learning."

Learning, for each of us, is a process of finding patterns that connect. In *Whole Language: Getting Started . . . Moving Forward,* Dr. Crafton demonstrates how whole language connects children and teachers, home and school, theory and practice, teaching and learning, as well as how what you are doing now connects with what you will be doing tomorrow to improve the teaching of reading and the language arts.

The personal nature of learning and whole language is why some people say that whole language is a theory of voice. In addition to the voices of children and parents we hear from seven Chicago-area teachers who tell how they took whole language and made it their own. The portraits they paint illustrate the connections they made and demonstrate that there is no one way to do whole language. The portraits they paint invite teachers who don't believe it will work in their schools to make connections and begin.

In this volume Dr. Linda Crafton and the teachers with whom she collaborated share their stories of getting started and moving forward. Theirs are messages of hope, of history, of invitation, and of basics. We join the authors in hoping that readers, too, see it as the stuff from which new worlds for children and teachers can be built.

Jerome C. Harste
Carolyn L. Burke
Indiana University
Bloomington, IN

Preface

In the past few years, the number of books about whole language has skyrocketed. When I began this book two years ago, there were already many creditable descriptions of whole language classrooms. I recommended many of them and listed them on the bibliographies I circulated, but the one thing that was missing for me was one book that highlighted each critical dimension of whole language teaching while helping to develop a *personal* theory/practice connection. I wanted a book that provided a strong vision for whole language while remaining sensitive to the realities of the classroom. And I wanted to be able to hand the same book to both novice and veteran whole language teachers and say: "There's something here for each of you."

Each chapter in *Whole Language: Getting Started . . . Moving Forward* emphasizes the individual choices teachers can make while maintaining a common learning perspective. The first two chapters of the book provide the larger setting for whole language curriculum while giving specific examples of its application. The chapters on "The Role of the Teacher" and "Inquiry and Integration" encourage teachers to find connections to themselves and their students so that personal interest and community support form the basis for learning. The chapters on "Management" and "Ownership" present alternative ways to organize whole language classrooms while sharing content and process decisions with students. Chapters Seven and Eight, "Evaluation" and "Other Realities," discuss the many ways whole language teachers have handled some of the thorniest problems related to assessment, parents, administrators, and basals.

Part II of the book highlights the idea of personal transition by presenting a number of "Small Changes that Make a Big Difference" and twenty-five "Whole Language Strategies" that teachers can try out and adapt to their own situations. "First Days, First Weeks" tells the individual stories of seven teachers and the ways they establish themselves and their classrooms at the beginning of each school year. The book ends with a "Personal Change Plan" which presents all of the critical dimensions related to whole language and encourages teachers to explore them based on their own needs.

Teachers have so many complex realities to deal with—parents, tests, reluctant students, discipline, time management. A useful book on whole language has to recognize and deal with those realities while supporting a new level of professional awareness. *Whole Language: Getting Started . . . Moving Forward* provides an image of a whole language ideal while demonstrating through teachers' eyes how that image can come to life. This is a book about classrooms and teachers and theory in action.

Whole Language: Getting Started . . . Moving Forward is a book that teachers can begin with and go back to year after year, transition after transition. The literature is beginning to fill with profiles and case studies of teachers' professional evolutions. Adopting, adapting and creating are terms that Andrea Butler uses to describe these 'stages' of development. Adopting is characterized by borrowing others' ideas and trying them out in the same form; adapting refers to changes teachers make based on personal style, grade level considerations and student interest; creating underscores the truly collaborative nature of whole language in which teachers and students develop curriculum and community together.

These labels *do* represent quite different passages in a whole language teacher's life—we all change as we gather knowledge and confidence. But there is an underlying mechanism that slides teachers forward. Constant reflection on what is and what can be is the primary tool of transition. If we miss this reflexive part, we can, like the tin man, be rusted into one position for "oh, the longest time." What can *be* resides in the understanding of whole language as a theory of learning. What is *now* depends on trying out good ideas and strategies and making them your own. This book was written to help teachers deal with the present and the future.

Acknowledgments

The ideas in this book began with my introduction to Carolyn Burke over ten years ago. Not long after I met Carolyn, Jerry Harste steamrolled his way into my life. Their early mentoring and long-term support have made a world of difference to me and my professional development. My first heartfelt thanks goes to them.

My second thank you goes to a wonderful group of teachers who entered my life many years ago. Most of them were my students and all have long since become colleagues and friends. They have enriched me personally and professionally and I am indebted to them for their contributions to this book. More times than I can count, I called Carol Porter, Kathleen Visovatti, Pat Riordan, Barbara Lindberg, Penny Silvers, Pat Miller, and Dan Powers to press them for new writing, revisions or 'just one last thing' to meet my newest, self-imposed deadline. They never blinked, they never complained, they only smiled and did what I asked. I am enormously grateful to all of them for their patience, their giving of themselves and their classrooms, and, most of all, for being *professionals* who continually demonstrate the incredible joy and satisfaction that whole language brings to teachers and kids.

I never guessed that reviewers could have such an impact on my thinking. Nancy Bertrand, Shirley Crenshaw, Debra Jacobson, and Virginia Pierce went through my early manuscript in great detail and gave their most thoughtful responses. Their comments came at a time when I was frustrated and ready, too early, to call it a book. I want to thank them for their time and insights. They strengthened my resolve to hang in there.

I am grateful to Richard Owen for believing in my work from its inception and to Susan Goldberg who has to be the most organized, meticulous project editor any author could have.

And, finally, of course, my family. The sacrifices it takes to write steadily over a long period of time do not belong solely to an author. My husband, Paul Katz, never complained of the long nights and lost weekends. Instead, he encouraged and worried and waited patiently for it to be over. Now that it is, I want to thank him lovingly for all of his support and for the things he never said that would have made a hard job even harder. And, to my daughter, Samantha, I am grateful for the times her laugh, her demands to play, and her emergent literacy pulled me away from my desk and helped me remember one of the reasons I wanted to write a book in the first place.

L.K.C.

Contents

Introduction

In the ten years I have been talking with teachers about whole language the questions I have been asked most often are: "I like the idea, but how do I get started?", and "I have a few whole language activities in place, but how do I move forward?". What has surprised me most about these questions is that they have often followed an in-service focused on those very concerns. Even when I think I have answered the questions, described the theory, demonstrated strategies, set up personal learning experiences, the questions are often there—loudly, tensely, predictably there. Perhaps when they come, the construction of the larger theoretical picture has occurred too quickly, or maybe the personal experiences don't carry the expected persuasive power or, maybe there just isn't enough time to soothe the inevitable feelings of anxiety, not enough ways to say: "It's important to go ahead, to continue to take steps, whether it is your first or your tenth, important even if you feel nervous or think you don't know enough. Even a small change can make a big difference in teaching and in learning. The pieces will begin to fall into place. Just get started and keep going."

Professional change can begin at a snail's pace or shoot forward like a racehorse out of a starting gate. Ultimately, however, change is a complex business. *Whole Language: Getting Started . . . Moving Forward* is about beginning and continuing as a whole language teacher. This kind of change is not just a professional transition, it is a deeply personal one, too. Whole language is not just about language, not just about teaching; it is a way of thinking about people and how they best grow—in every sense of the word. A change in your classroom will inevitably mean a deep change in you.

Along with the questions about getting started and moving forward, I often get protests about too much theory. Those comments seem to be increasing as whole language becomes more and more institutionalized in the profession. Teachers feel they know what whole langauge is and they just want to move forward with the application. It's an understandable position to take for educators who are constantly under the gun to prove themselves. But while many parts of this book answer the immediate questions about what to do tomorrow, it is also a book committed to the belief that the best long-term professional change occurs when teachers consistently move into practice based on theory.

When I first encountered whole language a decade ago veteran theorist/ practitioners like Ken Goodman, Yetta Goodman, and Frank Smith were just beginning to focus on writing process and the social dimensions of learning. They were using new theory to direct their changing perceptions of language and learning; they were using instructional and real-world research to refine their philosophical stances. For all professionals, theory and practice are inseparable. They form a tight, strong bond from the beginning, even when the practitioner is not that aware of their symbiotic nature.

As you initiate (or continue) your own change toward a more holistic curriculum, keeping the basic principles underlying whole language instruction close at hand can make the difference between a steady change that leads to a solid, theoretically consistent curriculum and a halting start that goes nowhere. In the end you want your classroom to be more than a collection of new and interesting activities.

When I decided to write this book I asked six practicing whole language teachers at different grade levels to join me. Because I believe whole language theory has practical implications for all learners, the book needed to be broad-based. Some of these teachers are still in the early years of "getting started," but most of them got started with whole language a long time ago and continue to move forward every year. Nevertheless, in a real sense, they must start all over again each fall with a new group of students, building new communities, creating new curriculum. Through their writing, these teachers share with you the initial parts of their transitions, how they literally get started with whole language each year, and what their process-based curriculums look like. Most critically, they let you into their heads and their hearts as they discuss instructional decisions that make the teaching work.

These teachers, including myself, represent a range of experience and personalities. Some have declared they "couldn't stand the noise" (and now don't think there is much learning going on without it). One teacher feels the philosophical foundation was always a part of her instructional mindset, while another slowly embraced the theory and even more slowly released her grip on her beloved teacher's manual. Several of these teachers painfully made the change alone while one has been part of a schoolwide evolution. Their histories and their versions of whole language are all unique, but they share the same vision for themselves as professionals and for their students as educated, literate people able to deal effectively with a complex world. Whatever their profiles, they bring to this writing and to their teaching a commitment, as you do, to a pedagogy firmly anchored in the best knowledge we have about language, learning, and kids. As you read the chapters, you will get to know them.

Pat Riordan is a first-grade teacher in one of the most culturally diverse schools in Chicago. Pat tried whole language when she first started to teach many years

ago, but she was constrained by a traditional setting. Now Pat is responsible for initiating a schoolwide K–8 change to whole language in her school.

Kathleen Visovatti is a second-grade teacher who has gained a local reputation as a model whole language teacher. Parents, administrators, and peers truck in and out of her classroom to view the dynamic learning environment she has created for herself and her students. Past students come regularly from the upper grades to visit and to ask why she doesn't teach anything besides second grade.

Pat Miller is a third/fourth-grade teacher in an economically depressed area. Pat has developed her notions of process learning through her work in math, as well as reading, writing, and the content areas. Because she is so skilled at focusing on students' existing and developing strengths, she and her students consider their classroom filled with experts in areas as diverse as dog training and rainbows.

Penny Silvers is an elementary school reading resource teacher, literacy consultant, and teacher leader. Penny was a strongly traditional reading teacher before she discovered whole language. Now she is one of the most respected whole language professionals in her geographic area. She not only shares her impressive knowledge base with her students but with other in-service teachers as well by teaching graduate courses and by organizing seminars for teachers getting started with whole language instruction.

Dan Powers is a sixth/seventh/eighth-grade language arts teacher. Dan started his whole language program with writing process and expanded his curricular ideas from there. Seeing—and feeling—many of the problems with traditional instruction he moved quickly to set up a student-centered classroom while transforming his own role in the classroom. Dan has become a skilled facilitator of his students' learning, while they have the freedom to read and write and think about topics that excite them.

Barbara Lindberg is a junior high remedial reading teacher in a suburban school. For years Barbara described herself as a "closet" whole language teacher, closing her door to set up the kind of curriculum that empowered her reluctant reader/ writers. Her years of careful reflection, change, and independent learning have, in the end, empowered *her.* She now shares her thinking through articles published in professional journals, district workshops, and state conferences.

Carol Porter is a high school reading/writing lab teacher. Carol began her transition to whole language as a junior high school reading teacher and recently moved to a high school setting. In this book she shares experiences from both schools. Carol is always checking her instructional decisions against a philosophical base that grows stronger with each article she writes, each collaborative research study she completes, and each professional presentation she makes.

When I invited these teachers to write with me I asked them first to consider, in an open-ended way, their own whole language stories. As the book progressed, I asked for more specific writing, writing that highlighted areas of strength and expertise, writing that would picture their students and their classrooms directly for you. While most of these chapters can stand alone, I've tried to weave the contributors' writing across chapters so you can get a strong sense of them as individuals who share a common philosophy. You will "hear" them talk about the first changes they made in their classrooms, the obstacles they encountered—and still encounter—how they get started at the beginning of each school year, how they set the tone for a trusting learning environment, how they build a sense of community, what strategies they have found to be most productive, how they ensure that those fragile first weeks lay a strong foundation for the rest of the year, and how they become learners in their own classrooms.

Both beginning and continuing with whole language means understanding the basis for the practice, jumping in and trying out new ideas, looking for individual ways to apply the theory, and adapting what other people are doing to your situation. Whether a novice or a veteran, whole language means an ongoing personal evolution. It is not only about changing the way you teach; it is about changing what you believe and who you are. The scope of this book is intentionally wide-ranging so that readers can enter at different points, so you can find where the theory and practice fit *you,* as well as the other way around.

When you walk into whole language classrooms you see various surface manifestations of a common theory. Much like the multiple routes to comprehension, teachers have different starting points and proceed along different paths to achieve a common purpose. Your whole language classroom *will* look different from that of the teacher next door, the teacher in the next school district. It's a point with which to relax, an understanding from which to draw personal strength.

—L.C.

BECOMING A WHOLE LANGUAGE TEACHER: WHAT CHANGES

Part

The Essence of
the Change

1

This is a wonderfully exciting time as teachers reclaim their classrooms and experience the joy of interacting in genuine ways with their students. But it's also a time of confusion for many teachers. "I think there's room for a little bit of everything," I was told by the thousandth unsmiling teacher just a while ago. The "unsmile" becomes a permanent frown when, hearing the rumble of a quiet revolution (Harste, Woodward, Burke, 1984), teachers try to add a few new activities to an already overcrowded curriculum. Then a little of everything translates into more of the same.

There is, in fact, a world of difference between traditional, product-oriented, teacher-controlled pedagogy and whole language. Compared to more traditional teaching whole language is student-centered, process-driven, and language-based. Whole language and traditional teaching exist as philosophical opposites, standing in stark contrast to one another. Illinois Writing Project Co-Directors, Steve Zemelman and Harvey Daniels (1988), put it this way:

> If I, as a teacher, spend the class period telling you rules for good writing, I am doing something profoundly different from what I do if I engage you as an active participant in a writing workshop, a growing community of writers. These are not minor differences of pedagogical styles; they are the essence of the matter (p. 12).

If you look around you'll see that there are many efforts to convince you that without much thought you can simply combine traditional and whole language teaching: a phonics program hiding behind a "Literature First" title, a workshop persuading you that you can learn to be a whole language teacher step by step—in five days!—or a basal program that now includes a writing process kit. Becoming a whole language teacher is not about making a few minor shifts, adding a little literature here and a little process there. It's about changing your teaching foundation, re-examining your role in the classroom, and reflecting on what is central to effective learning. It is a major transition for most teachers, but it doesn't have to be an overwhelming one. You can enter the world of whole language teaching with one decision, a shift in attitude, a choice about who you talk to or what professional material you read; but a sustained and substantive change means an awareness of a set of beliefs that guide whole language teachers.

GUIDING PRINCIPLES

The interest in whole language has focused on a re-definition of reading and writing. In actuality whole language applies to all areas of the curriculum, content learning as well as literacy learning. *All* teaching is grounded in assumptions about how people learn. Understanding the assumptions that you are currently making and the ones that whole language teachers in general make is a critical first step in getting started.

There are six principles related to language and learning that capture the whole of whole language for me. These are the pillars that whole language teachers embrace, the ones they keep protectively at their sides as they gather strength and consistency in their teaching. These ideas guide veteran and novice whole language teachers and inform professionals at all stages of transition. In fact, moving forward often depends on revisiting these critical curricular dimensions. They will tell you if your instructional decisions are consistent; they will help you see the gaps in your curriculum. In one form or another these principles have been developed, researched, and discussed by major interdisciplinary scholars. Primary among them are Carolyn Burke, Ken Goodman, Yetta Goodman, Donald Graves, Jerry Harste, Shirley Brice Heath, Judith Newman, Frank Smith, Lev Vygotsky, and Gordon Wells. The general applications presented immediately after each principle below begin to highlight their interwoven nature.

I know some of you will be tempted to skip this section, to quickly go on to something more specifically "practical." And, because you have pressing instructional questions, for now and for tomorrow, that's understandable. But the answers for now and for tomorrow begin here, because they reside largely in the principles themselves. These ideas not only inform you about the potential rightness of a particular instructional procedure, they also help you determine the flaws, why something didn't work, and what you can do to make it more effective. Theory isn't something only college professors think about. It is the conscious set of beliefs that drives every practical issue in the classroom. Theory *is* practice. For that reason the practical part of the book begins now.

PRINCIPLE 1: ORAL AND WRITTEN LANGUAGE DEVELOP WHOLE-TO-PART

This is probably the principle most closely associated with whole language. The notion of whole-to-part literacy development has its genesis in what we know about how children learn to speak. From birth, young children deal with language wholes. Parents speak to communicate whole meanings and strain to hear wholeness in their children's early speech. A baby's introduction to language comes in a complex whole with form and grammar and meaning operating at the same time. Child language research shows that parents maintain a steady stream of speech as they care for their children and introduce them to a wide, new world. Bits and pieces of language in isolation would baffle young children, but they are not put off by the intricate relationships within even a brief segment of ongoing conversation. In fact, they are drawn to the give and take, the inherent socialness of people talking to each other. It's inviting to them and they are quick to join in, sorting out the parts as they attempt to communicate wholes.

Our brains, we have learned, prefer the complex to the simple. Now our research, pioneered by Ken Goodman's miscue work, is confirming a well-grounded, multidisciplinary theory: *We learn things naturally and best when we have a chance to see and experience them in all their complex wholeness.*

This whole-to-part principle contrasts easily with the part-to-whole, skill-based view of literacy most prevalent in today's schools. Our instruction has been dominated by the belief that if we get students to master enough of the right skills (phonics, words, comprehension skills in reading, spelling, grammar, mechanics, text structure in writing), they will eventually be able to put those parts to use during real reading and writing. Many of us have seen the flaw in this reasoning through painful experiences with students who have indeed mastered any skill we cared to put in front of them but still could not comprehend or compose with reasonable success.

This part-to-whole model is filled with broken promises because, in reality, the parts have definition only in relation to the whole. For example, *t* functions very differently in the word "Tim" than it does in the words "the" or "station." The word "had" means very different things in the sentence, "Mary had a little lamb," when Mary is a little girl in a nursery rhyme or when Mary is a mother sheep in a story about a budding veterinarian. Seventeen-year-olds choose different vocabulary, grammar, and meanings when the topic is drugs but the context is grandma's medication rather than a Saturday night party with friends. Relationships are what is important in language. When a complex process exists as a natural, organic whole, simplifying distorts it and drains it of its purpose. Frank Smith (1986) reminds us that in an effort to make reading simple, we have made it hard. And, for too many years, we have done the same thing with writing and other kinds of learning.

Application: Materials for Learning Need to Be Whole, Intact Texts

From the very beginning students need to read and write texts that have all the characteristics of real language—no excerpts, no abridged versions, no papers with spaces to be filled in. Whole language classrooms are overflowing with a wide range of materials written for and by students. The focus on all of this written language is the understanding gained, the meanings constructed. When parts are examined, if at all, it is only in the service of meaning and only in relation to the larger whole.

Once, when my niece, Amie, was reading a story that involved a courtroom scene, she encountered the word "innocent." While she could have chosen to try a meaningful substitution or skip over the word and read on—both viable strategies used by proficient readers—she chose to apply her knowledge of phonics. Her first attempt produced a three-syllable word with the emphasis on the second syllable: "i-NOS-ent." Her voice sounded flat, the word meaningless to her. Next, she repeated the word using the same inflection, only quietly, listening carefully to the sounds: "i-NOS-nt." Then, she repeated once more, this time sounding annoyed: "i-NOS-nt??!! That doesn't make sense!" Now she was determined, and repeated the word over and over to herself, clearly trying to discover another pronunciation that would fit into what she knew and her developing understanding of the story. Suddenly, she got it: "i-N-ə-sənt! Okay. That makes sense." Then she continued reading.

Amie's phonics strategies were useful to her only in that they helped her decide on an appropriate phonetic alternative that fit into the narrative context. Had she encountered this word in isolation—apart from ideas like crime and guilt, courtrooms and juries, judges and attorneys—she would have had no way to judge whether her attempts at reading the word were successful or not.

The application of the whole-to-part principle is true in writing as well. Spelling and grammar make sense, and students gain greater and greater control over them when they are considered as tools to help convey the messages of stories and essays and letters and poems and all the other genre open to students as developing authors. When the whole-to-part principle is in place, teachers value interpretation before detail, a general understanding before individual words, immersion in reading good literature and writing of personal importance before control of specific items. When the whole-to-part principle is in place, young children have the chance to develop the joyful sounds of literature before they are asked to think about the abstract, variable sounds of letters. And with this principle, there is no worry about transfer or the reason for learning.

PRINCIPLE 2: LANGUAGE AND LITERACY ARE SOCIALLY CONSTRUCTED

For a long time we've had it wrong about reading and writing: They are not solitary activities; they are socialized learning events. In a very real sense, when you curl up in an overstuffed chair to read the latest bestseller, the author curls up beside you for a little chat. Reading and writing are part of an ongoing dialogue— with an author, with oneself, with other reader/writers. Ideas that begin as unformed thoughts need time and language and other people to move them forward. I'm impressed over and over with the evolution that can occur in composition and comprehension when people are given a chance to think with others about the meaning possibilities in a text.

While I need time to read and write and think by myself (my own personal dialogues), there is nothing that can match the excitement or the richness of sharing my interpretations or hearing the perspectives of others. To one degree or another it is a natural part of the way people process information. For example, my husband and I read the same book simultaneously so we can wonder, predict, comment, and take pleasure from the reading experience together while Barbara Lindberg talks about the frustrations of reading the Sunday newspaper with her husband because he insists on reading interesting sections out loud to her while she is trying to read to herself.

When reader/writers talk to each other they take those exchanges back to the texts they are reading and writing, able now to think in different ways, ready to move forward with altered stances. In that way learning becomes a perpetual social spiral.

Application: Students Need Opportunities to Learn from Each Other as well as from Teachers

In the classroom it's easy to strip literacy of its social nature—writing that's drafted solitarily, handed in to the teacher, given back with only a few notes and a grade or reading that's completed without any real talk about feelings, new ideas, personal connections, or varying interpretations. Historically, classrooms have separated students, physically and cognitively. We have warned them about keeping their distance, reminded them not to "borrow" anyone else's ideas. Recognizing the impact of oral language on cognition, whole language encourages collaborative learning and places a high value on students thinking together. In Carol Porter's high school classroom, comprehension of adolescent literature develops in Reading Discussion Groups* as students play off one another's individual understandings. Kathleen Visovatti's second-graders often choose to write about the same topics. When this happens, Kathleen reminds the young authors just how flattering it is that peers would think a topic interesting enough to try it out themselves.

At the end of an in-service day I asked a group of teachers to write Exit Slips* about one thing they had learned and one question they still had about whole language. Ninety percent of the things learned centered around this social principle. The teachers were surprised and excited by the idea that talk could be so

---

* All asterisks throughout the book refer the reader to Chapter 10 where full strategy descriptions can be found.

important to learning. Why had they spent so much time trying to keep their students quiet?

The next time we were together we began to plan how they could integrate more oral and written exchanges into their school days. They started by teaming students to read the same books, encouraging them to talk along the way at whatever points they chose. I encouraged teachers to choose their own student partners so students could begin to see firsthand how more experienced readers think. Many teachers felt enormously freed by a few simple, social changes.

The application of this second principle underscores the importance of collective thought and encourages students and teachers to think together, to build on one another's ideas. It's tough *not* to assume a different perspective, achieve a deeper understanding, extend or refine an idea if there are opportunities to talk before, during, and after a literacy event. Reading and writing need to be looked at as extended activities where each process begins and ends in a social setting with exchanges built into the process itself. Classrooms that are alive with purposeful talk keep the interactive part of development intact.

Who does the most talking in your classroom? It's probably a good index of who is doing the most thinking.

PRINCIPLE 3: LITERATE BEHAVIOR IS LEARNED THROUGH REAL, FUNCTIONAL USE

When young children use language they always have a personal agenda—to connect with someone they love, to get a cookie, to explore a developing concept, to manipulate Mom or Dad. They notice early in their lives that oral and written language are not arbitrary; they aren't created at someone's whim to decorate the environment. Symbols, in whatever form, have a purpose: Stop signs convey a clear message to the driver of a car; McDonald's logo conveys another message; nursery school teachers write names on paintings for a reason; and letters from Grandma and Grandpa are different from the grocery lists made by Mom and Dad. Language outside of the classroom doesn't exist without a real purpose; there is always some personal reason to read or write or speak or listen.

Language in the classroom doesn't always have the same clear, solid function that it has outside of school. We can contrast real language use to language study—grammar texts, spelling books, phonics workbooks. Studying language is what linguists do—voluntarily. There is not much interest or value here for young children. They want to know what to do with it. They want to know how it can help them negotiate within their families and their world. In the movie, *The Dead Poets Society,* Robin Williams insisted that his students tear out the introduction to their poetry texts because the author advocated a rigorous dissection of the poems rather than an individual transaction and personal response. Williams' L. L. Bean-clad prep school students were horrified. Analysis, they thought, was the reason for literature, not experience. These students were used to written language devoid of purpose but the teacher in the movie had another idea.

Application: Students Need Personal,
Authentic Reasons to Read and Write

Students learn and need to use language for a variety of functions (Halliday, 1975). This range of functions needs to be consistently represented in the classroom. Students should not only read and write stories, they must also read and write newspapers, plays, poems, lists, menus, maps, environmental print, magazines, letters, persuasive material, commentaries, editorials, chapter books and their own texts. These, however, cannot be "practice" literacy. The idea here is to think of all the ways in which you and others use literacy in your everyday lives. Those are the same uses that have to be represented in the classroom if students are to become literate in ways that will benefit them outside of school.

Literacy use is authentic when the student has personal intent related to the literacy event (Edelsky, 1989). That is, there has to be choice and a reason to engage. Authenticity must also take into account a genuine audience beyond the teacher. In Dan Power's classroom his sixth-graders choose a topic and work together to create magazines. When the magazines are finished, they are duplicated for other grades and brought to Dan's university graduate classes for other teachers to read. In Pat Riordan's first grade, students make lists of things they must do to plan a field trip. One of the tasks is to write a letter to the principal to make sure that they have his approval for the trip. In Penny Silvers' resource room children alphabetize the books they have written about pets in order to set up a mini-class library. Once the books are in order the children can check them out and take them home in a plastic book bag. In Carol Porter's high school reading/writing room she does research along with a senior who is interested in collaboration. Together they examine why this is an effective way to learn. Carol and Brian are writing an article together and plan to submit it to a journal with a national audience.

This notion of authenticity reminds us that school is not for getting ready to do the real stuff of life sometime in the distant future; it is for *doing* real things, for real audiences, and for ourselves, right now.

PRINCIPLE 4: DEMONSTRATIONS
ARE CRITICAL TO LEARNING

Proficient reading and writing can be a baffling mystery to a novice. It all looks so perfect—those beautiful, published books with inviting illustrations and glossy covers; those dramatic, polished oral readings. At the time that learners view or experience finished language products, the trail of thought that led to the final version has long since vanished. Authors don't tend to show the world their messy, in-process struggles and readers usually keep their comments and interpretations to themselves. It's easy for less proficient language users to get the idea that the ultimate goal of reading and writing and, perhaps even speaking, is to get it right the first time. Learners can assume too quickly that messing around with meaning is not an inherent part of the process and that it is something to be avoided.

Psycholinguist Frank Smith argues that process demonstrations are an essential component of learning. Demonstrations are different from our old idea of modeling where we show students how to do something and then expect them to aim for a perfect repetition. Demonstrations are real engagements that show novices the potential paths that can be taken. What people see in the world outside of the classroom are alternative ways of developing and displaying highly skilled behavior. During Chris Evert's career in tennis her tightly controlled baseline play was dramatically different from Martina Navritilova's aggressive net strategy, but certainly no less skilled. If Evert and Navritilova would let us on the court with them as apprentices we could develop an inside understanding of expert tennis and how the pros vary their strategies from one match to the next. In one form or another, less experienced players and students have to have a chance to get close to the masterful executions and the behind-the-scenes intricacies that make the behavior work. Our students have to see the possibilities.

Application: Teachers Need to Read and Write and Learn Along with Their Students, Sharing Their Thinking as the Experiences Proceed

One dimension of whole language is a shift in emphasis from products to processes. It is time for us, along with our students, to look inside the slick veneers of finished compositions and final draft comprehension. As skilled readers and writers and problem-solvers, part of what we have to do as teachers is demonstrate the ins and outs, the ups and downs of our proficiencies. We have to find ways to learn along with our students, and to let them inside our heads as we are constructing meaning.

This demonstration principle is about sharing our best strategies with our students. It's about demystifying literacy by making our thinking an integral part of classroom life. We can no longer ask our students to do things that we don't also do. In Pat Miller's third/fourth-grade classroom her students meet regularly to talk about their writing—the problems they are having trying to capture an experience, what topic they should write about next, how to get the writing to sound more alive, if they should abandon this text and move on to something else. Sometimes they just want confirmation that what they think they are communicating is indeed what the listener is hearing.

Pat always writes with her students and she is an integral part of their conference groups. When her group meets, she is not there to direct or to keep them on task. She comes, as they do, to share her writing, to ask for advice, to get confirmation. When she solves a problem or experiences a success, Pat is careful to share her thinking with her students. Demonstrations in Pat's classroom, however, are not confined to the teacher. Her students learn the jargon of writing from the beginning of the school year, and use it every day to talk about their composing processes. By doing what students are doing *as* they are doing it, teachers and students together can make process demonstrations an important part of the curriculum.

PRINCIPLE 5: ALL LEARNING INVOLVES RISK-TAKING AND APPROXIMATION

What was the last new skill you decided to learn? My husband is exploring conversational Japanese. I have a friend who is interested in yoga and has been taking classes for quite some time. My older brother and sister now have brown belts in karate, and expect to test for their black belts soon. These are people who are learning—and taking risks and making approximations in the process. They are beginners, trying things out for the first time, or more experienced learners, continuing because they have felt some success and because the activity holds meaning for them. What is common to all of them is that they don't see their learning as ended. And they never will. Even when my brother and sister receive their black belts, are considered experts in their own rights, and can go no further in their formal training, their learning will continue. Their chosen activities will always be characterized by experimentation, approximation, and refinement of a more mature model.

Learning involves constant risk-taking and, because we are forever trying out things we have never tried before, it also involves approximation. The trick is to make risk-taking and the accompanying approximations so comfortable that the learner will want to continue the activity. In toddlers' worlds, where no one expects more than "cute" attempts at adult behaviors, they are free to test hypotheses about how things work. This kind of secure experimenting shows up best in early speech. When a two-year-old points to the sky and says: "Wook! Airpwane!" no parent would respond by saying "How many times do I have to tell you?! L-o-o-k is pro-nounced luh-ooo-k. And please try to speak in complete sentences!" The adult response is more likely to be of a positive nature: "Yes, honey, I see the plane. Remember when we went to Grandma's on the airplane?" When the attempt at communication is affirmed and even celebrated, young children want to continue. Then the testing and exploring, approximating and revising move at a pace that leaves us all marveling at how quickly children learn. Negative responses, probably more common in classrooms than any of us would like to admit, do more to shut down development than to move it forward.

Application: Students Must Be Encouraged to Take Risks and Approximations Need to Be Expected and Valued

Playing it safe is a dead end when it comes to language and learning. Being able to try things out in a nonthreatening environment is the key to increasing language facility. To a great degree risk-taking is a trust issue. I know which peers will respond to my work in ways that help me focus on my message rather than on my ability to achieve my goal. Likewise, I know which peers will be so critical that I feel like abandoning the effort. Reading and writing and learning in general require so much rough-draft thinking that it's easy to feel vulnerable.

Students will try new literate behaviors on for size only if they trust that their thinking will be valued and encouraged. And, if they see their approximations treated as signs of growth, indices of real learning, and reasons to celebrate, they will continue to take the risks necessary to grow as language users.

When this principle is applied in the classroom, varied interpretations in reading are highlighted, invented spellings are respected at all grade levels, and written drafts are displayed along with finished pieces. When the environment is socially supportive, risk-taking becomes a natural strategy.

PRINCIPLE 6: LEARNERS MUST TAKE RESPONSIBILITY FOR THEIR OWN LEARNING

Experts in the field of process instruction emphatically point to the pre-eminent importance of students taking responsibility for their learning from start to finish. Much of the theoretical shift that occurs in whole language teaching is related to responsibility. When learners of any age initiate their own learning, the intent and purpose of the experience are clear. With self-initiation comes a greater degree of ownership, involvement, and commitment to the activity. The learning, then, really belongs to the participant.

That people must ultimately take control of their learning is tied to a strong belief in people being natural learners. Even under the most adverse conditions, we independently seek cognitive stimulation and strive to see the world in different ways. As in all human conditions, the drive to be actively involved can be suppressed. In certain contexts people quickly learn to be passive; they learn to wait for others to initiate their experiences. Other-directed learning results in decreased levels of involvement, and the ability to sustain interest is greatly diminished.

Learning to speak is the best example we have of children taking the major responsibility for a complex learning task and succeeding at it quite well. As we have seen, young children initiate the forms and meanings they will try out and control the revisions that result in more standard language. As learners control their progress, they are in the best position to determine the specific direction the learning should take.

Application: The Learning Context Should Offer Open-ended Opportunities and Student Choice

During my first years of teaching I was convinced that the amount of learning that took place was in direct proportion to how hard *I* worked. I spent long evenings and most weekends preparing worksheets, organizing materials, grading papers, reading and rereading my teacher's manuals to make sure I didn't miss anything. From start to finish the publishers and I made all the important learning decisions. Mine was an example of rigorous instruction, all right. Never mind the students. I certainly knew how to put myself through the paces. I left teaching for a while before it occurred to me that it wasn't the profession that had caused me so much discomfort, produced so much anxiety, and so little satisfaction. It was my lonely view of how learning should proceed. I saw the teaching and the learning as *my* responsibility. Because they both belonged to *me,* there wasn't much joy in it for anyone.

Now my graduate students choose their own projects and even the texts they will read. They design the methods by which they will learn and how they will share their learning along the way. In another whole language setting Barbara Lindberg's junior high students come to class every day knowing that they will orchestrate their time and their activities. While Barbara makes recommendations and occasionally suggests directions, the students know that it is up to them to choose what they will read and write and with whom they will learn.

From beginning to end learners need opportunities to exercise responsibility for their learning. That means choices in reading and self-selected topics in writing. It means a schedule that allows the necessary time to read and reread, to revise one time or twenty, to talk things through at individual points of discovery or confusion. Sharing the decision-making and allowing students to direct their learning is paramount if teachers are to encourage independence and self-direction.

The kind of beginning-to-end responsibility embodied in this principle has to start with you and the professional changes you are considering—you, seeing yourself as a learner, willing to take risks and to move at your own pace. If you start moving too fast or feel someone is pushing you, step back and remember that it is *your* learning, and then take back control. Step back one more time and remind yourself that your students need the same power over their development.

The principles just described comprise the basic set of beliefs underlying whole language instruction, and attempt to define a whole language teacher. Whole language is a perspective on language and learning. It is that perspective that makes the difference between traditional, skill-based instruction and whole language teaching—not the materials, not the activities, not the desks in circles—the perspective.

CONNECTED TEACHING

You know those days when you walk away from your classroom and feel a special closeness to your students, an inexplicable warmth inside? What happens then? Why are those days different from the ones that end with you feeling drained and ready to enroll in law school? I used to reflect briefly on those special times and simply say: "I did a good job today. I guess I'm a pretty good teacher." I'll bet if I had asked my students, many of them would have told me they had a special feeling too. And if we had examined the day more closely, we might have found that my goals were their goals: We planned together, thought together, achieved together, felt the satisfaction of changing together. On those days it wasn't a teacher telling, it was a group of learners exploring.

In their book, *Women's Ways of Knowing,* Belenky, Clinchy, Goldberger, and Tarule (1986) call it connected teaching. For me, it is another essential dimension of successful whole language teaching. Connected teaching means two things: Trying to be in touch with yourself as a learner, and connecting with the essential pivotal parts of your students—their language, their interests, their struggles, their passions, their instructional pasts. Belenky and her colleagues tell the stories of 135 women and their struggles for intellectual independence. As the authors looked for patterns in the women's evolution of self, voice, and mind, the individual voices became a collective outcry that echoed their anger at having to fight so hard to see themselves as capable of constructing knowledge.

When I first read their stories, their anger mirrored my own as I tried to understand why any student, male or female, should have to overcome a multitude of obstacles to discover the power of mind. These narratives were filled with descriptions of teachers who aggressively attacked the women's thinking in ways that made them want to hide their thoughts rather than examine them. The authors talk about instructional settings that made the learners want to retreat into silence. When these women *did* speak of growth-producing learning experiences, they described teachers who sanctioned the amorphous nature of their thinking in progress and who encouraged them to keep the process moving. One teacher said: "What you are thinking is fine—but think more" (p. 218).

Whole language is a model of teaching/learning that removes the obstacles, quiets the anger, encourages the individual as well as the social voice. It is a qualitatively different kind of teaching. Whole language encourages connections to students and to oneself in a way that traditional instruction never did, never could. With its focus on whole people and the integration of cognition and affect, whole language, by definition, encourages a linking of minds in which teachers and students make genuine efforts to enter into one another's experiences; or, at the very least, to recognize them as real and viable. Whole language implies a respect for the learner, the kind of respect that nudges toward independence, the kind of respect that gives over responsibility while offering support for new ways of thinking. Part of the strength in this kind of connected, responsive teaching comes from a willingness on our parts as teachers to open our minds to our students, to show them what our thinking looks like—how it begins, under what conditions it continues, and how it ends up. It's a vulnerable way to teach—it takes courage to reveal our imperfect thinking processes and to share curricular control. But, as Carol Porter notes: "I've never felt so alive, so fully involved in my teaching."

Getting started and moving forward with whole language and connected teaching involves a basic alteration in focus—from language study to language use, from teacher control to student responsibility, from learner deficits to learner strengths. This book is about curricular development with language use and student strengths as a basic foundation. In her book *Caring* (1984) Nel Noddings talks about seeing through students' eyes:

> Suppose, for example, that I am a teacher who loves mathematics. I encounter a student who is doing poorly, and I decide to have a talk with him. He tells me that he hates mathematics. I do not begin with dazzling performances designed to intrigue him or to change his attitude. I begin, as nearly as I can, with the view from his eyes: Mathematics is bleak, jumbled, scary, boring, boring, boring. From that point on, we struggle together with it (pp. 15-16).

Carol Porter is currently a high school reading/writing teacher who spent many years in a junior high classroom. Her transition to whole language occurred over many years, as her seventh- and eighth-graders struggled with their own transitions toward more literate behavior. Connected teaching is at its best when teachers like Carol come from behind their "Big Desks" (Atwell, 1987) and become an integral part of the learning going on in the classroom:

> A worker from the Dean's office came into the classroom the other day with a pass for one of my students. I heard Jim say, "She's back there reading." She walked to the back of the room and, as she handed me the pass, she said, "I couldn't find you. You weren't at the teacher's desk at the front of the room."
> I'm rarely at the teacher's desk in the front of the room anymore. I used to be there all the time—talking. Talking about reading and, less frequently, writing. But always, incessantly talking. I've given that up to a great degree, along with my teacher's perch at the front of the room. And, so, now when you walk into my classroom, you'll hear lots of voices, not just mine.

Not long ago Carol and some of her high school students were interviewed by a local journalist writing an article on whole language. This excerpt from one student's conversation highlights the notion of connected teaching from the learner's perspective:

> I have been in reading classes most of my years in school. And I have truly hated them. Let me explain. Most of my grade school reading classes were the same for me. For example, when I was in 5th grade I would have to sit in the corner of the room and read aloud Dick and Jane stories! Yes. That's what I said, Dick and Jane stories. All the years up until 8th grade were the same. And all this did was turn me away from reading. I hated reading more than ever because of this system.
> The reason everything started to change in 8th grade was my teacher. I was not in reading classes anymore; I was in an English class that did a lot of reading. This teacher had a different view about how students should be taught to read. This changed me from a person who didn't want to read into a person who enjoys reading. The teacher was Mrs. Porter.
> When I entered high school everything went back to what it was before—me having to read books that I was embarrassed to be seen with, reading the same old

low level books and doing the same stupid worksheets. After all, the school has its system. I thought I would have to continue this way but I was wrong about that. Mrs. Porter is now a high school reading teacher! We read books that are close to the level that we should be reading and there are no worksheets. We write to Mrs. Porter about how we feel about what we read. I enjoy this. I no longer hate reading. I love to read. I spend more time reading now than I do watching TV or anything else.

I have to add something to this. I do believe this system is the best reading system I have ever been a part of, but there is one other thing. The system would not work without Mrs. Porter. You need a teacher that is going to get down on the students level, talk to the students as if they are your equal and not try to intimidate them. You need a teacher that tries to understand how it feels to have a low reading level and most of all a teacher who cares for their students, not one that is just waiting for the next check.

During one of my first days consulting in an eighth-grade classroom the teacher and I were discussing the mechanics of setting up interest groups for reading novels the students had selected. She had expressed some concern about the potential noise level in the room (at that time, talk during class was prohibited), and I was trying to point out the value of discussion to comprehension. Her response cut me off in mid-sentence: "Oh, I don't *mind* the noise *IF* they are doing what they are *supposed* to do. And I just don't think they will if I'm not watching over them."

This is every teacher's greatest fear—that students won't do what they are *supposed* to do every minute. Time on task has become a treacherous notion in our classrooms. It has helped us forget that we are dealing with human begins, not learning machines. We are surprised and even offended when our students try to develop and maintain relationships with others during a learning activity. We wonder at their insistence on exchanging personal information or responding in emotionally appropriate ways when they are supposed to be learning. The literature on group dynamics helps us understand the importance of a connected base for our teaching. It convincingly shows that socially, psychologically, and emotionally connecting with others is actually necessary if a group, any group, is going to work together productively.

A TIME TO BE PATIENT

Penny Silvers gave up a lot when she decided to make a transition to whole language. Her long history of traditional instruction was marked by a visible confidence in her ability to diagnose and remediate reading problems. Her masters degree rounded out her experience and confirmed her authority as a specialist. Penny's introduction to whole language teaching came when she decided to take a few courses "just to find out what was happening in the field." Looking at students' strengths instead of their weaknesses made sense to her, and her own social nature made an interactive paradigm infinitely more attractive than one characterized by isolated decision-making. After several years of whole language teaching Penny's enthusiasm about her profession and about her students rivals any I've seen. If her convincing arguments about the value of real reading and writing for her "remedial" students don't get you, her winning smile will. But Penny will be the first to tell you that substantive professional change, while wonderfully gratifying, is likely to be slow. And, that's okay; it's more than worth the time.

> Once I believed that the basal program was inviolate . . . that the stories were only a vehicle for applying the skills, that the sequential order of the skills had to be followed and that the system had to be managed as it was written. I believed that students had to follow the program and adapt to it— whether or not it made sense or worked for them. Gradually, as I learned more about whole language, my teaching began to change but I gave up my traditional skill-based approaches slowly and painfully. I felt as if I was starting to learn to teach all over again.
>
> I learned to demonstrate the reading strategies that I used, encouraging risk-taking and celebrating the successes in reading and writing. Most of all, I knew instinctively, and then through theory, that students needed many opportunities to read a variety of real literature in a variety of contexts. They needed to become comfortable with language. The reading program had to adapt to the students' needs—not force them to fit the program. I also learned that I needed to look at what the student already knew, and the process of learning, rather than judging what wasn't known, looking only at the final product.
>
> Even with the change in philosophy, the actual implementation took a long time. And today, after several years of holistic teaching, I feel I am still an emerging whole language teacher rather than one who has fully arrived. Once in a while I find myself looking at the product instead of my students and their learning. I still feel the urge to control the instruction but have become more skilled at recognizing and following their lead while gently encouraging, responding, and celebrating in the learning. This has been the greatest revelation for me. It has been a source of unending stimulation and continued wonder at the amount of information, the breadth of knowledge, and the insights that students are capable of bringing to a learning situation.

I have often called upon Carol and Penny and the other whole language teachers in this book to come into my graduate classes and talk about their evolution toward a new way of teaching. I ask them, as I asked them for this book, to chronicle their professional histories, to discuss their difficulties in implementing whole language in traditional contexts, to share curricular insights, and to demonstrate basic strategies. At a time when this kind of teaching is still a radically new idea for many, these veteran educators help me assure other students that no one has all the answers and that change is a slow-moving, complicated animal. We expect to be at it for the rest of our professional careers. As you begin, or continue, your change to whole language, remember that no one expects it to happen all at once, so don't expect it of yourself. Take it a step at a time, reflect, talk to colleagues as you go, and be sure to celebrate your own risks and approximations along the way.

Personal Reflection

Whole language starts with people's strengths. Begin with your own. What are you already doing that is consistent with the principles outlined in this chapter?

Whole-to-Part Learning

Social Meaning Construction

Functional Reading and Writing

Demonstrations

Risk-taking and Approximation

Student Responsibility for Learning

Inside the Home/
Inside the Classroom:
Natural Learning Contexts

2

For years researcher Yetta Goodman has encouraged teachers to engage in "kidwatching" as a way of understanding what students can do and as a way of connecting with them. In my years of whole language teaching and thinking about kids I've done my share of kidwatching, but lately I've been doing a fair amount of "parentwatching."

One night we had friends over to dinner and I listened carefully to the nature of the conversation as we talked about our preschoolers. Except for one five-minute discussion bemoaning the frustration and embarrassment of the lay-down-and-kick-and scream-in-public type of tantrum, the exchanges revolved around the startling and wonderful development that had taken place in our children since we had last seen one another. We talked about new personality dimensions, their amazing social adeptness (WE were never THAT social at three), their resilience when faced with harsh words or difficult friends. We shared the generous compliments from their nursery-school teachers, and laughed at their invented words. In all of this there was joy and celebration and, maybe less visible, a strong belief that our kids would keep growing and developing in positive ways.

Researchers often look to the home and to parents to give them new perspectives on learning and to help them understand the complexities of a nurturing learning environment. The assumption has been that home is, after all, the place where kids learn more with greater rapidity than at any other time in their lives. And a child's greatest achievement during the early years, learning to speak, is accomplished with such great ease that we call it natural. Natural learning, however, does not mean that there is no teacher involved or that it is accomplished without thought and effort. The fact is, it occurs in an easy, happy manner under the tutelage of parents who don't intend to teach their kids anything; they only want to talk to them.

Perhaps the greatest insights from child language research have revolved around the role of the parent related to the phenomenal learning of preschoolers. Researcher Gordon Wells calls parents' intuitive tracking of language as they communicate with their children "leading from behind." Parents support and extend learning in very specific ways, and, in the process, give children the kind of information they need to keep the learning cycle going. For example, when a young child points to a carton of milk sitting on the kitchen table and says, "milk," the parent is likely to respond by confirming the expressed meaning in an adult form: "Oh, you want some milk? Here, I'll get a cup for you, and you can sit in your high chair while you drink it." All the time the parent is speaking, the language is supported by action—pointing to the milk, getting a cup from the cabinet, lifting the child, and putting her into the high chair.

While we are fond of saying that a parent is a child's first teacher, the kind of teaching that many parents do tacitly is very different from the traditional idea of instruction, in which the teacher is an expert whose goal is to pass along knowledge to a novice. Effective parental "teaching" doesn't fit with the idea of a passive learning model. When the culture encourages it, parents create active and interactive learning environments, urging their children to try things out, to think through problems. The conditions many parents unwittingly put into place sustain a dizzyingly rapid rate of learning.

What is it, then, about those homes in which learning takes place in a powerful and happy way? What is it about parents and their responses that make them such highly effective teachers? Learning in the classroom should not look so different from learning outside of the classroom.

This chapter will consider new perspectives on language, learning, and kids by taking a look at the learning in one home and how similar contexts are created in whole language classrooms.

IMMERSION

IN THE HOME

Samantha is three now, a passionate and demanding toddler. Sometimes, when her face is just at the right angle, I am startled to see my own profile mirrored so perfectly. She has been surrounded by language—speaking, reading, and writing—since she was born. Actually, this was so even before she was born. I wasn't sure if it would make a difference or not, but I wasn't taking any chances. I figured that my belief about immersing children in language simply couldn't start too soon, and so I started reading Margaret Wise Brown's *Goodnight Moon* to her as soon as

I found out I was pregnant. What with our talking and reading it must have been noisy in there during those nine months. But she came out to a world filled with even more noise—and it was her job to begin to make sense of it.

Our early conversations centered around what we were doing or how she was feeling. Now there is a lot of talk about talk (What did you say? I'm not sure what you mean. Where did you hear THAT word?), about reading and writing (Isn't this like the other book you have about going to bed? Would you like to write your grandma a get-well note?); but, mostly, a lot of talk about ongoing daily activities. My husband and I initiate some of the conversation but, just as often, she selects the topic (or the book) and we are happy to follow her lead.

During her first two years her mornings were difficult and I learned to use books along with talk to ease her into the day. By the time she was up fifteen or twenty minutes, we had often read at least two or three books. Intermittent reading throughout the day was established early as an important part of her daily routine.

There is a flow about her life now, and language in one form or another gently sweeps her along—from morning till night. She helps maintain her own immersion these days. She selects books and reads them to herself, to us, or to her fifty-two stuffed animals and dolls that sleep with her, eat with her, go to nursery school with her. They are her talkmates and reading partners when her dad and I are not around. She initiates her own writing—notes and letters, grocery lists, and birthday cards. In her preschool world it's language all day, every day.

IN THE CLASSROOM

Kathleen Visovatti is one of those lucky teachers who has taught more than one grade. She was a whole language teacher before the name was in vogue. When you enter her classroom you can't help but be impressed by all the energy—hers as well as her students'. Student talk and functional reading and writing have always been in every corner of her teaching—in her eighth-grade classroom, in sixth grade, and, now, in second. She knows that in a very real way if she limited any of these expressions she would risk sacrificing meaningful dialogue and, ultimately, many opportunities to think. A class of thirty, however, is not a home of one.

Consequently, organizing her classes to respond to this driving social need for expression, exploration, and exchange of ideas is one of the real challenges Kathleen has met head on. Because she understands the importance of language, Kathleen strives to immerse her students in language all day long.

> I shudder when I pass a quiet classroom where children are working silently. I wince when I overhear a teacher say, "No talking. Do your own work." My classroom is still for only ten minutes each day—at the start of our daily writing time when we have SSW (Sustained Silent Writing) so that I can model writing uninterrupted and so that each child can concentrate on getting started without any distraction on whatever writing task she or he has chosen first for the day— maybe writing a letter to a classmate (we have a class post office) or making an entry in his or her Dialogue Journal (we write back and forth to one another), or working on a current piece. Some students are in the middle of publishing books; others use the time to think—they gaze into space and occasionally jot down ideas on their Topics sheet.
>
> The rest of the day the classroom is full of talk—sometimes a quiet undertone of a few earnest conversations here and there, frequently a steady buzz from lively discussions at each activity center, usually a constant hum emanating from all clusters of desks.
>
> I encourage talk because I believe children learn from talking. They clarify their own thoughts, discover new ones. They help one another by explaining concepts and directions, offering suggestions. Brainstorming, planning, analyzing occur spontaneously. But there's no way to see this, no way to understand the richness of the exchanges unless you join a group and talk and listen as a member—not a teacher.
>
> My students talk: They exchange writing ideas, verbalize math concepts in their own words, talk about what they remember from field trips, talk as they conduct experiments, talk about what they're reading—summarizing for others, drawing connections.
>
> Talk is important in my classroom because I believe in its power. I respect children's thoughts. Sure, some take advantage of the open structure to socialize. But a gentle reminder puts them back on task. And, who knows? Perhaps what appears to be idle chatter on the surface may well prove to be the subject of someone's next story or the encounter of a new idea that will lead to hours of informal research, maybe even a career choice! I stop myself from stopping their talk.

REFLECTIONS

Kathleen recently sent me some writing samples from her second-grade students. As I read through them I was struck by the range of concerns these seven-year-olds have. They wrote about a bus driver who had died of cancer, making dinner with a Brownie troop, a sister throwing up, summer school, going to the zoo on a field trip, not getting responses to letters, tadpoles, Halloween, how to get home after school. I wondered what would have happened to these ideas and feelings if Kathleen had not been sensitive enough to provide an avenue for them. Maybe they would have been shared in other ways, but the greater likelihood is that they would have remained unexpressed, amorphous, with no chance of becoming fully formed. When language is so imperative to thought, and to the establishment of trusting relationships, I wonder that students who are expected to sit quietly throughout the school day while the teacher talks aren't bursting with their own needs to communicate. In some junior high and senior high classrooms it looks as if the teacher is expending all his or her energy keeping the lid on a bubbling pot. There's an explosion of language just under the surface for all our students; we just have to find ways to help them harness and direct by means useful to them.

EXPERIMENTATION

IN THE HOME

For Samantha it's time to try things out. She tries and tests and modifies in cycles of learning that are sometimes hard to observe because of their simultaneity. We were in the kitchen together one night when I heard her say: "Weedidawus!" (Ridiculous). I looked up from my magazine. Her dolls and animals were spilling out of the sides of her white wicker stroller but she was trying to stuff one more bear in with the others. Exasperated, she looked at me and said: "*I'm* going to get a magazine, Mom." A few minutes later she came back into the kitchen huffing and puffing and staggering under the weight of a basket filled with books. She picked up *Geraldine's Blanket* (Keller 1984) and said to me: "Great big magazine, Mom!" I laughed and she started to read a few pages to herself. Soon there was a big sigh: "This is weedikawus, Mom! These aren't magazines!" She walked out of the room muttering over and over to herself: "Weedikawus. Weekidawus. Weekidawus." As I silently watched her go, I sighed too, marveling at her personal invention and feeling the wonder of watching a new idea gather strength with each attempt to use it meaningfully.

I've come to expect that not long after Samantha encounters a new concept through speaking or reading or writing, she will begin trying it out—on her own terms, within a context she determines, approximating the adult version. She builds competence with each attempt, and I wonder how many I miss. Her experimentation and approximation in oral language is now an observable strategy with books and writing. She scribbles thank you notes, takes messages on the notepad beside her play phone, reads favorite books using what theorist Ken Goodman calls "holistic remembering," altering words and sentences as she goes along but faithfully reconstructing the story line. On her bedroom door she has posted a sign that says, according to her translation: "Stay Away, Monster" (*see* Figure 2.1).

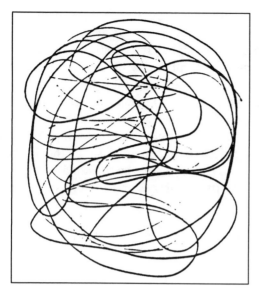

FIGURE 2.1
Translation of Message Written by 3
Year-Old: Stay Away Monster

FIGURE 2.2
Translation of Message Written by 3
Year-Old: No Boys Allowed. Except Daddy

For months her scribbled message has kept at bay the monsters lurking around our house. Recently she posted a new sign next to her old monster message: "No Boys Allowed! (Except Daddy)" (*see* Figure 2.2). This latest directive looks decidedly different from the earlier one. Unlike the scattered, erratic, crisscrossed lines in the first, it has neat rows of controlled, wavy patterns with an occasional letter interspersed throughout. In the middle of the paper is a big yellow heart that contains the "Except Daddy" portion of her writing. Samantha's experimentation is paying off. Her oral and written language are developing and changing with each effort. She has learned that she can communicate whatever she wants—in some form that is always acceptable to us.

IN THE CLASSROOM

In her junior high classroom Barbara Lindberg has created a safe and accepting environment for her students. There is a warm and welcome feeling as students walk in the door, greet her, and quickly go about their business. Almost immediately Barbara is beside one or two students, talking quietly, helping them plan or reflect. Barbara feels a major part of her job is to support her students as they experiment with reading and writing as a means of learning about life and literature. But many of her remedial students, systematically silenced over the years by careless labels and low expectations, have ceased to take any kinds of risks.

Barbara gently tries to draw them out, contributing when she judges they are ready, backing away when she knows it must be their decision to move forward.

Early in the year 8th grade students were busy with their Writing Folders.* Some were adding to their ideas for writing topics; others were busy with first drafts. Monika, however, sat with her eyes down, obviously not lost in thought. I did a Donald Graves [writing researcher] tour of the room: "How is it going, Tom?" "What are you writing about now, Jane?" "Where are you now in your draft, Alison?"

Monika looked at me blankly when I asked her, "How is your writing going?" She is a quiet girl who receives speech therapy weekly, and I was surprised to find out that English was not only her first language; it was her only language.

"I can't think of anything to write about," she murmured. We looked in her folder where students keep a list of possible topics to write about. Her list was made up of two items: "My vacation in Poland" and "Visiting grandpa in the hospital." I probed a little about Poland. She answered with shrugs and I don't remembers, so I tried her grandfather. When had he been in the hospital? Had he been there long? Was she able to visit him there? It was a one-sided conversation, and before moving on I suggested that she look at what others were writing and at their idea lists.

I kept an eye on her, but nothing was happening, and as much as I wanted to support her it seemed that her inability to find a topic and write came from her sense of inadequacy in using language. And then a germ of an idea came to me. Writers are readers first. After our class had read *Sarah, Plain and Tall,* for her Extension* of the book Monika read several other books by Patricia MacLachlan and she had written in her journal about the author's simple writing style. I scurried around the room and found MacLachlan's *Through Grandpa's Eyes,* a new acquisition, and Cynthia Rylant's wonderful books, *Waiting to Waltz* and *When I Was Young in the Mountains.* These are books intended for a much younger audience, but because they are beautifully written and illustrated are a delight for any age. I was taking the risk that Monika might be offended by being given "picture books," but I was willing to take that risk with the hope that those special books would support her as a writer and help *her* to start taking a risk—to start writing. Without any expression she took them and started reading. She read to the end of the class period and to my surprise did not return the books to me but put them in her Writing Folder.*

The next day Monika came into the room, took out her Writing Folder and the books and started to read and reread. I lost track of her until the last moments of class, when I noticed that she was no longer reading but writing.

The next day she returned the books to me and continued writing. I was dying of curiosity, but only reminded Monika that her writing group was ready to confer with her whenever she needed them. She smiled shyly and shook her head. Monika wrote, revised, and edited by herself, finally producing a finished piece. The spelling as it appears here is all Monika's, but is quite different from her early

---

* All asterisks throughout the book refer the reader to Chapter 10 where full strategy descriptions can be found.

drafts of this same piece when her experimentation focused on ideas. When the time came for us all to share our writing Monika startled us by volunteering to read her piece. She stood up, and in a voice that caused the class to lean forward straining to hear, she read "Moment of Sadness."

MOMENT OF SADNESS

Moment of Sadness was when I moved into a new neighborhood.
Moment of Sadness was when my parents yelled at each other.
Moment of Sadness was when my brother got his hand stuck in a fence wire.
Moment of Sadness was when my family and I left America to visit Poland.
Moment of Sadness was when my father went to visit Poland by himself.
Moment of Sadness was when I was going to kindergarten.
Moment of Sadness was when my cousin was taken by an ambulance.
Moment of Sadness was when my sister was having an operation.
Moment of Sadness was when my grandfather was in the hospital.
Moment of Sadness is when I read all these moments of sadness.

We were stunned—and touched. But after a moment of silent admiration the class burst into applause and Monika, the writer, sat down.

REFLECTIONS

A few days ago I was walking down a corridor in a local high school. On one of the doors this sign was prominently posted: "A mistake means that someone was trying to do something." Learning can't move forward, nor has it any place to go unless the learner is willing to experiment, to engage in the risky business of language learning. Risk-taking is certainly a natural part of the way three-year-old Samantha approaches literacy; it is the same strategy that works so well for her in oral language learning. However, it is not just the willingness to take risks, to experiment that produces growth in language. It is the adult acceptance and celebration of approximations as well. While there is inherent satisfaction in the discoveries that come from trying things out, the desire to continue is fueled when the people around you validate your attempts.

Traditional literacy instruction does not encourage inventiveness in the same way it is encouraged when young children are learning to speak. The result has been an unfair emphasis on perfect language—too early or too soon. Teachers need to understand that invented spellings, invented or no punctuation, nonstandard use of capital letters, and so on, are approximations of conventional written language in the same way that "weedikawus" is an approximation of the conventional spoken word. This is not to say that whole language teaching ignores standard English. Rather it recognizes the necessity of experimentation for all of us as we come to terms with new ideas and new ways of expressing them.

It's a shame that thirteen-year-old Monika forgot, if only momentarily, the one strategy, experimentation, that guarantees her movement forward as a reader/writer. Sometimes when I see Samantha experimenting with language I support her efforts in the same way I helped her figure out the pedals on her tricycle; but, at other times, I sit back and watch the learning process take care of itself. Skilled teachers like Barbara make conscious decisions about when and how to encourage experimentation.

GETTING THINGS DONE

IN THE HOME

One day Samantha and I were on our way home from a doctor's appointment. She was reading a coloring-book version of a story she already knew well. In the middle she turned to me and said, "Do you know *why* I'm reading this, Mommy? To find out if there is an Easter egg hunt."

Samantha reads and writes with me or reads and writes by herself because it helps her get things done. At three she *uses* reading and writing for lots of different reasons. She explores ideas and action: "Let's see what these dinosaurs are doing, Mom." She theorizes: "I wonder why Grandfather closed the gate on Peter." She soothes: "It will be all right, Grandma. Your broken leg will feel better soon." She gets information: "Wait! Don't put the pizza in! Let's see what the directions say." She role-plays: (pen poised above paper with a pouty look on her face pretending to be in first grade) "Do I *have* to do my homework, Mom?"

Reading and writing are embedded in the fabric of her daily life, and the range of functions alone is impressive. At three that's the primary thing she knows about literacy—you use it to get other things accomplished.

IN THE CLASSROOM

Pat Miller teaches a split third/fourth grade in a small, blue-collar suburb. This year she was convinced by Pat Colfer, another whole language teacher, that having a class animal throughout the school year gives an outside world dimension to the inside world of the classroom—and provides one of the best ways to integrate language and content. So, this year, Pat Miller started with a caterpillar.

> We found our huge green pet in the early fall leaves and immediately transported it to our classroom. All of us were unsure about the specific care of a caterpillar and that gave a focus to our initial questions. After some discussion we finally decided to line a large bell jar with leaves and twigs, and Bobby settled down to lunch in his new home. We settled down to write.

During the next half-hour we wrote of what we knew or had guessed about our pet's identity and needs. Some individuals chose to sit and observe, taking notes on Bobby's behavior as they watched. Two students reflected on our mistake in tampering with nature, and began to write an editorial. Most of us posed questions we wanted answers to. We thought we would have time to answer our questions at a reasonable pace, but when we observed that Bobby was shrouding himself with silken threads, we felt an urgency about our learning.

We took Bobby and some journals and traveled to other classrooms and the office. We conducted brief interviews as we went to see what others knew of caterpillars and cocoons. Often the interviews yielded more questions than they answered (for example, "Do you know if Bobby is going to be a moth or a butterfly?").

We made our decisions to investigate further with books, and a few days later moved our science class to our school library. We collected fiction and nonfiction books on caterpillars, cocoons, butterflies, and moths (*see* Appendix A). We took a short walk to our public library, searching through reference materials and insect anthologies.

We decided to form research teams, with each group focused on individual questions. Some children read independently, many drew pictures and diagrams. Like all good scientists, groups visited each other to check progress. The subsequent sharing and responding in our discussion circle was used to determine future directions.

Our interest in Bobby started permeating other parts of the curriculum. In their daily writing Bobby began to appear as a main character in stories with fact and fiction ingeniously woven together. His portrait was the focus in art and he was even the object of story problems in math. I read out loud daily of caterpillar and cocoon poetry, of a luna moth's life story, and of Carle's [Eric Carle: *The Very Hungry Caterpillar*] gluttonous caterpillar.

In the process of answering our questions we learned about caterpillars, moths, and butterflies; of molting and life stages; metamorphosis; habitat; food supply; reproduction; and the origins of Bobby's relatives.

Our fiction and nonfiction writing taught us of our pet's purpose, beauty, and place in the natural world from which we had taken him.

The saga does not end here. As I write [mid-December], Bobby is still in his cocoon. Long ago we cut the bell jar to allow for his anticipated 5-inch wing span when he emerges. The jar, plus cocoon, have been placed inside an old fish tank covered with leaves, branches, and a screen. His home is now outside within easy view, so our observations can continue. Letters to our pet still appear spontaneously, wishing him safe passage into his adult life. The two environmentalists are composing a lengthy "Ode to Bobby," certain that we interfered in our pet's destiny. All of this—and for a pet that has been immobile for almost our entire acquaintance! Next I plan to have a pet that *moves,* a gerbil or a snake or a bird . . .

REFLECTIONS

Professor Carole Edelsky has been concerned about real reading and writing in the classroom for a long time. In a recent conversation she said: "I don't think we will ever get this whole language stuff right unless we pay attention to authentic literacy." When Edelsky and Smith (1984) talk about the difference between authentic and inauthentic writing, they describe how the children they observed had to be "coaxed and prodded" into doing writing that served no purpose for them or for anyone save the teacher's ongoing evaluation. Book reports are the classic example of writing that is ". . . written to fulfill the assignment, though supposedly to interest others in reading the book, never actually used by the others in choosing a book, actually written to prove to the teacher that the book was read" (p. 31). There was no coaxing or prodding to write/read/research in Pat Miller's room when the cocoon formed a central part of their curriculum; there is no pushing to get the Message Board* filled in Pat Riordan's first-grade classroom. It is not the infamous threat of a bad grade that fills the pages of the reading journals in Barbara Lindberg's junior high reading class. And, when Pat Riordan asks her first-graders to talk about the books they are reading, she hears a chorus of "Okays," not moans and groans.

It must seem very strange to have thousands of meaningful encounters with reading and writing as a preschooler and then suddenly discover that school reading has little to do with personal meaning-making. Four- and five-year-olds come to school with a very well-developed notion of functional literacy, and *that* is a basic place to start, a point that all students understand, an instructional beginning that draws immediately on strength.

CONNECTIONS

IN THE HOME

Samantha made her first connection between real life and reading at eight months when the picture of a lightswitch and the accompanying "on/off" text prompted her to try to turn off the light in the book we were reading. "On/off, on/off, on/off" she repeated as she scratched the picture with her index finger.

Elements of the literature that Samantha and I read show up in so many ways, so many places, I often lose track, even though I keep journals of her development. Just recently, now a ripe old three years and nine months, she pulled a small pink brush from a bathroom drawer and, holding it close to her face, she purred: "Oh, what a beautiful pink brush, the Mommy said." In her oral language she borrows from many authors to get her points across:

> Early one winter morning, I was at my computer writing, she toddled into my office. Crowding me, she got her face close to the screen. "I see the cursor, Mommy! Could I try to write my name—pleeeeeese—just one time and that's it!" Sensing that I was ready to say no, she added, "Oh, do, Mommy, do!" (From *Mommy, Buy Me a China Doll* Zemach, 1966).

Samantha borrows whole patterns to make jokes.

> [laughing] "Oh, Mommy, Mommy won't you marry me?
> "With your musket, fife and drum?"
> "Oh, no, sweet maid I cannot marry you
> "For I have no Samantha to put on."
> (From *Soldier, Soldier, Won't You Marry Me?* Langstaff, 1972)

Part of my talk about books is making comparisons to other books and to life experiences: "Does that rhinoceros remind you of the one in the little boy's tree?" (comparing *May I Bring a Friend* deRegniers, 1964 with *It Didn't Frighten Me* Goss & Harste, 1981). "What happened when we went to the parade last summer?" (connecting to *Up Goes Mr. Downs* Smath, 1984). And now Samantha is doing it, too: "Mom, this greedy zebra is just like greedy cat." (comparing Joy Cowley's *Greedy Cat* with Hadithi Mwenye's 1984 *Greedy Zebra*). Contexts overflowing with real reading and writing and speaking inspire connected, literate thought.

IN THE CLASSROOM

Inside Carol Porter's classroom, she tries to insure that the curriculum encourages a wide range of connections.

> I know how important it is for my students to bring what they know into the classroom and make personal connections to whatever we are reading or writing about. I encourage long chains of connections by using Text Sets* as the basic underlying tool in my classroom. The sets I have developed (*see* Appendix A) usually begin with a focus on genre, theme, or author. Over the summer I planned an author study set focusing on the novels written by Chris Crutcher. As I read his books I tried to identify themes and connections that my students might make as they read and discussed the books. I generated a list of novels and short stories relating to these topics, and a folder of information on the author and how his personal life relates to his writing. But it wasn't until my students and I read, wrote about our reading, and discussed the first book, *The Crazy Horse Electric Game,* that the Text Set developed into a network of our personal connections.
>
> Fiction and nonfiction materials on topics such as acquired brain damage, physical disabilities, runaways, SIDS, death, baseball, and divorce are now included in the set, as well as *Running Loose* and *Stotan!,* two other books by Crutcher. Maps, personal snapshots, and travel brochures of Montana, Idaho, Washington, and California have been posted at our classroom learning center so that students can locate specific scenes from the book. Audiotapes of songs mentioned in the books are also available at the center, along with printed versions of the songs. Students found that the song, "A Boy Named Sue," was written by Shel Silverstein. This prompted them to ask for books of poetry by that author. Two weeks ago Corey brought in a photocopied page from *Julius Caesar* showing a quote that Crutcher turned into a play on words in *The Crazy Horse Electric Game.* An article from the

The English Journal about the use of Crutcher's book in an Advanced Placement classroom for seniors concerned about the 4.9 reading level of *Running Loose* was added to the set recently.

REFLECTIONS

In their studies of the relationship between background knowledge and comprehension, schema theorists have helped us understand that learning is basically a process of making connections. In reading, we comprehend when we make connections to past experiences, including other books we have read or pieces we have written. Encouraging a life/literature and literature/literature connection was a professional interest that I brought home to my daughter, and it's something that whole language teachers keep alive in their classrooms. Donald Graves hypothesizes that "lifelong readers are found in children who connect their reading with life events" (1989, p. 781).

EXPECTATION AND CELEBRATION

IN THE HOME

My husband and I had no doubts about Samantha learning to talk. Not only did we expect it from the beginning, we treated every formless sound as highly polished speech, skillfully delivered. What a little thespian! And our friends were no different. We all ooohed and aaahed over the slightest babble, and returned each attempt with a validation of successful communication.

Our celebration of even the smallest change in Samantha's speech has extended beyond our immediate home. One of my greatest satisfactions has been sharing the things that she says with her grandparents, our brothers and sisters, and friends who will tolerate the gloating. Our ooohing and aaahing have extended also. Now it's Samantha's reading and writing and art that we encourage and celebrate at every opportunity. We treat her as a proficient reader/writer/artist, respecting her opinions and interpretations of stories, mailing out her scribbled messages to the intended recipients, displaying special drawings on the refrigerator door. And, like her speech, which is developing quite nicely, we have a solid expectation that eventually she will read and write in adult form.

IN THE CLASSROOM

I asked Carol Porter to comment on the changes, if any, in her expectations of students as she transformed her traditional teaching into instruction based on whole language principles.

There was a time when I expected my students, who had learned to hate reading and writing and school so much as to be resistant to any activity, to fail; to do little, if any, homework; to turn in few assignments; and to cause me nightmares when it came to discipline and classroom behavior. Sure enough, they met all my expectations and I felt justified in what I believed about them.

Now I expect the opposite—that they will read and write and complete the activities they commit to. At a conference last fall a teacher asked me what I did about students who refused to do the work in my whole language class. I didn't really know how to answer her without sounding smug, but all I could come up with was, "If you expect them to do the work, they will." I'm not sure she believed me, but every month I expect my students to read at least one novel and several short stories, write journal entries for their reading, publish [in school] at least one piece of writing, and contribute to discussions related to their reading and writing—and they do. I also expect them to read and write at home. I know it may be hard to believe, especially for students who have long histories of not reading and writing and giving teachers a hard time, but doing the work (or not) just isn't an issue any more. Again, they meet my expectations.

I do know there is more to it than a change in my expectations; they have expectations of themselves that they didn't have in the past. Through reading and writing choices and making firm commitments to peers about group discussions and goals, they now take the responsibility for their learning—and that makes all the difference.

REFLECTIONS

Brian Cambourne (1984) talks about expectations as very subtle forms of communication to which children are highly sensitive. Think about those areas of your life in which you have excelled, and those in which you have failed or have only performed at a mediocre level. My own images of success are filled with adults, teachers or peers, for whom I had a great deal of respect and who respected me enough as a learner to communicate high expectations regarding my ability to achieve. Expectations, positive or negative, are incredible influences on performance. When they are coupled with student choice and ongoing celebrations of risk-taking and sincere effort, they can virtually mold a developing learner.

FROM HOME TO SCHOOL

Samantha is in nursery school now, and the year after next it will be kindergarten. I admit I am nervous about her formal schooling. Like every parent I want her school years to be happy and productive, but I'm worried that all the strength she has gathered in her few years of living somehow won't be recognized: her solid oral and written language foundation; her risk-taking strategies; her ability to connect life and literature; her view of speaking and reading and writing as functional tools that help her get things done; and her image of herself as a capable learner, reader, and writer.

The transition from home to school for Carol Porter's daughter, Michelle, has been anything but smooth. Below Carol talks about the problems and anxieties both she and her daughter have faced:

> As I read Nancie Atwell's *In the Middle* and listened to Kathleen Visovatti describe the writing that her second-graders do, I was saddened because my daughter has not had the experience of being in a whole language classroom. Michelle strives to please, which has made school life difficult for her since she's always trying to figure out exactly what the teacher wants from her. She is not a risk-taker anymore—she was when she entered school. Now she's afraid of being wrong and, while she receives teacher rewards, I feel that she is stagnating academically.
>
> This past year much of our studying time was spent memorizing facts for science and social studies. Michelle's note cards for a social studies report on her ancestors received a grade of 89 percent with a comment of "Great Job!" Her final draft received a 96 percent for oral presentation, 95 percent for final copy, and 98 percent for language. The comments were: "Well done!" and "Well written, presented and organized. You can be proud of a fine effort." She was not proud, however. She just kept wondering what she had done wrong—and what she had done right. She felt little ownership in the project itself because every part of it was prescribed from the beginning—no room for her to put a personal stamp on it. The cover of her report had to be drawn in a certain way with the name "Porter" on it, even though the research was not done on that side of the family. Michelle was even afraid to include some wonderful transcriptions of Italian records and pictures we had taken on a trip to show her where her ancestors lived when they arrived from Italy. It wasn't until I said I would take full responsibility if she was graded down for it that she agreed to slip them in at the end of the report.
>
> Working on school projects could and should be a nurturing time for us, but it usually causes pain since her efforts are totally focused on figuring out the correct response, while I am encouraging her to ask her own questions and follow her own interests.

Literacy researcher Denny Taylor says: ". . . we need to bridge the gap between home and school so that reading in one is reading in the other." (1983, p. 19). I think her statement needs to be broader: Living in one should look like living in the other. Our challenge as effective teachers is to begin to bring the successful learning conditions that exist in the home and other places outside of the classroom into our schools. Whole language can help us do that.

Personal Reflection

How can I begin to create contexts in the classroom that are more like the natural learning that takes place outside of school?

The Role of
the Teacher

3

When Carolyn Burke and Jerry Harste first introduced me to whole language, I was at the end of my masters degree. I was enrolled in a summer practicum experience and spent each morning in a school helping other teachers teach reading. The seminars prior to the in-school experience had convinced me totally, unequivocally that whole language made far more sense than the abstract, skill-based model I had been using in my basal program. Here was an explanation of language and learning that was exciting, all-encompassing; one that looked at development in an integrated, whole child way. I embraced the theory quickly, even passionately, and couldn't wait to get my hands on some kids so I could try it out. But the morning I walked into my assigned school I was jolted by the realization that I really had no idea about *what* I was supposed to do. While the theory seemed crystal clear to me, the implementation and, particularly, *my* role in doing it, were unclear.

I decided to go with the one thing I did understand—that whole language meant reading whole books (how could anybody miss this?). Perhaps *that* was my primary role—acting as a resource for good literature. Armed with that hypothesis I spent the first part of my summer reading good children's books, passing them out to students, and then standing along the cinderblock walls hoping Carolyn or Jerry would not come in to observe my "teaching." Eventually, they did. Carolyn sauntered in one hot, summer morning just after our students had finished watching a videotape of *The Red Balloon.* My co-teacher (also an M.A. student) and I looked at each other nervously and Carolyn's teaching assistant scuttled across the room to us: "Do you have a copy of *The Red Balloon*?" she hissed. As we scrambled to find the written counterpart to the video, I wondered uncomfortably for the thousandth time since my introduction to whole language *what else* I should be doing as a whole language teacher. Surely, this new model of teaching was about more than being a good librarian.

As it turned out, defining my role as literature resource person was a reasonable place to start. But as the weeks rolled on I began to refine my undifferentiated beginning. What I learned about my new role I learned primarily from watching Carolyn Burke. I observed her interactions with kids, and I scrutinized her responses to us, the teachers. I discovered that from first grade to graduate teaching her role never varied. She taught me the meaning of master teacher as she answered questions directly when she deemed it appropriate, pushed for independent solutions when she did not; acted as a resource and, at the same time, encouraged learners to reach beyond her toward their own goals. It wasn't called empowerment then, but she empowered us nonetheless—and she empowered equally the young students with whom she worked.

It took me a while to understand that it was a complicated, well-developed social model of teaching/learning we experienced that summer. It rocked my passive view of what it is that "good" teachers do. The part of Carolyn's behavior that stood out above all the rest and the part that was most valuable to me was that while we were frantically asking questions about language-based teaching, Carolyn was busy asking her own professional questions. She saw herself as a learner, a teacher in perpetual motion, always changing and growing, always moving forward. Her strongest message to me that summer was that teaching is learning; this understanding helped me relax with the things I didn't know.

Back in my own classroom that fall I stopped waiting for a teacher's manual to tell me what to do. I started by taking a long hard look at my students. Miraculously, they all had language competency and real-world knowledge. I had never seen that before, and I felt as if someone had been holding out on me. I told them that we would be learning together—about each other, about reading and writing. Slowly, my curriculum began to gather a strength, a consistency, and a child-orientation it simply had not had before.

This chapter is about changing roles in a whole language classroom. Moving toward whole language means that our roles as teachers are dramatically different, yet we are no less critical, no less central, to our students and the curriculum. Whole language teachers are not managers of programs or distributors of materials; we are not technicians implementing packages planned by some faceless Other. We are learners and demonstrators and facilitators, recapturing the excitement of forever being a student as we use our expertise to create optimal learning environments.

While many things change on the way to whole language, the one thing that doesn't change is our position as instructional leaders. In fact, empowered with new understandings of the teaching/learning process, our role as professional decision-makers is a bright light that has dimmed for many other educators. It yields a new feeling of strength derived not from getting students to play the game *our* way but from skillfully creating a game we can all play.

TEACHER AS LEARNER/DEMONSTRATOR

When Kenneth Torbeck edged warily into Carol Porter's twelfth-grade reading class for the first time, he expected that he would have to "read the same old low-level books and do the same stupid worksheets." Most likely stupid is the way he felt doing them. But this time he was wrong. There were no worksheets or low-level books. Instead, he found a teacher who respects her students enough to give them choices about what they read; he found a teacher who joins groups and reads and writes along with her students, sharing her insights and her changes as a literate person.

In her classroom Carol Porter is at once a learner and a demonstrator. She constantly strives to connect with her students on a human level by joining in their reading and writing endeavors. She reads the books her students read; she wonders out loud with them about the reasons for a character's actions; she shows students how she relates personally to an emotion; she talks through her comprehension snags; and she makes sure her interpretations are seen as only one possibility. During literature discussions the questions she asks are those for which she needs clarification as a reader seeking meaning, not questions for which she already has the answer. Both the students and Carol prepare for reading discussions by starring or highlighting items in their Reading Journals*, to share for confirmation or differing opinions. When they come together for discussion of writing in progress, Carol receives help with her pieces along with the other writers. Here is an excerpt from a discussion Carol had with one of her reading groups. It shows how she enters into the discussion as a real reader, a bona-fide member of the group, demonstrating her process through genuine interactions with her co-readers. Pat, a tenth-grader, initiates the group discussion.

> PAT: Is the Salmon Lake in this story the same as the Salmon Lake in the last book we read?
> COREY: We don't know, but since both stories are written by the same author, and it's near where he grew up, they probably are.
> PAT: We tried to find it on the map and never could.
> COREY: What I didn't get was why did Louie call his parents by their first names? I grew up in the South and you just don't do that down there. It's disrespectful.
> CAROL: One of the things some of my colleagues and I have been discussing is if students should be able to call teachers by their first names after graduation. What do you think of that?
> COREY: I could never do it, but I think it depends on the two people and what their relationship is.
> PAT: Maybe they aren't really his parents; you know, stepparents or something.

---

* All asterisks throughout the book refer the reader to Chapter 10 where full strategy descriptions can be found.

CAROL: I thought that too at first, but then I asked myself what might the author be trying to say about a kid who calls his parents by their first names—maybe they have a close relationship or the parents are just real progressive?
COREY: That makes sense based upon what happens at the principal's office. The dad stands up to the principal and sticks by Louie like a friend would.

Commenting on her role in these group meetings Carol says:

> It's no different than any of the other members' roles. I read through my journal and star what I want to talk about to the others in the group. I do not formulate questions to assess their understanding of the material or to push them to higher levels of thinking, but the kind of thinking I'm interested in almost always occurs as we explore together what we have read. And, it is *self*-initiated, not teacher-induced. Instead of questions, I do what I would do if I were discussing a book with a friend: I make statements concerning my opinions and feelings, make personal connections to the reading, and ask for clarification when I need it."

About her role in general, Carol states:

> To me there are three major benefits to being a whole language teacher: I really get to know my students. I have time to read adolescent and content-related literature and . . . I get to continue being a student myself. There's no chance for burnout here. I have too many exciting things to read and learn and talk about.
>
> I expend at least as much energy as a whole language teacher as I did when I was a more traditional teacher, but the work is very different. Rather than preparing worksheets, tests, and grading papers, I am reading novels and short stories, writing letters to my students about my learning and theirs, writing in my own journal about my reading, writing and revising my own texts, and planning reading and writing Mini-lessons.* I used to spend my summers planning units and lessons for the coming year. Now I spend my summers reading and trying to find books and short stories that high school students will enjoy reading.

In Pat Miller's combined third/fourth grades she, too, becomes a learner beside her students. Because her school draws heavily from a nearby naval base, her students' language and experience are wide-ranging. Pat sees this as a tremendous advantage, and taps into the diversity every chance she gets. When teachers like Pat continually experience learning on a personal level, they are more likely to incorporate a similar kind of learning into the curriculum (Crafton, 1987). Pat calls taking a learner position in the classroom an "inside view."

> I see the learning possibilities when I take the pupil role. It might be reading my own book along with the class, trying a new algorithm for math subtraction, or revising a story I've drafted. It's the reason we seldom do the same activity twice in our classroom, or year to year. When it's a new learning experience for all of us,

> I can understand how it feels from the inside. It's the same when I take the collaborative role. When I think out loud with my students and remain open to their influence, I can see that the meaning gained from interaction stays uniquely our own but is richly shared.

Participating in the learning events going on in your classroom means that you not only intimately understand the strategies and struggles that your students are confronting but you have an opportunity to share your thinking, your interpretations, and your decisions, as you encourage them to share theirs. These are the process demonstrations mentioned in Chapter 1 of this book. For the most part, our classrooms at all grade levels are devoid of them. Amazing that we give so much lip service to teaching our kids how to think but rarely give them a glimpse into the intricacies of the very thing we want them to do.

A freshman science teacher asked me not long ago if there is a place for research papers in whole language instruction. After I assured her that there was, she expressed her apprehension about the assignment she had just given her freshmen. "They've never done a research paper before. I'm afraid most of the papers will be poorly researched and poorly written." We talked for a while about the importance of her students *reading* the kind of research they were expected to do and about the impact of self-selected topics and collaboration. We talked of the possibility of bringing a researcher into the classroom to discuss the generation of research questions and how that researcher goes about doing systematic inquiry. As I was leaving, I asked her what topic she had chosen to research and how she would share her own research procedure with her students. She looked at me blankly.

While a teacher demonstration of inquiry process would have helped these freshmen researchers, demonstration is not the exclusive domain of the teacher. Students need opportunities to share their thinking as well: How do they choose a topic in writing? How do they select the next book to read? How do they tighten, add detail, insert new ideas, rearrange old ones? How do they come to terms with confusing texts? And on and on. The idea is to get into the curriculum multiple demonstrations of how to approach a learning activity and how to think your way through it. In a reflective letter one of Carol's students wrote:

> I have learned to look at different ideas in a story—in other reading classes we had to see the story the way the teacher saw the stories. When the teacher prepares questions you only learn the same thing about the story the teacher has learned.

How many times have you told your students about the part you had to reread because the sentence was just too complicated or the idea too unfamiliar? How often have you allowed them to think along with you as you compose a letter, a story, a "To Do" list, an essay, or even a grocery list? When students and teachers talk together about their thinking, they begin to form an interpretive community. Because process demonstrations are a daily part of school life, one of Pat Miller's students remarked: "There are very many smart people in our classroom, not just Ms. Miller. That is why our questions will be answered."

TEACHER AS FACILITATOR

Several years ago I became fascinated with the long-distance swimming feats of Diana Nyad. I followed her days of preparation before she tackled the grueling miles around Manhattan Island. I marveled at her training and her commitment, and was all the more impressed because I assumed that she was in this alone. One night on the news, however, I learned the real story. During all of her ultra-athletic undertakings, she always had a small lifeboat purring quietly beside her. The boat was filled with emergency equipment, sustenance, and two watchful supporters, ever vigilant, constantly calling words of encouragement to her.

When a classroom becomes child-oriented and student-directed, teachers no longer assume primary responsibility for the learning that occurs. They do, however, climb into lifeboats and float alongside, watching for opportunities to support, looking for openings to offer encouragement. When teachers help their students along, lead them from behind, instead of doggedly pushing them in a predetermined direction, they are making a distinction between facilitation of learning and traditional instructional control. Facilitation is the essence of responsive teaching.

Facilitating learning is the opposite of controlling it. One of the toughest things you are likely to encounter in whole language teaching is giving up control in your classroom. Not because you are necessarily a controlling person but because the system itself is enmeshed in the idea of transmission teaching (Barnes, 1975) in which we dole out our expertise to our students in a steady, predetermined script. In Margaret Donaldson's brilliant book, *Children's Minds,* she captures the tension between rule-driven, formal education and child-centered, progressive education. She sees the conflict between the two as being intimately related to control: "I can only see one way out of this dilemma: it is to exercise such control as is needful with a light touch and never to relish the need" (1978, p. 126). Most teachers have a deep-seated concern about students and their development, a fervent wish to help them grow in positive ways. For these teachers the realization that our teaching is less than it can be—for us and for our kids— is often enough to send them down a different, more facilitative, less-controlling path.

In this wave of educational change, which is slowly gaining momentum, the major shift, I believe, has to come at this point—it may all come down to issues of control and shared responsibility and teachers who are willing to allow students to direct their own learning. It can be a scary, painful proposition when you get right down to it. Nancie Atwell calls the change she made from teaching reading curriculum to teaching eighth-graders "pure heartache" (1987, p. 19). We have so much invested in the other kind of teaching, but because we can't identify up front what will set a young mind in motion, where it will go and how it will get there, giving up control and sharing the curriculum is necessary. Like so many other changes, it can happen a little at a time.

Dan Powers started his change to whole language while teaching language arts in grades six, seven, and eight. He talks about his slowly changing perceptions, about his facilitative role in the classroom, about how he started the shift and what has happened along the way.

> I used to wonder what a whole language classroom would look like—and what I would look like in it. As I talked to other teachers and read books like Douglas Barnes' *From Communication to Curriculum,* I began to perceive my job as teacher as one in which I needed to spend more time creating environments and situations in which students could *use* literate behaviors, rather than master a list of skills.

> Literate behavior, I decided, would require me to give students more time to discuss their reading and writing than I had been doing in the past. That meant I was going to have to turn over more control to them and learn to keep my mouth shut more often. That scared me. How would the kids know what to learn if I didn't tell them what was important!!!?

> I didn't have answers at that point, but I was committed to exploring possible ways to set up new structures to encourage more independent learning. If I wanted them to buy into the curriculum and take some ownership in their development as language users, I was going to have to give them enough room so that it could happen.

> It really was Barnes' book that got me to begin to view student talk in the class as a positive, rather than a negative. His point about talk as a means of learning led me to attempt to set up more and more small-group interactions where I was not the central figure. I had already set some of this in motion though, so my students could talk about their drafts in writing, but I began to look into ways to incorporate it into their reading experiences.

> Initially, I determined the groups and charged them with a task: to compare the theme of one story to another, or discuss possible motives for a character's actions. But by my third year of change I was willing to let the reading groups self-select.

> The idea was simply to put out several books at a time and then do a little advertisement, a Book Talk,* for each of the books being offered to a class [at this time, I was teaching two classes each of grades six, seven, and eight]. Within this introduction I would try to give high points to intrigue my students, I would comment on the complexity of the piece; potential problems; connections to previously read stories, authors, genres.

> I began with only two books and worked up to about four at a time per class. There was often overlap, but it wasn't unusual to have seven or eight books going at once. This became possible because the students were taking over much of the group responsibilities that I had previously believed must be handled by the teacher.

> After the Book Talks,* students would write down their choices. If there was a big mismatch between reader and book, I would conference with the student, but I would never deny them the right to try a story. I feel strongly that if we want students to take intellectual risks, we must arrange a psychologically safe environment.

> Once grouped by their selection of a particular book, the groups met to discuss how to begin. Guidelines included how much they would read for the next meeting.

They were also asked to bring in discussion questions and/or comments, which were written in their journals. The last ten minutes of each class was used for follow-up journal writing in which they would reflect on the discussion that had occurred within their groups. [Between checking their journals regularly and occasionally listening to group discussions, I found I was quite capable of keeping track of individual's participation and development.]

From the beginning I was worried that they wouldn't really engage in serious discussions if I weren't there prodding, pushing, and generally leading them forward [maybe I had been confused about teaching and animal training]. I couldn't have been more wrong about this. While observing these heterogeneous groups in action, I found that not only did they discuss the stories but they actually helped each other comprehend and interpret. If someone was having trouble, the group often would help by explaining where the person had gotten lost. Sometimes this was in the form of vocabulary help, thinking through a difficult passage, finding a main idea, sorting out details, reorganizing a confused sequence of events, filling in gaps in a reader's background so that he or she could understand a reference, and so on. If a group was really stuck and they felt they wanted my contribution, or needed direction, they let me know and I would join them.

Dan often chooses to have discussions with individual students as the group meetings are going on. He feels that the individual exchanges he has with his students allow for a more natural and realistic literary interaction. Whether he joins a small-group discussion as a member sharing his thoughts and interpretations, or is involved in an intimate discussion with an individual reader, he finds the thinking "far more significant and sophisticated" than the old days of teacher-directed comprehension.

It would be easy to believe that these kinds of student-generated discussions could only occur at the junior high or high school level, but Kathleen Visovatti, Pat Miller, Pat Riordan, and Penny Silvers have all found that their younger students are quite capable of interacting in a productive, open-ended manner with the books they read. While sometimes the teachers join groups to contribute their own thinking, which can help facilitate the exchanges, the classroom contexts themselves are facilitative of the kind of learning these whole language teachers value.

One day I took Samantha into Kathleen's second-grade classroom to videotape and to talk to some of Kathleen's students. We walked into the classroom during writing time and all of the students were engaged in one writing project or another. Samantha said hello to Kathleen and a few of the children and then turned her attention to the activity in the classroom. After a short time she came over to me and whispered: "Mom, could I have some paper?" Kathleen helped me gather up markers, pencils, and recycled paper from the bin and we settled her into a chair at a low table. A half an hour later she was still writing.

Activity in literate contexts is contagious, but the facilitative nature of these environments is not accidental. The high level of engagement in whole language classrooms is due to a great degree to the careful preparation of the learning setting by the teacher.

WHAT ABOUT DIRECT INSTRUCTION?

There is an old joke about walking into a whole language classroom and not being able to find the teacher. A concern about blending in too well with students has caused many teachers to keep their distance from whole language, viewing it with an anxious eye. The fear, it seems, is that whole language teachers somehow lose their identities amidst all the collaborating and contextualizing. This is an unfounded fear. Whole language teachers do indeed "teach," but their teaching takes a different form.

Jerry Harste stresses the idea that whole language teachers are in the middle of the classroom, not out the door. Writing researcher Lucy Calkins talks about high student input/high teacher input. Nancie Atwell cautions us not to be afraid to teach. These educators underscore the centrality of a whole language teacher—teachers who have intimate knowledge about literacy and learning and who direct their energies to the development of effective learning contexts, to meaningful discussions with students, to strong demonstrations of proficient literacy and skilled problem-solving. Whole language teachers have a different notion about what it means to teach, but because of the responsive nature of the pedagogy they are indispensable to their students.

Seeing the major contrasts between traditional teaching and responsive teaching may help you understand and reconsider what you have done in the classroom in the past, and the ways you would like your role in the classroom to change now.

In our personal lives we embody multiple roles: teacher, spouse, lover, friend, athlete, and so on. Depending on need and focus, one role gets highlighted over the others, but most often they transact. It is the bringing together of such roles that allow curriculum to be created. That is the topic of Chapter 4, but, first, a final word from Dan Powers about the beginning of his changing role.

THE ROLE OF THE TEACHER

Traditional	Whole Language
Transmitter of information	Facilitator of learning
Focuses on product	Focuses on process
Teaches skills in isolation	Highlights strategies in functional contexts
Emphasizes direct instruction	Emphasizes demonstration, engagement, and reflection
Controls the learning	Places responsibility for learning on students
Builds curriculum on deficits	Builds curriculum on strengths
Minimizes social learning	Maximizes social learning

I began to realize that as I turned over some of my control to the students they were becoming more empowered, which appeared to make them more involved. Yet I was also gaining a type of empowerment because I was, for the first time, beginning to get real glimpses into their thinking. Sure, it was work, but I felt I had finally discovered what teaching was all about. I began to feel more and more confident about not slavishly following some preconceived curriculum that didn't seem to meet the needs of my students. I began to see myself as the decision-maker in my own classroom—funny that it took me awhile to see that as a problem.

Have I mastered this? No. Will I ever master it? I doubt it. BUT, it's exciting in a way my other teaching never was, . . . and it has kept me in teaching. A major discovery that I've come upon in my development as a whole language teacher is that in order to teach reading and language (and anything), I had to learn how kids learn. The only way to do that was to watch them, and talk to them about what's going on in their heads. That can't be done when they are never asked to think beyond filling in a workbook page with answers that they guess the teacher wants to see.

If we want real readers we must help students develop a sense of control over print; if we want real learners, a sense of control over their ideas. We must give them the power necessary to do that. As for us, we must act, as Roger Taylor says, as guides on the side rather than sages on the stage.

Personal Reflection

Reconsider the contrasting lists regarding "The Role of the Teacher." What changes can you make in your teaching to move you from the traditional side toward whole language?

THE ROLE OF THE TEACHER

Traditional	Whole Language	Your Change
Transmitter of information	Facilitator of learning	
Focuses on product	Focuses on process	
Teaches skills in isolation	Highlights strategies	
Direct instruction	Demonstration, engagement, reflection	
Controls the learning	Student responsible for learning	
Deficit curriculum	Strength curriculum	
Minimizes social learning	Maximizes social learning	

Student-Centered Learning: Beginning Inquiry and Integration

4

In 1975 a tornado hit the small southern Indiana town of Hanover where I grew up and where I was teaching at the time. The high school was damaged beyond repair, and when I waded into my elementary classroom I watched the costumes my students were going to wear in their Easter play bobbing on the flooded floor alongside chunks of wall and ceiling. The decision was made to find a makeshift school for third grade and higher so the students could resume their reading and math instruction.

I talked recently to one of those third-graders, now a college junior preparing to student teach. Jeff talked about the impact the tornado had had on him, his family, and friends. And then he showed me a short story he had written about it called "Reading Destruction."

In Jeff's story he described going back to school, the first day still a vivid image as he recalled seeing friends for the first time after the storm and anxiously inquiring about their families. Sitting next to one classmate, he leaned over and asked if anyone was hurt. "Yeh, my grandma. Her leg. How about you?" As they were talking the teacher's voice came sternly from the front of the room: "Boys! Stop talking about the tornado and get back to your reading workbooks."

After experiencing firsthand the pain and anxiety caused by a natural disaster, Jeff and his friends had questions: Did anyone close to them get hurt? Did anyone in the small town get killed? What was the extent of the damage? What were people doing immediately before the tornado hit? Was this a tornado of major proportions? Why did it rain for so many days after the tornado? What causes a tornado to form? And how would Hanover ever get back to normal? Jeff's teacher missed a golden opportunity to respond to her students' fears, to help them answer their questions, to encourage them to use reading and writing and talking to explore and extend their inquiries. Instead, she silenced their voices and got back to the "real" stuff of school.

In their book, *Whole Language, Inquiring Voices,* Watson, Burke, and Harste (1989, pp. 40-66) present a number of curriculum stories. In these brief accounts students and teachers *create* curriculum as they go about exploring real-life questions through reading, writing, talking, and research. One teacher was interested in encouraging alternative thinking through experience centers, so she invited students to explore books that highlighted the idea of perspective. One entire class brainstormed questions they wanted to do research on following the earthquake in Soviet Armenia. Everyone chose a research partner, including the teacher, and they proceeded collaboratively to answer their questions and share their findings. A second-grade class, a sixth-grade class, and a group of preservice teachers all teamed up for a pen pal project. The undergraduates learned about writing processes, while the children answered questions about their development through self-evaluation.

Chapter 4 is about teachers and students answering questions—their own and others'. And it is about the kind of deep learning that occurs when the curriculum is integrated across content areas, language processes, and experiences.

INQUIRY

In part, whole language is a reaction to packaged curriculum, uniform activities, and ideas hammered out in studentless and teacherless places and then transplanted into a thousand different classrooms to be used with a thousand different learners. Not only are these standardized activities based on other people's interests and questions but they are often short activities that are also disconnected. For many, school has become a kind of cognitive runaround. In our primary grades, our intermediate grades, and our high schools, students are jumping from one story to the next, one chapter to the next, one topic to the next, most of them at a pace that is too fast—a pace that doesn't give students a chance to come to terms with specific content or to make the critical connections among language expressions. Writer Donald Graves calls this the cha-cha-cha curriculum, and it just doesn't work. Some of our students engage, but most of them put on their academic best and perfunctorily work through tasks that hold no meaning for them and, consequently, have no long-term impact on them.

Schools, not teachers and students, have long served in the role of question-asker: What materials are appropriate for our first-graders to read? How much time should be spent on math? When should high-schoolers be introduced to the Civil War? How should spelling be taught? What words should be learned? Questions, and even the means to answer them, are produced apart from kids and classrooms.

One year I subbed in a sixth-grade classroom for a full semester while the permanent teacher was convalescing. Time after time these tough kids from migrant families questioned me about the reading and writing topics being imposed on them. Why, they wanted to know, did they have to read a story on public art in New York City? It didn't have anything to do with them. Good question. Why was I asking them to write a different ending to a story they didn't like in the first place? Because the teacher's manual suggested it. It was one of my most uncomfortable times in teaching. I didn't have reasonable responses to give to these twelve-year-olds. I had not figured out that effective curriculum has to represent students' lives and passions at least as much as it takes into account the topics and content prescribed by the textbook or school.

The topics and questions that are pursued in any classroom need to come from four basic sources: students' interests, teacher's interests, grade level/school/state requirements and incidental occurrences (*see* Figure 4.1).

When each of these sources is considered, many whole language teachers find a great deal of overlap in them. Kathleen, for example, asks her students at the beginning of each year what they would like to learn about in second grade. Animals is often a topic that is mentioned, and is one that Kathleen has loved to set up as an area of inquiry for her past second-grade classes. It is also an area covered in her science text. Because it is a strong topic area, important to everyone involved in deciding curriculum, she often begins her year with an animal research unit (*see* Figure 4.2). The process and content of this unit are described in the "Fact and Fiction" section later in this chapter.

Another strong topic area in Kathleen's classroom this year has been endangered species. This inquiry

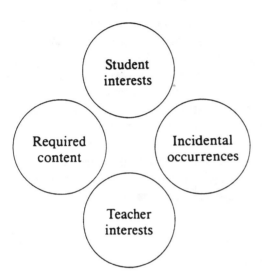

FIGURE 4.1
Sources to Consider for Identification of Curricular Content

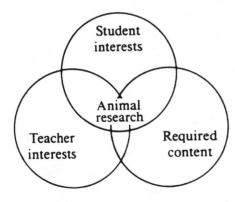

FIGURE 4.2
Overlap of Student Interests, Teacher Interests, and Required Area of Study to Determine Curricular Content

began with a chapter in the science textbook. Many of Kathleen's students were outraged when they found out about the murder of baby elephants, while disappearing dolphins intrigued a number of students. Their concern, which has become a passion, was channeled into an Interest Club* that has been meeting twice a week since the beginning of the year and is showing no signs of slowing down.

The Endangered Species Club has become a social force in the school and beyond—eight-year-olds to be reckoned with. After reading the textbook chapter students started collecting other books and articles on the topic. From that information, each of the club members chose an endangered animal and wrote a book—this writing often took place during the morning writing workshop. When the students learned that dolphins are endangered because Japanese fishermen use them as above-water cues to schools of yellowfin tuna, they made and posted signs in the halls that read: BOYCOTT TUNA AT LUNCH. Their cafeteria serves yellowfin tuna for lunch every Wednesday. Students also wrote letters to the cafeteria staff urging them to replace the yellowfin with white albacore. The cafeteria manager has not yet responded.

These young activists have also collected money in order to join Greenpeace and the World Wildlife Fund; wrote to President George Bush urging him to be more sensitive to the plight of endangered animals; became pen pals with another Endangered Species Club in Kittye Copeland's Columbia, Missouri, classroom; and, finally, set up a consulting business. The second-grade Endangered Species Classroom Consultants* have business cards and professional brochures (*see* Figure 4.3). So far, they have been asked to speak in several other classrooms, and have made presentations at a local children's museum. They are now in the process of doing research on the possibility of "adopting" a zoo animal.

Now there are three Interest Clubs* going in this classroom: Endangered Species, Sports, and How to Become a Doctor. Kathleen is hopeful, however, that a field trip to a local Health Center planned in the next few weeks will spark new areas of inquiry (many health areas are mandated by the states to be covered at different grade levels), and that the new clubs will consider inviting health professionals to their classrooms to help them answer students' questions.

Kathleen has made collaborative inquiry a way of life in her classroom. Recently she saw that *National Geographic* would send a packet of material on the environment on request. The environment is an important issue for her, and she knew that it also was for another fourth-grade teacher in her building. Kathleen suggested that they team the classes to do research on environmental issues.

Kathleen and her colleague started the inquiry by gathering materials they thought the students might need. The *National Geographic* packet suggested that they form committees on Land, Air, Water, and Energy Resources. Students chose their groups with an equal number of second- and fourth-graders on each committee. Their first task was to pair up with partners from the different classrooms, and

---

* All asterisks throughout the book refer the reader to Chapter 10 where full strategy descriptions can be found.

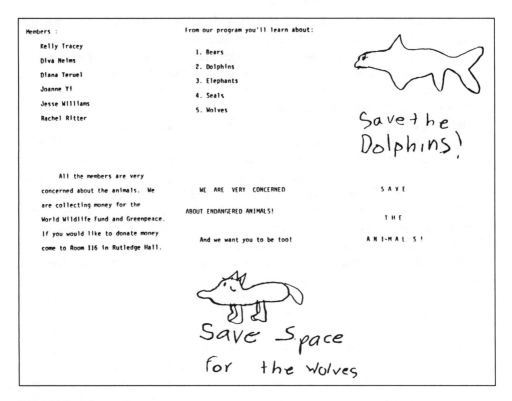

FIGURE 4.3
Classroom Consultants' Business Card and
Professional Brochure

use the available materials to pose an environmental problem and a possible solution. Each pair made a poster with the problem on one side and the solution depicted on the other, using writing and art. These posters were put up all over the school.

During an early committee meeting of the whole group, the students brainstormed projects. Because the community has recycling interests, one committee decided to show just how much waste there is by counting and charting the cans their families saved. They also put boxes in every classroom and encouraged people to put paper in them, flat and clean side up, so that it could be reused. Abbey, one particularly zealous environmentalist, put notepads together from paper her dad had brought home from work. Abbey had seen the Endangered Species business cards and longed to be businessperson, too. (Kathleen found this out one day while reading Abbey's journal.) Kathleen suggested that perhaps Abbey could sell the notepads. Now Abbey not only has her own budding business but has other classmates and committees making notepads as well. They often gather at recess to produce them. They plan to use the money to buy trees to plant on International Earth Day.

In Carol Porter's classroom many of the areas of study for her students come from Incidental Occurrences. This year a kindergarten teacher inadvertently

FIGURE 4.3 *(Continued)*

launched a group of Carol's high school students into a three-month study of children's literature, and the writing and producing of a play for kindergartners called "Make Believe Miracles."

When teachers remain flexible enough to follow the excitement of an unplanned event, the incident itself often influences student and teacher interests so that there is a coming together of these sources with the incidental occurrence (*see* Figure 4.4).

We know that students are more involved when they share in the identification of content to be learned. When they feel passionate about something, they can get hooked and hold on for a long, long time—reading, writing, talking, and sharing their information. Much of Kathleen's curriculum is built around student and teacher

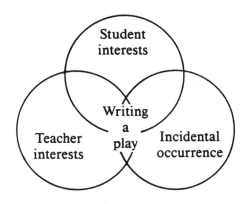

FIGURE 4.4
Coming Together of Student Interests, Teacher Interests, and an Incidental Occurrence to Determine Curriculum

interests, but Kathleen has figured out ways of introducing required topics so that often her students choose to study them.

Try starting your year more open-endedly by listing student interests, teacher interests, and required areas of study. You may find that there is a great deal of overlap, and then you can proceed to prioritize the topics, the themes, you and your students will explore throughout the year. If the common area is not there as much as you would like, negotiate with your students about when and how you will study the required areas, and when you can get on with issues you've identified as a class. One possibility is to alternate throughout the year what you as a class would like to study and what you are expected to study.

Don't forget to value your own questions. Your enthusiasm about taking flying lessons, and your questions about the incredible changes in the Communist world can light a fire and set the stage for some wonderful collaborative learning. And you certainly don't have to abandon those topics you've used successfully in the past. In fact, on closer examination, those may be the ones you've tended to use more open-endedly, drawing the students into your excitement, while respecting their need to explore individually identified questions related to the topic. Yet those may also be the ones you've put so much time and energy into that there isn't much room for student-generated questions. So, be careful and be honest with yourself and your students.

In one in-service session a veteran middle-grade teacher said, "I thought after twenty years of teaching I would have it down so well that I could pack everything up in June and simply take out my well-preserved units in the fall and start all over again. But this year I've done more thinking and planning and developing of new curriculum with my students than ever before." Real learning can't be put into mothballs, taken out, dusted off, and reused.

Once your initial lists are in place, keep adding to them, but be careful not to lock yourself or your students in too rigidly. There will always be tornadoes blowing, Saddam Husseins bellowing, and Berlin Walls tumbling down. There will always be broken legs, new siblings and new pets, overnight snowfalls that break previous records, changes in the power structure of the district schoolboard, and special parents who are willing to bring their areas of expertise into the classroom. All of these are possibilities for creating curriculum collaboratively. You'll want to feel that you can temporarily abandon existing agendas to pursue the spontaneity of life. Within the expected study areas encourage your students to identify specific concerns related to the overall topic; those questions, then, can be the focus of their inquiries.

INTEGRATION

One of the byproducts of whole language teaching is that you start to think in larger terms—language moves beyond speech, and curriculum reaches out to include process, as well as content, and the learner, as well as materials and teacher. When you think about reading, you also begin to think about writing;

when you think about literacy, speaking and listening push their way to the front of your mind and take their rightful places alongside reading and writing. As you consider the connections among language expressions you begin to come to terms with the fact that they are not areas of study in and of themselves but rather tools to use when studying other things, skills that help change human beings into something more than they are. Researcher Ken Goodman defines whole language as the integration of oral and written language for concept learning. That definition has implications at every grade level, in every learning context.

Integrating the language arts and the content areas can be a natural result of an inquiry-based curriculum. When kids read a story or do research on a particular topic, and then write about it, their learning is naturally extended. When they write a story or report, and talk about it in the process, they begin to read their own thoughts and pull in elements from past literacy and content experiences. As numerous research studies have shown, readers not only learn to read by reading, and write by writing, they also learn about reading through writing, and writing through reading (K. Goodman and Y. Goodman, 1979; Eckoff, 1983).

Encounters with language in any expression have the potential to impact on how meaning is constructed in future reading, writing, speaking, or listening experiences. That's why, for example, when children are repeatedly exposed to the contrived language of a basal reader, they are likely to use the same structures in their writing. But it works the other way as well. When we provide good, quality literature and other reading materials, our students' writing tends to reflect the more complicated, literary elements they are used to reading. Diane DeFord looked at this relationship (1981) and found it to be startlingly direct. Children who had been exposed to the short, vocabulary-repetitive language in basal readers produced writing that looked the same as that material in form and content. In contrast, children in a whole language classroom wrote about personal experiences and current events using language that was richer and visibly more sophisticated than did the children using basal readers.

Expressions of language are naturally integrated and can develop in a parallel rather than a serial fashion (Burke, 1984). Separating language in the classroom (reading from writing, writing from reading, talk from both) weakens the ties that can form so easily when a curriculum juxtaposes one expression with others, when a teacher encourages movement and negotiation among them. In integrated classrooms reading and writing, speaking and listening play off each other as a means of learning content through language.

FACT AND FICTION: AN EXAMPLE OF INQUIRY AND LANGUAGE INTEGRATION

In Kathleen's second-grade classroom she helps her students find their inquiring voices quickly. Once the areas of inquiry are identified, students are invited to explore the themes through reading and writing. Here is an example of inquiry and process integration in action. As you read Kathleen's description of her students' research project on animals, notice her role, the kinds of theory-based decisions she makes, and the enormous amount of incidental skill and strategy learning that occurs as students pursue their questions.

Every year I ask second-graders what topics they are interested in learning more about. Every year animals are at the top of the list. I go to the public libraries to collect hundreds of books on animals. I make sure that there are at least three nonfiction and three fiction books per animal, and that there are many more animals than children.

When the children enter the room these Text Sets* are stacked all over. The children browse until they've made a first and second choice about the animal they want to study. If two people want the same animal, they negotiate, or decide to join forces. If they do research on the same animal, they often gather their information independently and then come together to compare facts.

After the animals are chosen, students gather the appropriate books and look at them more carefully, commenting in any way they would like. This tends to pique interest, trigger prior knowledge, and helps frame specific questions.

After a while I ask them to separate fiction from nonfiction. If there are some questionable decisions, neighbors help. Two "tests" the children have devised are: 1. look at the illustrations (nonfiction usually has photographs; fiction has drawings); and 2. read the first sentence to see if it sounds like a story.

We talk about the differences and purposes of fiction and nonfiction. This discussion lays the groundwork for the narrative and expository writing about their animal that they will do later. They talk about what they know in relation to specific animals and what they would like to learn. The group brainstorms the questions they hope to answer about their animals.

I introduce the term research and demonstrate how I can look for the same information in different books, and how I can take facts from all of them in order to make my own report. I ask if they would like to create a book about their animal based on the facts they find in their stack of nonfiction books. No one has turned me down yet. We shelve the fiction books in alphabetical order by animal names (a major production, by the way, with much incidental learning like "which comes first, dog or deer?"), and begin to look through the nonfiction books for answers to our questions.

I introduce and demonstrate scanning by asking, "If you're trying to find out what your animal eats, will you need to read every word on every page? What shortcuts could you take?" We discuss the books' table of contents, the index; and I show them how to scan pages for key words by using the opaque projector; and then I float around the room, assisting people who need help. Speaking of key words always leads to a discussion of synonyms. The children are intrigued by scientific terms, such as habitat, appearance, and lifespan, and soon incorporate them into their speech as well as their sight vocabularies.

We talk about how to keep track of the information we find. This leads to note-taking. The children are given 5×8 notecards that they carry around (rubber-banded) protectively for the next few weeks. Some use them as bookmarks —scanning all the pages, then going back to write. Others take notes as they go along. We talk about plagiarism, and practice putting only key words on cards. (I demonstrate this on an overhead projector with my own research.) We discuss what to do when the same information appears in all the books, or when answers to our questions vary from book to book.

I give my one-hour block of reading time in the morning every day for research. The whole process takes several weeks and each researcher works at his or her own pace. Parents volunteer to come in and assist. The children feel important and quite grown up as they develop the research skills of locating information, notetaking, organizing, and reporting their findings. They learn to be flexible—answers don't come in the order in which the questions were brainstormed; not all questions can be answered; new questions come up through the research process itself.

Once students complete their notetaking, they spread all the cards out and group them (for example, all "enemies" cards together) and then decide on a sequence for their writing. We talk about how to start and the logic of putting certain cards together. When the cards are in order, the child chooses three separate people to listen to him or her tell about the animal. By telling about the animal many times, children understand their information better and better, gain confidence about their expertise, and rely less and less on their notecards. In oral sharing they also experiment with different ways of expressing the same ideas; they develop a unique style of delivery, a voice, a mood. This activity is prewriting for the next step, which is to use the information they have gathered to create a nonfiction book.

The children go through the usual stages of the writing process—fast write, content conference, revision, self-editing, editing conference, publishing. Parent volunteers type the finished manuscripts. Authors are thrilled to see their final drafts transposed into professional pieces! They then illustrate their books and make covers for them. Their published works include a table of contents and an acknowledgments page. Some authors choose to include a dedication, an index, and an "About the Author" page.

Now the children turn to fiction books. As they read, they spontaneously contrast these and the nonfiction they have just finished. After some formal, as well as informal, comparisons, I ask them to write a story about their animal. It may be realistic fiction or fantasy, but it needs to incorporate some of the facts they have recently learned.

We talk about story structure. They plan a beginning, middle, and end. They decide on a problem, and plot its resolution. There is much discussion before any writing—and during it. Pieces go through the same process cycle described before and, again, parent volunteers type the finished manuscripts. But this time the fiction is attached to the nonfiction piece and they become one book. Children illustrate the fiction portion and then have great fun exchanging books and reading each other's (*see* Figure 4.5).

Proud authors lend their books to the school and public libraries, arranging their displays and often including in the exhibit a soap carving or mask or clay rendering of their animals.

While bookmaking is going on in Kathleen's room, the animal theme pushes its way into every other part of her curriculum through her students ongoing questions. If you walk into her classroom while the animal research unit is in full swing, one thing you are sure to be struck by is the level of excitement and the

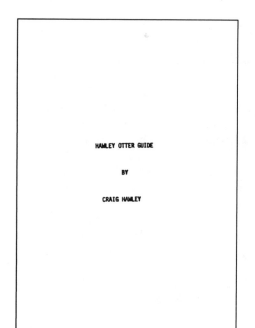

HAWLEY OTTER GUIDE

BY

CRAIG HAWLEY

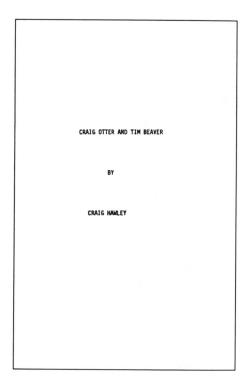

CRAIG OTTER AND TIM BEAVER

BY

CRAIG HAWLEY

FIGURE 4.5
Example of a Fact/Fiction Book on Otters
Written by a Second-Grade Researcher

If an otter's fur gets dirty, its hair sticks together and the chilly water chills his skin and he can die. If that doesn't happen, some otters live to be fifty years old or older.

Animal Research Fact

Once upon a time there was a furry brown otter named Craig. He loved eating mussels, sea urchins, crabs, clams, squid and abalone. He also loved swimming. He was considered the best swimmer. Tim Beaver was the second best at swimming.

Tim was too sad to be on this page. So turn the page to see him.

Animal Research Fiction

willingness and ability of her students to talk about what they're learning. Her inquiry-based curriculum never fails to yield the very things we seek in our students—passionate interest, long-term commitment, deep engagement. And, as if that weren't enough, these seven-year-olds top it off by becoming more skilled readers and writers than they were before.

GETTING STARTED WITH STUDENT-CENTERED LEARNING

Inquiry and integration can begin at many different points—a piece of good literature, an interesting theme, a textbook chapter, a current event. Making your curriculum more inquiry-based, with an eye toward increasing integration, takes, as all of whole language does, a shift in attitude, an altered perspective on curriculum. A major part of the change is recognizing that curriculum does not have to be (should not be!) developed in detail before students get involved. In whole language classrooms units are not planned apart from students because learners must be integral contributors to the decision-making process, not passive sideliners waiting to implement someone else's best-laid plans.

Teachers do, however, need to sketch a tentative frame. Professor Dorothy Watson calls it "planning to plan," and it refers to the initial decisions that a teacher can make to get the inquiry ball rolling.

Kathleen was involved in planning to plan when she ordered the *National Geographic* packet and when she arranged the health center field trip. Planning to plan forms the basis for deciding what gets explored, the strategies appropriate to the investigation, and the resources that need to be tracked down (Watson, Burke, and Harste, 1989). The point to be remembered is that themed studies, content explorations, or literature units will have less of a chance of succeeding if the bulk of the decisions are made before your co-inquirers have a chance to contribute. The idea is that ". . . the curriculum can't be in place before the learners are in place" (p. 49). Those beautiful teacher-made units can now be replaced by the beauty of creating with your students. And, here is the overriding key point about the relationship between inquiry and integration: GENUINE INQUIRY LEADS TO NATURAL INTEGRATION. Don't worry about pulling in *every* subject area related to a theme or topic—let the questions, the curiosity, the unknown lead the way.

You may want to choose a starting point (literature, current event, content topic, and so on) and try it out with your students as a way of seeing the possibilities for whole language, inquiry-driven curriculum. Once a point of departure is established, plan to plan by making a list of questions you and your students have—what would you really like to know about the topic? Narrow down the list and ask students to choose their top three. They can write these on 3 × 5 cards and research groups can be formed by placing students in groups based on their primary interests. Now, what kinds of strategies would help you answer those questions? And what materials would be useful? How about other resources beside print materials? Are there any classroom experts? Parent experts? Professionals you could call or

FIGURE 4.6
Planning an Inquiry
Source: Adapted from Watson, Burke, and
Harste, 1989

interview in person? What about videotapes and audiotapes? Now everyone needs a plan of action. Who in the groups will begin to find books? Develop interview questions? Track down videotapes? See if anyone in the class knows about the topic? Figure 4.6 summarizes these planning steps. Appendix A has a list of topically-related materials that can support many areas of inquiry.

In Figure 4.7, the initial planning to plan for student/teacher interest, "Chicks and Quails," is shown in the innermost circle around the starting points. The broken lines extending out from the inner circle of the diagram indicate that students and teacher together moved beyond the initial decisions made by the teacher *and* all of the planning by the teacher did not get played out. The curriculum develops as the topic is explored, and the appropriateness of varied strategies and resources become apparent. The planning to plan for studying "Chicks and Quails" was done by Pat Riordan.

When I look at "whole language units" that have been developed by teachers (often over the summer), I have been struck by two things:

1. While objectives, content, and resources have been meticulously identified, the kinds of reading and writing strategies in which students will be involved to learn the content and use the materials is often left out.
2. There is no room for students to make decisions, no provision for adding their questions and interests.

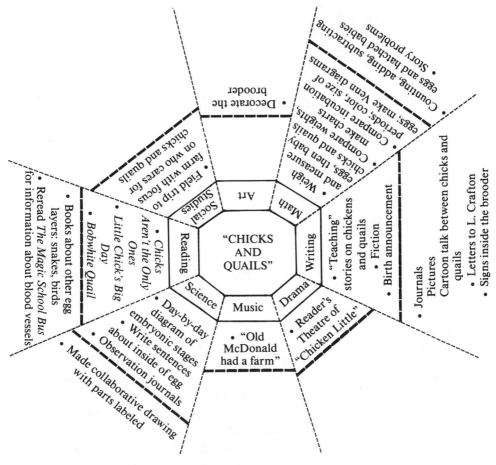

FIGURE 4.7
Planning to Plan for Inquiry and Integration
Related to "Chicks and Quails"

While gathering materials and predicting natural areas of exploration are important parts of preplanning, don't invest too much of yourself. Your students may very well want to move in directions you could not predict; they will ask questions that have not occurred to you.

Once the inquiry has been completed, be sure to plan with your students some ways of sharing what has been learned, a culminating project or presentation. This is a wonderful time to invite parents into the classroom to see what you have been doing (for example, *see* Family Histories*).

Personal Reflection

Where in the curriculum can I encourage more choice so students can pursue their own questions?

Ownership

5

In *Toward a Psychology of Being* psychologist Abraham H. Maslow writes that every human being carries within himself or herself two conflicting forces— the desire for security and the desire for growth. The first makes every person afraid to take chances, afraid to jeopardize what he or she already has. The other impels us forward toward wholeness and uniqueness of self, toward full functioning of all our capacities. The process of healthy growth, Maslow concludes, becomes a never-ending series of free-choice situations.

The freedom to make choices—it's what life in this country is supposed to be about. It's not, however, what classrooms are usually about. Once I asked a fifth-grade teacher what kinds of choices she gave her students. Looking at me strangely, she thought for a moment and then said: "Well, on Fridays, sometimes, they get to choose what they want to write about and . . . oh, yeah, when we go to the library I encourage them to choose their own books." Then she quickly added, "But I have to watch that closely, of course, because many of them choose books that are just too hard for them." Of course.

WHOSE LEARNING IS IT?

By and large we are a protective lot. With all good intentions we don't quite believe that our students can handle the full challenge of responsible learning. There is something about them that won't allow independent choice of activities in order to move their development forward. They are (your turn to choose):

1. too young,
2. too dependent,

3. used to too much structure,
4. don't have enough self-control.

And so, with a thousand different assumptions and as many good intentions, we take the learning away from our students or, at least, restrict the possibilities. We select their writing topics, designate the number of pages, transcribe their stories, point out their errors, choose their reading materials, determine the content they should learn, and designate what strategies they should use to learn it.

Many of our students, regardless of age, are in situations that make them appear to be extremely dependent, in need of careful guidance and tight hand-holding. But as we seek to "support," we find ourselves whirling endlessly in the proverbial vicious cycle—we encourage their dependence by making decisions for them; the more decisions we make for them, the more dependent they become; the more dependent they become, the more we feel we need to make decisions for them.

Our dependency training begins early. In *Language Stories and Literacy Lessons* the authors Harste, Woodward, and Burke guide us through the cognitive constraints imposed on Alison during her first few weeks of first grade. Alison came to first grade reading books at a third- and fourth-grade level. And she had been writing her own texts for some time. Despite these strengths, one of her first school activities was a worksheet that contained two sentences supplied by the teacher: "Here I am. My name is _____." The new students were to underwrite what the teacher had written and then supply their names. They were also asked to draw a picture of themselves.

Another activity also involved overwriting. This time students were given parts of a story written by the teacher, asked to assemble the pages in order, and overwrite the teacher's composition. (If you are hoping that at least the story itself might have some merit, the page shared by Harste, *et al.* reads: "Run, Pug. Mother, see Pug run. Run, Pug, run. Oh, Pug!").

Alison's initial experiences in first grade were not deviations from a curriculum that usually recognized and built on students' strengths. They were representative of the kinds of activities Alison would have to complete throughout her first year in school; experiences in which her teacher made "the significant creative decisions" (p. 6).

It seems to be a teacher's right, part of an invisible document that we receive along with the teaching degree, to judge what our students should read, write, and think. Yet, when we take responsibility for important learning decisions that should rightfully belong to our students, it is the antithesis of good teaching. In contrast to Alison's first-grade teacher, Pat Riordan offers open-ended activities from the very beginning of first grade: choice in topic selection for writing, choice of books to read and partners with whom to share, which math games and activities to be involved in, and what Extension* activities to complete.

---

* All asterisks throughout the book refer the reader to Chapter 10 where full strategy descriptions can be found.

In Pat's classroom even when the activity is not one chosen by students, she makes sure they are still involved in the major decisions. Last year her twenty-six first-graders planned their own field trip. In collaboration with another first grade they formed committees to decide on the necessary tasks, wrote letters to potential chaperones describing the trip and outlining the responsibilities, wrote to the principal asking permission to take the trip, and called the bus company to arrange for transportation.

In Kathleen Visovatti's second-grade classroom she has turned over all of the morning "housekeeping" chores to her students. From 8:30 to 8:50 every morning her students are responsible for class business. They handle attendance and lunch count, and then take both to the office; they change the calendar and report the date and weather; they water the plants and change the Sustained Silent Reading seating chart (they take turns in alphabetical order reading on soft, whistle chairs, in the teepee, and in the Private Place, a corner of the room sectioned off by a tall cardboard partition that hides a table and chair). Other jobs are done later in the day, such as line leaders to guide groups to special classes, and lunch (the hands-down favorite of them all), and board-washing. Those who don't volunteer for a job one week, will do so the next. Children take weekly turns with jobs. By the end of the year everyone has done every job at least once.

Kathleen says:

> Sometimes they improve on the original list of tasks, decided by group consensus, when they determine a chore is not needed. For example, people were carefully hanging up their coats and putting their papers in back packs, so the hall monitor job was discontinued. They also add new jobs. We now have a bookshelf guard to supervise the neat return of books at the end of SSR because that had become a class problem. Those who aren't involved in specific responsibilities are writing in their journals or putting notes on the Message Board.*

Kathleen and Pat and the other whole language teachers portrayed in this book encourage independent decision-making from the beginning of the school year. They believe that ownership in learning and living and handling social situations will enable students to deal with the complexities of life outside of the classroom. It makes sense, but it is not what John Goodlad (1984) found when he looked inside American schools.

In his book, *A Place Called School,* Goodlad surveyed junior-high school classes to determine the axis of decision-making. Ninety percent of the time he found decisions related to "seating, grouping, content, materials, use of space, time utilization, and learning activities" (p. 229) were made by the teacher.

Many of my graduate students, strong and independent individuals for the most part, feel uncomfortable, even hostile, when they first encounter my open-ended curriculum. Reflective journals that encourage personal response are foreign to them and they, too, want to know how many pages when I ask for a paper. It takes a while for them to believe I'm not going to direct their learning and that I really don't know how many pages they should write. I only have some of them as students for one semester. That's not very long for people who have spent a lifetime in teacher-controlled institutions. Some of them never quite relax, never settle into their own learning. When students are given the opportunity and the reassurance of making their decisions, they often rise to the occasion with admirable strength. From kindergarten through graduate school, the dependence that has been fostered at every level can be eradicated by a determined and patient teacher. In the following story, called "Teacher's Kisses," Barbara Lindberg describes her efforts to get one of her junior-high school students to take the first steps toward responsible literacy.

TEACHER'S KISSES

He came into my 8th grade reading class having demanded his way out of a self-contained special education room. He didn't survive in the mainstream long, but he remained in my class.

Our beginning was rocky. When school started I was apprehensive. He had a reputation for being volatile and disruptive. My classroom is a place where students are risk-takers and therefore vulnerable, so I worried about how he would fit in. Within days, my worry shifted focus and grew. He was no academic risk-taker! He would not do anything that could be responded to. His notebook cover was chewed, his pen was an attack weapon, singularly capable of making hard rock insignias.

I read "The Most Dangerous Game," a sure hit with boys. We wrote and talked about it, minus the one who kept his head down and etched. As we read other short stroies, I suggested that instead of writing, he draw his responses. He produced simple looking pictures, but as he described them, it became clear that he understood the stories and had a surprising grasp of significant details.

I tried everything to get him to write. He sometimes would start, but the words grew large and soon fell off the page. I remember one day when he said he didn't know how to start a response, I humorously put my hand over his, both of us holding the pen, and wrote "I didn't like this story because . . ." We laughed, and he said he could go on alone, but he could not.

One day in desperation, I took him to a corner and "read" Mercer Mayer's *A Boy, a Dog and a Frog.* He "read" it and then I asked him to write an accompanying text. He wrote for *HICCUP* and *ACHOO* and for Fernando Krahn's *The Great Ape* and *The Creepy Thing.* His first texts were short and picture dependent. Sentences like "The boy left." "The frog jumped." were common. Gradually his writing expanded and he began attributing feelings and motives to the characters. When we looked at his first story, he commented on his growth as a writer. To his credit and my surprise, he never said our reading and writing was childish.

Uncertainly, I suggested that he start a writing idea list (Atwell: *In the Middle,* p. 73). Finally he had three ideas, chose one and it was time to start writing. He spent the rest of the period staring at the paper, but at least he did nothing else, no insignias nor tearing. On his way out, I asked how it went. "Okay" was the response. My apprehension grew when he sat the next day. I stopped him on the way in the third day and asked what he planned to do. He responded that he had finished thinking and now he was going to write. He composed in his head and then wrote! Writing was laborious for him but he finished and we conferenced. He had written about his sister, but had stopped, not ended his piece. We talked about that, he agreed and added "That is the way she is, and nothing will ever change." When he read his piece to me he realized that he had mentioned her boyfriend in two different places and those parts needed to be together. He learned to revise by cutting and pasting. His draft looked like a disaster, but his writing was exciting: "The clothes she wears make it seem like every day is Halloween."

Now, two months later, he has written a piece on World Peace. He is revising and expanding it, but more importantly, it looks like the beginning of a series he will write on world problems. His writing is far from polished, but it is also far from where he started. The metamorphosis has begun.

In student-directed learning patience is truly a teacher virtue. Whole language teachers like Barbara have given new meaning to the idea of "wait time." And, in the process, have breathed new meaning into the life of their students.

CHOICE AND OWNERSHIP

When Goodlad studied our public schools and classrooms he uncovered a fear that many teachers have: If students have too many choices, if they are allowed too much say in their learning, teachers will lose control and, once lost, it may never be retrieved. This fear of losing control can be a driving but unrecognized force in the development of curriculum and the organization of a classroom. When Goodlad glanced inside classrooms across the country, he saw a surprisingly uniform picture: teachers behind desks; or, chalk in hand, standing at the chalkboard writing and talking; students sitting silently in rows, taking notes, looking at the teacher, or gazing out the window. This scenario of teachers talking and students silent is not always a bad one; indeed, I've learned many things from teachers talking to me. But it is a problem when the majority of students' time in school is spent writing facts that someone else has constructed on a topic selected by the teacher or mandated by an outside committee.

When Carol Porter asked seventeen-year-old Dave about the changes she had seen in his reading behavior during his senior year with her, he said: "Well, it wasn't that I couldn't read before I came into your class. I just didn't want to." And he didn't. Before meeting Carol, Dave was part of the growing group of aliterates in our schools—people who can read, but rarely do. Now Dave uses his ability to read and write on a regular basis. When Carol asked Dave what made the difference for him, why this year was different from the previous eleven, he said: "Getting to choose my own books."

Recently Carol talked with several of her former eighth-grade language arts students who are now entering their junior year in high school. Without exception, they felt that being able to choose, even a portion of the time, what they read and what they wrote made the critical difference. They no longer had a reason to resist, and because *they* made the choices, they felt more committed, took more ownership of the learning process itself. After ten years of schooling the learning finally belonged to them.

Most teachers are not in a position to allow students to choose everything they learn. While Carol's teaching situation is more open-ended than many, it still has its set of constraints. Carol, however, has found ways to make them work for her instead of against her. S. E. Hinton's *The Outsiders* is required reading for high-school senior reading classes. Carol begins her year with this popular novel. Because there are no ability groups in her classes all of her students have the opportunity to read the same material. By starting with one novel she can give them a common experience. Once Hinton's book has been read and discussed, the real choices begin. Now students select related reading and writing that are Extensions* of their individual interests.

Two years ago the whole class wanted to read another book by Hinton after they got their first taste of her writing. Kristie, Laura, Jim, Angel, Tim, Tracie, Bill, Lisa, Chip, and Ken chose *Tex.* The rest of the class—Ty, Brian, Lon, Salvador, Todd, Dave, and Jeff—chose to read *Rumble Fish.* Carol read both books. When this second novel was almost finished students began making plans for subsequent reading and/or writing.

Kristie and Laura became a group of two reading another contemporary novel with females as main characters, and writing about their reading. Jim, Angel, Tim, and Tracie followed a theme from *The Outsiders* by reading about gangs in sociology books and current newspapers and magazines. Then they wrote about what they had read and expressed their opinions about gangs. Bill and Lisa decided to read a third book by Hinton and chose *Rumble Fish,* which they had not read earlier. Then they wrote about all three books, comparing and contrasting across the novels. Ken, Carol, and Ty read articles about Hinton's life, discussed how her beliefs have influenced her writing, and then wrote their own experience stories.

A crossover of members from the *Tex* and *Rumble Fish* groups occurred when Chip, Brian, and Lon decided to read contemporary short stories written and published by teenagers close to Hinton's age when she published *The Outsiders* (she was seventeen). Salvador and Todd wrote extended fiction incorporating gangs similar to those encountered in *The Outsiders* and *Rumble Fish.* Jeff was confused and frustrated by the symbolism in *Rumble Fish,* but Dave enjoyed the challenge of figuring it out; they joined forces so they could talk and write about what each symbol meant. Dave then wrote his definition of a hero, and used the stories he had read to support his opinion. Jeff wrote a personal experience story. Figure 5.1 tracks the individual and collaborative choices made by this class during the Hinton unit. Related materials and themes are included in Appendix A of this book under the Fiction category.

There are several factors in place in Carol's classroom which help guarantee that choice does not become chaos and that students are responsible for their choices once they are made.

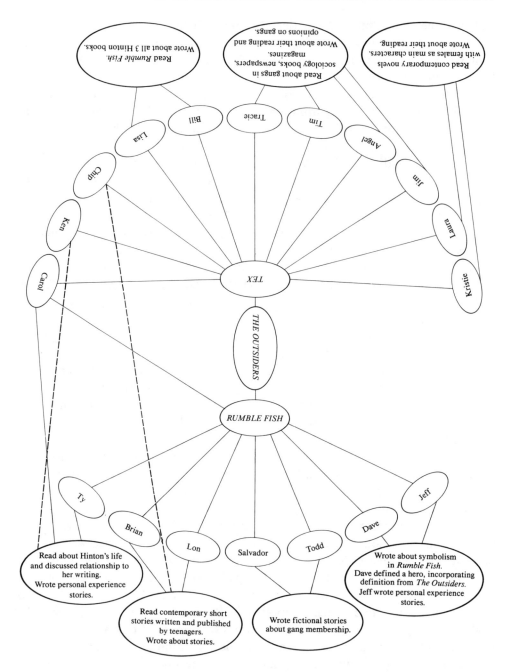

FIGURE 5.1

Individual and Group Reading/Writing
Choices Made by High-school Students
Following a Common Reading Experience

1. Choosing to do nothing is not one of the choices. When a student does not seem to be productively engaged for a period of time, Carol sees it as an opportunity to have a conference so that, together, they can determine what the problem is and set specific goals for the next few days.
2. Reading/Writing Contracts encourage a solid commitment. Once the choices are made, Carol uses a Reading/Writing Contract that we developed (*see* Figure 5.2). The contract includes both content and process decisions (What will you read? What type of writing will you do during reading?); social decisions

---

READING/WRITING CONTRACT

Name _____

Partner or Group Members _____

_____

_____

Reading Choice: _____

Writing Choice: What type(s) of writing will you do as you are reading?

_____

_____

_____

How often will you discuss with your partner and/or group?

_____

Will you do anything else together?

_____

_____

How will you share what you have read with the whole class?

_____

_____

Due Date: _____

_____   _____
Student Signature   Teacher Signature

CONTRACT
D2D6

FIGURE 5.2
Reading/Writing Contract

(Are you reading/writing with others? How will you proceed?); and a commitment for completion.

In the contract, writing choice often refers to journal responses made during reading or letters that Carol and her students write back and forth to each other as they are reading the same books.

The final question in the contract (How will you share what you have read with the whole class?) can take any form: a written piece, a Book Talk,* skit, videotape, poster, talk show, and so on.

Different kinds of Celebrations* of reading take place on a regular basis in Carol's classroom. The completed contract is signed by both teacher and student with the express understanding that all parts of the contract are negotiable.

GROUPING AND OWNERSHIP

You know that stomach-tightening feeling when you witness something that is flagrantly unfair but you are powerless to stop it? A few months ago I was visiting a second-grade classroom. I had asked the teacher if I could come in and help with the process writing she was trying out for the first time. When I entered the room there were seven or eight students busily writing at their desks, another group in a front corner discussing a story, and one group conspicuously missing.

I waved to the teacher as I came in and started circulating among the writers to see if I could get a sense of what they were doing. I stopped at the desk of a little freckled-faced, pony-tailed girl named Christie and asked her what she was writing. As she talked about her topic the classroom door opened and in rushed another second-grader. The little girl breezed by and whispered to Christie, "We're making clay!"

"I know," Christie said quietly with her head down.

"Why are they making clay?" I asked.

Christie explained that because this group was on a certain story in their basal readers they got to do something special. It sounded like one of the enrichment activities—the ones the slow readers never get to.

"When do you get to make clay?"

"Oh, I don't know if I'll get to. I have to get through two more books first."

Christie, as you've guessed, is in the low reading group. Her reading ability isn't the only thing that is "low." So are her spirits—and her self-esteem.

John Goodlad states that students who are homogeneously grouped are systematically denied access to knowledge. The lower ability group simply do not get the same quality of information that higher ability groups do. Nor are the exchanges within those groups at the same level. When expectations are low, performance usually follows. Homogeneous grouping is characterized by one person, the teacher, making uniform decisions for diverse individuals—what material gets covered, the pace at which it's covered, the questions that get asked, the amount of time to spend on each story, who gets to make clay and who does not. For too long we have allowed many of our most accepted practices in education to remain unexamined. In my opinion this is not only one of the most widely accepted, it is also the most widely destructive.

In her discussion of tracking in junior-high schools teacher Nancie Atwell points out that homogeneous groups don't lead to increased achievement; they lead to the acceptance of low levels of learning. The literature repeatedly warns us of the dangers of homogeneous grouping:

1. Kids who are tracked don't get better. They tend to stay at the same self-concept-depleting level, learning over and over again that they don't measure up.
2. When teachers teach the low-ability groups, they ask qualitatively different questions and expect far less than they do from children in higher ability groups.

Those are not *conscious* decisions made by teachers; they are the subtle influences of a negative management tool.

When we know so well that an educational practice is damaging our kids, it is truly educational malpractice to continue with it. "BUT," one of my graduate students protested recently, "Ability grouping is so practical. It's the easiest way to manage thirty children." I watched her dig in. Heterogeneous grouping wasn't something she was going to consider easily. I explained the basic alternative: "Let your students self-select into interest groups. You'll be surprised at the richness of the collective thought and, most likely, your low students will suddenly look smarter."

She glared at me over half-sized reading glasses: "It won't work."

"Have you ever tried it?"

"No. But it won't work."

Irene seemed skeptical, too, when I suggested that we stop using reading groups and basal stories and try self-selected literature groups in her first-grade classroom. When she wanted to get started with whole language instruction, I gave her Ken Goodman's *What's Whole in Whole Language* (1986) and Judith Newman's *Whole Language: Theory in Use* (1985) and suggested we read and talk for a while before she made any instructional changes.

She started with a Message Board* and then slowly added writing process. (Writing process is described more fully in the last section of this chapter.) In a few weeks the children in her class were selecting their own topics, drafting, pairing up to read and get responses to their writing, and sharing their stories with the whole class. The rest of her curriculum was still very traditional, including a time for isolated phonics and spelling, but she was anxious to make changes. She had talked to her principal and he had agreed to let her try some new things. Materials were a problem, so I volunteered to go to the local library to try to find multiple copies of books that the students could use. I chose several sets of predictable books and fairy tales (*see* Appendix A) knowing that the strong patterns and familiar story lines would make for immediate successful independent reading.

As a demonstration of one way to initiate literature groups, I pulled the class together one morning and called on the children to give quick reviews of fairy tales I had in hand. As they told the familiar stories we talked about different versions and wondered together which versions would be told in the books I had selected. I wrapped up the literature meeting by reading a predictable book I guessed was unfamiliar to them. Then I asked them to choose which books they would like to read, and the heterogeneous interest groups were set. Irene took over from there.

I think it took only a week or so for all of Irene's skepticism to disappear. I walked into the classroom one day not long after we had started the literature groups and saw one group in the corner reading favorite parts of *Little Red Riding Hood* out loud to one another. Another group was in the back talking about their book, and a third group in front was doing a Shared Reading* with Irene. I asked her later how it was going and she reported that she had never seen a group of first-graders so excited about reading, and that the discussions were better than she had imagined they could be. She was clearly excited, too. In one fell swoop we eliminated the ability groups in her classroom. I don't think anyone could talk her into organizing in that old way again.

OWNING THE CLASSROOM

In New Zealand all teachers are expected to apply whole language principles in their classrooms. This country enjoys one of the highest literacy rates in the world. Whole language consultant, Margaret Mooney, says that in these days of "whole child" teaching in New Zealand, it's impossible to find any wall space in the classrooms. They are covered with student work, personal prizes brought in for sharing, and oh so much language. The chalkboards are invisible as well, anachronisms relegated to another time when teaching in that small country was given more attention than learning and the classroom was still a teacher's well-protected territory.

One day Pat Riordan asked me to come into her classroom to see what I could make of her current organization of the writing process. She had expressed concern about editing and so I suggested setting up an editor's table (Harste, Short and Burke 1988) and volunteered to kick off the discussion on editing with her students.

I selected a piece a little girl in another first-grade class had written, made my overhead transparency, and sauntered into Pat's room one gorgeous winter morning. I asked if she had a projector so I could show the writing. Her head turned slowly, looking around the room: "Uhh, yeah, . . . but I don't know where to show it . . ." As I perused the wall space I could see the problem: Every inch was covered—mostly with the children's work.

"Oook. How about if I just brainstorm with them and we'll write it on the chalkboard?" Her head started moving that way again: "Uhh . . . Well . . . Why don't we take these stories down for the moment and maybe we can find a little space here." We both started laughing.

So far this chapter has been about the sociopsychological ownership that helps define whole language classrooms. Now physical ownership completes the picture from a student perspective. We tend to move from one extreme to the other as kids proceed through the grades—from beautiful, personalized, "Land of Oz" kindergartens to high-school classrooms that have a depressing sameness about them with hardly a visible sign of the content explored there. Students need to bring in pieces of themselves—favorite books, personal collections, photographs, and so on. The personal artifacts that they create in the classroom—the writing, the literature extensions, the art—should claim a space on the wall or the chalkboard or the ceiling, and serve as a reminder to them and to everyone who comes in the room that there are multiple owners of this small piece of real estate.

TEACHER OWNERSHIP: UNDERSTANDING LITERACY PROCESSES

Ownership in whole language classrooms does not only refer to student learning, it encompasses teacher understanding as well. In traditional classrooms materials and publishers own the classroom to a much greater degree than do teachers. In these settings, texts, not teachers, direct the learning. In whole language classrooms teachers feel they have the power to make informed decisions because they know their students in intimate ways that publishers never could. Whole language teachers own their classrooms in another important way: They strive to develop an understanding of reading/writing processes so that they, and no one else, can guide the development of a process-oriented curriculum that is appropriate for their students.

Developing an in-depth understanding of reading/writing processes takes time, study, and observation. But part of whole language teaching is seeing reading and writing as acts of individual meaning construction guided by the learner's language and experience.

READING/WRITING PROCESSES

Ken Goodman defines reading as a long-distance conversation between author and reader. When writers write, they use their languages and background experiences to construct meaning while anticipating their audiences' needs. When readers read, they bring their language and prior knowledge to the text and, using them as a basis for comprehension, actively construct meaning from the written materials. Because both reader and writer are actively engaged in meaning construction, they are both authors in a real sense. It is our recent understanding of the role of the reader as an active contributor to the reading process that has helped us re-conceive reading instruction as the opportunity to encourage reading as a personal thinking process. Similarly, writing is an act of personal communication in which authors must conceptualize, re-think, and revise their messages as they proceed through the text.

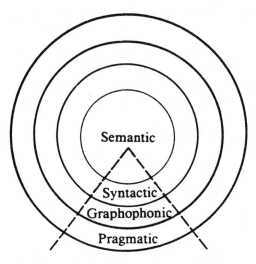

FIGURE 5.3
The Four Major Language Cueing Systems

In reading and writing four major cueing systems are involved: semantic, syntactic, graphophonic, and pragmatic (*see* Figure 5.3). These systems are the sources of information that readers and writers must use if they are to comprehend and compose.

As Figure 5.3 shows, the semantic system is at the core of the processes because the intent of literacy is the communication of meaning. Without it, reading and writing would be purposeless nonsense. Meaning cues come from readers' conceptual backgrounds. The semantic system is far more than word meanings; it is a network of conceptual knowledge developed through language and real-world experience.

The syntactic, or grammatical, system is the structure of language; the interrelationships of words, sentences, and paragraphs. Young children possess a significant store of syntactic knowledge developed through oral language and listening to books. Readers and writers must draw on extensive understanding of syntax to construct meaning.

The special, interdependent relationship between syntax and semantics can be seen in this classic psycholinguistic example: "Green clouds sleep furiously." Syntactically, the sentence is fine. Semantically, however, it makes no sense. When readers read and writers write, they are constantly checking on this inseparable relationship. Does this sound like language (is the syntax acceptable)? Does it make sense (is it semantically acceptable)? While this is sophisticated linguistic knowledge, it develops quite early. When preschoolers listen to a book being read, for example, they can easily detect a deviation that doesn't sound right or doesn't make sense—and will quickly tell the reader so!

The graphophonic system refers to the sound/symbol knowledge that readers have about the marks on a page. In an alphabetic system like ours, graphophonics includes the sounds of oral language (phonology) and spelling (orthography), and the complex relationship between the two. In the development of effective readers this system gets a lot of credit it doesn't deserve. If effective readers actually slowed down and used the graphophonic system as painstakingly as traditional skill-based instruction would have it, they would lose all sense of what they were trying to understand. To be efficient, readers have to learn only to sample from this system as they are reading. For example, the first letter or two of any word is the most significant graphic cue for a reader; final letters are a close second. Consider this sentence from *Strega Nona* by Tomie de Paola:

As soon as Strega Nona w___s out of sight, Big Anthony went inside, pulled the pasta p___t off the sh_____f and put it on the fl_____.

If readers over-rely on graphophonics and cue into every letter and every word, a bottleneck results and meaning is lost (Smith, 1978).

Knowledge of graphophonics is largely a result of experience and intuited understandings, not direct instruction. Proficient readers who have had no intense phonics instruction are a good example of how this system develops through the reading experience itself. No reader needs to understand all of the complex rules in our spelling system to be effective as a reader. Reading programs that put a strong emphasis on graphophonics through isolated phonics instruction risk producing readers who have a word or even a letter focus as they read. While often considered a critical instructional issue in reading, the graphophonic system is best developed within the context of writing and spelling. It is there that learners slow down and pay more consistent attention to the component parts of written language. Still, it is a writer's desire to capture a message that makes her want to pay attention to this system in the first place.

The pragmatic system takes into account the context in which language occurs. Language, in fact, does not exist outside of a particular context of situation. The three language cueing systems just described depend on the context to determine how they are used and the relationships among them. My language is different when I speak to Samantha, when I talk with graduate students, and when I am having a private dinner with my husband. Every context has its own set of constraints, and all language users vary their language based on their perception of the pragmatics involved. Just as the pragmatic system exerts an influence over oral language, it influences written texts as well. Students approach and respond differently to worksheets than to trade books (those found in bookstores); fiction and nonfiction vary in vocabulary, layout, tone, and style; menus look decidedly different from standardized tests and require different strategies on the learner's part even though both involve a series of choices. In order to understand and better use the pragmatics unique to each type of written material, students must have opportunities to experience a range of texts.

Yetta Goodman, Dorothy Watson, and Carolyn Burke (1987) discuss the relationship among the cueing systems:

> Each of the language cueing systems has its function and its place in relation to the other systems. While they can be separated for the purposes of discussion, research, or definition, they cannot stand alone or be isolated from the others during actual use. They must all be available for comprehension to occur. This is one of the most important principles of a holistic view of reading. *All four language systems must be intact and interacting whenever reading occurs* (p. 29).

The cueing systems develop as learners try to *use* them to comprehend and compose. It is the effort toward communication with all systems operating simultaneously that allows legitimate exploration and refinement of each. Readers select what they need from these systems depending on the demands of the reading/ writing event.

Using the cueing systems interactively takes strategic thought on the part of the reader/writer: When do I go back to re-read or revise? How do I tie this current information in with what I already know or what I have written? I don't understand this part; what do I do now?

There are three basic strategies that all learners use to construct meaning effectively: predicting, confirming, and integrating. Readers and writers use these problem-solving strategies to process cues from the semantic, syntactic, graphophonic, and pragmatic systems. Like the utilization of language cues, predicting, confirming, and integrating are used interactively and often simultaneously. These strategies are not unique to reading and writing. They are part of a larger cognitive process. Our daily lives are filled with prediction, confirmation, and integration of experience.

Predicting means using what we know to anticipate upcoming events. We predict the ends of movies; we anticipate what someone is going to say and finish their sentence; we wake up and consider how the events of the day are likely to unfold. We use the same strategy in reading and writing. In both expressions of language, reading and writing, we predict on many different levels at the same time: the next word the author could use, what event may happen next in the story, how a main character will behave.

Predicting strategies are based on the inferences that readers make using information from all of the cueing systems (Goodman, Watson, and Burke, 1987); confirming strategies are based on how meaningful the prediction is, given the surrounding context. To see predicting and confirming strategies in action—and, at the same time, a reader's interactive use of semantics, syntax, and graphophonics—consider this example from Kevin, a second-grade reader.

While reading *Lon Po Po* (1989), a Red Riding Hood Story from China, Kevin reached a point in the story where two children, thinking it was their mother knocking at the door, had let the wolf into their house:

>   Toy
> The old wolf held Tao. "Good child, you are
>   pleasing   Patsy
> so plump." He embraced Paotze.
>
> "Good child, you have grown to be
>
> so sweet."

(Kevin read the text as written except for the substitutions written above the printed line.)

Throughout the book Kevin read "Toy" for "Tao" and "Patsy" for "Paotze," as he did here. When Kevin reached the word "plump," he predicted "pleasing." Kevin's substitutions on the children's names in the story show that he knows the words are names, and he knows how they function in the text. He was comfortable with his predictions and, because they were acceptable syntactically and semantically, he was able to confirm them and continue reading.

Kevin's prediction of the word "pleasing" was based on simultaneous information from all four cueing systems: He sampled the graphophonic information at the beginning of the word ("pl"); at the same time he inferred that an adjective was the appropriate syntactic structure; and he used semantic cues to produce a word that made sense in the context of the story and the sentence. When Kevin read the next sentence, "Good child, you have grown to be so sweet." the meaning relationship between "sweet" and "pleasing" most likely served as further confirmation of the appropriateness of his prediction of "pleasing" for "plump." The pragmatic cues from the context of the story, then, also helped confirm his prediction.

Kevin's deviations from the print on the page are called miscues and are an expected part of any reading event for *all* readers. Ken Goodman coined the term "miscue" to be used in place of "error" or "mistake" to indicate that deviations are the result of readers using language cues to make reasonable predictions. Miscues are not mistakes, and they are not random behaviors to be eradicated. Readers have good reasons for what they say and think during reading. Miscues are a natural part of a process that involves prediction based on language knowledge and world experience.

When readers like Kevin produce miscues that don't disrupt the meaning of the whole for them it is a strength when they continue to read, leaving their predictions intact. However, strong readers correct miscues that don't make sense. Teachers who understand the reading process help students to see high-quality miscues, those that make sense within the larger context, as effective decision-making.

A third strategy that readers use is integrating. Integrating is operative when a reader reconciles what he or she knows and believes with his or her interpretation of the text being read. Not all information is integrated during the reading process; readers select what they remember based on the compatibility between their knowledge base and the author's. Because readers have different backgrounds, experiences, and purposes for reading, the construction of meaning for any given text is different for different readers. For this reason readers cannot be expected to retell what they have read in exactly the form another reader (teacher) might expect. Every reading event is a unique transaction (Rosenblatt, 1985).

Predicting, confirming, and integrating are the basic strategies used in writing as well as reading (Shanklin, 1981). As in reading, prediction occurs in writing on a number of different fronts at the same time. Writers predict globally what they would like their messages to be and, then, as they are writing, they predict on a smaller linguistic scale; that is, they anticipate what they will say next and how they will say it. Effective writers always keep the larger picture in mind as they are dealing with focal predictions. Confirming in writing relates to making sense. Writers monitor their writing to see if it makes sense to them and to their intended audiences. Just as readers use confirmation to determine whether they should continue reading, or stop and re-read or re-think, writers use confirming

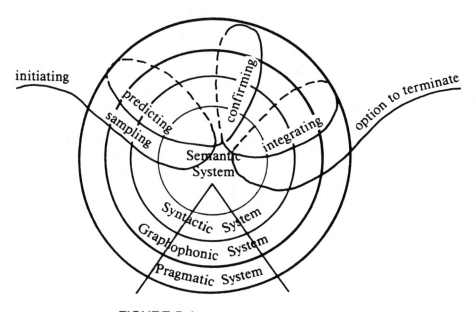

FIGURE 5.4
The Continual Interaction of the Language
Cueing Systems and Strategies

Adapted from Goodman, Yetta M., Dorothy
J. Watson, and Carolyn L. Burke. *Reading
Miscue Inventory: Alternative Procedures.*
N.Y.: Richard C. Owen Publishers, 1987,
p. 29.

strategies to decide when to keep writing and when to stop, re-think, and revise. Integration in writing is based on how authors perceive readers' backgrounds, beliefs, and interests and how well they can integrate those with their own to accomplish their intended purposes.

Reading and writing strategies interact continually with information from the language cueing systems shown in Figure 5.4.

Reading and writing are analogous processes. Understanding how they work is critical if teachers are to own their classrooms, if they are to feel empowered enough to make the best learning decisions for themselves and their students.

Personal Reflection

How can I make the learning in my classroom more collaborative?

How can I continue to increase my understanding of reading/writing processes?

The Management
Question

6

Nancie Atwell tells the story of Don Graves coming to visit her writing workshop in Booth Bay, Maine. After spending the day watching her and talking to her students, he said: "You know what makes you such a good writing teacher?" Smiling inwardly, Atwell happily anticipated Graves' comments—maybe he would say something about her intelligence or her sensitivity or her commitment. Instead, he said: "You're so damned organized."

That is the consummate compliment for this kind of teaching. No teaching works well without organization; whole language instruction would be impossible without it. It's true that you often *do* have thirty students moving in thirty different directions, but it is deliberate, purposeful movement. They know where they are going; and you can help all thirty of them get there. There are some keys, however, to making it all work well. In the following section Kathleen Visavotti shows us how it works for her.

TIME AND STRUCTURE

Kathleen believes that the most important first step toward whole language and good management is to simplify the schedule by consolidating areas of study.

> Instead of teaching the language arts as separate entities at different times throughout the day, bring them all together in the context of young reader's/writer's work during a daily language workshop—the biggest block of time you can provide given the constraints of the school day. Start by revising your schedule so that it includes extended periods.

Kathleen's daily schedule reflects her belief that real development can't occur unless students have a chance to stay with something for a useful period of time. Each morning, after their usual class business (discussed in Chapter 5 under "Ownership") from 8:50–9:15 A.M., Kathleen's second-graders know they can count on a block of time to write, then a block of time to read—these surrounded by plenty of opportunities to choose, to think, to talk, and to share.

Writing Workshop gets the first sixty minutes, followed by recess, and then another hour is given over to Reading Workshop. Storytime precedes SSR (Sustained Silent Reading), when each of the second-graders select three books from the class library (many have been written by the students themselves and are displayed on a book rack in the back of the room) and read independently.

Within Kathleen's Writing/Reading Workshop time, there is an invariant structure. Her students know what to expect. They can depend on a sequence of activities and can make their decisions accordingly. The predictability gives her students the independence they need. Functioning apart from the teacher is no problem (even if you are only seven or eight years old) if you have a clear idea of where you are going from one moment to the next, and what is expected of you once you finish one thing and are ready to move on (*see* Figure 6.1).

With an eye toward both student and teacher responsibility, Kathleen describes the internal workings of Writing Workshop this way:

> Writing Workshop always begins with a prewriting activity. I often read aloud a book that may influence the children's own writing. Afterward, the book is placed in the reading area so that individuals may refer to it during writing and

Writing Workshop

Minutes	Workshop Activity
	Read literature out loud to whole group
10	PREWRITING or BRAINSTORM TOPICS
10	UNINTERRUPTED WRITING (SSW)
30	CONFERENCES, WRITING, TALK ABOUT WRITING
10	WHOLE GROUP SHARE

Materials: Unfinished Writing Folder
              Writing Topics Sheet
              Unfinished Pieces
            Finished Writing Folder
              "Pieces I Have Written" Sheet
              Final Drafts
            Spelling Folder

FIGURE 6.1
Kathleen's Writing Workshop Schedule

reread it during SSR. Sometimes we brainstorm writing topics. The list of these is then posted for future reference. There is a weekly "go round" in which each student reports what he or she is currently writing. This often results in a spontaneous exchange of ideas. Everyone has a "Writing Topics" Sheet in their Unfinished Writing Folders. Students are encouraged to be on the lookout for writing ideas at all times, and to record topics whenever they think of them.

The next ten minutes we call SSW, Sustained Silent Writing. Many find the quiet conducive to concentration. As with SSR, the procrastinators soon get involved because there's nothing else to do but, in this case, write. They can't while away the time with chitchat or lament, "I don't know what to write about." They have their Topics Sheet for ideas, and no distractions.

I write at this time, too. It's always hard to pull myself away, but when I do set aside my journal and quietly call the day's small weekly conference group to the table in the writing area, that is the signal that it is now permissible to talk and to leave one's desk to get writing supplies or deliver messages.

It is an easily observable fact that a writing process classroom is filled with talk. Students write independently yet cannot help but give and get ideas from one another. From Day One we talk about talk—that they should limit themselves to talking about writing during writing time, saving socializing for recess. Lots of good topics pop up in the course of conversation. Writers come to realize that *it is a compliment if someone likes an idea well enough to write about it, too.*

During Writing Workshop students are free to: write on self-selected topics (expository or narrative), write in their journals, write letters to classmates or pen pals, or read and take notes on a topic on which they are doing research. While individuals are writing any and all of the above, volunteer writing aides meet for conferences, one at a time, in the Writing area (*see* Figure 6.2 Kathleen's Floor Plan). This is an alcove with table, chairs, and easily accessible writing supplies. The aides are trained parents who come to the class at least once a week. Basically they meet with individuals in order to listen to drafts or to help with editing.

At the same time I am with a weekly general conference group in the meeting area. I divide the number in the class by the number of days on which writing is scheduled and meet with a group each day. For example, five become known as the Tuesday group, and gather every Tuesday to discuss their writings. On a given Tuesday one child may be selecting a topic; one may be in the midst of a piece of writing; one may be ready to read a completed piece and receive feedback on its content; one may need help with the mechanics of a revised piece; and one may be publishing, that is, writing a revised and edited piece in final form. All the children interact—reading to one another, giving praise, asking questions, offering suggestions. All take an active role in each stage of the writing process, their own cycles, and those of others.

After about fifty minutes of Writing Workshop I ask everyone to put their writing folders in order (work in progress in the light blue Unfinished Folder, completed pieces in the dark blue Finished Folder, their personal spelling dictionaries back in the manila Spelling Folder) and place them neatly in their desks. Finally, it's time to share.

During the Whole Group Share time volunteers read sentences they've composed that they really like. I always make a positive comment about each one. If

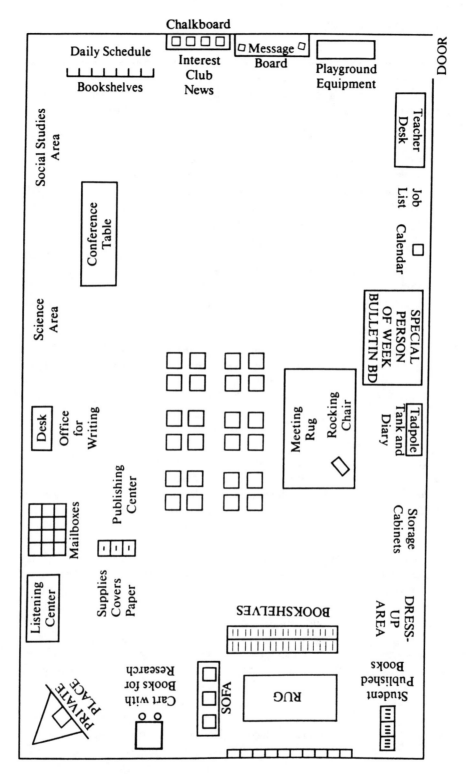

FIGURE 6.2
Kathleen Visovatti's Second-grade
Classroom Floor Plan

someone has completed a publication and has met with the writing aide for final editing, she or he sits in the rocking chair on the rug. The class gathers at the author's feet as the book is read aloud. Afterward, the book is proudly added to the classroom library to be enjoyed during SSR until the end of the school year, when the writer takes it home.

Kathleen runs Reading Workshop as much like Writing Workshop as possible. Again, she pays attention to the importance of time and structure while highlighting process.

During our one-hour Reading Workshop there are individual, small group, and total class activities; a great deal of self-selection of materials; and an emphasis on process rather than product. Over the year I have developed a number of literature units based on themes (friendship, family, peace), genre (folktales, poetry, mysteries), and authors (Tomie de Paola, Eric Carle, Leo Lionni; *see* Appendix A). Which I adapt—or what new ones evolve—depends on the interests of the students. Each year is different.

As with Writing Workshop, each session begins with the whole group meeting on the rug. Sometimes I introduce a book by asking questions to elicit their prior knowledge and to encourage prediction. Other times I give Book Talks* on a number of titles, then students choose which they want to read. Most of the time they self-select books from the library or classroom or read ones they have brought from home. I have collected hundreds of paperbacks and cultivated the friendships of local public librarians who can make requests all over the state for fitting titles and are able to grant long-term loans. The class set of district-adopted basals are another resource I use—but very selectively. For example, I'll occasionally use a selection as a jumping-off place. We'll all read a mystery, talk about its contents, then everyone chooses other mysteries from the classroom library and independently compares them to the one in the basal.

The opening talk about reading is also a time for students to share their goals for the day. By verbally committing themselves to a task in front of the others, each becomes a group conscience for others. It is also a time when I can present a Mini-lesson* as the need arises. For example, "I notice in some of your journals problems identifying clues early on in mysteries. Let's practice a bit. Here's a mystery. Listen for hints to a solution as I tell it. Raise your hand whenever you hear one. . ."

Reading Discussion Groups* meet weekly. We keep notes in our journals as we talk. The day after a group meets, they refer to their journals as they share highlights of the discussion the day before with the whole class. For example, "We talked about books in a series. Here are some we compared. . ." "We noticed that every book has a copyright on the back of the title page. How old are your books?" "We thought of unusual, attention-getting titles." "Some events in books could never really happen. They're called 'fantasy fiction.' Others seem so real, but they're made up. They're called 'realistic fiction.'" Thus, literary concepts are reinforced for the reporting group, as well as introduced to the whole class.

---

* All asterisks throughout the book refer the reader to Chapter 10 where full strategy descriptions can be found.

The bulk of the time in Reading Workshop is spent reading. Students sit wherever they would like, books in hand, Reading Journals* on their laps. Everyone keeps a journal in which the students and I carry on a written dialogue about what each of us is reading. Their responses over the year document their growth as thoughtful readers. They read; they jot down ideas; they also talk about their reading spontaneously to the person next to them: "Hey, listen to this . . ." "What's this word?" or, "You know, something like this happened to me . . ."

Readers keep a blank Bookmark* handy as they read. When they come upon an exciting or descriptive or moving passage they want to remember to share, they write the page number and an exclamation point on the Bookmark. If they are confused by a section, they jot down the page number followed by a question mark. Any words they don't know and can't figure out through context, synonym substitution, structural analysis, or some other means, *and* that are important to the meaning of the text, are recorded on the Bookmark along with the page on which they appeared.

These Bookmarks are a handy reference when discussion groups meet and for all the class to share. They are also an incidental way of documenting the number of books read and the level of difficulty and enjoyment—a blank Bookmark often indicates an easy, perhaps boring book; whereas, one with many page numbers and question marks may mean the book is too difficult. Both conclusions have to be verified by the reader, however, and most children usually stop reading either kind of book after a chapter or two with no prompting from me. (One child filled a Bookmark, front and back, with every page number followed by an exclamation mark! Quite a recommendation! Needless to say, many others chose to read this book, too!)

In addition to individual musings, small groups meet once a week to respond to their reading. Open-ended and teacher-directed discussions occur. Everyone contributes, although each may be reading a different book. Some topics are continued from week to week; others arise and are concluded in one sitting. During the discussions there are no wrong answers. All contributions are valued, and I speak only to facilitate, not to offer opinions.

Reading Workshop

Minutes	Workshop Activity
	Whole group prediction of new material everyone will read
10	PREREADING Book Talks on a number of different titles for self-selection
20	UNINTERRUPTED READING Writing about Reading Journals
20	INFORMAL TALK, WEEKLY CONFERENCES
10	WHOLE CLASS SHARE

FIGURE 6.3
Kathleen's Reading Workshop Schedule

Also, a number of specific strategies are used. Again, time is provided at the end of the hour for a Whole Group Share. This time we focus on surprises during the workshop hour, new strategies tried out, or comprehension problems solved. Students make final journal entries if they would like, and we clean up (*see* Figure 6.3).

Kathleen's time distribution and internal writing/reading workshop structure give only one organizational possibility—you'll see others in Chapter 11 "First Days, First Weeks." However, paying attention to extended time for reading and writing, and getting a simple, predictable structure in place are important first management steps.

REFLECTIONS ON TIME

I always find it ironic that the very institutions that are supposed to nurture literacy, the places where our children and our teenagers should have a formalized opportunity to immerse themselves in reading and writing, give precious little time for extended, uninterrupted reading and writing every day. Our students have learned to think in episodes—if they miss "The Cosby Show" or "Alf" one week, no matter; they don't necessarily have to tie one half-hour segment to the next to understand what's going on. We encourage episodic, sit-com type of thinking with our choppy curricula that move students too quickly from one lesson to the next, and give them a fast dance from subject to subject. While short bursts of creative brilliance are occasionally possible with brief encounters, it's sustained time that allows for more complicated thought patterns to develop.

Our students read and write so little in school. Think about your own school day. Do a quick calculation on the percentage of time your students actually read and write. (It's not fair to include teacher-directed basal reading instruction—that's not the kind of real, sustained reading you see outside the classroom.) The statistics from the last National Assessment of Educational Progress show that the average high-school student completes a piece of writing longer than a paragraph only *once a month!* Illinois Writing Project Co-Directors, Steve Zemelman and Harvey Daniels, have this to say about the findings: "Now, how could anyone build competence at an activity so complex and demanding as writing by practicing only nine or ten times a year? Clearly, one of the main challenges to all teachers is to devote more student time, more learning time, to actually doing writing" (1988, p. 21).

Ditto for reading. Teaching kids to concentrate is also a time allotment issue: Increased powers of concentration are related to experience, not discipline or some innate ability. When students have daily opportunities to immerse themselves in reading and writing for long periods of time, continuous, independent engagement is more and more possible.

In Carol Porter's junior-high-school reading class she, too, gave long periods of time for reading and writing. All of her eighth-graders entered her classroom last year aliterate, only capable of reading for short periods of time ("My eyes get tired after about fifteen minutes"). Most of the students left the class able to read for an hour or two at one sitting, and all voluntarily read outside the classroom. Here's an incredible discussion about the growth of a few readers and writers from that classroom:

> TANYA: I remember I never had read any novels except Nancy Drew mysteries. Now I read all the time. All different types of books.
> SEAN: Yeah, she always has a book in her purse. It drives me crazy. They're really thick, and she pulls them out during science class and shows me how much she has read since the day before.
> TRACEY: That's true. Before eighth grade I read, but not very much. Now I always have a book with me.
> SHAWN: I remember our suspense unit. Can you believe that some of us came back to school on a Friday night to watch a suspense movie?
> TANYA: And what about when we went to hear [Robert] Cormier speak in Chicago after we had read all of his books and the night our parents came to school to discuss stories with us and when that lady came in and we could discuss religious themes in *A Wrinkle in Time?*
> DAVE: You [Ms. Porter] could tell everyone how obnoxious I was at the beginning of the year and how I turned into one of your best students. I didn't believe it when you said that we wouldn't have any worksheets and that there were a lot of good books out there. I remember saying: 'Yeh, well, we sure haven't seen any yet.'

They did see them though. Through Carol's commitment to showing every student the wonders of reading, and through her strong belief in time to read and talk about reading, the class grew as readers and learned to revel in the deep involvement, the transcendent pleasure of reading. In a final reflective letter, shown in Figure 6.4, Dave lauds Carol's connected instruction, and proudly underscores the changes in his own literacy development.

Let me join the ranks of educators who insist, encourage, and demand more time for real reading and writing (Graves, 1983; Zemelman and Daniels, 1988; Calkins, 1986; Harste, Short, and Burke, 1988; K. Goodman, 1986, Atwell, 1987; Edelsky, 1989).

Even if you have to close your door to critical peers and administrators, give more time for real reading and writing. If you have to go to confession to get rid of your guilt for not "teaching," give students the chance for more extended involvement. If you only have small blocks of time—such as Barbara Lindberg in a junior high school (37 minutes per class!); or Carol Porter, who is now teaching high school (40 minutes); or Penny Silvers with her pullout remedial program (30 minutes); or the millions of teachers whose basal programs have a stranglehold on their time—you *can* give more time for literacy. Students come into your class, then, knowing, expecting to pick up where they left off the preceding day. When there is prolonged thinking time within a day and/or across days it is far more likely that students will continue their thinking outside of the classroom—they will "write" when they are not writing (Graves, 1983), "read" when they are not reading.

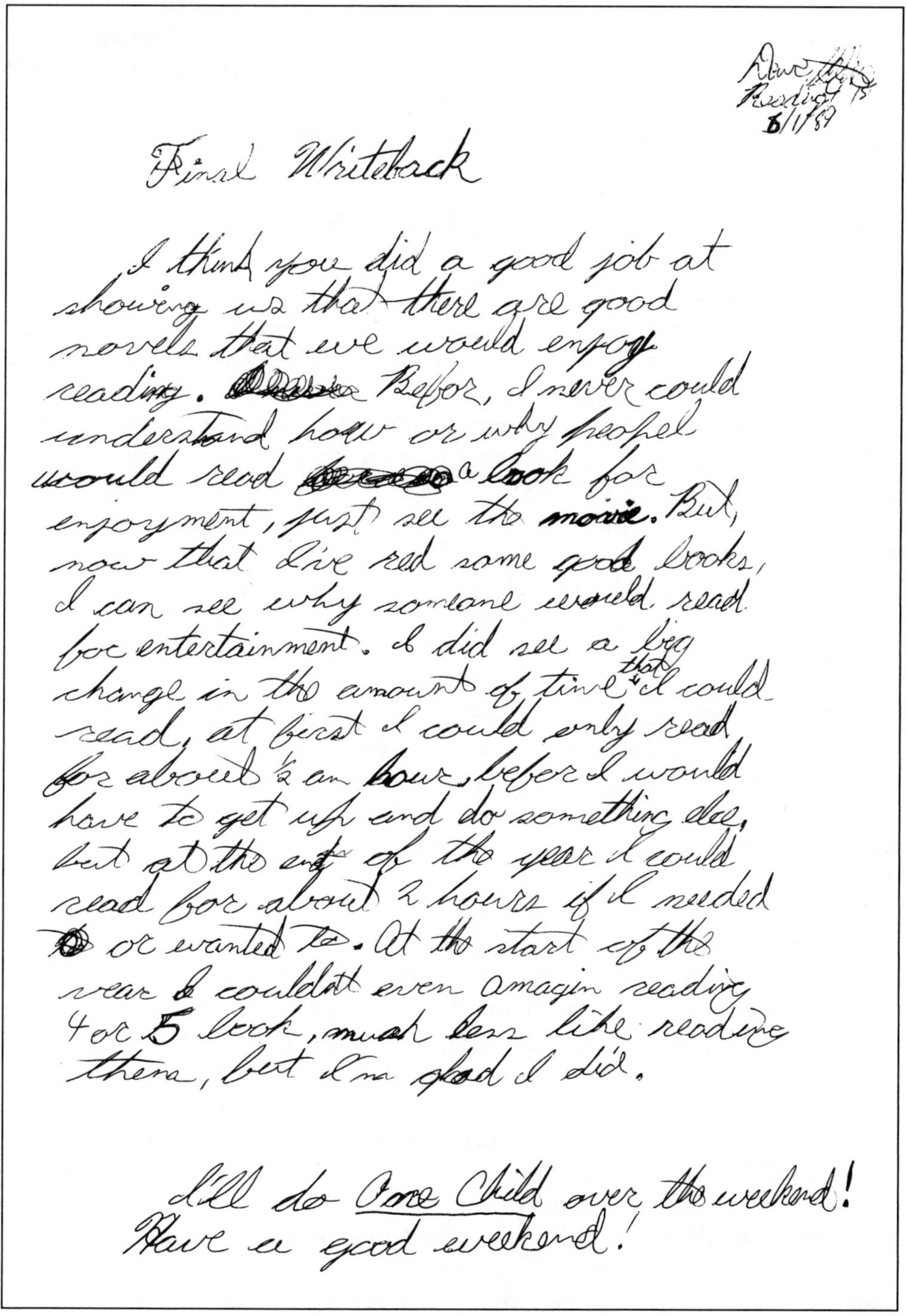

Dorothy
Reading 9
6/1/89

Final Writeback

I think you did a good job at showing us that there are good novels that we would enjoy reading. ~~Before~~ Befor, I never could understand how or why people would read ~~a book~~ a book for enjoyment, just see the ~~movie~~. But, now that I've read some good books, I can see why someone would read for entertainment. I did see a big change in the amount of time that I could read, at first I could only read for about ½ an hour, before I would have to get up and do something else, but at the end of the year I could read for about 2 hours if I needed ~~to~~ or wanted to. At the start of the year I couldn't even amagin reading 4 or 5 book, much less like reading them, but I'm glad I did.

I'll do _One Child_ over the weekend! Have a good weekend!

FIGURE 6.4
Student Letter on the Value of Time to
Development

We know that people get better at something by simply engaging in an activity at which they want to become more skilled; teachers can't pretend that knowledge doesn't exist. Allowing students time to "just" read and write may be the most important instructional decision you make all year long. And it may be the best response to the question: "What's the first step in whole language instruction?"

REFLECTIONS ON STRUCTURE

When Dave was asked by a teacher how the independent reading and writing and small group discussions fit together in Carol's classroom, he said: "It's really simple. You choose a book and then your group decides when you will meet to discuss and how far you will have to read. We also write and pick pieces we want to publish. Then we meet with a group to get ideas for what we want to change."

This is a clear, predictable framework that Dave and his peers learned quickly and then used throughout their eighth-grade school year. While giving time is critical, providing structure for that time relieves students and teachers from figuring out a direction whenever a new book or project is started. It also gives everyone a sense of security so necessary when the processes themselves must be filled with risks and errant movement.

Because of the research on reader contributions, we know that reading begins long before the reader opens a book and continues long after the book is closed. Similarly, we have found that writing includes cognition and language before, during, and after composition. While Prereading/Prewriting, During Reading/During Writing, and After Reading/After Writing have been used as a means of encouraging students to connect more intimately to literacy events, and to extend them beyond the reading/writing experience itself, it is also a useful way to think about a whole language organizational plan (*see* Figure 6.5).

The time before reading and writing can be focused on selecting books and topics or talk about process strategies. You, or one of your students, can simply talk about your reading or writing, a kind of Process Share.* Sharing problems that have been encountered and how they were solved or major strategies that are useful to any reader/writer (*e.g.,* rereading, predicting, questioning, revising, talking to someone, and so on) strengthens a process-focused curriculum tremendously. These demonstrations should be brief, with the goal of highlighting a strategy or a literacy decision that may support others' composing or comprehending.

"During Reading/During Writing" can begin with uninterrupted reading and writing. This should be the primary activity. Some days you may want to do only this with little talking and few teacher/student or student/student interactions. On other days, you may encourage a more active exchange in which students choose to read as partners or pair up to discuss comprehension problems or meet in small reading circles to interpret material together. Start slowly. You always have time to build a core of good process procedures with your students learning along with you. But, no matter how sophisticated you become with whole

Reading/Writing

Before	Select and discuss topic	
	Talk about process strategies	
During	Uninterrupted engagement	
	Focus on process	
	Reading	*Writing*
	Reading Journals*	Peer responses
	Reading Conversation*	Teacher Responses
	Reading Discussion Groups*	Revision
		Editing
		Publishing
After	Whole group share	

FIGURE 6.5

Beginning Organization for Reading/Writing Time

language teaching, the extended involvement that you start with, the uninterrupted reading and writing time that you build into every day, is always the dimension to keep faithfully in place.

Using strategies during reading/writing that help maintain a steady focus on process is one of the hallmarks of whole language teaching. Many veteran teachers like Kathleen and Carol have found that some of the simplest strategies are still the best. Strategies like Written Conversation,* Reading Journals,* and Reading Conversation* are interactive procedures whose simplicity belies their power. They can be put into place tomorrow and, when they are, they compel reflection, encourage personal connection, and help students go beyond text-based responses to interpretive levels of comprehension. Many of the "thinking skills" found in traditional teacher's manuals can be encouraged and driven by real, whole sense-making. These meaning-based procedures can also be used to track process changes and development and help give you the documentation you need of your students' literate behavior (*see* Chapter 7, "Evaluation").

Educators like Graves, Calkins, and Atwell, who have pioneered and refined instruction in process writing, have also found that simple, interactive procedures during writing are the most effective. Be sure to begin the "During" phase of writing by writing yourself—your own writing will become an invaluable resource for sharing and talking about process strategies before pen-to-paper writing begins, not to mention the solid display of proficiency you are providing. After some uninterrupted writing of your own, you may want to circulate among the other writers, just taking enough time to touch base: "How is it going?" "Would you read what you have written?" "Are you having any problems?" "What do you plan to do next?"

You want to keep the process in the hands of the owner, so don't worry about direct teaching at this point. In fact, you may be much better off not even to look at your students' early draft writing. The temptation to jump in and point out all that's wrong is too great. Maintain a steady gaze at the writer's face while you are listening, respond briefly and genuinely to the content, and then move on. From time to time you may want to compare early drafts to later ones, just to see how much was taken care of in the process itself. In any case, your role is to show interest, to plant some keep-going messages, and perhaps to take some process notes that can be used later for brief lessons or "Before Writing" discussion.

Always allow time for sharing and talk after reading and writing. Whole group volunteer sharing is the easiest, but students have to know that only a few can be heard each day. Usually that's not much of a problem if you've been careful to structure time for talk in the "During" phase. Partner and small group sharing gives everyone a voice and a chance to explore process and content. Be sure that "Whole Group Shares" include process discussions. To facilitate these discussions you may want to ask students to note on a 3 × 5 card a process strategy they used during reading/writing time. Students bring their cards to the whole group Process Share,* and volunteers talk about their strategies. Students who have the same idea written on their cards, talk about how they used it in different contexts. Try designating at least one day a week for process sharing, until students are talking about process as much as content. If you have many process issues on any one day, they can always spill over into tomorrow's "Before Reading/Writing" time as a way of preparing for the day's literacy work.

THIRTY STUDENTS/THIRTY DIRECTIONS: KEEPING TRACK

It may not be thirty; it may be twenty-five or fifty or 150, but in whole language classrooms teachers face the tough, sometimes formidable task of tracking processes that can move in many directions. Even though the basic cycles of literacy processes do not vary, individuals vary greatly in their quest for meaning construction. Tracking all of that mind movement creates a pressing need for clear, large-group management formats. Described below is one procedure, "Status of the Class," which has proven useful for many whole language teachers.

STATUS OF THE CLASS CHART

Adapted from Don Graves, Nancie Atwell refined this management device for writing. It is just as useful for reading. Basically it works like this: Write all of your students' names on the left side of a sheet of paper (legal size if you have a large class). Across the top write in the dates for a full week. Designate "Reading Workshop" on one form and "Writing Workshop" on a photocopy. Make enough forms for each week of the school year.

At the beginning of Reading and Writing Workshops do a quick inventory of the entire class, asking each student what she or he is working on or what they plan to do during Workshop on that day. If you have regular group meetings (such as Kathleen's Monday-Friday conference groups in writing), students can simply be reminded to join you at the conference table when you check the status of the class. You can also see what reading/writing activities are likely to be carried over from one day to the next and you can just check in with those students to confirm that they are still working on their "Grandma" story or still reading *Across Five Aprils* with a partner.

Even if you have a very large class the status check only takes a few minutes once you get an abbreviated notetaking system worked out and your students learn to report to you in a shortened form as well.

Reading about or walking into a fully functioning whole language classroom can be overwhelming, even intimidating. How do they know what to do? How did they learn to be so independent? What is the invisible structure? Like any other part of the whole language curriculum, developing an effective, smoothly operating management system takes time—and preparation. It is, however, worth all the time and energy you can give to it, because effective management can make the difference between purposeful movement and chaotic misdirection, between a controlled sense of panic and a peaceful sense of productivity.

Personal Reflection

How can I increase time for uninterrupted writing?

How can I increase time for uninterrupted reading?

What beginning organizational plan can I use for reading and/or writing?

Evaluation

7

In Miriam Cohen's book, *First Grade Takes a Test,* Anna Maria is assigned to a gifted class because she "did good on the test." When the other first-graders hear about this, they start calling each other, "Dummy, dummy." Jim says it quietly to himself: "Dummy."

"Listen to me!" The angry sound of the teacher's voice startles them.

> The test doesn't tell everything. It doesn't tell all the things you *can* do! You can build things! You can read books! You can make pictures! You have good ideas. And another thing. The test doesn't tell you if you are the kind of person who helps your friend. Those are important things.

The teacher is right; the tests don't tell us everything. But, as a profession, we have been inclined to treat them as if they do. No doubt about it, we are obsessed with tests and with evaluation in general. It's one of the less-than-virtuous outcomes of the back-to-basics movement in this country. In the face of an ever-increasing demand for accountability, teachers have felt forced to turn their attention more and more to how the children perform on THE TESTS. However reluctant, teachers have become more and more accountable to numbers and less and less accountable to kids.

One of the many goals of whole language is to change the very face of evaluation; to help move it in a different direction, toward process, toward reflection, toward self-knowledge, directly toward the positives so that all students understand their strengths and never think to call themselves "dummy." During in-services and graduate classes, institutes and seminars, questions about evaluation are always among the first ones I get about whole language. I used to think that it was a question to be put off, an issue to think about once the "real " curriculum was in place. But because evaluation influences the other parts of the curriculum so directly, so inevitably, I've learned that it has to be an issue that's dealt with from the beginning, along with authentic reading and writing, right up there with student choice and ownership.

The discussions we've had so far in this book about process become useful as you start paying attention to the increasingly complex behaviors encouraged by whole language instruction. You need ways to hold on to them; you need tools to help you see, track, and report the changes. Evaluation, like math and spiders, makes a lot of people nervous. But you should know that qualitative evaluation is new for almost everyone, and we are slowly working out the systems that are needed to capture process behaviors across time and in varying contexts. This chapter will introduce the idea of whole language evaluation and give you enough options to get you comfortably started or move you a little further along. First, it helps to have a working definition of what evaluation is and what function it serves.

EVALUATION: WHAT IS IT?

Trish Peppler is a wonderful fourth-grade teacher in Pat Riordan's school. I was in her classroom not long ago talking to her students as they engaged in her effective version of Reading/Writing Workshop. Her students outlined their goals for a forty-five-minute block of time and then proceeded to accomplish them. Two or three students were at their desks reading alone; several were involved in individual writing; but most of the class had gathered into small groups to work on collaborative story writing or play scripts. Trish moved around the room conferring as she was needed. A little black-haired girl named Lucille tapped me on the shoulder: "Would you listen to our story?" I listened to a sensitive narrative about a new girl in school who had no friends. Afterward, I asked Lucille and her partner why they had chosen the topic, how it had worked for two of them to write together and what they had learned. They seemed ready for the questions and were able to reflect on the process that had resulted in an interesting, coherent story. A few minutes later, I eased over to a group discussing the strengths and weaknesses of a play they had written and rehearsed. Trish was part of this group and I watched as she skillfully led them through the same kind of process reflection I had observed in Lucille and her co-writer.

In *The Whole Language Evaluation Book,* Yetta Goodman writes: "In our classrooms, as we critically examine what students do in order to help them grow as educated human beings, we become consciously aware that at the same time we are seeing a reflection of ourselves." (p. 3) As I listened to Trish's students think about their writing experiences, I was, to a great degree, seeing Trish. If you ever want to get some insight into the instructional practices of a teacher without actually observing the teacher in action, listen to the students. Student responses and behavior are a reflection of teacher decision-making. Examining the change that occurs as a result of classroom interaction is evaluation. The only way to see that change is to observe process, which often means looking at students and learning in a very different way.

If you pick up any of the old classic texts on evaluation you will see the chapters built around two ideas: formative and summative evaluation. Formative evaluation is meant to influence learning, to change the direction of a student's thinking, to encourage a change. Summative evaluation "sums up" what has been learned, gives us a report that can be handed to parents and administrators—or to the media. Summative measures often become the force that drives the curriculum. Numbers are used as powerful and intimidating indicators of the social climate of district classrooms. Despite the carefully developed discussion in graduate teaching courses about evaluation as an ongoing enterprise, evaluation has become an idea almost synonymous with outcome and product. To no one's surprise, but everyone's concern, instruction is insidiously test-driven.

Evaluation is summative in most classrooms. That's not an earth-shattering observation. Summative evaluation is consistent with everything that is going on in traditional classrooms: It helps measure mastery of the little bits of learning that comprise curriculum. Some teachers who are getting started with whole language feel they want to leave the question of evaluation until they have other parts of their curricula in place, then they can concentrate on assessing what they and their students have accomplished. But like other notions of teaching and learning, this idea no longer fits with a new paradigm focused on interactive concepts of teaching and learning. Evaluation is supposed to help us achieve a qualitative difference in our personal pedagogy. Evaluation is supposed to have something to do with instruction. If we gather information on our students it should, in some way, inform our teaching and help us decide what to do next. That's the acid test for any evaluative procedure. When we evaluate kids' learning or ask them to evaluate it themselves, there is only one reason to do so: to help them learn more.

BASIC GUIDELINES

In the March 1989 issue of *Reading Today* researcher Bill Teale recommends two basic guidelines for the evaluation of reading and writing: Minimize the use of group standardized tests and maximize the use of informal/observational methods. In a nutshell the problems with group standardized tests revolve around the fact that, as Teale points out, they don't help teachers teach: "Especially the statewide criterion-referenced competency tests—teachers often feel compelled to teach to the test. The effect is a sad one. Teachers feel the anxiety of test scores as much or more than their students and so they end up overemphasizing what standardized tests measure, the only thing they can measure: fragmented reading and writing, isolated skills and rote memorization."

Standardized tests are way behind the times. They are based on behavioral research of at least thirty years ago (Heald-Taylor, 1989) and have hardly changed at all for decades. They don't reflect *any* of the current research on language and learning (Farr and Carey, 1986; Valencia and Pearson, 1987), and are, in fact, downright dangerous: Not only do they give a distorted profile of a student's learning, they can also lull us into a false sense of security about our teaching (Valencia and Pearson, 1987) when we draw conclusions about our curricula based on how well students perform on the test.

It's fine, you may be thinking, to bash the tests, but they are my reality; I *have* to give them. And in a world where numbers count, sometimes more than the quality of teaching or the level of real learning, it's a fair objection to raise and it's also fair to ask how students in whole language classrooms are doing on the tests. How are they faring on formal assessments when how they are taught and how they are assessed are worlds apart? When asked that question teachers writing for this book gave a resounding response: "They are doing fine!"

Kathleen Visovatti says that her principal gave her the freedom she needed to apply her whole language beliefs—with one caveat: Her students must perform as well as the other second-graders on the standardized tests. And they always do.

Up until last year Pat Riordan's first-graders received respectable scores on the California Achievement Test. Last year was different for Pat because she refused to give her students the CAT. She argued that it was too much time away from learning, that it traumatized some of the children in her class, and that, anyway, the test gave her no real information to help with instructional decisions. After many heated discussions her principal validated her right to take that politically sensitive position.

Whole language teachers who *do* give standardized tests make different decisions about how to prepare their students for them. Some wait until the week before, and then familiarize students with the structure and the questions. Other teachers prepare students in short blocks of time, making sure they have multiple exposures before the actual exams. Whatever procedure you choose, be sure to relate what you have been doing in the larger curricular, reading/writing context to the isolated bits students will encounter on the tests. Knowing where to fit the pieces and what purpose they have in real literacy events will help tremendously in sorting out the narrow abstractions represented on the tests.

While it may be comforting to some degree to hear that students in whole language classrooms are doing fine on standardized tests (it soothes the nerves of many principals and parents), it's certainly not enough for a teacher who wants to know how students are changing and growing in the more complex ways of process reading and writing. Test scores give a grossly incomplete picture of a student's language learning, and do little to inform the necessary responses and modifications in a dynamic, student-focused curriculum. Whole language assessment, in contrast, tells you about the strategies and behaviors students are using in different reading/writing contexts. It tells you how well your curriculum is supporting the kind of proficient decision-making necessary for continued growth and language development.

The rest of this chapter is about making process observations and using alternative evaluation procedures that will support the other dimensions of your whole language curriculum.

SEEING DIFFERENTLY

In Cynthia Rylant's new book, *All I See,* a painter looks out over a small lake and creates beautiful pictures of whales. When his young, new friend asks him why he paints only whales, he laughs and says: "It's all I see." One of the wonderful things about whole language is that you start to see kids and their learning differently—instead of focusing on their weaknesses, more and more you see their strengths until that's all you can see.

Perhaps remedial and special education teachers are taught, even more than the rest of us, to look at the problems, the "don't knows," the "can't dos." With Penny Silvers' gradual transition to whole language came an altered sense of what to look for, what to validate in her reading lab students. But the negative aura created by a traditional deficit model of learning has been a constant battle to be fought.

> Looking at a student's strengths is very different from emphasizing the deficits—the skills that the student does *not* seem to know. As a reading specialist I was trained to evaluate mistakes, to focus on what was wrong and to plan a remedial program that provided drill and practice until mastery could be shown, usually on a test. When there seem to be many deficits, the student becomes deficient in the teacher's eyes. Students are treated as flawed individuals who do not know, rather than people who have the potential to learn and to become literate. As I worked with students I began to see how much they really did know, how proficiently they used language, and how effectively they used strategies when reading a book of their choice. I noticed, too, how different this reading was from the slow, plodding, often incoherent reading exhibited in regular classroom reading groups.
>
> At first it was difficult for me to explain how a student who was reading below grade level, like fourth-grade David, could become so absorbed in science-fiction books, discussing UFOs so intelligently, writing reports, and contributing information so willingly to his peers in the reading lab. How could he do research on the Black Hole and read about the Bermuda Triangle when he was unable to pass the basal unit tests in his classroom or answer comprehension questions accurately enough for his homeroom teacher? In his classroom he often failed comprehension tests, did minimal work, wrote sparsely, if at all, and felt defeated in comparison to his peers.
>
> During his year in the reading lab I saw very little of this remedial behavior. David was the "expert" on UFOs. He was reading and writing freely and with confidence, using the group of six other fourth-graders to listen to his drafts. This was in marked contrast to his classroom behavior where he was in the "lowest" reading group and rarely completed any assignments. In the reading lab David was reading, writing, contributing to projects that the group became involved with, learning reading strategies, making decisions, taking risks, and behaving in all the ways in which literate people behave.
>
> In the spring of that year David took the CAT test given to the whole school. He took the test confidently, and I was surprised that his total reading score was below grade level. Even though the score obviously did not reflect any of the successes he had experienced in reading and writing in the lab, I began to feel guilty that I had

not done more isolated skill instruction and even questioned the validity of my holistic beliefs. As I thought about why David's scores did not seem to reflect the successes he had experienced in reading and writing in the lab, I began to question what I knew he had really accomplished, what I was doing to help the students, and the rationale for my literature-based program. Ironically, I knew that not only was David gaining proficiency in literacy processes but he was *excited* about reading and writing—unlike his performance in the regular skill-based classroom.

It wasn't until I started reviewing my process notes about him as a reader and writer that I began to balance what I knew about his strengths as a learner with the skill deficits reflected in his test scores. I could see that isolated skills did not address his learning strategies or his literate behaviors. While this knowledge didn't change his scores, it enabled me to confirm again that David's reading and writing processes and his attitude about them were the critical components in the total assessment of his learning. With this validation I was able to continue to plan his literacy experiences in a way that allowed him to continue to make choices and assume responsibility for his learning.

Whole language curriculum is built on student strengths, not weaknesses. It is a giant leap away from the diagnostic tools and screening devices based on deficit models, which are intended to uncover what it is that kids *don't* know, what they *can't* do, rather than what they do know and what they can do. These deficit views can creep in and, before you know it, we are trying to find out what's wrong with first-graders, then kindergartners, and now those preschoolers who are high risk —wondering what's wrong with these young learners before they've had a chance to show us what's right.

The perspective from a deficit model is to start curriculum by assessing the problems, and then teach to the knowledge gaps. Funny thing is, once those deficits are identified, they tend to follow students around during the rest of their school careers. They even increase as we test and retest in an effort to uncover more of what is wrong, identify ever more closely the minutiae of the disability, so an entire curriculum can be built around it and students' learning energy can be expended on it.

Consider the following journal entries from Dave, a senior in Carol Porter's reading class. He is responding to two chapters from *The Outsiders*.

While these are *reading* responses, it would be easy to focus on all the things that are wrong in Dave's writing. In fact, when Carol asked a colleague to look at Dave's responses, she took a red pen and marked only problems—misspellings, poor sentence construction, lack of specificity, and so on. Her deficit evaluation totally missed the point of his writing! When I asked Carol to assess the entries, she said: "Well, I want to look at them from a reading perspective first and then consider what he is doing in writing." This is what Carol noted about Dave's responses:

As a reader Dave is actively constructing meaning by:

- using previous text information to determine symbolic meaning,
- connecting text with life experiences,

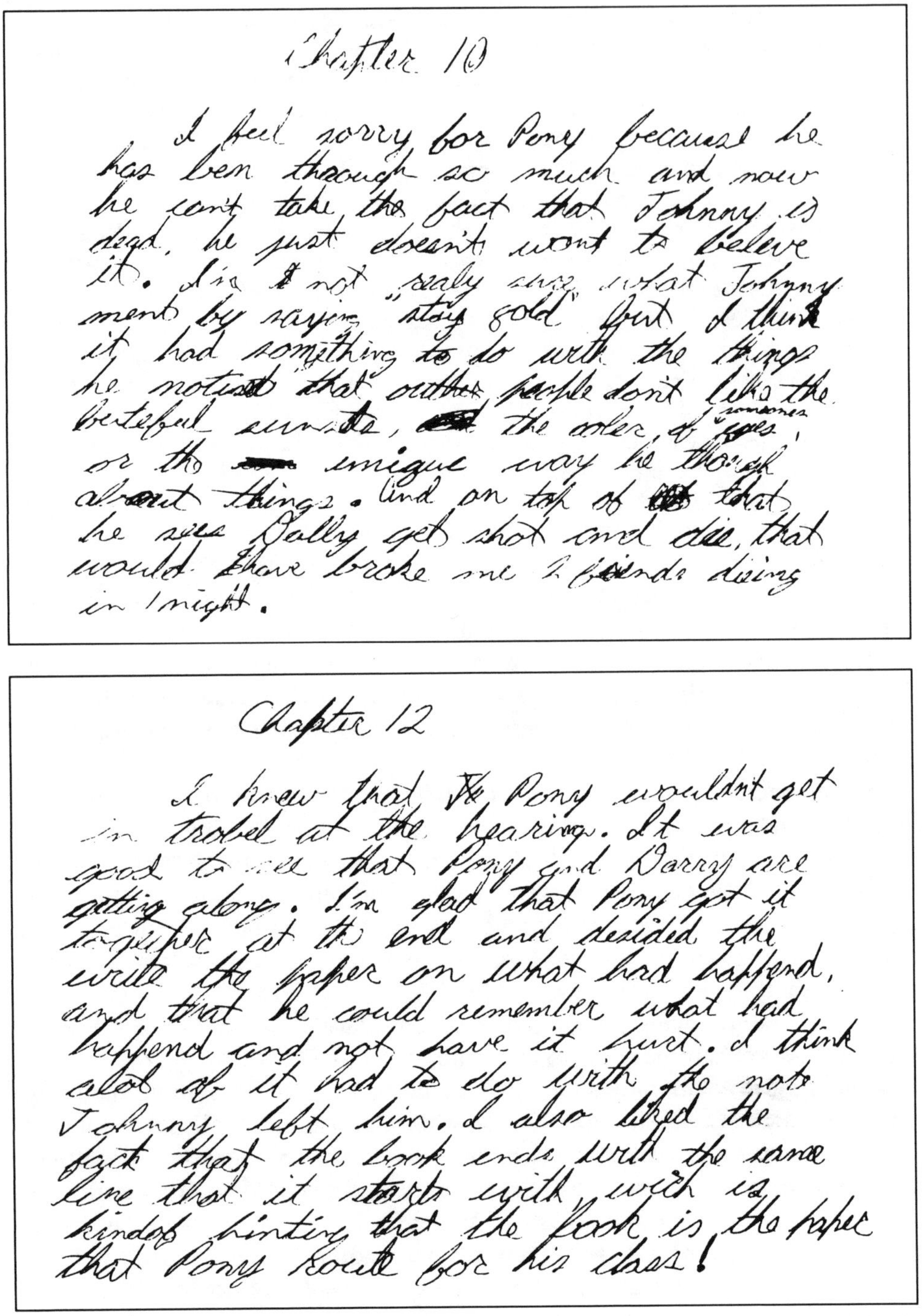

Chapter 10

I feel sorry for Pony because he has been through so much and now he can't take the fact that Johnny is dead. he just doesn't want to believe it. I'm not realy sure what Johnny ment by saying "stay gold" but I think it had something to do with the things he noticed that outher paple dont like the besteful sunsets, the coler, or yes, or the unique way he thougt about things. And on top of that he sees Dally get shot and die, that would have broke me 2 freinds dieing in 1 night.

Chapter 12

I knew that Pony wouldn't get in trobel at the hearing. It was good to see that Pony and Darry are getting along. I'm glad that Pony got it togupor at the end and decided the write the paper on what had happend, and that he could remember what had happend and not have it hurt. I think alot of it had to do with the note Johnny left him. I also liked the fact that the book ends with the same line that it starts with, wich is kindof hinting that the book is the paper that Pony route for his class!

FIGURE 7.1
Dave's Responses to Two Chapters from *The Outsiders*

- making predictions,
- confirming predictions,
- aligning himself with a main character,
- analyzing character actions,
- taking risks with interpretation,
- determining a resolution to conflict,
- identifying change in the character as a result of the reading experience,
- making connections back to the beginning of the book,
- recognizing cause and effect,
- expressing opinion.

As a writer Dave is:

- making in-process revisions with the reader in mind,
- distinguishing between journal writing and other formats (that is, final copy for publication),
- developing complex sentences,
- punctuating sentences properly,
- using quotation marks appropriately,
- using contractions correctly.

Pretty sophisticated stuff! I hope Carol's responses encouraged you to go back and look at Dave's writing with a fresh eye—to note the complexities of thought and language that produced these brief entries. Carol doesn't use this kind of fine analysis on all of her students' journal entries, but she has a skilled grasp of strengths and process from systematic observations of her students.

What kind of instructional information do these process notes give Carol? She has abundant evidence from these entries alone that the Reading Journals* she is using are encouraging a special kind of thought, and are giving Dave repeated opportunities to use salient reading strategies important to his development. Over time Carol will be able to tell how Dave's comprehension is changing, which strategies are his strongest, and which behaviors she can encourage even more.

As a teacher I would want to keep him in a strong learning context like this, make sure there were many of them in place, and track the changes over time. I could then see not only how my curriculum is supporting his development (for example, how he has daily opportunities to engage in real, extended reading and writing, doing the things proficient readers and writers do) but what growth is occurring.

This shift to a process perspective, this striving to see learning in a different more positive way, gives teachers a new sense of students as learners. When you start to look at your own students in these ways, your curricular decisions can

---

* All asterisks throughout the book refer the reader to Chapter 10 where full strategy descriptions can be found.

begin with the intent to support what the learner is attempting to do, whatever she or he is trying to sort out; that is developmentally appropriate instruction and accountability in the truest sense.

OBSERVING PROCESS

The first step in whole language evaluation is not an evaluative step at all; it's a learning step, an observational move aimed at sharpening your eye toward process. You've already started considering what good literacy strategies are and how you can begin to get them into place. Once situated, you can settle down to learn what process looks like. Recently I heard someone tell a story about a student talking to her mother about a narrative she had read in school and how deeply it touched her: "You know, I was crying so much, I could hardly answer the comprehension questions." The impact and the depth of this learning experience were no doubt lost in an evaluative effort to *prove* that the student had comprehended.

Carol Porter remarks that her students have "spent their whole lives trying to prove they've read a book."

When you begin, you may have to remind yourself that you are trying to see learning in a different way, that automatic responses and asides during reading and writing can tell you more about meaning construction than answers to questions can. Another part of observing process is to keep an eye out for the decisions students are making in various contexts. To develop a habit of observing strengths and process, you may want to choose one student and focus on him or her for a period of time. Watch as reading is initiated; listen carefully as material is discussed; pay extra attention to journal entries and invented spellings. Concentrate on observing and recording only what the student *can* do. An extended period of time with individual students can have a rich payoff.

At the beginning of this school year Pat Riordan identified evaluation and process observations as areas in which she would like to become more skilled. I suggested that she make a copy of her daily schedule on the lefthand side of a blank sheet of paper so that she could list the general contexts in which her students were involved throughout the day. On the right she left extra space between each instructional time for the process notes she would keep. I also suggested that she divide the righthand side of her page into independent and interactive observations to get a sense of how one student was functioning alone, with peers, and with her.

Pat started her process observations with Alison. For one full day she took special note of what she was doing and how she was doing it. Figure 7.2 shows some of her process notes and the contexts in which she observed Alison. Figures 7.3 and 7.4 show examples of Alison's work that day.

You are likely to find as Pat did that it's impossible to track everything. Process is often fleeting and you still have other students to deal with. But the experience is wonderfully enlightening and is important if you are to become a skilled observer of

	Alison	
	Independent	Interactive
8:25 Class Meeting		
8:45 Songs, Chants, Poems	Listened to Raffi tapes	
9:10 Reading Workshop	During Shared Reading, chose ① <u>Down by the Bay</u> (read w/ friend and alone) ② <u>Wheels on the Bus</u> ③ <u>Animals Definitely Not Wear Clothing</u> – used picture cues to construct meaning – meaningful substitutions	
10:05 Writing Workshop	Wrote her own <u>Animals Should Def. Not</u> … book	Shared book with peers as she assembled pages —
11:00 Lunch		
11:45 Read Aloud		
12:00 Gym		
12:40 Math		Chose 'Restaurant' – Customer, read from menus (clear schema for structure & language in menus/ restaurants)
1:05 Science		Contributed to How Animals Keep Cool chart: "They go underground during the day."
1:30 Independent Reading	<u>More Spaghetti I Say</u> <u>10 Crocodiles</u>	
1:45 Journals/Sharing	Wrote about Reyne's birthday	Shared Entry
2:10 Class Diary		

FIGURE 7.2
Pat Riordan's First Attempt at Making
Process Observations During One School Day

FIGURE 7.3
Page from Alison's Book *Animals Should
Definitely Not Wear Clothing.* Translation:
A Porcupine Would Look Silly in Clothes

FIGURE 7.4
Alison's Journal Entry

process. If you find you have trouble concentrating in your own classroom for initial observations, arrange with a colleague to trade off time while students are in music, gym or some other special class. Also, be sure to talk about what you see with some mutually interested party—it will go a long way to sharpen your evaluative eye.

Don Graves reminds us (Atwell, 1987, p. 8) that it is entirely possible to read about students and teaching and learning, even have a reasonable grasp of literacy research, and still be completely unaware of students' reading/writing/learning processes. It takes some heavy duty, up-close kidwatching to become aware of the processes you want to observe and understand and encourage. Process awareness can be heightened enormously if you engage in the same activities that your students do, and then reflect on your own decision-making and strategies.

BASELINE INFORMATION

It helps if you have a sense of where your students are developmentally when they come to you. The beginning of the year is the logical time to gather baseline information, but the following procedures will yield valuable data any time during the year. Once you gather an initial profile it's a good idea to repeat the surveys and interactive assessments at least once or twice during the year. That way, you and your students can develop a literacy profile by looking at the responses together to see what changes have occurred.

Good evaluation doesn't interfere with instruction; it is an integral part of the curriculum. For that reason the procedures suggested below are, first and foremost, sound learning activities as well as useful assessment tools.

READING SAMPLE

Reading Samples can be collected in a number of different ways. Using the Say Something* strategy with individuals can give immediate insight into students' comprehension and interpretive abilities. Because it is also one of our favorite thinking activities, evaluation is not separated from instruction. Carol Porter worries that "teachers are so busy trying to get kids to be partners with each other that they forget to be a partner to every student." Carol uses Say Something* repeatedly throughout the year to gather process information and to demonstrate her own thinking to students.

Audiotapes of oral reading can give you and your students a sense of how well they are using meaning strategies. When you collect an oral reading sample, choose a text that the reader will find challenging, but comprehensible. Explain that you want them to read out loud so that you can look at their reading and see what you can discover together. Tell students that you cannot help them during the reading and so, if they come to something they don't know, they should just do whatever they usually do when they are reading independently. Also inform them that you will ask them to retell the material when they finish.

While the student is reading, have a copy of the text in hand so you can simply follow along as they read. You may want to take a few notes as you listen, but stop if you notice that it is making the reader nervous.

After the oral reading simply discuss the material as you would when participating in a Reading Discussion Group.* If you follow up with any questions, make them few and open-ended (for example, "Do you remember anymore about . . . ?")

Once an oral reading is collected, listen to it *with* the student so you can notice and discuss together what was happening in-process.

1. What did the reader know about the topic before reading that influenced miscues and the reader's overall comprehension?
2. What did the miscues look like? Did they make sense?
3. Were there areas of difficulty and confusion? What happened here?
4. Did the reader reread and self-correct? When and why?

Following your discussion both you and the student should write up your observations and discoveries and put them in the student's personal reading portfolio. (Portfolios are discussed in greater detail in the next section of this chapter.) A more detailed description of taping an oral reading and of miscue analysis can be found in *Reading Miscue Inventory: Alternative Procedures* (Goodman, Watson, and Burke, 1987).

WRITING SAMPLE

Written Conversation* is a great way to collect an initial writing sample. Like the Say Something* strategy, Written Conversation gives you that individual, close-up look at a writer while having an opportunity to engage in a meaningful interaction with the student. The first part of a Written Conversation I had with a first-grader is shown in Figure 7.5.

Rachel and I had not met before we had this written exchange late in the fall. From this twenty-minute interaction I learned that Rachel could read my writing, reread, revise, borrow from my language to create her own message, initiate a topic, and take risks with her spelling and punctuation. I learned that she was aware of sentence structure, the give-and-take in conversation, and various spelling patterns (for example, the silent "e" at the end of words).

A student's first piece of writing on a self-selected topic can also serve as a baseline for writing. You and your students can use this as a beginning point and compare future writing against this one.

READING/WRITING SURVEY

A reading/writing survey that focuses on literacy strategies and attitudes is also a good way to gather baseline information on students. These surveys can be used

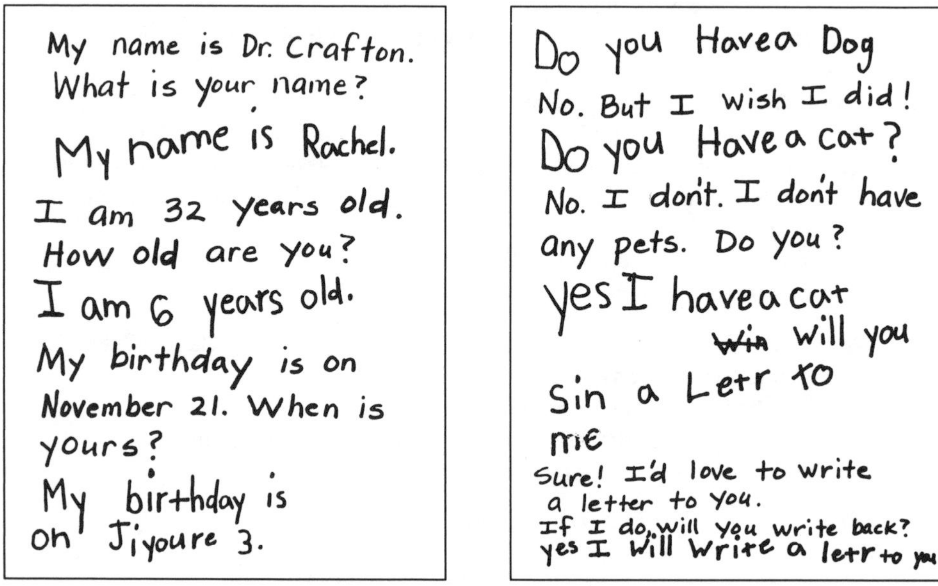

My name is Dr. Crafton.
What is your name?
My name is Rachel.
I am 32 years old.
How old are you?
I am 6 years old.
My birthday is on November 21. When is yours?
My birthday is on Jiyoure 3.

Do you Havea Dog
No. But I wish I did!
Do you Have a cat?
No. I don't. I don't have any pets. Do you?
yes I have a cat ~~Wia~~ will you Sin a Letr to me
Sure! I'd love to write a letter to you.
If I do, will you write back?
yes I Will Write a letr to you

FIGURE 7.5
Two of Three Pages of Written Conversation with a First-Grader

at the beginning of a school year and again at the end. Carol Porter and I used Carolyn Burke's *Reading Interview* (1987), Nancie Atwell's *Writing Interview* (1987), and our own interests to come up with the Reading/Writing Survey shown in Figure 7.6.

MANAGING PROCESS OBSERVATIONS

Once you start regular process observations you need a system for managing them on a daily basis and a central place to keep them. There are many workable solutions to the problem. A Process Notebook in which each student has an individual section devoted to them is one idea I have used successfully. A three-ring binder works well for this because you can keep adding looseleaf paper during the year. As process observations are made each day, they can be jotted down on small "post-it" pads and transferred later. If you decide to use a binder, start with two to three pages for each student with name tabs for easy location. Divide the pages into sections for Context, Independent, and Interactive observations with a space on the far left for the date. Don't forget to save a section in the back for notes on *your* process—questions, reflections and concerns.

Kathleen Visovatti prefers individual folders for each student but still makes her daily observations on small notes. Norma Mikelson recommends ordering large index cards on a clipboard so that each student's name is visible at the top or bottom. Anecdotal notes, then, can be added throughout the day by simply flipping to the appropriate card. When filled, the cards can be organized in a main file box.

Kathleen describes her organization and the use of her process notes:

> Before school starts, I write each child's name on a folder and put a few blank sheets in each. Every day I try to record something about each child. Sometimes it's a reflection at the end of the day, but it usually occurs throughout the day as I jot down anecdotes as they occur—or hastily put a few key words on a "post-it" and stick it on my desk. After school I write up the incident in detail. I reread the entries to help prepare for parent conferences and report cards. Occasionally I make copies of significant student writing to put in the folder if it gives insight into the child's attitudes or behaviors. I date everything in these folders and keep them in an easily accessible file on my desk.

Notes in your "Process Notebook" should be simple, systematic recordings of student behaviors over time and across different learning contexts. Remember not to overwhelm—or exhaust—yourself with unreasonable goals about process observations. While you need to make sure you capture a range of behaviors in a range of situations, some days you may find few things worth recording. Don't worry about it. But do make sure that at least every week or two you write something significant about every student. I have found that trying to get down verbatim responses and exchanges give me the most insight when I am trying to

Reading/Writing Survey

Name _____

Date _____

1. What types of reading have you done this past year (novels, short stories, newspapers, magazines, etc.)?

1. What types of writing have you done this past year (English compositions, test essays, letters, writing for enjoyment, etc.)?

2. What are some of your favorite types of reading, titles, and/or authors?

2. What were some of your favorite pieces of writing?

3. On an average, how many hours per week would you say that you spend reading?

3. On an average, how many hours per week would you say you spend writing?

4. How many books would you say you have read in the past year?

4. How many extended pieces of writing have you completed in the past year?

5. Do you see yourself as a "reader"? Why or why not?

5. Do you see yourself as a "writer"? Why or why not?

6. How do you decide what you will read?

6. How do you decide on topics for writing?

7. Do you do anything special before you read?

7. Do you do anything special before you write?

8. What types of things do you think about as you are reading?

8. What types of things do you think about as you are writing?

9. What is difficult for you as a reader?

9. What is difficult for you as a writer?

10. What is easy for you as a reader?

10. What is easy for you as a writer?

11. When you are reading and you come to something you don't know, what do you do?

11. When you are writing and something stops you, what do you do?

12. Who is a good reader that you know?

12. Who is a good writer that you know?

13. What makes him or her a good reader?

13. What makes him or her a good writer?

14. If you knew someone was having trouble reading, what would you do to help?

14. If you knew someone was having trouble writing, what would you do to help?

15. What would you like to do better as a reader?

15. What would you like to do better as a writer?

FIGURE 7.6
Reading/Writing Survey

Carol Porter & Linda Crafton, August 1989.

Source: Adapted from C. Burke, and P. Atwell.

see changes in thinking and literacy strategies. I have also found that using a journal with a few key categories listed (for example, Risk-Taking, Sharing, Initiating) makes my long-term evaluation easier and gives me the framework I want to understand and discuss my observations.

SELF-EVALUATION

The real question in evaluation is how to help students judge how well they are growing; knowing how well they are doing is a reflection of how well we as teachers are doing. Daily self-evaluation is one of the best ways to empower your students, to give them ownership over their learning. Whole language curricula are ongoing cycles of doing and reflecting (*see* Figure 7.7).

The easiest way to get self-evaluation into place is to plan for it systematically throughout the day and use open-ended questions to guide the reflexivity. For

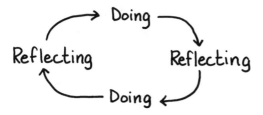

FIGURE 7.7

Cycles of Doing and Reflecting as Consistent
Parts of Whole Language Curricula

example, at the end of uninterrupted
reading or writing time, the following
questions can raise student learning to a new level of awareness and
solidity:

1. What was one thing that surprised
   me in my reading/writing today?
2. Did I have any problems? How
   did I solve them?
3. What do I know now as a reader/
   writer that I didn't know before?

Portfolios, discussed in the next section, can be a prime opportunity for students to self-assess. Portfolios contain student-selected literacy artifacts from the
entire year. Questions such as: "What can you do now that you couldn't do earlier
in the year?" can do wonders for all students. Learners need to have a vision of
themselves as people capable of intellectual transformation. Give your students
time to grasp a sense of what they have accomplished and where they are going.
"When students are actively involved in planning, executing and evaluating their
own learning, they become self-directed and independent" (Goodman, Goodman, and Hood, 1989, p. 239).

Self-evaluation is for the young and old alike. Don Howard, a transitional
first-grade teacher, has his young reader/writers reflect on their reading as a
natural extension. He talks to them about the reading process and encourages
them to talk about their miscues. If you walk into his classroom during reading
time you are likely to hear these six-year-olds making comments such as: "Oh! I
just made a miscue. That one wasn't so great." Or "That one was okay because it
still makes sense."

Carol Porter's high-school students also know a lot about themselves as reader/
writers. Following any discussion of a book, short story, poem, or any other piece
of literature, she asks them to look back and think about what occurred:

Reflections

Consider these four questions as you reflect on your learning. We would also be
interested in hearing any other thoughts you might have about the discussion that
do not fit under one of these questions.

1. What were some of the topics discussed in your group?
2. Were there any issues that people had different opinions on? What were they?
3. What questions or things that you weren't sure about became clear for you?
   (How did you revise your thinking based on the things you heard?)
4. What were one or two new ideas that you gained from the discussion, things
   that you had not thought about before?

Carol and I developed the following "Reflective Evaluation" form (*see* Figure
7.8) that she has been using at the end of each grading period with her students.

Reflective Evaluation Form

Conference Time _____

Name _____
Date _____

* = Quite a Bit
+ = A Fair Amount
√ = No Evidence Yet

	Reading		Writing		Reading Comments
	Self	Teacher	Self	Teacher	
Independent Learning					
1. Draws on personal experience					
2. Takes risks by trying out new ideas and/or process strategies					
3. Sets goals for growth in learning					
4. Strives to meet goals					
5. Pushes thinking so that pieces make sense					
Social Learning					Writing Comments
6. Shares thinking with others					
7. Asks others genuine questions					
8. Supports peers					
9. Revises thinking					

One thing that I'm doing better.

One thing I'm having trouble with.

One thing that I would like to work on in the future.

FIGURE 7.8
Reflective Evaluation Form

Source: Linda Crafton & Carol Porter

We intended this self-evaluation to be a summary type, not something that could be used if students were not reflecting daily on their reading and writing and their independent and social learning processes. Carol fills out the "Teacher" section; students mark the section on "Self," then they come together to discuss their observations. The open-ended questions at the end are used to set goals for the next grading period. When Carol and her students come together six weeks later, they pull out the previous form and start with the identified goals.

In my graduate classes I have replaced final papers with self-evaluations. They are often the major piece of reflective writing in my classes now. In preparation for the evaluations and the individual conferences I have with each student, I review my process notes and student projects; they use their own Reflective Journals.* We both consider open-ended questions related to Level of Effort, Involvement, Risk-Taking, Support of Peers and Personal/Professional Change. Once everyone has had a chance to think and to prepare a draft profile, we meet to talk about their growth and change during our months together.

SELF-EVALUATION: PORTFOLIOS

Cynthia is my one artist friend. She has taught me about perspective, positive and negative space, and has influenced my ability to see the world in different ways. In preparation for her freelance work she developed a portfolio of her mosaics. In the brown binder that showcases her projects she carefully selected photographs to display her crowning achievements and to chronicle the depth and breadth of her creativity. Often, next to a picture of a complete work of art, she includes a closeup of the work so the viewer can consider the beautiful, intricate detail that signals the painstaking attention she gave each part.

Portfolios such as the ones that Cynthia and other artists use are becoming more and more popular in whole language classrooms. Like artists, readers and writers need a place to gather their best work, a place they can turn to periodically in order to reflect on and celebrate their growth. Portfolios are collections of student-selected reading/writing/thinking artifacts that help create a complete picture of students' developing literacy abilities.

In classrooms where teachers strive to capture individual growth, Portfolios* have the best chance of representing the strengths and changes across a variety of situations. In a recent article Sheila Valencia (1990) outlines the virtues of Portfolios:

1. They are anchored in authentic reading/writing. The things that go into a Portfolio come from the real literacy events that are an ongoing part of the curriculum. Assessment, then, is not something separate; it is an opportunity to reflect on the learning itself.
2. They encourage evaluation as an ongoing enterprise. Portfolios help us shift our focus away from simple product assessments to the process of learning over time.

3. They are multidimensional. Because portfolios include a range of reading/ writing samples produced for different purposes in varying contexts, they represent literacy as a complex process. Portfolios can give a more reliable and valid profile of learners.
4. They provide for reflection on the learning that has occurred. Using portfolios, teachers and students can come together to collaboratively think through changes, strategies, and struggles.

In addition to the four dimensions listed here portfolios provide ownership of the learning for the learner. Valencia points out that, "No single test, single observation, or single piece of student work could possibly capture the authentic, continuous, multidimensional, interactive requirement of sound assessment" (p. 339). With portfolios, students have a chance to look at themselves from many different angles; they have an opportunity to take altered stances on themselves as readers and writers. Portfolios represent the multiple dimensions of a learner and the learning process itself.

Portfolios for reading and writing need to include a range of materials. These items may come from writing folders where students keep current and past writing (in-process work as well as final drafts), Reading Discussion Groups* transcriptions, Reading Journals,* Dialogue Journals,* spontaneous writing samples like notes for the Message Board* or letters to an author, collaborative work, research projects, anecdotal observations, audio- or videotapes, Celebrations,* and so on. Portfolios can also include important items from the students' life outside of the classroom. Like the whole language curriculum itself, the possibilities are limitless and so it is up to you and your students to determine where to start and how much to include. As always, it's better to start with one step and a few decisions, and progress from there.

When your students start using Portfolios,* help them select items that come directly from process strategies and other whole language areas of the curriculum you are developing. For example, once writing process is in place, and students have generated a number of finished pieces, ask them to consider what work highlights their learning—effort, involvement, tough problems solved, collaborative thinking, shift in organizing, coherence, detail, overall ability to tell a story, and so on. It's fine for them to include their "best" writing, but keep reminding them that Portfolios should represent their learning process and not just their finished, polished products.

Ask students to reread their Reading Journals* or any other records that they use to capture their responses to literature. Encourage them to keep an eye out for written comments that represent a shift in thinking, the use of a new strategy, or a particularly insightful personal connection—one that helped them to see the reading or the experience in a new light. Because you will keep your own portfolio in the classroom, you can always use it to demonstrate what parameters you use to select different items for inclusion. Together you and your students can choose from anecdotal notes to put in the Portfolios.*

Carol Porter has been experimenting with self-evaluation of selected writing with her high-school students. They choose several pieces they are particularly proud of and make final revisions and editing changes if the pieces are not already in published form. Once selected, the writing, including all revisions, is physically spread out on the classroom floor so the writer can consider change across pieces of writing. Carol asks that her students include their first piece of writing during the grading period to use as a baseline. She sets aside time to confer with each student as they consider questions in relation to each piece (*see* Figure 7.9).

After students have considered the evaluative questions Carol asks them to write a description of the changes they see in their writing over time. These summary evaluations are included in their Portfolios.*

Audiotapes and videotapes are another powerful way to see learning in action, and can be included in Portfolios. Audiotapes of oral reading, including reflections on the process, can give a strong sense of a student's thinking during

---

What frustrations did you have with writing earlier in the year and how has that changed?

What currently frustrates you as a writer?

How did you come up with ideas for writing?

How do you decide on ideas now?

How did you revise your pieces of writing earlier this year? (For example: Rewording, adding content {details, expanding ideas, examples}, rearranging, fixing mechanical problems . . .)

How do you revise now?

How is your first piece of writing different from your best piece?

What makes your best piece best?

How do you write for an audience now compared to the way you used to consider the audience while writing?

Are there any other observations you would like to share with us?

FIGURE 7.9
Questions for Students to Consider in
Evaluation of Their Writing Changes

reading. Audiotapes can also be used at different points during the school year, as students reflect on their learning. Videotapes can be used to highlight major projects and presentations.

During the school year Portfolios should come out quickly when you are discussing individual student progress with administrators and parents. The positive nature of Portfolios is contagious, and they effectively show continuous evaluation and how students are at the center of the learning process.

At the end of the school year students and teacher can collaboratively review the contents of each Portfolio, deciding which items should stay and which can be sent home. Many districts are moving toward passing Portfolios on to the next teacher. After students have had a chance to review their Portfolios and celebrate their strengths and learning activities over the school year, learning profiles should be written and placed in the Portfolio.

Writing samples and self-evaluations may be added three to four times a year and may coincide with report cards. Combining Portfolios with more traditional assessment helps to give critical balance to an otherwise narrow, relatively meaningless reporting procedure, such as report cards.

When students select items for their Portfolios their reasons for the selection should be clear. Consider making a sheet for each Portfolio that includes the date a piece was selected and why it is part of the collection:

PORTFOLIO SUMMARY SHEET

Date	Description of Item	Why It Is Included

The following list of potential Portfolio items may be helpful, but what is actually included depends on individual learners and how they perceive their learning. When I talked to one of Carol Porter's students about his Portfolio, Carol thought his Bookmarks* would be rich with information about his reading process and strategy utilization. When I asked Doug, however, he said, "Noooooo . . . I just did those for Mrs. Porter." He then turned to his journal and started pulling out examples that expressed changes in his learning from his perspective.

When I discussed the incident with Carol she pointed out the transitions in Doug's development from not doing anything to pleasing the teacher to taking ownership of his learning.

Examples of the items listed can be found in Tracy and Abbey's portfolios in Appendix B.

Possible Artifacts to Include in Portfolios

1. Writing samples (drafts and published work)
2. Audiotape of student reading self-selected material
3. Responses to reading (writing, art, and so on)
4. Photographs and accompanying reflections
5. Ongoing list of books/other materials read and pieces written

6. Periodic self-evaluations
7. Learning profile.
8. Items from home.

GRADES AND REPORT CARDS

Grades and report cards are institutionalized artifacts of an outdated view of learning. Our current reporting systems don't reflect changing curricula that are increasingly more meaning-centered and student-driven. Despite the fact that "Dick and Jane have grown up and changed along with our knowledge of literacy development and reading/writing processes" (Bailey, 1988), grades and report cards are likely to be with us for a long, long time. Many teachers are meeting the limitations they feel grades and report cards place on them by drawing their students into the decision-making and by developing supplemental ways to communicate what their students have learned.

Like most whole language teachers, Kathleen Visovatti is required to give grades. Because letter grades could never capture the dynamic learning going on in her classroom, she is always busy keeping alternative records and encouraging her students to self-evaluate. When report-card time rolls around, she pulls her second-graders into the process:

> A week before the report card is distributed, I pass out blank copies to the class. We go over the different categories (subject areas) and the itemized skills and the significance of the grades. I ask each student to think about how she or he is doing —not compared to others—but individual efforts in relation to abilities. In the course of the ensuing week I meet with each child for a private conference. We fill out the report card together. Thus, grades are not something mysteriously "done" to them or arbitrarily assigned by an authority figure. Because my students may have other teachers for reading, I explain that I'll be adding the grade from the other teachers because they don't have time to meet with each child in the school, but that any teacher will be happy to talk to them if they have questions.
>
> The conference is very insightful. I learn much about passions and frustrations, pride in successes, and what's really important to each of the children. I discover metacognitive awareness—or the lack of it. Perhaps the biggest payoff is that our collaborative relationship is enhanced as together we select "Excellent," "Satisfactory," and "Needs Improvement" marks for social and personal development. At the parent conference the children do most of the talking and both parents and I are impressed with their ability to reflect and honestly self-assess.

With the collaborative grade conferences just described, Kathleen has turned a difficult, theoretically inconsistent part of her curriculum into a learning experience much more compatible with whole language philosophy and her beliefs about kids.

Carol Porter also holds conferences with her high-school students about grades, and I use a conference procedure before grades are finalized in my graduate courses.

Many whole language teachers include a narrative insert in the report card. Some teachers are writing individual narratives at report-card time. Kathleen has chosen to write a general one that is included in each student's grade card when it is sent home (*see* Figure 7.10). At some point you are likely to feel that your reporting system *has* to begin to reflect more of what is going on in your classroom, more of what you know and observe in your students. If you complete a supplemental form or narrative sheet, you may find the grades much easier to determine.

Dear Parents,

I really don't need to give report cards. You and I communicate frequently:

at conferences
at open houses
when you call on the phone
when you send a note to school
when you visit the classroom
when you join us on a field trip
when you pick up your child
when I call on the phone
when I send a note home

I feel good about the way we share good news and concerns, our personal contact.

The weekly newspaper comes home every Friday, which reviews all that we've done during the week. Your child is always mentioned at least once.

I keep a lot of records which I am happy to share with you when we have a conference. My notes document your child's progress and level of participation.

Your child also can show you his or her accomplishments when you visit the room. She or he keeps a journal. You can see the growth over time in written expression (fluency, clarity, legibility, spelling, and mechanics). His or her writing portfolio is a collection of all the stories your child has written this year. Looking through the folder shows you the variety of topics and types of writing your child selects. All this work will come home the last day of school, but it is work in progress so it needs to stay in school until then. The books your child has published are in our classroom library. They, too, will go home in June, but currently are being read by classmates during SSR, our daily independent reading time.

FIGURE 7.10
Example of a Narrative Report to Parents

The demonstration of your child's understanding of science concepts is evidenced in culminating projects for the hall and classroom. Science as a process is emphasized—investigating, hypothesizing, evaluating. Often these projects are turned into big books for the classroom library after being on display. Your child will eagerly show you his or her part in these endeavors, and explain their overall meaning whenever you visit the school.

Social Studies concepts are also reviewed through final projects. Our working definition of social studies is the many ways people are alike and different. We study ourselves, our families, and our community. History, geography, reference, and map skills are acquired as needed in the context of children's explorations. The Interest Clubs provide an opportunity for children to pursue topics of interest to them in a cooperative learning setting. The wealth of information they share with you demonstrates not only what they have learned, but also the enthusiasm they have for the act of learning itself. You will also see evidence at home of increased social skills as your child learns to share, to value the contributions of others, and to be tolerant of differences.

Math concepts and their applications are mastered in a low-key, individually paced setting. Lots of talk and demonstrations with concrete objects precedes all paper and pencil computation. The emphasis is on hands-on experiences. Basic facts are practiced through computer games. Much time is devoted to the development of a variety of problem-solving strategies for the real world. Your child is expected to take full responsibility for completing all assignments and making any necessary corrections. You know your child is doing well in math when she or he can divide the food evenly and knows how much change should come back. I really don't need to give report cards.

Nonetheless, I am required to do so.

A traditional report card is not an appropriate assessment of your child's progress in my class. How can a little mark in a box capture your child's enthusiasm, her or his insight into human nature, the joy of learning, the sense of accomplishment for a task well done? I don't give tests. I don't assign a numerical value to an individual's contributions. I don't rank order student's work. We don't compare. We don't compete. We are a group. We cooperate. We learn together.

However, I believe in compromise, in making the best of every situation; therefore, I would like to meet with both of you and your child to explain the report card, and to talk holistically about all that is going on in the classroom. Would the following time be convenient for the three of you?

Sincerely,

Mrs. Visovatti

FIGURE 7.10 *(Continued)*

KEY POINTS TO REMEMBER ABOUT
WHOLE LANGUAGE EVALUATION

1. Evaluation doesn't interfere with learning; it is an integral part of the learning processes represented in the curriculum.
2. Process evaluation requires a different definition of learning. Evaluators, teachers, and students must learn to see differently, focusing on the strategies and decisions that learners make during the learning process itself.
3. Evaluation informs instruction. The observations that are made as readers and writers learn and think are used to evaluate the context in which the learning occurs. Adjustments can then be made to make the learning situations more supportive of the learner.
4. Evaluation is continuous, occurring across learning contexts.
5. The major goal is self-knowledge. Students, then, must be involved in each facet of evaluation.
6. Everything that's evaluated becomes curriculum. Qualitative measures are maximized; quantitative measures are minimized or eliminated.

Personal Reflection

How will my students and I begin systematic process observations?

Parents, Administrators, Basals, and Other Realities

8

The challenges of whole language teaching go beyond the practical and philosophical issues we have discussed so far. There are other realities: expensive new basal programs, purchased, in place, and expected to be used; administrators who are wary of teaching that is so nontraditional, a challenge to the status quo; parents who are nervous about test scores, skills, and spelling mistakes. These social and political concerns are real, forceful, and impossible to ignore. It doesn't work to simply "close your door and do what you want." Nor may we expect that major changes will be met with open arms and immediate acceptance from those outside of our classrooms. The American public believes that schools and, to a large degree, individual classrooms belong to them, at least as much as they belong to the people who inhabit them day in, day out. Being guardians of our children's minds and our nation's future means that demands for accountability can come from any number of sources—parents, administrators, legislators, and even peers.

This chapter will take a brief look at some of the problems and realities that you are likely to encounter as a whole language teacher and some of the responses/solutions teachers quoted in this book have found useful.

MAKING PARENTS YOUR ALLIES

Not long ago I learned an important lesson from one of my graduate students. During class one evening we were discussing the challenge of educating parents about the value of whole language. The exchange had centered around how to communicate basic whole language philosophy to parents, around specific changes in the curriculum, what parents might expect to see in papers brought home by students, and about a new definition of homework. Tom, a high-school teacher, had been leaning back in his chair, listening but not contributing to the discussion. After a while, he said: "The key to all of this is not just to tell them things but to draw them in as your allies. Make sure they know that just because your teaching has changed, or is changing, that your goals and hopes for their children have not. I ask my students' parents what they want from me and from this year in school and, after they tell me, I show them how I *am* doing *exactly* those things—and more."

Tom is right. Parents can be our strongest supporters, our most vocal allies. But, just as we have to be gentle with ourselves and our students, we must also be careful not to push parents along too quickly in our desire to educate them. Here is another place to start slowly, moving along only as quickly as you—and they— feel comfortable. After you have made a few changes—perhaps launched Writing Workshop, Reading Discussion Groups,* or journal writing—consider your level of comfort with these initial steps. When you are ready, confident of the procedure and the wonderful learning occurring as a result, consider how you will communicate your changing curriculum to parents.

Some of the ideas discussed below may help you to develop your own first steps. However you decide to reach out, be sure to let parents know in as many ways as you can that:

1. your professional decisions are well thought out,
2. whole language has a strong research base,
3. you are joining a growing group of forward-looking teachers across the country.

COMMUNICATION WITH PARENTS

Throughout the year invite parents to school for informal discussions of pertinent issues. Be sure to send information or articles home prior to parent conferences so that parents can come prepared to discuss their questions in an informed way.

As often as you can, send letters to the parents. Penny Silvers communicates frequently with parents of reading lab students. In this letter, written early in the fall semester, Penny alerts parents to the fact that her students will be bringing home writing with "mistakes," but that, she tells them, is part of a larger writing process (*see* Figure 8.1).

In a more recent communication Penny discusses the learn-to-read-by-reading idea and encourages the parents to read with their children (*see* Figure 8.2).

---

* All asterisks throughout the book refer the reader to Chapter 10 where full strategy descriptions can be found.

Dear Parents,

The students in the reading lab do a lot of writing as well as reading. Research has shown that reading and writing complement each other and that they often occur together.

From time to time you may see some story writing papers with words spelled incorrectly. Do not be alarmed. The first step in story writing is to "draft" your ideas. In this first draft the students are encouraged to use invented spelling. This is any spelling they can figure out easily and quickly so the idea or thought they are trying to express won't be lost. After their ideas are written down, we conference, revise, rewrite, and *then* edit. It is in the editing phase that correct spelling is stressed, along with correct grammar, punctuation, and all the mechanics of conventional print. Not all of the stories and papers students write are taken through the writing stages to editing. This is reserved for those pieces of writing the student likes best and wishes to "publish" or make public.

In the reading lab I use first draft work for diagnosis of spelling, phonics, and language that needs to be worked on. Students correct their papers and also keep a list of frequently used but often misspelled words to be learned. It is important to help students understand that spelling needs to be correct when others are going to read what they have written.

We know that spelling and language are best learned in the context of the students' own reading and writing, rather than in isolated drills of lists and words. The words they see and use often in their writing are more meaningful to them, and, because they are used often, the motivation to remember them is quite strong.

I am constantly emphasizing conventions of language, and am interrelating reading and writing. The children know they are "authors" and have a responsibility to write as clearly and correctly as possible because other people will read what they have written. This is a very important part of the curriculum and the ultimate goal for all of the children is language proficiency and confidence in one's ability to communicate effectively.

Sincerely,

Penny Silvers

FIGURE 8.1
Letter to Parents Explaining Writing Process
as Part of the Larger Curriculum

Dear Parents:

There is no substitute for reading to and with your child. All the current research is saying that the more pages and chapters a child reads from real books, the better reader the child becomes. Reading together with your child is a wonderful and meaningful way to spend quality time together. Not only will you be enjoying the story together but you will have ideas to talk about, "what-ifs" to think about, and will be developing a very special bond with your child.

Reading together also provides you with an opportunity to model how literate people read. You are setting an example by reading to your child, as well as sharpening his or her auditory processing and listening skills. You will also be guiding his or her thinking by your questions and the discussions that are generated from those questions.

In school it is often difficult to fit extended blocks of reading time for pleasure into the already stretched curriculum. In the reading lab, as in the classrooms, reading for pleasure is encouraged and a love for books and language begins to be developed. However, more time needs to be spent on reading real books than can be provided in school. That is why the parent-connection is such an important component of learning to be a better reader. Your involvement in sharing reading experiences with your child will make the difference between a child who can read but chooses not to, and one who will enjoy reading for the rest of his or her life!

The best books in children's literature are rich in language and vocabulary. Some words may be unfamiliar to your child. Nevertheless, the exposure to excellent poetry and literature will enrich his or her word knowledge and help heighten an appreciation of the beauty of language. Research has shown that there is a lot of carryover into the child's own writing from listening to stories and reading good books. Furthermore, well-loved books are enjoyable when read more than once, and are worth the investment in order to build a home library of quality children's literature.

I have enclosed some information on excellent children's books and added a few of my own favorites. Also, Jim Trelease's *Read-Aloud to Parents Book* is an excellent resource for finding books that appeal to children with a variety of interests at all grade levels. What better way to survive a winter in Chicago? Enjoy!

Sincerely,

Penny Silvers

FIGURE 8.2
Letter to Parents Describing the Philosophy
Behind the Reading Resource Program

Favorite Books (Reading Lab Choices)

Grades K–2:

Clifford stories—Bridwell
Curious George Stories—Rey
The Stupids—Allard
The Forgetful Bears—Weinberg
Morris and Boris—Wiseman
Where the Wild Things Are—Sendak
Alexander books—Viorst
Lyle Crocodile books—Waber
Ira Sleeps Over—Waber
George and Martha books—Marshall
Anastasia books—Lowry
Q Is for Duck—Elting
Katy No-Pocket—Payne
Frog and Toad books—Lobel
And any books by: Tomie dePaola, Leo Lionni, and Paul Galdone

Grades 3–4:

Miss Nelson Is Missing—Allard
Little House books—Wilder
Sarah, Plain and Tall—MacLachlan
Paddington stories—Bond
James and the Giant Peach—Dahl
Nate the Great books—Sharmat
Encyclopedia Brown books—Sobol
Pippi Longstocking books—Lindgren
Tuck Everlasting—Babbitt
And any books by: E.B. White, Beverly Cleary, Judy Blume, or Chris
    Van Allsburg

There are lots more books waiting to be discovered by you and your
children. Those listed here are already well-loved. Please share with me
any new books that you would like to recommend. It will be appreciated
by everyone.

Thanks!

FIGURE 8.2 *(Continued)*

Pat Miller uses a short form that she sends home weekly with each of her students, which lists their accomplishments for the week. Her lists are so impressive it's hard to imagine that any parent would question the level of learning going on in her classroom.

In the following excerpt Kathleen Visovatti discusses the class newspaper she sends home every Friday. It is her primary vehicle for keeping parents abreast of the learning going on in her classroom.

> Because work doesn't go home—everything stays in the room to be shared and to document progress—parents wonder what we do all day. The Friday newspaper is a way to communicate the week's events through the kids' eyes—what they consider important and what I want to highlight—announcements, rationales, etc. I circulate around the room, interviewing each student as I go.

Figure 8.3 shows one of Kathleen's Friday newspapers.

You'll want to find as many ways as possible to communicate to parents just how powerful your curriculum is from a learning perspective. This list may help:

1. Have children take student-published books home. Many whole language teachers use plastic book bags and encourage students to check out their favorites to read to parents. Put a pad in the bag with a note from you asking parents to notice something particularly well done in the writing, (for example, "When you are reading this latest book by Darren Miller, notice the character description. It's his best attempt yet. And, by the way, your daughter is experimenting with some great character profiles of her own.") Close the note by encouraging the parent to write to the author.

2. Present your program at an open house or PTO meeting. Be sure to include descriptions of your reading/writing program, using students' responses and work to showcase the kinds of thinking strategies they are involved in daily. Capture a Reading Discussion Group* on video or audiotape and track published pieces of writing from first draft to final editing.

3. During parent-teacher conferences show Writing Folders* and Reading Journals.* Discuss growth of individual students and show how you keep track of it. Ask parents if they have noticed their children reading or writing more often outside of the classroom.

4. Ask parents to choose a book to read with their sons or daughters. Carol Porter tried this in her junior-high school language arts class. She set up an evening when parents could come to school and join a small-group discussion of literature. Later they spent time reflecting on what had happened during their discussion, and Carol talked about her curriculum.

When parents begin to ask how they can support what you are doing in the classroom, invite them in to watch—and join in. They will be able to give support a hundred times more effectively if they have a stronger sense of what's happening

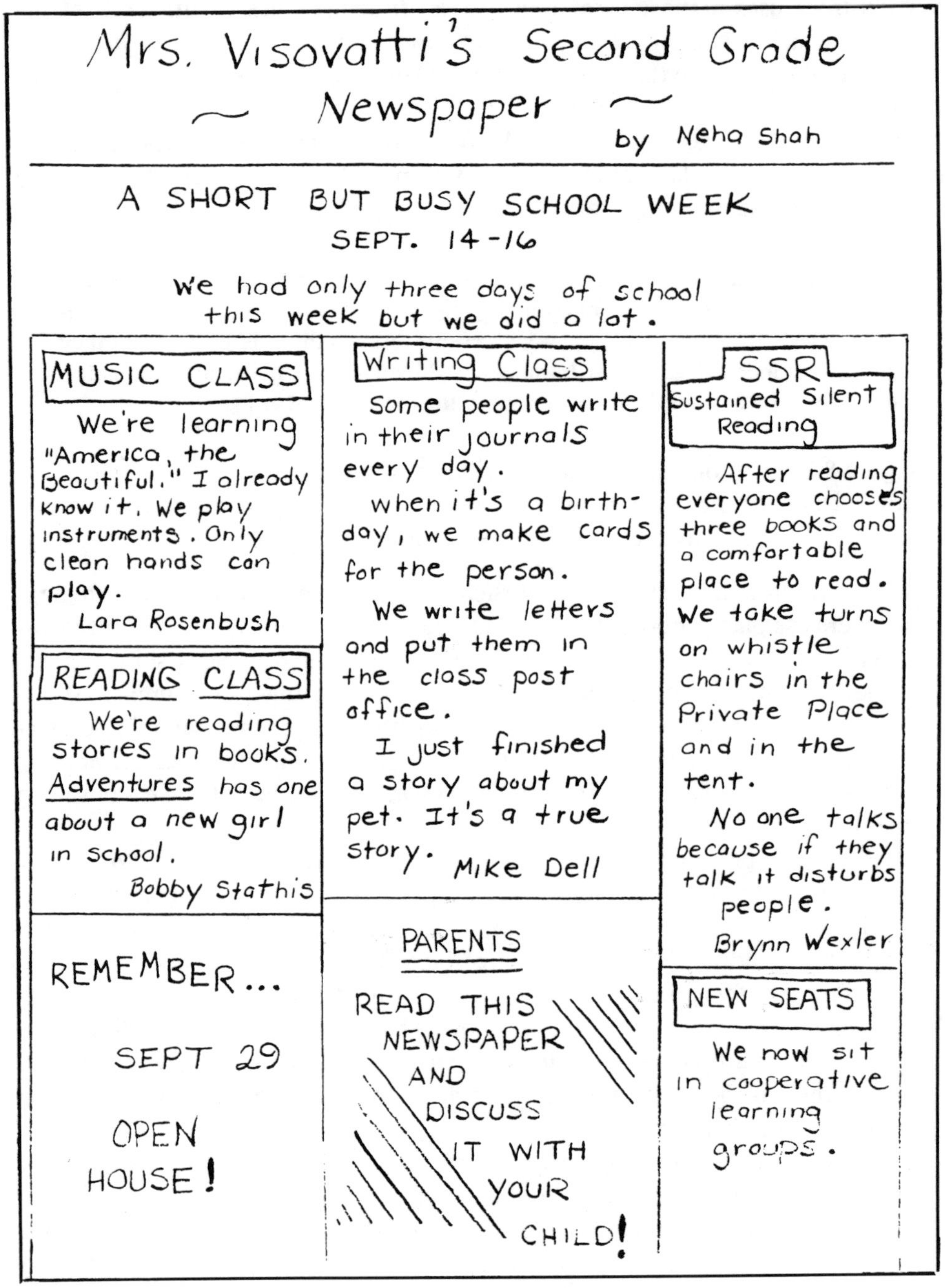

Mrs. Visovatti's Second Grade ～ Newspaper ～
by Neha Shah

A SHORT BUT BUSY SCHOOL WEEK
SEPT. 14-16

We had only three days of school this week but we did a lot.

MUSIC CLASS

We're learning "America, the Beautiful." I already know it. We play instruments. Only clean hands can play.

Lara Rosenbush

READING CLASS

We're reading stories in books. Adventures has one about a new girl in school.

Bobby Stathis

REMEMBER...

SEPT 29

OPEN HOUSE!

Writing Class

Some people write in their journals every day.

When it's a birthday, we make cards for the person.

We write letters and put them in the class post office.

I just finished a story about my pet. It's a true story. Mike Dell

PARENTS

READ THIS NEWSPAPER AND DISCUSS IT WITH YOUR CHILD!

SSR
Sustained Silent Reading

After reading everyone chooses three books and a comfortable place to read. We take turns on whistle chairs in the Private Place and in the tent.

No one talks because if they talk it disturbs people.

Brynn Wexler

NEW SEATS

We now sit in cooperative learning groups.

FIGURE 8.3
A Weekly Newspaper for Parents

in the classroom. Also send home careful descriptions of what parents can do at home. Here are just a few examples:

SUPPORTING WHOLE LANGUAGE CLASSROOMS FROM THE HOME

1. Reading aloud is still the best way to support reading development and a love of literature and learning. No matter what age your child happens to be, preschool through high school, read to them as often as you can.
2. Set up real writing opportunities for your child. Notes in lunch boxes or on refrigerators; letters to relatives and friends; writing birthday invitations, grocery lists, and so on—all encourage authentic and/or interactive writing.

    Once the opportunity is in place, however, parents' responses are critical! Be positive about the effort, even if the product isn't in standard adult form. The quickest way to shut down writing is to point out mistakes. Always focus on the message and what your child is trying to say. Remember that writing, like speaking, needs time and experience and lots of support to develop.
3. Saturate their environment with print. Buy them a variety of reading materials. Subscribe to a children's magazine or an environmental magazine, a car or travel periodical—whatever interests them and you. Have books at home for them. Go to the library regularly and have them get their own library cards as soon as they are allowed to have them. Books make the best long-lasting presents! Don't worry about always buying "good" literature; buy what you think they will enjoy.
4. Read yourself, for yourself. The strongest teaching is done through demonstration. You may want your child to be a good reader, but children want to do what grownups around them do.

The primary concerns that parents seem to have about whole language are skill development and a structured, disciplined learning environment. How many times have you heard a parent say, "I'm glad my child is in so and so's class; she's/he's tough and organized and my child *needs* that." You may have to find ways to assure parents that you, like these other teachers, are as concerned about skill development and rigor as anyone. You've simply found a way to insure skill development while also insuring growth toward proficiency and a love of literacy. You'll want to explain to parents the level of self-direction, independence, and involvement that whole language engenders, and how different that is from learning in more traditional settings.

Parents must be informed of the growing number of whole language teachers who report that they have fewer behavior problems than ever before because students have far more ownership in their learning.

Remember that parents will most likely be concerned about the changes you are proposing in your classroom. And, like everyone involved in a transition, they will need positive and patient support.

ADMINISTRATORS: OPERATING FROM STRENGTH

The teachers in this book have had a range of experiences with administrators. Pat Riordan's principal, Tom Eber, was intrigued with whole language from the time Pat first passed an article about it along to him. Three years ago he began a school-wide transition to whole language. Tom started slowly and has encouraged teachers to move at their own pace, while supporting them in as many ways as he could.

Penny Silvers, on the other hand, has encountered many obstacles along the way, and has often been in a position to defend herself and her whole language curriculum. She has tackled her difficult situations with admirable strength and has succeeded over and over again because of her decision to be proactive with her administration. Penny spends a lot of time talking about what she does and the value of her resource program to students who are performing poorly in regular classroom settings.

One day her superintendent was wandering around her building with his five-year-old son. Penny's first-grade group had just finished reading about a flea who outwits larger animals to become king of the mountain. They had decided to re-enact the story when the superintendent appeared on the scene. Penny grabbed the superintendent and invited him and his son to participate in an Extension* of *I'm the King of the Mountain*.

Everyone joined in the quick transformation of story to play, choosing characters, writing dialogue, and making signs to identify the animal role each (including the superintendent) would assume. Following the drama, Penny took the superintendent aside and pointed out the high level of involvement, self-initiation, and decision-making that had occurred in the group. She was careful to underscore the importance of experiences like these to skill, strategy, and overall literacy development. Penny has planted seeds of understanding with exchanges like these, and is seen by her administration as a knowledgeable professional.

Carol Porter has also made it a point to interact with her administration from strength. When she feels that something is likely to work to her disadvantage, she has found ways of turning it around. Teacher evaluation is a good example of how Carol has made sure she is seen in the best possible light, while being surrounded by traditional perspectives.

> Writing professional goals yearly is a requirement in my district. Last year I decided to write my goals so they clearly reflected the kind of development I value in myself. I stated that each month I would implement at least one innovative teaching idea that I had gained from professional journals or conferences. The innovation, however, had to be consistent with my whole language views, and so I would be required to constantly review my theoretical base while considering practical application. My accomplishment of this goal would be assessed by writing about the idea, summarizing and critiquing the presentation or article, and explaining the learning results to my supervisor.

Pat, Penny, and Carol have discovered how important it is to be proactive with their administrators. They are constantly talking about what they do—and why. Even if their principals, supervisors, or superintendents don't agree, the teachers' assertive stances have helped to establish them as thoughtful, up-to-date educators.

SHARING CHANGES WITH ADMINISTRATORS

It's not easy to take a strong stand when you are in the process of remolding your own belief system. In the beginning you are likely to feel vulnerable. Give yourself the time you need, whatever that is, to establish your new professional self with no one but yourself. Empathetic peers can be invaluable to you during this early transitional time but, eventually, you'll want to establish how you and your students are changing as a result of your professional efforts.

When you are ready, start sharing what you are doing. Be ready to articulate the reasons for the changes you are making. The worst thing is to feel anxious because you are worried that administrators will see you doing something with which they disagree or which they don't understand. Let administrators know what you are doing, and try to keep them abreast of the changes in your teaching and thinking. This can be as gentle as sharing the revisions in a piece of writing or the multiple drafts produced by a reluctant writer. It can be as subtle as sending student-written notes to the principal as part of a larger author Celebration,* or asking the principal if he or she would like to join a Reading Discussion Group.*

When you are ready, invite administrators into your classroom. But first prepare them for what they will see. Again, talk to them and put it in writing:

Dear_____:

It's important to me that you know what to expect when you come into my classroom. As you're aware, I'm trying some new process-based, whole language instruction. I've made a list of the things you are likely to see and those things I'm trying to eliminate from my curriculum that you probably won't see anymore.

What You Might See in My Classroom and Why

1. Students in small groups discussing the content area reading or literature they have just finished. WHY? Discussion groups help support and enrich comprehension because students can see interpretations other than their own and can modify their understandings and sort out confusions.
2. You might see ME in a small group, talking and sharing in the same way my students are. WHY? My best teaching (and their best learning) is done when I can show them how a proficient reader THINKS and what strategies she or he uses before, during, and after reading.
3. During writing time you might see some of us writing, some of us talking about our writing, and some of us getting ready to publish. WHY? Writers are always at different points in the writing process. On any given day some people will

need time for uninterrupted writing; others will need people to listen and respond so they can rethink and revise.

What You Probably *Won't* See Anymore

1. You probably won't see me in front of the class lecturing. WHY? I've changed my ideas about what it means to be a good teacher. I no longer think that telling is teaching. Now I try to do more showing and demonstrating and setting up authentic literacy experiences for my students so they learn by doing.
2. You won't see my students in ability groups. WHY? The research shows that when students are ability-grouped, teachers lower their expectations for the low-ability groups and instruction is inferior because of that. When students are heterogeneously grouped, by interest or purpose, the level of thinking tends to look more like that of the higher-ability groups. Heterogeneous grouping is a much more effective way of maintaining a high level of learning in my classroom while eliminating the stigma that goes along with ability-grouping for less accomplished students.
3. You probably won't see my students quiet, and you definitely won't see them in neat, straight rows. WHY? We know from research that talk and interactions with other learners are critical for learning to move forward; classroom organization can encourage (or minimize) the social dimension of learning.

Please come in when you get the chance and then we can talk some more about my classroom. I'm eager to share more of what I'm doing and why, and my students would be happy to talk about their learning, too.

Sincerely,

PROFESSIONAL READING

Start gathering information and materials that give support and authority to your whole language teaching. Photocopy articles and keep them in a professional notebook; write down quotes; track down appropriate research; know the giants in the field—theorists, researchers, and practitioners. Empower yourself in every way that you can, and your knowledge will come back to you in the form of increased confidence and a sense of professional ownership. Administrators who are strong themselves look for confident, articulate teachers.

PEERS: GETTING SUPPORT AND GOING IT ALONE

One wonderful extension of the whole language movement has been the development of teacher support groups across the country. Our first local TAWL (Teachers

Applying Whole Language) group started with a handful of teachers who were applying whole language theory in varying degrees, and desperately felt the need to talk about what they were doing—and thinking. During our first year Barbara, Penny, Carol, Dan, Evelyn Hanssen, and I met once a month in the evenings in Barbara's living room. We explored strategies, interpreted theory, listened to individual school-based problems, and, generally, felt united by a common goal. We increased our professional strength with those small group meetings.

In the past four years our TAWL group has grown to over one hundred. Now we meet on Saturday mornings at a public library, have a board of directors, pay dues, and sponsor an annual conference which drew over six hundred educators last year. There are many TAWL groups in the area now, and I often get calls from teachers (sometimes principals) wondering about how to get a support group started. I always tell them about our beginnings—just a few interested people who agreed among themselves to meet regularly and share their classrooms, their problems, and new articles and books about whole language.

We stress the importance of peer support and the opportunity to talk about learning, especially if there is no one else in the school involved in a whole language transition. There is no official act that makes a group a whole language support group, but we do have a coalition of groups under the auspices of "The Whole Language Umbrella." Information about joining the Umbrella and how to get a TAWL group started is available from Center for Establishing Dialogue in Teaching and Learning, Inc., 325 E. Southern Avenue, Suite 14, Tempe, AZ 85282.

Reaching out to peers takes many different forms. When Barbara Lindberg started her change to whole language we had not yet started a support group, and she was very much alone in her school. I asked her to write about how she handled getting started alone.

It is ten years since I struggled to understand what Linda meant by sociopsycholinguistics. I had taken a reading course at a local university because I was a junior-high Social Studies teacher who could not make the text readable for my students. Reading course followed reading course and my search for help led to the master's program. In the last course I began to get a glimmer of how to help students read better and, then, I was back alone at my school with exciting discoveries and no one to share them with.

I was laughed at when I brought up educational ideas in the teachers' lounge. By then I had been taken out of the Social Studies department and given the Remedial Reading assignment. Instead of opening up all departments to me, as I expected, my new assignment isolated me. This turned out to be a blessing and a curse.

No one expected much from classrooms full of remedial readers. If the teacher could survive with a minimum of disruption to others in the school, that was accomplishment enough. This gave me freedom to experiment, which was reinforced by the wise refusal of our assistant superintendent to allow a basal for these students. Publishers were flooding the market with skills kits, low-reading workbooks, and controlled vocabulary storybooks. They looked impressive, and I tried using a few of them, but found their primary usefulness was in controlling students through highly structured work. They were management programs that had little to do with reading. I decorated the room with them because I could not discard them.

I became known as the weird reading teacher and I felt more isolated than ever. I decided my one salvation might be to continue to enroll in college seminars that I knew would have the whole language perspective. Those were few and far between, because Linda was the only person at her university talking about whole language and I couldn't find any others in the Chicago area. What I did find, though, was a few other teachers who wanted to experiment and talk about their classrooms. That, plus the professor, was critical for my continued development—and my sanity.

I learned of conferences, newly published books, new ideas. I could tolerate my reputation at school, but I could not have survived without the contact with others in the field of reading who were exploring a new way of looking at language learning. In January of 1985 I took a major step and enrolled in the three-week summer program at the University of New Hampshire. Then in 1987 I went to UNH for six weeks to study writing process. These were expensive undertakings, even when my district helped underwrite my second trip. They required a big time commitment by me and my family, but they proved to be invaluable experiences professionally and personally.

These outside explorations gave me the knowledge I needed to continue to try to develop a whole language classroom, and the confidence to be able to defend my position with parents, as well as other educators. Yet even when I was being evaluated, I was not able to discuss the philosophy that underlay my classroom activities. As long as what I was doing "worked," and I didn't cause waves, I was left alone.

I continued to dust off the kits before school open houses, but forgot about them as my personal library grew. Used bookstores, garage sales, and resale shops were my primary sources. When a traditional, respected, "gifted" Language Arts teacher in the next room retired, he gave me three classroom sets of books that were one of the nicest presents I ever received; and I learned that there were ways of getting money to buy multiple copies of trade books. When PTA or special funds are not available, I buy sets myself.

In time, some faculty members began to notice the difference between my classroom and others, and they began to see changes for the better in my students' reading abilities and attitudes. This happened first among the special education support staff. It was also evident in building conferences and staffings, where teachers and administrators gather to discuss specific students' needs. As we talked about a student it often seemed as if I had mistakenly spoken of someone else—certainly my description of strengths did not match the deficit profile created by other teachers. But, over the years, I had gained enough confidence and knowledge to stand my ground; and then I noticed that students were being put into my classes who did not qualify as remedial but were in need of "special" treatment.

About five years ago I began making presentations at local conferences, and then received invitations to present at regional conferences. I am still seen as different, even as other teachers strive to integrate trade books and the writing process into their classrooms. At a recent retirement dinner for our principal I was introduced as the faculty member who speaks a strange foreign language—whole language.

The change from being a closet whole language teacher to one who offers workshops in the district has taken place over almost ten years. It has been rocky at times because really new ideas cause turmoil. But I feel that it has been and continues to be worth all the effort. I take the condition of education in this country to be a part of my personal responsibility. Effective changes can be made only by classroom teachers. I'm not alone anymore. My support group has grown from two people to hundreds of teachers who belong to local TAWL groups and who share my commitment to whole language. Becoming a whole language teacher may not be easy, but with wonderful references, research, professors, and teacher support groups, it becomes easier every year.

Carol Porter feels that other teachers are not always as supportive of whole language as we would like because they don't understand it. With that assumption in mind, she invites other teachers into her classroom to participate in the curriculum so they can get an inside view of what's going on. She sees this as "another one of our jobs as whole language teachers."

When the history teacher in Carol's school was covering the Civil War, Carol's students read historical fiction and short stories on that time period. The history teacher started visiting Carol's class during his free periods, bringing in books from his personal collection. Like Penny, Carol has repeatedly found that a little personal involvement goes a long way in explaining her program to peers and administrators.

BASALS: JUST ONE MORE RESOURCE

Basal reading programs are a reality many of you are likely to face for years to come. While the ultimate goal of whole language from a reading perspective is to use a wide variety of real, intact materials, basals in and by themselves need not make or break a curriculum. As with all other materials it depends on how basals are used; and, that use is based on the teacher's philosophy of literacy and learning or his or her willingness to unquestioningly adopt someone else's philosophy.

Basal programs represent a theory antithetical to whole language. Basals and isolated phonics programs are built on the assumption that the road to literacy is paved bit by small bit, skill by skill, brick by brick until the whole structure is unshakably in place. These structures, we now know, are no stronger than the little pig's straw house, if they get built at all. Many of them fall down before they are completed, and their builders end up in remedial classes.

The good news is that basal publishers, more and more concerned about an imminent demise of their current product, are making a genuine effort to incorporate more literature into their existing programs. They are also showing an increased awareness of the place of writing in reading and vice-versa. While some of the literature and the reading/writing connection activities may be worthwhile, the basic programs are virtually useless to a whole language teacher. If you must use some part of a basal program make sure *you* are in the driver's seat, deciding what to use and how to use it. Penny Silvers comments on the use of a basal in her school.

We are trying to develop curriculum around different themes. Some of the newer basals have already identified themes and have literature available to extend the basal stories. However, we are still using an older basal in which there are no themes, and stories are not connected in any way. In order to move our instruction away from dependence on the basal, we started to identify themes within each grade level that were a part of the social studies or science curricula. We also added themes that seemed to emerge consistently from students' interests and interactions. Themes like feelings, courage, friendship, growing up, neighbors, dinosaurs, etc., all became part of a master list. First we identified quality trade books (multiple copies of paperback books, as well as library books), poetry, nonfiction books, and related art and music. Finally we looked at the basal as another possible resource, and carefully selected the literature to be included.

Slowly we are gathering a collection of paperback books with money from reading grants, PTO, and materials' budgets. Our thematically-based Text Sets* will be able to stand on their own soon.

For management purposes (and for really anxious teachers), skill checklists may be kept and used while observing students in their daily reading and writing activities. It's reassuring to many who want to use the basal less and less to see that the skills are being learned through real language use.

When Carol Porter was teaching junior-high school she, too, decided to examine the reading materials in the basal as one small resource to tap for her thematic units.

Rather than looking at the required basal as the thing holding my program back, I looked at it as a source of short stories that could be used in the developing units. Stories were categorized by genre and/or theme. I also went to other anthologies and magazines to find additional materials that would fit into the same categories I had identified. For example, in a biography/autobiography unit the stories were divided by historical figures, accident victims, celebrities, people in the news, etc. Students were able to choose stories in each of those divisions to read with a partner. They also used strategies such as Written Conversation* and Say Something* as they read. These activities replaced the traditional checktests and worksheets for reading.

The librarian and I put together a collection of novels relating to the same themes and genres from which the students could choose. For some units I read a related novel aloud.

USING THE BASAL WITH CARE

If you plan to use the basal for a while longer, scrutinize the materials carefully. The first step is to decide which materials are worth an investment of your students' precious reading time. Even though most new basals glowingly market the "literature" in their programs, a large percentage of the material is excerpted or revised in some way. Why bother, you may wonder. If they are going to include good quality literature, why not just present it in its entirety? Usually the answer is embedded in the overall goals of basal programs: They are not about the development of literate behavior through the use of rich, extended literature; they are about teaching skills.

Bernard Waber's wonderfully sensitive book, *Ira Sleeps Over*, is a good example of basal publishers' disregard for the literature itself. *Ira Sleeps Over* is about a little boy sleeping at his friend, Reggie's, house for the first time. Both boys have a hard time containing their excitement about this new adventure, but there's a hitch—Ira always sleeps with his teddy bear and he's afraid if he takes it along, Reggie will make fun of him. The story is filled with indecision. Ira wavers back and forth. His parents encourage him to take the bear; his sister insists that Reggie will think he's a baby. In the end Reggie sneaks out his own little secret teddy bear, and the two boys sleep happily with their stuffed animals. Waber has written a beautiful story with rich, natural language and detailed illustrations of a young boy dealing with a tough childhood issue.

One basal publisher decided to use a version of *Ira Sleeps Over* in a recent edition. In an effort to simplify the text the publisher deleted many of the charming exchanges between the two friends. The vocabulary and syntax were watered down and even the illustrations were altered so that their supportive role in the story was enormously diminished. All in all, it's a sadly stripped down imitation of the real book.

Basal publishers often give information about the literature they use at the beginning of the teacher's manual, where the acknowledgments are listed. Usually they tell you in fine print if the stories are abridged or excerpted, but NOT ALWAYS. You can first rule out stories you don't want to use due to "revisions," and then check out the other possibilities. Invite one or two of your peers to help with your investigations, and then together you can discuss what is worth using. Occasionally you may want to use the modified versions to compare with the trade books themselves. Even kindergartners are linguistically sophisticated enough to perceive the differences in real and contrived language.

The material you do select can be part of a larger theme you are trying to develop with your students, or it can be the kickoff for a focused unit of some kind. One of my graduate students, Susan Streuve, used a dinosaur story from a basal to begin a unit on dinosaurs, a study area her students had voted for. Her students formulated questions; gathered trade books and diagrams; speculated about the dinosaurs' demise; and celebrated their learning with presentations, dioramas, and bookmaking. These students spent weeks directing their own learning. The experience made Susan question even more seriously the value of using the basal program at all in her classroom.

INTERACTIVE LEARNING OR
SKILL-FOCUSED PROCEDURES

By and large, basals deal with single texts, presenting one story, analyzing and questioning it ad infinitum, and then going on to another story. Whole language is much more interested in connected learning, and so encourages the use of sets of conceptually related materials (Crafton, 1983). If you are using a basal or one content-area textbook, it is important to branch out and consider the larger learning picture. Written material on a topic should span genres. Broadly conceived, conceptually related Text Sets* should include art, music, and videos, as well as poetry, newspaper articles, nonfiction trade books, biographies, magazine articles, and so on (*see* Appendix A for examples).

Beyond the selection of materials there are certain qualities of interaction and process that have been highlighted throughout Part I of this book. These are dramatically different from the skill-focused procedures suggested in the teacher's manual of basal readers and which comprise the heart of any basal program. The so-called "enrichment activities" still found in many basals are the only parts of these books that may be theoretically consistent with whole language. But unless these are used with student choice and intent in mind, they, too, should be disregarded. For teachers moving toward a whole language classroom, using the basal is, at best, an intermediary step on the way to developing a classroom library filled with a range of materials and a classroom curriculum focused on process, not skills, and students, not programs.

Where does the skill instruction that is so dominant in basals fit in? It fits in as an integrated part of any reading your students are doing. In whole language learning skills become strategies—the plans and decisions in which readers and writers are involved to make literacy happen. Skill development and application traditionally assume a passive reader, one who learns "the skills" through repeated exposure and drill and then applies them invariably from one reading/writing context to another.

Literacy is anything but passive. Readers and writers constantly have to make global and local decisions as they are constructing meaning. Because these operations vary from one reading/writing setting to the next, even young language users have to sort out the differences and strategic demands of reading and writing stories versus reading and writing nonfiction, reports, newspapers, menus, commentaries, and so on. The application of strategies must be reader/writer-determined and is the major part of "process" that must be learned primarily through multiple reading and writing experiences themselves. Don Holdaway puts it this way:

> The major difference between "skills teaching" and "strategy teaching" concerns the presence or absence of self-direction on the part of the learner. In skills teaching the teacher tells the learner what to do and then "corrects" or "marks" the response. In strategy teaching the teacher induces the learner to behave in an appropriate way and encourages the learner to confirm or correct his own responses—*the teacher does not usurp the control which is crucial in mastering a strategy* (1979, p. 136).

Another shift in our understanding of literacy (in fact, any learning) is that strategies *must be used* in many contexts for many different purposes for a reader/

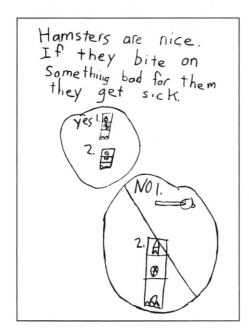

FIGURE 8.4
The First Four Pages of
Diana's Book, *Hamsters*

writer to become secure with them. If you closely examine a student involved in an entire, authentic reading or writing event, you can begin to see the incredible range and depth of thought and strategy utilization that must occur if comprehending and composing are successful.

One day I was visiting Kathleen's classroom and admired a student-published book called *Hamsters*. The next time I was in the classroom Diana, the author, presented me with my own original copy of the book. In Kathleen's classroom students choose their own topics, draft, get responses to their content, revise, and then publish. Knowing the authoring cycle that her students go through, I used Diana's book to track the strategies, linguistic information, and real world information that she had to use to create her brief text. Figure 8.4 shows the first few pages of Diana's book. Figure 8.5 lists some of the strategies and decisions she had to make as an author.

Reading has its own set of strategies and decisions. The point is that literacy development requires rich reading material and strategic thought, not stripped-down, synthetic language and automatic skills.

Don't worry that your students won't learn to read if you replace the basal with real literature. Literature-based reading programs in Canada, New Zealand, Great Britain, and Australia demonstrate every day that students can learn from authentic material from the very beginning. Another point, made repeatedly throughout this chapter, is that teachers and students, not publishers and programs, need to be in control of their classrooms.

Selection of personal topic

Focus for the writing

Development of personal expository structure

Sequencing events

Integration of personal experience and fact

Rereading

Revision

Relationship between text and illustrations

Segmenting text

Punctuation decisions
    Capitals
    Periods
    Commas
    Apostrophes

Spelling decisions (89 different words)

FIGURE 8.5
Partial List of Decisions Made by One
Second-grade Author for One Publication

All of the sociopolitical issues with which teachers are concerned—parents, administrators, peers, basals—are best dealt with out of strength, strengths that are developed through a willingness to take risks and a willingness to take back authority and responsibility in the classroom.

Personal Reflection

How can I begin to communicate with parents about the whole language changes in my curriculum?

How can I share my changing philosophy with administrators and peers?

What new decisions do I want to make about my reading program and use of materials?

CREATING A
PERSONALIZED
WHOLE LANGUAGE
CURRICULUM

Part

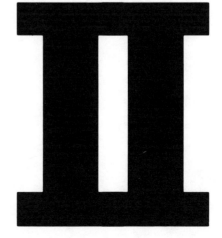

Small Changes That
Make a Big Difference

9

ot long ago a first-grade teacher asked me to help her get started with whole language. Irene is an active professional who attends local conferences, reads education journals, and tries new ideas in her classroom. She was convinced that her basal reading program was not providing the exciting experiences that would nurture a love of reading in her students. We talked several times about whole language, its philosophical base, its focus on literature and process. I chose a couple of books that I thought would be useful in giving her a stronger sense of the overall picture. After we had talked about them, I suggested we start with a Message Board.* Irene chose to use the bulletin board in the back corner of her classroom, and then explained to her students how the note exchanges would work. After a few days she said to me: "This is wonderful! They are writing all the time." Then, laughing, she added, "But now that I have it started, how do I get it stopped?"

Irene found that one small change in her classroom launched her toward a more interactive curriculum. She saw quickly that her students could initiate their own writing and that she could communicate with them in authentic ways. It was an easy, nonthreatening, productive way for everyone to begin with whole language. There are many small changes you can make immediately in your classroom that will make a big difference to you and your students: Message Boards can be a place to start authentic writing; letters can quickly draw you into your students' lives, hearts, and minds; talking about a book you are currently reading can give a new perspective on literacy and can begin a shift in your role toward teacher as

---

* All asterisks throughout the book refer the reader to Chapter 10 where full strategy descriptions can be found.

learner/demonstrator; extending the amount of time your students (and you) engage in uninterrupted reading and writing can quickly strengthen your literacy program and student development.

Try any one of the following "small changes" and, most likely, you won't stop there. But, don't forget, a series of small changes will not make a classroom "whole language". This kind of teaching is not comprised of little, holistic-like activities, it is defined by a specific set of beliefs about language and learning.

1. *Give choices.*   Whether you are totally literature-based, using a basal series, bound to mandated textbooks, or somewhere in between, you can make your classroom more student-centered by giving additional choices in the learning activities in which your students engage. For example, after reading a required book or chapter, present several pieces of related literature and let students decide which to read (be sure to make your own choice as well); after reading, develop several alternative writing extensions and let students choose one; peruse a required text with your students and together identify the topics you will study, giving reading/writing choices along the way. Choice is a critical issue when it comes to learning and involvement, but it doesn't mean a free-for-all. Bob Wortman, a principal in Arizona, advises teachers not to give choices they can't live with, but to always give some choice.

2. *Read a book you've never read before along with your students.*   Most of the time teachers read literature or textbooks so they can choose what is best for their students. While it's important to be familiar with a range of age-and-interest-appropriate materials, reading something for the first time with your students gives you the opportunity to talk about your initial impressions, predictions, and interpretations. There's nothing like it to pull you in as a genuine member of a Reading Discussion Group,* and your students benefit enormously by hearing about your first-encounter thinking.

3. *Forget your teacher questions and have a genuine discussion with your students.*   This can be a great first step toward giving up control and sharing the responsibility for learning in your classroom. In the literate world outside of the classroom people talk about their reading and only answer questions that are an integral part of a discussion, never to prove that they have read or comprehended in a certain way at a particular level. (Discussions can give you that information if you want it.) And, besides, real exchanges give students, even kindergartners and first-graders, the chance to see alternative perspectives and to play off each other's thinking. Teacher-constructed or basal-composed questions just can't do that.

4. *Read out loud to your students EVERY DAY.*   Reading out loud is one of the simplest, most important, most powerful strategies for all grade levels; but probably the one most overlooked, most often ignored. No matter how full your day is, how demanding your curriculum, FIT THIS IN. Jim Trelease makes a strong case for sharing good literature in his *Read-Aloud Handbook.* If you can keep the books you read out loud in a central class library, students can read their favorites during a free choice time.

5. *Share classroom problems (noise, management, materials, and so on) with your students and work toward collaborative solutions.*   Ownership in the classroom can take a number of different forms. Classrooms simply function more effectively when everyone involved has decision-making power. For example, I've seen some teachers eliminate small-group work and other kinds of student interactions because it sometimes gets out of hand. If the exchanges are stopped, the social learning potential is lost. A better direction is to discuss the problem with the class and brainstorm solutions. Settle on one that you can all live with, and expect that, from time to time throughout the year, you may have to negotiate a different solution to the same problem.

6. *Sit in on group discussions making process observations your only goal.* Observing group dynamics and collective thinking is an important part of your new role with process-based instruction. You are in a wonderful position to help students reflect on their developing strategies. Set up a simple system for yourself to make sure that you observe Reading Discussion Groups,* writing workshops, or any other learning settings in your classroom on a regular basis. Always allow time to share your observations with your students.

7. *Replace worksheets and dittos with uninterrupted reading or open-ended journal writing.*   Many teachers seem quite willing to give up worksheets and dittos, but aren't sure what to use in their place. Start by replacing them with more time to read and write. If your students have trade books in their desks, or access to literature in a class library, it's easy and not disruptive to give them the time to simply read while you are meeting with a discussion group or engaged in a conference concerning writing in progress. The same is true for writing—journals can be kept in desks or in a central file box in the classroom so students can retrieve them at a moment's notice, freeing you to present a Mini-lesson* to a small group or have a content or editing conference with individual students.

8. *Organize the literature you use into conceptually related sets.*   Comprehension is enhanced when readers make connections across texts. That kind of thinking is highlighted when sets of materials are used. Instead of focusing on the reading and comprehending of single pieces of literature, start thinking in terms of Text Sets.* Start with some of your favorites or the Caldecott and Newbery award-winners. Build sets around prominent themes, books by the same author or the same genre. This is a good place to include selected stories from your basal, if you are still using one. Try to get multiple copies of books so that students can explore sets together. They can read all or choose only a few.

9. *Get real, functional writing into place quickly with a Message Board,* *mailboxes, and sign-in sheets.*   Message Boards and mailboxes are great ways to encourage interactive exchanges. Put them up at the beginning of the school year with a note or letter to each student. Sign-in sheets can be placed on a table or attached to a bulletin board near the classroom door. For younger students it's one more opportunity to write their names for a real reason; for all students it's a way for them to take over the responsibility of attendance-taking.

10. *Ask your students what they would like to learn, and follow their interests at least some of the time.* While most teachers have required content and/or developed units they would like to use, student interests and the topics that excite them can't be ignored. Start the year by talking about questions your students have about the world, or topics they hope to study this year in school. Once the areas are out on the table, plan time to pursue the most popular ones, and time for individuals to do research on at least one burning question or topic. Both you and your students can start gathering materials to support these projects and, when you are ready, plan the learning together. Because these student-selected areas of study tend to yield the best learning, you may find that, once you start, your curriculum moves increasingly in this direction.

11. *Be sure your students are writing for audiences beyond the classroom.* When writers write for genuine and varying audiences they have a chance to think about effective communication and the strategies they need so that different kinds of readers understand the ideas they are presenting. If students write letters to authors, mail them; if they have political issues to explore, help them find the names of their local representatives; if students are interested in writing a class newspaper, be sure the principal gets a copy and that it goes home to parents; if they do research on a topic in depth, help them find ways of sharing their new expertise, perhaps at a local children's museum, open house, or PTO meeting.

12. *Have a written conversation with at least one student every day.* As teachers we are always trying to find ways to get closer to our students, to understand them better, to see some of their thinking up close. Written exchanges are one way to do this. Take five minutes—at the beginning of the school day, before lunch, while other students are doing uninterrupted writing or reading—to have a Written Conversation* with one student. Post a list of class names each week with the days of the week beside the five names so that students will know when it's their turn. You may want to initiate the first conversation, but, after that, ask students to come up with topics they would like to talk/write about. Occasionally, give over an afternoon or a whole day and make it Written Conversation Day with everyone writing back and forth on topics they choose.

13. *Begin a classroom library.* Developing a collection of good trade books is crucial to any whole language program. There are inexpensive ways to begin: Ask your students if they have books they would be willing to donate to a class library; talk to your principal and PTO to find out about funding; check professional journals for grants and awards that can be used to buy literature; go to garage sales.

14. *Talk less and listen more.*

Whole Language
Strategies

10

This chapter includes instructional procedures that have been used successfully by other educators moving toward similar learner-centered goals. Used reflectively and judiciously, classroom strategies can increase your understanding of the whole of whole language and help us, as a profession, fine-tune our effort toward a practical theory of literacy.

For emphasis and assurance I'll begin this chapter with an old caveat: Whole language is a theory, not a method, and even though every whole language classroom incorporates strategies into its curriculum, whole language is not a collection of holistic-type strategies. As you consider experimenting with the ideas presented in this chapter, also consider and be aware of the principles that are highlighted in each: whole-to-part literacy, authenticity, social learning, process demonstrations, choice and ownership. Don't forget the importance of *your* ownership in any instructional procedure. As you read through these, be alert to modifications that would suit your context better while maintaining the theoretical integrity of the original strategy.

BOOKMARKS

GENERAL DESCRIPTION

Active readers respond to text as they read. They monitor comprehension, predict, agree and disagree, recall related experiences, ask questions, connect life with text, and make connections across texts. Strategies that encourage reader/

text interaction can result in higher levels of understanding and increased reader involvement.

Bookmarks is a simple procedure that allows readers to capture their responses quickly on small pieces of paper. For many, the Bookmark strategy serves as a kind of go-ahead activity when the reader is confused or encounters unknown words and concepts. Readers can use their Bookmarks to note struggles as well as other transactions with the material, and then continue to read, comfortable in the knowledge that they will have a chance to talk about their problems and interpretations after reading.

BASIC PROCEDURE

1. Students should have many opportunities to talk about their responses to literature before the strategy is introduced. The teacher needs to join into discussions as a reader, highlighting personal responses to material.
2. Cut regular sized notebook paper or construction paper into strips about two inches wide.
3. The teacher should demonstrate the procedure by sharing his/her own written responses on Bookmarks. If the range of genuine responses is narrow, the teacher should share responses to a number of different selections. This kind of teacher demonstration should continue from time to time.
4. Students should be given several Bookmarks and asked to choose a piece of literature to read. Bookmarks can be stapled together.
5. The teacher should provide an extended uninterrupted reading time. Students are asked to write their comments, responses, interpretations on the Bookmarks and to note the page number. Additional Bookmarks should be made available so students have easy access to them as needed.
6. Students should voluntarily share with the whole class examples of their responses, and then hand them in to the teacher with the clear understanding that they will not be graded.
7. The teacher should read through the Bookmarks with an eye toward responding to questions, sharing similar reactions, or asking the student questions to encourage rethinking or rereading. Teacher comments can be written directly on the Bookmark and handed back to the reader (*see* Figure 10.1).

VARIATIONS

1. Barbara Lindberg color codes by days the Bookmarks her junior-high school students use. For example, Monday is green; Tuesday is yellow. Her students also put a page number on the paper only if they want a specific response from her.
2. Kathleen Visovatti asks her second-graders to use Bookmarks in an abbreviated form. When students start a new book they get a blank Bookmark from

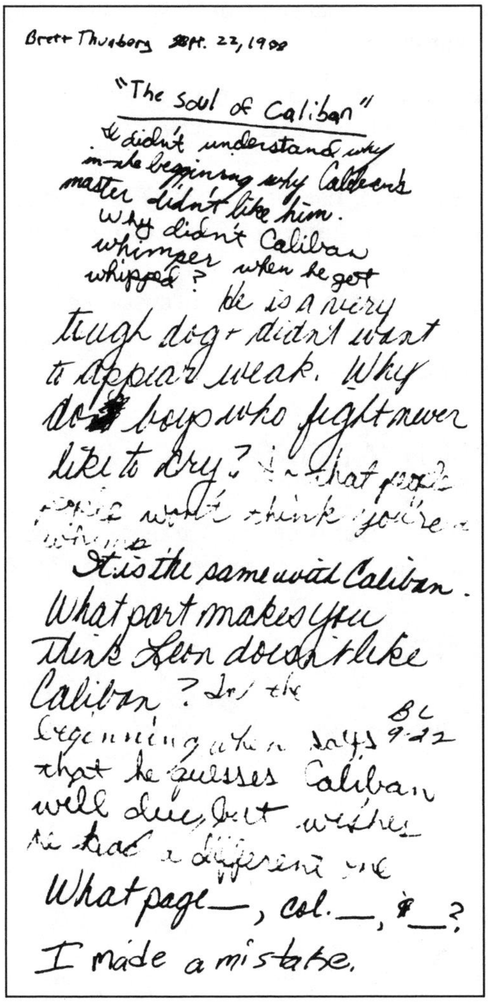

FIGURE 10.1
Bookmark Strategy: Teacher Comments in Response to Student

FIGURE 10.2
Example of Bookmark Strategy by Second-Grade Reader

the recycled paper box. During uninterrupted reading time, they keep their Bookmarks handy to respond in different ways:

a. For passages they like and want to remember to share in their Reading Discussion Group,* they write the page number and an exclamation mark beside it.

b. For text that is confusing (words, sentences, paragraphs, etc.), they write the page number, a few words to indicate the area of confusion, and a question mark (*see* Figure 10.2).

   These can be discussed with a partner, the teacher, or a discussion group. If readers solve the problems during reading (with or without help), they also share their problem-solving process.

PROCESS OBSERVATIONS

Teacher and/or students can keep Bookmarks over time and use them as a way of monitoring reading assignments and tracking changes in process strategies.

REFERENCES

The idea for Bookmarks came from Dorothy Watson's "Reader Selected Miscues" (1978).

BOOK TALKS

GENERAL DESCRIPTION

From the books that we choose to read to the natural discussions that arise from a text experience, reading is a social process. When it comes to selecting books, readers depend primarily on other readers for recommendations. Book Talks are used to whet the reading appetite, to call attention to good literature that others may want to read. Book Talks occur informally and regularly in classrooms where students are immersed in literature, but time should also be scheduled for more formal introductions.

BASIC PROCEDURE

1. Teachers should introduce the idea of Book Talks with varied demonstrations from different genres. Book Talks may center around: a brief retelling of story

---

* All asterisks throughout the book refer the reader to Chapter 10 where full strategy descriptions can be found.

highlights with the ending deleted; a picture showing the reader's favorite part, and shared while reading that section from the book; one character's perspective regarding a major event or relationship in the book; the personal impact a book had; how this book connected with other books by the same author or with the same topic; the author's skill as a writer (good dialogue, detail, evocation of feelings, unusual organization, and so on).

2. Following the demonstrations teachers and students should brainstorm the purpose of a Book Talk. Teachers should be careful to highlight characteristics like interest and appeal and the idea that Book Talks are not traditional book reports with complete retellings.

3. Book Talks should occur as students complete a book they are excited about and would like to recommend to others. Book Talks can be scheduled for a

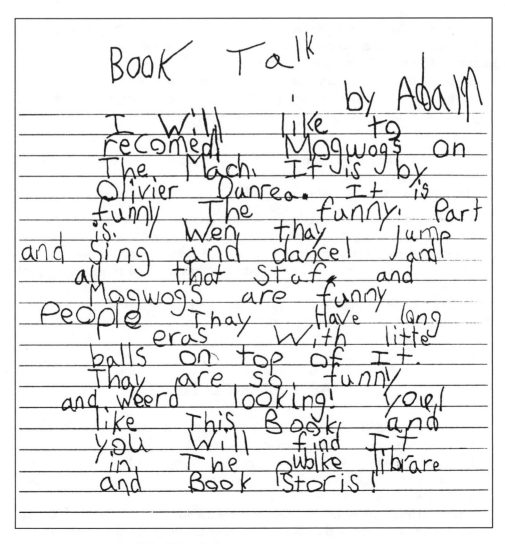

FIGURE 10.3

five-minute block of time at the beginning or end of Reading Workshop or when new Reading Discussion Groups* are being formed. Students should be encouraged to prepare for their brief presentations by drafting what they will say (*see* Figure 10.3), and trying it out with a peer who can respond and give advice. Students can also make posters advertising the book and/or dress in a costume which represents one of the book's more interesting characters.

CELEBRATIONS

GENERAL DESCRIPTION

Public observations of a job well done, the completion of a commitment or genuine engagement can all encourage a learner to engage once again. When public sharing is accompanied by audience response, learners have one more chance to stand outside themselves and see their work from others' perspectives.

Learning Celebrations are a common occurrence in whole language classrooms. They are, as the name implies, a time for joyous sharing. Celebrations serve one or two functions:

1. They laud the meaning-making process itself by calling attention to in-process thinking, and/or
2. They present learners' final interpretations, discoveries, or extensions.

Process Celebrations often take the form of classroom displays, which highlight in-process thinking (for example, multiple drafts in writing).

Culminating Celebrations are intended for audiences beyond the learners themselves, and are complete when the audience joins in with a respectful, appreciative response.

These Celebrations often look like the same kinds of gatherings outside of the classroom complete with invitations and invited guests. Example of Celebrations can be found in relation to various Text Sets in Appendix A.

BASIC PROCEDURE

1. At the beginning of the school year teachers should introduce the idea of a process-focused curriculum to their students. The value of personal authorship and decision-making in reading and writing should be emphasized. Teachers should highlight the notion that process will be celebrated throughout the year in many different ways.
2. Initial Celebrations of process can occur with students and teachers deciding together on areas of the classroom where rough drafts of writing can be displayed. Time should be given so students can briefly discuss their revisions

before the in-process writing is posted.

Other display areas of the classroom can show: Extensions* related to a theme or unit, such as drawings of favorite parts of the material being read; excerpts from Reading Journals*; or literature letters,* which are written exchanges between two readers reading the same work.

3. Culminating Celebrations for reading and writing should become a regular part of curriculum planning. These Celebrations should routinely include published writing. Other Celebration possibilities are videotapes, songs, skits, illustrations, audiotapes, scrapbooks, unit parties, dressing in character costumes for a day, cooking, authors' teas or luncheons, and so on.

4. When appropriate, invitations should be created to announce the Celebration (*see* Figure 10.4).

FIGURE 10.4
Celebration Invitation

VARIATION

Carol Porter celebrates her students' literacy growth by writing letters to parents. Following intensive conferences with her students, Carol drafts letters that not only discuss changes in reading and writing but goals students have met and new ones they have set. Students are invited to include self-evaluations or any other papers with the mailing.

CLASSROOM CONSULTANTS

GENERAL DESCRIPTION

Students need to have many opportunities to use reading and writing to learn about self-selected topics. When learners have been immersed in an area of study for some time, their expertise should be recognized in the same way it is valued in the world outside of the classroom. Classroom Consultants is a strategy that provides an avenue for students to share what they have learned with interested audiences who have invited students to serve in a professional role.

BASIC PROCEDURE

1. Individuals or small groups identify topics they would like to study. Identification can come from personal interests, experiences, field trips, textbook chapters, current events, parental occupations, and so forth. In this strategy the teacher is a group member or acts as a consultant to multiple groups, helping them gather information and organize their learning.
2. Learners begin to identify resources related to the topic. They decide what information they will need to become experts in their chosen areas: professionals they could invite into the classroom or interview over the phone, films or videos they need to secure, organizations or museums they could visit, books and other written materials they can consult. Resources should not be limited to print materials but should include a wide range of information.
3. Initial study sessions are spent perusing gathered materials, discussing resources, and deciding on specific questions to be explored.
4. Learners decide on procedures to be used to gather the information. This may be a time when individuals or groups need teacher support to help them determine learning strategies and procedures.
5. When learners feel they have enough information about their topics to call themselves experts, they work on various ways to present what they have learned. Planning should include what will be said, overhead transparencies, handouts for audiences, and so on. Presentations can be tried with other small groups, who are then asked to respond and give advice for revision.
6. When consultants are secure in their presentations, they develop brochures and business cards advertising their new professional status. Students disseminate these materials outside of the classroom to other classes announcing that they are available for consultation.
7. Audiences can help consultants refine their presentations by writing Exit Slips* that include one idea learned and one question they still have about the topic.

PROCESS OBSERVATIONS

Teachers should observe the group processes as much as possible, noting how expert groups organize, gather information, solve problems, and/or share knowledge. Informal discussions of these observations can help to facilitate ongoing studies and show learners alternative ways to pursue topics of interest.

VARIATION

Pat Miller starts her year by telling her third/fourth-graders that she is an expert in many other things besides teaching and that they, too, are experts. She shares her areas of expertise, careful to show that daily, taken-for-granted life experiences can turn one into an expert. She then invites her students to talk about their expertise. Some of her students are experts in babysitting because they are expected to care for their younger brothers and sisters on a regular basis. Some are experts in model building, others are experts in baseball, making dinner for a large family, skateboarding, people in their neighborhoods, taking bubblebaths, spotting rainbows, and so on.

Pat and her students make a large Expert List that she keeps in her classroom all year long so students can determine independently with whom they should consult about various topics or skills. This list grows as students gain knowledge about authors they read extensively, topics they choose to do research on, bookmaking, and other topics. Included in this Expert List are process strategies that students use skillfully. Pat's opening expert activity is a powerful way to build a sense of strength and community for students of all ages.

EXIT SLIPS

GENERAL DESCRIPTION

When reader/writers are encouraged to reflect on their learning, they come to understand and value the content and process in new and deeper ways. Exit Slips are a simple way to help students reflect on what they have learned and to identify areas that need further exploration. Exit Slips work well after any learning experience, or at the end of the school day, as a way of prompting students to review what they have accomplished.

BASIC PROCEDURE

If this is the first formal use of a reflective strategy, talk about the importance of thinking about what is learned (content) and how people go about learning things (process). Teachers should demonstrate by highlighting their own decision-making within a simple context; for example, writing a letter, deviating from a recipe, deciding what to wear, thinking about how to approach a friend about a problem, discovering what route to take to an unfamiliar destination, and so on. Students may need to talk through some of their processes before using the strategy.

1. Following the initial demonstrations and at the end of a school day, or any important learning activity, distribute one 3 x 5 card to each student.

2. Ask students to write one thing they learned during the day, or from a particular activity, on one side of the card. On the other side students are to write one question they still have. Present this part of the strategy in an open-ended manner so students are free to consider content or process issues in their responses.

3. Collect the cards for review.

4. Select several questions to use in a whole group setting the following morning or during the class meeting. Questions can be answered directly by the teacher, orally or by writing on the card, or students can be invited to respond. Selected questions can be put aside for future study or be used to inform the teacher about topics for Mini-lessons.*

VARIATIONS

1. Exit Slips can be used throughout the reading of a text, much like a written Say Something.* The first part of the strategy, then, serves as a reflection of what has been learned; the second part, a reader-generated question.

2. **Rapid Reflection** is a verbal form of Exit Slips. Throughout the school day—at the end of important discussions, demonstrations, Mini-lessons,* or any learning engagement—students can be asked to reflect on the experience quickly and, at random, call out a response. Responses can be focused by asking open-ended questions before Rapid Reflection begins:

   • What was surprising for you?
   • What were you thinking about the most?
   • What was one question that you have?
   • What is one idea you are excited about?

REFERENCES

Various forms of this strategy have been developed by Kittye Copeland, Jerry Harste, and Carolyn Burke.

EXTENSIONS

GENERAL DESCRIPTION

Reading is an extended process that begins long before a book is opened and continues long after it is closed. When students have the chance to extend their comprehension during and after a reading experience, their interpretations and meaning constructions are expanded and enriched. Extensions allow readers to take different stances on a text and to alter their perception of it. Extensions are any activity related to the material students are reading or have completed.

The starting point for an Extension is one text-related idea, theme, or problem. Extensions are important in a whole language curriculum because they reflect the understanding that reading is a personal act of inquiry and meaning construction.

This strategy makes a distinction between in-process Extensions (those occurring during reading) and after reading Extensions. In-process Extensions include connecting personal experiences to a text, asking someone for additional information or clarification, and any time readers consult an outside source so they can better understand what they are reading.

When the overall classroom environment encourages choice and individual interpretation, Extensions occur naturally during and after the reading process. After-reading extensions should consistently include choices related to forms of communication other than language—for example, music, art, drama—and should be used for content reading as well as literature.

Commenting on Extension activities, Carol Porter says:

> When I ask students to reflect on their favorite books over the semester, I have found that their choices are not made by considering the literature alone. It is our search for meaning by making connections or satisfying a curiosity through Extensions that determine the long-term hold that a book has.

BASIC PROCEDURE

1. Teachers should set the stage for in-process Extensions by gathering their own natural reading extensions to share. Natural extensions can include: discussions during and/or after reading; questions asked of peers or family members while reading; the use of maps, encyclopedias, and other reference materials; reading related material; etc. Teachers should discuss the idea of reading Extensions as an integral part of reading process.
2. Following discussion and teacher demonstration, students select a piece of literature or content material to read. Partner reading or small groups may be used.
3. Readers decide if they will read silently or orally and how discussions of the material will occur.
4. Following discussions, teachers should help readers reflect on their in-process Extensions. If students express a strong interest in knowing more about a particular issue, teachers can be prepared to support the Extension with print and nonprint resources and to encourage students to collaboratively extend from the reading. Teachers should be careful to share their own Extensions and to bring new ones to the next group discussion.
5. After discussions and in-process Extensions are completed, students can help develop a choice list of after-reading activities:

a. Read a related book on the same topic or by the same author.
b. Draw or paint a picture of your favorite part of the reading or of what the material meant to you.
c. Write a script for a TV show and produce it using a roller TV.
d. Form character groups in which each small group chooses a character and writes the story from his or her point of view.
e. Invite experts to discuss topics from the material (*see* Variations).
f. Create a puzzle or board game.
g. Make a book following the same form or format as the book just read; for example, a pop-up book.

VARIATIONS

Carol Porter makes sure that her students engage in multiple Extensions when they read any piece of literature. Carol encourages the many Extension opportunities that occur naturally during the reading process itself, as well as those that take place after the reading is completed. Some of the Extensions compel students to revisit a text one more time, rereading pertinent sections and constructing new meaning as they explore the writing in alternative ways. When Carol's students read Chris Crutcher's books, for example, they extended from the reading in the following ways:

1. Maps and travel brochures of Montana, Idaho, California, Washington, and Wyoming were ordered and displayed so students could work together to locate rivers, camp sites, small towns, and major cities. The students followed the travels of Willie in *The Crazy Horse Electric Game* as he ran away from home in order to come to terms with brain damage acquired from a skiing accident; and they located the towns and colleges where the swim team in *Stotan!* traveled to their meets.
2. The class called Northern Montana University and requested pictures of their swimming facility where the final swim meet in *Stotan!* occurred (the PE department had no pictures available so the secretary took her camera down to the pool, took some pictures, and mailed them to Carol's students).
3. A music center was set up in one corner of the room with "The Best of . . . Johnny Cash, Waylon Jennings, and Emmie Lou Harris because these artists' work was mentioned in two of Crutcher's books.
4. Students discovered that "A Boy Named Sue," mentioned in *The Crazy Horse Electric Game,* was written by Shel Silverstein, so his books of poetry were brought into the room and read.
5. Books and articles were collected about Crutcher and about acquired brain disorders.
6. One student brought in a copy of an act from *Julius Caesar* containing a quote used in *The Crazy Horse Electric Game.*

FAMILY HISTORIES

GENERAL DESCRIPTION

Connecting with ourselves, our past and current knowledge, and our larger world gives us all a stronger sense of knowing and belonging. Understanding ourselves from the inside out and the outside in can be enormously enhanced when we bring those closest to us into the process. Family Histories is a strategy that introduces students to a research process as it helps them uncover the richness of their heritage; it is content and language-as-tool-for-learning at their best.

Family Histories is an extended activity that can take a few weeks or span the entire school year. It involves interviews, note taking, summarizing, and reporting information in a number of different forms, as well as reading from primary sources. The strategy culminates in a major celebration in which students and their families come together to share the learning and to feast on favorite family dishes. Families leave the celebration with a large album filled with valuable artifacts collected and created during the Family Histories strategy.

BASIC PROCEDURE

1. Family Histories is considered an area of study within social studies, broadly defined as studying about ourselves and others. Students are introduced to this social studies strategy by learning about themselves and their families. For a period of time they collect different types of family information in a variety of ways. The information is shared along the way and accumulates in an oversized family album. Family Histories is worked on primarily during social studies time but the related reading/writing activities are often accomplished during Reading and Writing Workshop. Teachers participate in each part of the strategy with their students, collecting their own Family Histories, creating their own albums, and sharing their research processes.
2. Each student has an expandable file that can be added to as the individual parts of the strategy are completed. Files should be easily accessible so students can go to them at any time.
3. The first part of Family Histories is a questionnaire given to all family members. If the teacher's parents are available, one or both can visit the classroom to help demonstrate the interviewing technique. Teachers use the same form the students will use and show them how to reword a question for clarification, paraphrase what has been said to be sure it's understood, record responses that are too long for the space provided, and abbreviate long responses or difficult spellings.

1. Do you (or did you) have a nickname? How did you get it?

   _____

   _____

2. What were (are) some family sayings, proverbs, and phrases you can remember from childhood? What did they mean? Who said them?

   _____

   _____

3. What countries did your ancestors come from? Why did they come to the United States? What stories did they bring?

   _____

   _____

4. Do you remember a special moment with your grandparent(s) or great-grandparent(s)?

   _____

   _____

5. What are some of your early school memories?

   _____

   _____

6. Is there a skeleton in your closet or a black sheep in your family?

   _____

   _____

7. What was one of your most embarrassing, satisfying, happy, or sad experiences?

   _____

   _____

8. What is a story from your own life or your ancestors' lives that you are likely to pass along to younger generations?

   _____

   _____

9. Who told you your first stories? (Describe the person, the situation, and the stories.)

   _____

   _____

FIGURE 10.5
Family Ethnic Background Survey

4. After students have completed their interviews, the teacher demonstrates selecting an incident from the interview to share with the class and illustrates one incident for the album. Each time students complete one part of Family Histories, they are asked to share, illustrate, and immediately add it to the album. Album pages can be large pieces of construction paper on to which forms, pictures, and illustrations are pasted.

5. Next, students are asked to collect reports of favorite family rituals or celebrations. These stories are told to the class from a rocking chair or other honored place, then written up and put into the album. A special storytime can be set aside during the school day until all students have told their selected stories.

6. Surveys of each student's ethnic background are developed and taken home (*see* Figure 10.5). As students share these the whole class gathers around a globe and wall map to help locate and star the areas of the world from which ancestors immigrated. Children have individual maps to color.

7. Students now prepare to interview siblings or cousins. First they interview one another in class then take the same questions home (*see* Figure 10.6). The two childhood responses are compared as students share their findings.

Me	My Sibling or Cousin
When I grow up I want to be	When I grow up I want to be
My favorite subject is	My favorite subject is
I am good at	I am good at
I like to read	I like to read
My favorite lunch is	My favorite lunch is
My favorite game is	My favorite game is
The biggest mistake I've made	The biggest mistake I've made
The proudest I've been	The proudest I've been
The luckiest I've been	The luckiest I've been
What I remember most so far.	What I remember most so far.

FIGURE 10.6
Sibling or Cousin Interview

8. Interviews of Moms and Dads come in the form of "Tell me a story about something that happened to you when you were my age." Students write the stories, conferring with parents as they draft it; then they retell it to the class.

9. Grandparent interviews are next. Students are asked to audiotape these. When grandparents live in another city or state, interview questions are sent to them and they are asked to respond on tape (*see* Figure 10.7). From these interviews one incident is selected for transcribing, telling, writing in final draft form, and illustrating.

10. Each student is asked to bring a favorite family recipe and the story behind it. The stories are collected from parents or grandparents or whomever has the most information about the story behind the ethnic dish. Students share their stories by recreating them from notes taken during oral telling.

11. Students prepare the last entry for the album. Each person writes a love letter in which they tell why they are glad to be in this particular family. Students are encouraged to mention each family member in the letter.

12. Family Histories culminates in a potluck dinner to which each family brings a dish and multiple copies of the accompanying recipe. Students entertain with songs and dances and the teacher tells the "family" story of the class. Videotapes of highlights from the school year can also be shown. Albums are presented to the families with a picture of the family on the front.

REFERENCES

The Family Histories procedure was developed collaboratively by second-grade teachers Kathleen Visovatti and Jenny Pliska. The original unit was developed by Sue Gundlach, seventh-grade teacher. Kathleen and Sue have often planned the integrated unit together to include both age groups and variations, such as family history drama productions and shared quilt-making.

INTEREST CLUBS

GENERAL DESCRIPTION

People naturally come together to explore and share common interests. Informal and formal clubs contribute to our sense of belonging and community and can enhance our pursuit of new information. Interest Clubs are one way to encourage in-depth exploration in a particular topical area. Such clubs can emerge from any student interest, teacher interest, or required area of study. They are temporary groups that remain intact until club members decide they have explored their developing area of expertise sufficiently. Members use reading and writing as tools for learning about self-selected content.

An Interview with

_____

1. What year was it when you were 7 years old?

    _____

2. Where did you grow up?

    _____

3. What did you like to play?

    _____

    _____

4. What kind of toys did you have?

    _____

5. Was there a special pet in your life?

    _____

6. What kind of clothes did you wear?

    _____

7. What was your favorite food or treat?

    _____

8. What chores did you have to do?

    _____

9. What do you remember about school?

    _____

    _____

10. What was your favorite holiday and why?

    _____

    _____

11. What did your family like to do together?

    _____

    _____

12. What was the most mischievous thing you did as a child?

    _____

    _____

    _____

by _____

FIGURE 10.7
Grandparent Interview

BASIC PROCEDURE

1. At the beginning of the school year students and teachers brainstorm a list of topics they are interested in learning more about. Questions like: "What is the one thing you hoped to learn about in _____ grade?" and "What is one question you have always wanted to get answered?" are possibilities. These can help spark a lively discussion and generate a list of genuine interests. The teacher can also suggest required areas of study to see if there is enough interest to add them to the list.

2. A vote is taken on each topic to determine if there is enough interest among students to form a club. Groups as small as three and as large as eight can function productively.

3. Teacher and students work together to set regular meeting times for the groups.

4. Groups should decide on their goals for the club, specific questions related to the topic, and how they will identify and gather resources to pursue their questions and answers. Teachers should encourage a wide range of resources that include nonprint as well as print materials and experts in the field.

5. Students may form subcommittees based on student interest in a particular question. These smaller groups decide on varied learning activities—including reading, writing, interviewing, and hands-on experiences—to help then explore and learn more about their topics. This is the point where teacher input and support is most needed to help learners organize and pursue specific related issues. Different clubs should request information and resources from one another so that all class members, including the teacher, are contributing to a growing knowledge base.

6. Teachers should provide frequent opportunities for Interest Clubs to report on their activities and share the learning procedures they are using. If club members bring in resources that would be of interest to the entire class (for example, an expert in the area to speak to the club), all clubs may gather for the event.

7. When club members feel they have exhausted a topic or are ready to move on to another interest, they should plan a presentation and Celebration* of what they have learned. Students should be encouraged to consider a number of different forms of sharing: club magazines, videotapes, posters, displays, Classroom Consultants,* presentations to outside audiences, and so on.

VARIATION

Kathleen Visovatti's second-graders started their Interest Clubs at the beginning of the school year by looking through their science textbooks and choosing topics they really wanted to study. One of these Interest Clubs, the Endangered Species Club, continued during most of the school year.

Toward the end of the year Kathleen asked students to look at the chapters in the science text they had not yet covered and choose one they would like to study in depth. These groups delved deeply into their chosen topics and eventually set up hands-on learning experiences for the rest of the class so that everyone would have a chance to explore all areas in the required text.

JOURNALS

GENERAL DESCRIPTION

Writing functions in many different ways in our lives. Much more than simply communicating what we know, writing helps to clarify a complex world, allows for intimate exchanges of thought, lets us capture our in-process thinking so we can examine and revise it, and, most exciting, encourages a discovery of ideas and relationships. These varied purposes need to be represented in classroom activities. Journals are a learner-centered strategy that can be used in many different ways as an opportunity for students to explore their ideas and feelings.

Whole language teachers often point to journals as one strategy they couldn't live without—and for good reason. From kindergarten to high school, journals are a consistently powerful tool for getting close to students in ways that teachers may not have been able to before. Journals also encourage an unusual depth of thought and observation and provide a way for teachers to demonstrate their own literate thought in an authentic, individualized forum.

Teachers are not always involved in journal writing, but, when they are, their role is critical. Responses must be real and human, focused on ideas and feelings, not form, spelling, or mechanics. This may sound simple enough, but when teachers see themselves primarily as evaluators, it's often difficult to remember that genuine responses are what keep the writing and the writer going, not the ferreting out of grammar errors and nonstandard spellings.

Dialogue Journals

1. Students and teacher should bring to school either a spiral-bound notebook or a homemade journal with construction paper covers and blank sheets stapled inside.
2. The teacher should discuss the function of the Dialogue Journal. If students are familiar with Written Conversation,* they can easily see that these journals are an expanded version. The teacher may need to demonstrate a written dialogue on the board or overhead projector.
3. Initially it is a good idea for the teacher to be the major audience for journal entries so that he or she can demonstrate the kinds of responses that are appropriate (*see* Figure 10.8). Students can leave their journals in a box or central place in the classroom so the teacher can pick them up for reading and responding.
4. After all students have had at least two responses to their journal entries from the teacher, a whole class discussion takes place regarding the genuine content responses that the teacher has written. It should be pointed out that Dialogue

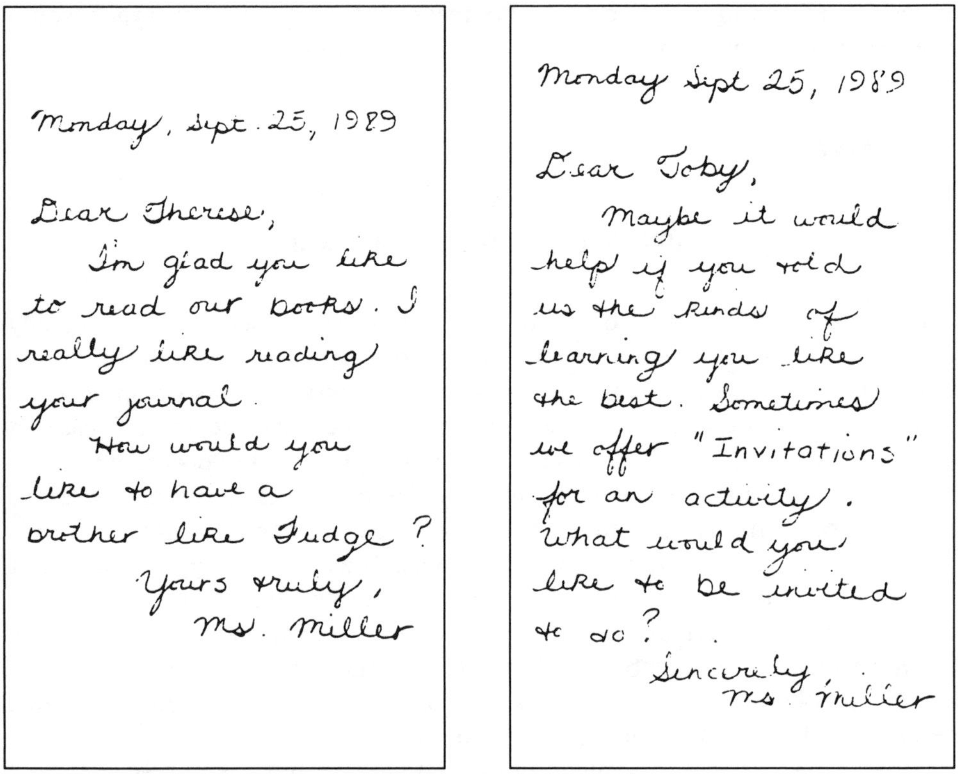

Monday, Sept. 25, 1989

Dear Therese,
    I'm glad you like to read our books. I really like reading your journal.
    How would you like to have a brother like Fudge?
        Yours truly,
        Ms. Miller

Monday Sept 25, 1989

Dear Toby,
    Maybe it would help if you told us the kinds of learning you like the best. Sometimes we offer "Invitations" for an activity. What would you like to be invited to do?
        Sincerely,
        Ms. Miller

FIGURE 10.8
Examples of Teacher Responses to Fourth
Grade Students' Journal Entries

Journals are never a time to call attention to problems in the writing. They are a time to exchange ideas, experiences, and feelings.

5. The audience for Dialogue Journals can be opened to include peers. At that point journals can be placed directly on desks for a response, left in mailboxes, or put into another box in the classroom where students can retrieve them at a certain time during the day.

6. Instead of designating a certain time for writing in Dialogue Journals, communication should be left to the discretion of writers. Dialogue Journals may be one writing choice during Writing Workshop.

Observation Journals

1. Students and teacher select an area of social studies or science they would like to observe firsthand. Classroom "pets"—such as caterpillars, chicks, worms, snakes, spiders, gerbils, or plants of any kind—are a natural for this.

2. Teachers inform students that they will be involved in original research as they pose questions, make observations, set up experiments, and use their Observation Journals to record discoveries.

3. The class brainstorms questions they might want to investigate related to the selected topic. Students and teacher self-select into groups of three to five based on questions of common interest.

4. Small groups are assigned to ten- or fifteen-minute blocks of time to begin their investigations. The time is used to observe, discuss, and record observations (*see* Figure 10.9).

5. Following the observation time, small-group members meet to generate new questions or refine old ones in preparation for their next observations. This is a time when groups may want to suggest experiments to help them answer their questions. Journals can be used to plan the steps for the experiments and to record explorations.

6. Students should be encouraged to analyze their observations and to draw conclusions.

7. Other experts and print materials can be used to confirm and extend students' understandings, but the emphasis should remain on their ability to investigate and uncover the information.

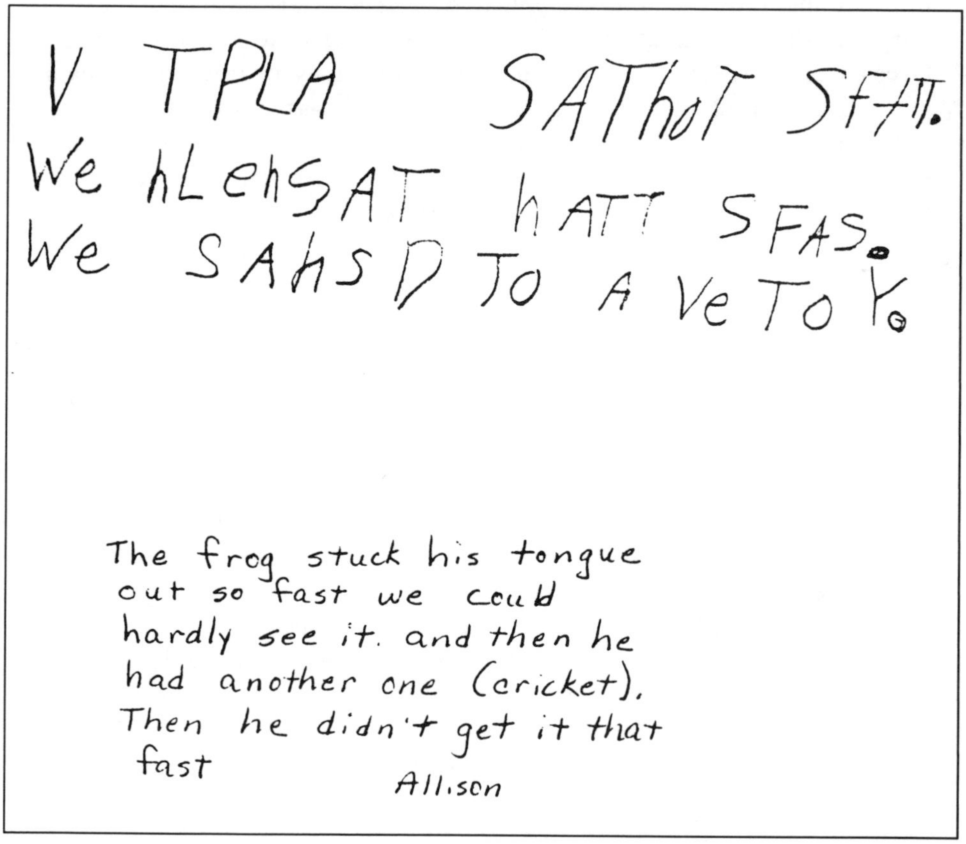

FIGURE 10.9
Example from a Kindergarten Observation
Journal

Private Journals

1. Private Journals can be introduced through the use of literature that includes this type of writing. *Dear Mr. Henshaw* (Cleary, 1983) and *Anne Frank: The Diary of a Young Girl* (Frank, 1967) are two good examples. (Others can be found in Appendix A.) Teachers should consider keeping Private Journals before introducing the strategy, so they can share selected entries.

2. Students should understand that Private Journals cannot be read by anyone else unless the writer decides she would like to share a particular entry and/or would like a response. Under those circumstances the page to be read can be paperclipped and placed on the respondent's desk or placed in a designated container. If the teacher feels a need to check the writing in some way, the dates at the top of each journal entry can be noted to make sure students are writing during the time set aside for journals.

3. A special time should be set aside each day for writing in Private Journals. Consistency in writing is extremely important to writers if they are to achieve greater depth and focus in their writing. Regular writing time also encourages thinking about topics and being prepared to write at a certain time during the school day. Teachers keep Private Journals and write while students are writing.

4. Occasionally, writers may simply run out of things they are interested in exploring in their journals. Those are times when whole-class brainstorming sessions can help, or when writers may want to read during writing time. Teachers should develop a Text Set of literature that encourages writing so they can recommend it during those "dry" times that all writers have.

Reading Journals

1. Teachers should introduce Reading Journals by reading aloud and demonstrating their responses to the literature as they read. These think-alouds can include predicting, recalling related experiences, commenting on feelings and ideas, connecting to other texts, extending, elaborating, summarizing, and expressing opinions. The important thing is that students see the range of responses that readers naturally produce when they are reading. Teachers may want to demonstrate think-alouds with a variety of materials to highlight the difference in responses across genres.

2. Students are given, bring in, or make Reading Journals.

3. Teachers explain that everyone (including the teacher) keeps their journals close by whenever they are reading. Before readers begin a new text they put "Before Reading" at the top of a blank page and write predictions about the content of the material. Predictions can be made from the title and/or by quickly perusing the whole text.

4. On the line below their predictions, readers write "During Reading." This section is used to record responses during the reading process. Teachers remind students that these responses will be like the think-alouds demonstrated earlier.

If responses tend to be limited, teachers may want to use incomplete sentences for a short period of time (*see* Figure 10.10). Teachers never impose a certain number of responses during reading. This is a prime time in which to highlight repeatedly that variation in quantity as well as kind is to be expected and is an integral part of a process that involves personal construction of meaning.

5. Readers also have an "After Reading" section in their journals for each piece read. This area is for reactions to the whole text, final interpretations (which may be expressed in writing or art), and lingering questions. This section can also be used so students can brainstorm Extensions* and/or identify related themes they would like to explore.

Reflective Journals

1. At the end of a discussion, any reading or writing activity, or at the end of the day, teachers initiate a brief whole-class discussion focused on what happened during that particular block of learning time. Students may talk about what they learned, discoveries they made, the significance of working with a partner or in a small group, or problems they encountered. Teachers share their own reflections.
2. Teachers are careful to point out that any learning activity involves process as well as content, and both are important for reflection.
3. Following the discussion, students spend time writing their personal reflections in a journal maintained only for this purpose.
4. Reflections can be shared with the whole group, in small groups, or with partners. Teachers also share on a regular basis.

---

1. I wonder what this means . . . .
2. I really like/dislike this idea because . . . .
3. This character reminds me of somebody I know because . . . .
4. This character reminds me of myself because . . . .
5. This part reminds of _____ in _____.
   (name of another book)
6. I really like the way the author wrote this part because . . . .
7. I wish the author had not _____ . . . .
8. If I were _____, I would _____ . . . .
   If I were _____, I would not have _____ . . . .

FIGURE 10.10
Open-Ended Sentence Examples to
Encourage Reader Response During Reading

5. When students are comfortable with reflection, the whole-group discussion at the beginning can be dropped.

VARIATION

Reflective Journals can be used any time there is a need to encourage students to stop and think about the topic at hand. Teachers can ask students to write in their journals in the middle of a discussion, presentation, Mini-lesson,* and so on; or while reading a complex text as a means of making personal connections, framing questions, or clarifying interpretations.

REFERENCES

Dillard, Jill. "Learning from First Graders How to Use Dialogue Journals: A Teacher's Perspective." *Dialogue.* vol. VI, no. 1 (April 1989).
Fulwiler, Toby. "Journals across the Disciplines." *English Journal* (December 1980).
Harste, Jerome, and Kathy Short with Carolyn Burke. *Creating Classrooms for Authors.* Portsmouth, N.H.: Heinemann, 1988.
Youngblood, Ed. "Reading, Thinking, and Writing Using the Reading Journal." *English Journal* (September 1985).

MAILBOXES AND MESSAGE BOARDS

GENERAL DESCRIPTION

Language users of all ages need to experience the functional, interactive nature of writing. Mailboxes and Message Boards are a simple way to highlight the social dimension of written language, while engaging students in authentic exchanges.

BASIC PROCEDURE

1. A central bulletin board is designated as the class Message Board, or Mailboxes are set up and each student is assigned an individual space. Mailboxes can be made from cardboard dividers that may be available from department and discount stores.
2. When students come into the classroom at the beginning of the school year each has a note on the Message Board or a letter in their mail slot from the teacher.

3. Teachers should initiate a discussion about the notes and letters that students have received in other settings. Once the interpersonal function of these forms of writing has been determined, teachers and students should decide together how the Message Board or Mailboxes will operate in the classroom. Many teachers leave the timing of these activities open so that students can write notes or send letters during any free time of the day—before school, at recess, before lunch, and so on. Some teachers include letter-writing as one choice during Writing Workshop time. Students may decide that the posting or delivering of messages may occur only at designated times.

4. Students should be reminded to sign their names to all messages and should also be told that hurt feelings are not allowed. Whenever inappropriate messages are sent, the Message Board or Mailboxes can be shut down for a time and then reopened with a review of the rules.

5. Teachers can use Message Boards or Mailboxes to help with direct, individual contact that is so valuable to students but so difficult with large numbers. Teacher messages can include personal notes about vacations, new siblings, change in dress; encouraging words about a difficult learning activity; noticeable growth in reading/writing strategies; new books the student might enjoy reading; or just a "Hi! How's it going?" message.

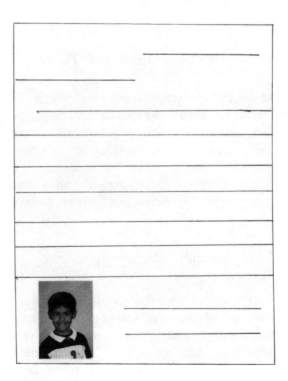

FIGURE 10.11
Personalized Stationary Used in a Second
Grade Classroom

6. When the flurry of excitement that often surrounds Mailboxes and Message Boards dies down, teachers may want to rekindle the interest by finding new uses for them. For example, Message Boards can be used for a while only to write congratulatory notes to classroom authors on newly published books, or letters can be limited to interview questions about families or other parts of students' lives.

7. Someone should be responsible for keeping the Mailboxes or Message Board stocked with appropriate writing supplies. Regular notebook paper can be recycled for use as note paper and kept in a small box near the Message Board. Personalized stationery can be made by the teacher or students (*see* Figure 10.11) and kept in Writing Folders* for easy access. Stationery and envelopes can also be brought from home and put into a container near the Mailboxes.

REFERENCES

The idea for Mailboxes is adapted from Vera Milz (1980). Message Boards was developed by Carolyn Burke.

ME BOXES

GENERAL DESCRIPTION

When reading and writing are based on personal interest and life experience, risk-taking is encouraged and predicting highlighted. Organizing learning activities that are highly personal and predictable gives readers maximum support for meaning construction. Me Boxes are collections of items that represent various dimensions of owners—their interests, families, experiences, and areas of expertise. When students have a chance to organize and then share their individual slices of life, they can more easily write and then read texts that reflect their immediate experiences.

BASIC PROCEDURE

1. During the first week of school the teacher brings a small box filled with special, personal items to share with the class. The items should represent family, hobbies, and professional interests so as to give students a sense of richness and variation in the teacher's life. Items could include personal pictures or ones of the family, artifacts from vacations or special times, favorite books, sports items, small household items (statues, diaries, childhood mementos, and so forth). The number of items should be relatively small for younger classes, increasing in number for older groups.

2. The teacher takes each item out of the Me Box and talks briefly about its significance.
3. At the bottom of the box is a story or description that includes the items and experiences shared (*see* Figure 10.12). The teacher reads the text to the class.
4. Students are invited to bring their own Me Boxes to class. Shoe boxes work well because they are easy to get and don't hold so many items that the strategy becomes unwieldy.
5. Students share their boxes with the whole class or in small groups. Whole-class sharing can be done over a period of days. While it can take a fair amount of time, sharing with the entire class is a highly effective way to start the year and to help develop a quick sense of intimacy and community. It also gives the teacher enormous insight into students' lives and interests.
6. After Me Boxes are shared, students write related stories or descriptions. All items need not be included, but the closer the match between personal items and text, the more predictable the material.
7. As students complete their writing, it is shared with the whole group.
8. Me Boxes should be displayed in a central place, with the completed writing at the bottom of each box. Students should be encouraged to look through the items in the boxes and then read the accompanying story or description.

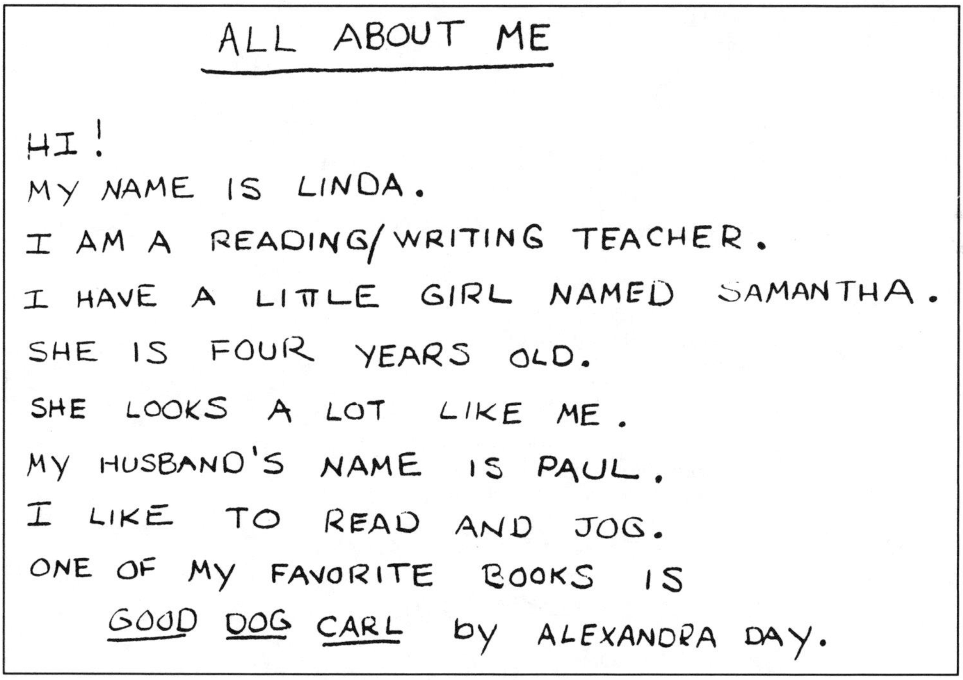

ALL ABOUT ME

HI!
MY NAME IS LINDA.
I AM A READING/WRITING TEACHER.
I HAVE A LITTLE GIRL NAMED SAMANTHA.
SHE IS FOUR YEARS OLD.
SHE LOOKS A LOT LIKE ME.
MY HUSBAND'S NAME IS PAUL.
I LIKE TO READ AND JOG.
ONE OF MY FAVORITE BOOKS IS
    GOOD DOG CARL by ALEXANDRA DAY.

FIGURE 10.12
Story Found at Bottom of Me Box. Items
Included Family Pictures, Trade Books,
Statue of Child Reading and Running Shoe

9. Students can use the individual items in their Me Boxes to start their Topics List for writing.

VARIATION

Me Boxes can be used to introduce and highlight the writing process. When teachers initiate the strategy, they should include one or two drafts of their personal stories, placed with the final draft at the bottom of the Me Box (*see* Figure 10.13). After items are shared and the final version of the personal description is read, the teacher should discuss the drafting, rethinking, revising process that occurred before the final version was produced. Drafts should be shared as the decision-making process is discussed. Whatever decisions were made from first to final draft should be shared—how the writing was started, what ideas were included and excluded, word choice, spelling changes, sequencing of description,

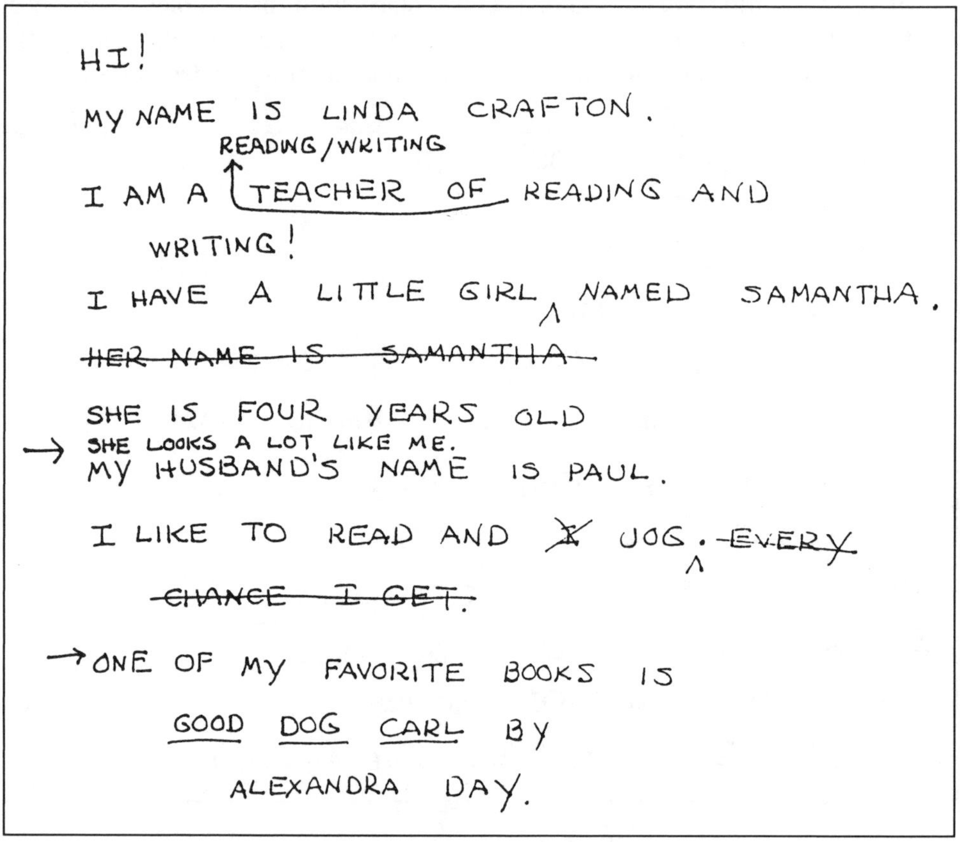

HI!

MY NAME IS LINDA CRAFTON.

READING/WRITING

I AM A [TEACHER OF READING AND

WRITING!

I HAVE A LITTLE GIRL NAMED SAMANTHA.

HER NAME IS SAMANTHA

SHE IS FOUR YEARS OLD

→ SHE LOOKS A LOT LIKE ME.

MY HUSBAND'S NAME IS PAUL.

I LIKE TO READ AND JOG. EVERY

CHANCE I GET.

→ ONE OF MY FAVORITE BOOKS IS

GOOD DOG CARL BY

ALEXANDRA DAY.

FIGURE 10.13
Draft of Personal Story Included in Me Box
as a Demonstration of Writing Process

and so on. Teachers may want to put the in-process drafts on an overhead transparency so students can easily follow the writing process being described.

Students can keep all drafts as they are writing, with time given to talk to the teacher and peers about the process decisions. Student drafts and final versions can be kept in the Me Boxes, along with a description of the writing process itself.

REFERENCES

Me Boxes was originally developed by Carolyn Burke for use as an individual reading lesson.

MINI-LESSONS

GENERAL DESCRIPTION

Learners benefit the most from instruction when it responds to what they are trying to accomplish and the areas of learning to which they are giving the most attention. When teachers observe a learning activity closely, they can see strategies that need to be strengthened and parts of the learning process that could profitably be highlighted.

Mini-lessons are brief discussions or demonstrations of some aspect of reading/ writing/content learning. They are designed to highlight rather than isolate the kind of thought or procedure in which a proficient language user might engage. Mini-lessons extend from teachers' observations of what students are trying to do. This is a time for students to see possibilities, not definitive steps; it is a time for teachers to encourage strategic decision-making. Mini-lessons, then, are presented as options, not as rules for everyone to practice and apply in exactly the same way. They are appropriate for whole groups, small groups, and individuals.

BASIC PROCEDURE

1. When students are reading or writing or engaged in any form of meaning construction, teachers should spend time observing what dimension of the process students are thinking about or struggling with. In writing, it may be topic selection or revision or editing. In reading, it may be rereading, difficult vocabulary, interpreting graphs and charts, or relating concepts to life experiences. Mini-lessons need to relate as directly as possible to students' current involvements. They can be procedural and organizational as well as process-focused. Reading/ writing folders, dialogue journals, discussions, and informal interactions are all

possible ways to see a process in action and to determine where students need support.

2. Using procedural or process observations, teachers should design a brief lesson to highlight one aspect of the learning activity. The emphasis here is on brevity. Mini-lessons are most effective when they are to the point and then quickly give the learner an opportunity for personal application. While some Mini-lessons will last only a minute or two, teachers should target five to ten minutes as the basic time frame.

3. The lesson should begin with the teacher alerting students to observations that lead to instruction. For example, "You know, yesterday when I was talking to Robert, Alice, and Toby about their writing, I noticed that their stories had a lot of detail when they talked about them but the detail hasn't found its way into their writing yet. Today I have a few examples of strong detail from other authors' work that I thought might help some of you in your writing."

4. Following the lesson presentation, students are asked if they see an opportunity to use the information from the lesson in their current reading or writing. One or two students should be asked to share what their application might look like. If there are no responses, students can be encouraged to keep the idea in mind for use at another time.

5. Following reading/writing/content time teachers ask students who used the lesson to reflect out loud about its usefulness: "Did it help? How? Will you use it again? In what other situations do you think it would work?"

6. When Mini-lessons have become a comfortable and regular part of the curriculum students should be invited to participate in designing the lessons by sharing their discoveries about reading/writing strategies and/or procedures that are particularly helpful.

7. Mini-lessons can be repeated throughout the year as teachers observe a need.

REFERENCES

Atwell, Nancie. *In the Middle*. Portsmouth, N.H.: Heinemann, 1987.

Calkins, Lucy. *The Art of Teaching Writing*. Portsmouth, N.H.: Heinemann, 1986.

PORTFOLIOS

GENERAL DESCRIPTION

When we look at the world around us and consider the range of productive work in which people engage every day, there is no evidence of formalized testing as a measure of success. Instead, the world is filled with examples of reflective self-evaluation that helps guide, support, and refine the pursuit of worthwhile goals: Artists collect photographs of their work to show the range of their skill; musicians keep journals to help them remember the nuances of successful performances; master actors keep reflective notes about the relationship between intentional dramatic variations and audience response. In an effort to encourage reflection as an integral part of learning, classroom evaluation should look more like the kind of intimate monitoring that skilled learners use outside of the classroom.

Portfolios are a collection of student-selected artifacts that represent growth over a period of time. They should be open and wide-ranging in their inclusions in order to capture a profile of the whole learner. While they can include a learner's "best," the emphasis is on students taking responsibility for reflecting on their learning and their lives and uncovering important changes. Portfolios, like other qualitative forms of assessment, are an integral part of an extended learning process and are themselves a learning strategy. They are there to give the learner information that can feed back into a developing sense of self. Portfolios assume a process-focused curriculum in which students are responding to written texts in some systematic way and are collecting drafts of their writing on a regular basis.

BASIC PROCEDURE

1. Teachers can introduce the idea of Portfolios by bringing artists into the classroom to share their portfolios, interior decorators' before and after collections, or scrapbooks that contain selected personal items that represent important life changes/experiences. A scrapbook that highlights a child's work from one grade to the next is useful in getting the idea of Portfolios across. More than one example should be used, if possible, to give greater depth to the idea of Portfolios.

2. Based on these examples, students and teacher should brainstorm a list of parameters regarding the function and development of a Portfolio. The brainstorming should be guided so that students consider a wide range of possible items to include in their Portfolios (related to their lives *both in and out of the classroom*): art, letters, notes, personal items—any personally significant artifact. Teachers should begin Portfolios early in the year.

3. Students are asked to consider their written drafts, reading responses and other artifacts from a change perspective. For example, they can be asked what they notice about themselves as readers/writers/thinkers as they look across drafts and responses. Teachers should join individual students to collaboratively study their literacy behaviors and suggest dimensions of reading/writing students might consider. It's important that teachers give students adequate time to reflect on and write their observations. It's helpful to learners when reflections take place on more than one day to give them a longer period of time to think about their processes.

4. Following the independent observations, a whole-group discussion can help give learners a broader perspective on self-evaluation. Teachers should share reflections on their own personal artifacts, written drafts and text responses.

5. Learners (students and teacher) can select one piece of writing, including all drafts, one or more reading responses and any other items as the first inclusions in their Portfolios. Selection should be based on learner judgment about the importance of the artifacts as a reflection of thought, change and experience.

6. Portfolios should contain an entry sheet with places provided for the name of the item, date it was included, and why the learner chose to include it (for example, what growth or change does it represent?).

7. At intervals throughout the school year, teachers should provide time for learners to self-evaluate and select items for the Portfolio. Items should not be limited to reading/writing samples. Portfolios need to show range as well as change, and can include art, audiotapes, photographs, projects, formal evaluation forms, personal items, and so on.

8. At the end of the school year learners need time to study the entire contents of their Portfolios with an eye toward creating a story about themselves as learners (*see* Appendix D). Narrative profiles are written and shared with classmates and parents and can be included in the final Portfolio.

9. Teachers should set aside time for a final conference with students about their learning and life changes over the year. In preparation, teachers can review Portfolios, reread learning stories, and write their own narratives about each student. Final conferences highlight the ongoing nature of change and learning as lifetime endeavors. Teachers and students discuss individual goals for future learning.

10. Portfolios and/or learning stories should be passed on to the teacher(s) at the next grade level.

VARIATION

1. Parents should be given the opportunity to write their own learning stories about their sons or daughters. If parents are involved in reflecting on the changes they see in their children throughout the school year, these narratives become a natural extension and expectation of parental involvement in the schooling process.

2. Carol Porter and Janell Cleland request that their teaching evaluations for the year be based on professional portfolios. Their collections include: descriptions of changes in their curriculums—both pedagogical decisions and the theoretical assumptions which guided the changes; photographs of the classroom with accompanying explanations; articles and other references which have influenced their thinking; insights from conferences or speakers they have heard; and, narrative profiles of their professional development.

REFERENCES

Carol Porter, Janell Cleland, Kathleen Visovatti and Linda Crafton's work contributed to the strategy description above. In addition, the following references helped to shape the ideas:

Eisner, Elliot. *Cognition and Curriculum.* New York: Longman, 1982.

Valencia, Shelia. *Reading Teacher.* January, 1990.

Wolf, Dennie. "Portfolio Assessment: Sampling Student Work." *Educational Leadership,* April 1989.

PROCESS SHARE

GENERAL DESCRIPTION

When people read or write or communicate in any form, they are involved in a series of decisions and problem-solving procedures. If learners are encouraged to examine and reflect on those process strategies, these are more available for future use during other literacy events. Whole language classrooms seek to make reflection an integral part of learning and process discussions a natural part of the curriculum.

BASIC PROCEDURE

1. Each day for a period of about one week the teacher sets aside a few minutes to discuss specific reading or writing strategies noticed during their personal literacy events. For example, while reading the newspaper the teacher may have reread a section to clarify meaning or may have noticed a miscue that disrupted comprehension. These are called to the students' attention and discussed briefly. The teacher shows the material being referred to and may want to make an overhead transparency or photocopies of the section being discussed so students can clearly see the larger context.

2. The teacher asks students if they have noticed similar behaviors in their reading. Time is allowed for students to brainstorm their observations about process.

3. After five or six days of the teacher's personal process sharing, students are told that at least one day a week is going to be set aside and designated Process Share Day. During that time students will bring up the strategies/decisions/problems they have begun to notice in their reading or writing. Teachers may want to alternate weeks with reading and writing or have Process Shares for both each week.

4. At the beginning of Reading/Writing Workshop, or any uninterrupted reading/writing time, each student has a 3 x 5 card to write down at least one process

behavior noticed during or immediately after the literacy engagement. The number of cards can be increased for older students and those experienced with the strategy.

5. On Process Share Day students bring their card(s) to a whole-group gathering at the end of the reading or writing time.

6. If students have more than one card they are asked to look through them and choose one they would like to talk about.

7. Volunteers share their process observations as long as time permits. Those who do not have a chance to share can turn to a person sitting next to them and talk through the selected behavior.

8. Teachers should keep track of those students who share so everyone can eventually have a voice in the larger group.

9. It's important that teachers continue to share their own processes on a regular basis, so students can see the strategic thought of a more experienced reader in various contexts.

10. Students can keep their process cards in a central place or transfer the strategies to a single master list entitled "Strategies I Use."

PROCESS OBSERVATIONS

During reading/writing time the teacher occasionally circulates around the room with a set of 3×5 cards on which to note in-process behaviors. This is especially useful for younger students and those who do not have a high level of process awareness. The cards can be used in talking to individuals or in highlighting specific strategies during Process Share. Teachers can add their cards to students' cumulative sets, maintain their own sets for individual students, or transfer the information to a Process Journal that contains space for each student. Process cards are one way to keep track of strategy use and change for each student.

PUBLISHING CENTER

GENERAL DESCRIPTION

Publication completes the writing process and makes the entire cycle functional. If writers, even very young ones, write without the expectation of a wider audience and repeated reading of their work, the engagement can lose its sense of purpose. A Publishing Center in the classroom gives prominent claim to the importance of this final phase of writing. Students understand that in this part of the room, the last editing and content checks occur and decisions for layout and binding of the work are made. Once the Publishing Center is introduced, and its function understood, it becomes an independently operating part of the curriculum.

BASIC PROCEDURE

1. Teachers and students decide on one area of the classroom to be used as the Publishing Center. A small desk or table with several chairs and drawers for supplies works well.
2. Supplies for the Center are gathered and carefully introduced to students:
   a. a box containing multiple copies of a proofreading sheet (*see* Figure 10.14) for content and mechanics;
   b. various sizes and colors of blank paper;
   c. materials to make book covers (heavy wallpaper, construction paper, cardboard from boxes, posterboard, contact paper);
   d. scissors, glue, rubber cement, stapler;
   e. typewriter (if available), pencils, markers, felt-tipped pens, and so on.
3. Rules for using the Publishing Center are established and displayed:
   a. Writers (teachers and students) can select one piece of writing to publish after a certain period of time or after they have written a certain number of texts (many teachers use three to four pieces as the rule of thumb). Students may want to ask peers or the teacher for final responses on a piece and take the writing through one more revision process before publication.
   b. After the piece to be published has been selected, writers go through a final Content and Editing Check using the form provided. The checklist can be modified depending on the age and experience of the writers.

Here are reminders about the meaning of writing and the mechanics to make it clear. Every time you finish a story, check it for every item listed below, then record it on the sheet attached before putting it in the Finished Work basket.

Content Checklist

Did I say what I wanted to say so that others will understand?

Did I arrange the sentences in a logical order?

Does my story have a beginning, a middle, and an end?

Did I make the people and events in my story seem real, interesting, and worth reading about?

Editing Checklist

Did I capitalize the first word of each sentence?

Did I capitalize names, titles, and other appropriate words?

Did I punctuate the end of each sentence?

Did I use punctuation in other appropriate places?

Did I spell each word correctly or circle words I was unsure about?

Did I use proper form on titles, margins, and other matters?

FIGURE 10.14
Proofreading Checklist

c. Following the self-check by the writer, pieces go into a box at the Center labeled "Ready for Final Editing." In conference with the writer, teachers can make final changes on the piece and make sure it is readable as final copy. During the conference the writer decides on the layout for the text and marks how much text should go on each page.

d. Writers can choose paper and cover materials from the Center, assemble the book, and write the final version. Illustrations can be added after the text is completed. If books are typed by the writer, teacher, or volunteer parent, pages should be typed before the assembly of the entire book.

4. Writers should have a special time to share their newly published books before they go on a revolving book rack or other special display area in the room. These books become a regular part of the classroom library and are read along with commercially published trade books.

VARIATION

Many teachers prefer to have blank books made and available for students when they are ready to publish. These books can be made in quantity by parent volunteers. If this procedure is used, the books can be sewn down the middle with a sewing machine and the covers can be made to resemble "real" trade books with hard covers (*see* Harste, Short and Burke, 1988, p. 238, for a full description of this kind of bookmaking).

READING CONVERSATION

GENERAL DESCRIPTION

Reading is a long-distance conversation between a reader and an author (Y. Goodman, Watson and Burke, 1987). The interaction occurring as readers construct meaning includes responses similar to the exchanges that people have when they are talking—agreeing, disagreeing, predicting, confirming, questioning, paraphrasing, summarizing, and so forth. Reading Conversation attempts to make readers more active participants in the reading process by building on the communicative strengths they have developed as speakers.

BASIC PROCEDURE

1. The teacher introduces the strategy by having a discussion about the nature of oral conversation—what people do, how they respond to one another when they are talking.

2. A list of responses are summarized and written on the board or on an overhead.
3. Students are asked to choose from two or three reading selections. The material has been cut into columns with sufficient space between them so students can write in the margins as they read. The passage or book should be relatively brief.
4. As students and teacher read their selected material, they respond to the author/ideas by writing in the margins. For example, one reader produced the following marginal comments while reading an article about Richard Nixon and his lack of concern for minority feelings:

"Nixon—yuk!"

"Unbelievable!"

"He had to be convinced of *that*?!"

"Sounds like the author is making a direct connection here."

"I don't have much background on Jackie Robinson."

5. Students and teacher bring their responses to small groups or large groups to use as a starting point for discussion. Later, readers can talk about the kinds of responses they used during reading, and the nature of their conversations with the author.
6. Readers can choose portions of their conversations and expand the ideas in a journal or any extended piece of writing.

PROCESS OBSERVATIONS

Conversational responses vary not only from reader to reader but from text to text. Teachers and students can categorize the types of responses that are made and compare the differences across materials. This kind of scrutiny is also useful for raising readers' levels of awareness about their reading process and to see what kinds of responses are more or less prevalent. Teachers can use the in-process information to track changes in reader interactions with text and see if there is a need to highlight particular kinds of reader/text exchanges (for example, relating information to personal experience) through Mini-lessons* or discussion.

REFERENCES

Barbara Lindberg and Linda Crafton have done extensive work with Reading Conversation in junior high school and in basic college classes.

READING DISCUSSION GROUPS

GENERAL DESCRIPTION

When learners have a chance to talk about their learning experiences, those experiences are extended, revised and enriched. Reading Discussion Groups give readers the opportunity to come together to talk about their reading in an open-ended forum. This strategy encourages the same kind of genuine exchanges that occur outside of the classroom in relation to all real world events. As a comprehension strategy, it is as powerful with kindergarteners as it is with advanced graduate students.

BASIC PROCEDURE

1. Multiple copies of various stories, trade books, or nonfiction material are collected.
2. The reading material is introduced by the teacher or a student. The students understand up front that they will have a choice of materials to read.
3. Students who have chosen the same material, come together in small groups to plan their discussion times. If the material is brief, students may read it silently in one sitting and then come together to talk about it. If the selection is longer, students may decide how much they will read the first day, second day, etc. If students are keeping Reading Journals,* they may respond in these journals as they read and bring their responses to Reading Discussion Group.
4. Once the reading or a portion of it is completed, the students come together to discuss their responses, interpretations, personal connections, etc. Students comfortable with risk-taking or familiar with open-ended discussions, are usually able to begin with no prompting, especially if they have journals to rely on to begin the discussion. Younger students may need a question or comment to get them started. Appendix C has examples of questions that have proven useful in literature discussions. After some experience with Reading Discussion Groups, even younger readers can begin their exchanges with little or no support from the teacher.
5. The primary role for the teacher is group member. Initially, informal monitoring may be helpful to keep the groups going, but, very quickly, the teacher joins a group from the beginning and remains a bona fide member, bringing journal entries and contributing genuine reader responses and questions.

VARIATION

See Text Sets strategy.

PROCESS OBSERVATIONS

Once the strategy is established, teachers can join a group as process observer. Students are told that ideas and exchanges will be written down as they occur so the discussion process can be explored later. After the group discussion, process notes are shared and everyone has the opportunity to reflect on what happened during the discussion and portions that were particularly helpful as a means of thinking through the reading experience. Appendix C gives one form that can be used to make process observations of Reading Discussion Groups using literature.

SAY SOMETHING

GENERAL DESCRIPTION

Reading outside of the classroom is filled with talk and questions and shared interpretation. Social exchanges during literacy events give readers an altered stance on the developing text meaning and help to focus their mental energy in new ways. When readers have opportunities to talk as they read, their in-process strategies, personal connections, responses, and overall evolving meaning construction are influenced. Say Something gives readers the chance to interact with other readers as they read the same material, highlighting the natural social dimensions of literacy.

BASIC PROCEDURE

1. The teacher introduces several brief reading selections to the class and asks students to choose one they would like to read.
2. Students identify a partner who has chosen the same reading selection.
3. Partners should look through the selection together and then decide how much of the text they will read silently before stopping to say something to each other. Exchanges may be comments on what was read, the author's style or tone, predictions about upcoming text, comprehension problems, personal connections, and so on. The teacher may want to demonstrate the strategy with a partner before asking students to try it.
4. Readers proceed through the material stopping at designated points to Say Something, and then decide on how much more to read before stopping again.
5. Students should come together as a group from time to time to reflect on their responses and the impact on comprehension. These reflective sessions give the teacher an opportunity to:
   a. underscore strategies that are particularly useful to proficient readers;
   b. encourage students to extend or challenge partners' thinking;
   c. validate alternative interpretations.

PROCESS OBSERVATIONS

Capturing students' in-process behaviors is not always easy. Say Something makes visible for examination otherwise invisible thought. Teachers or individual students can join pairs of readers to observe how thinking evolves during reading and is enhanced by the social impact of the strategy. As readers are using Say Something, process observers write down the salient parts of the exchange. Observers can then help readers reflect on the behaviors that were particularly effective, making them more available for future use while reading with a partner or alone. Readers should know beforehand that process observers are not there to evaluate but to help them think about their thinking related to meaning construction. Before students act as process observers, they will need to experience process observations in their own reading.

Partners can also audiotape themselves using Say Something and other comprehension-based, interactive strategies, and then listen to the tape to consider the strategies they were using, how effective they were, and how reader exchanges impacted on one another's comprehension.

A simple observation form like the one found in Appendix C can be developed and used for process observations.

REFERENCES

Say Something was developed by Jerome Harste, Carolyn Burke, and Dorothy Watson. A description can be found in Harste, Jerome, and Kathy Short with Carolyn Burke. *Creating Classrooms for Authors.* Portsmouth, N.H.: Heinemann, 1988.

SHARED READING

GENERAL DESCRIPTION

Sharing the responsibility for reading decreases the risk for all readers and encourages the use of supportive strategies. When meaningful, predictable materials are used as the ownership is shared, the learning environment provides maximum support. Shared Reading brings predictable books and shared responsibility together to create one of the most mutually beneficial strategies available for young, developing readers.

Shared Reading has been translated into many different versions, but successful variations involve the same basic foundation—multiple readings with readers helping each other through whole, predictable texts. The strategy is patterned after lap and bedtime reading done by parents in the home, followed by the child-initiated repeated reading of old favorites. Don Holdaway (1979) developed the idea of increasing the size of predictable books (called Big Books) to accompany the Shared Reading strategy, so that large groups of children could have the same kind of intimate interaction with a book that young readers have while snuggled up to their parents.

BASIC PROCEDURE

1. Teachers introduce a book for Shared Reading to the whole class by reading the title and asking students to predict the content. Big Books are often used to facilitate Shared Reading because all students can see the words, the illustrations, and their relationship. During the first reading the teacher takes the primary responsibility for reading the text, but encourages students to talk about the pictures and content and to continually predict the text from what has come before and from the picture on the page. Many children will naturally join in the reading of repeated text during this first time around.
2. Following the first reading, teachers are careful to allow time for students to discuss the story, extending and elaborating on selected parts and comparing and contrasting with other books or characters they know.
3. Immediately following the first reading, students are invited to participate in a rereading. This time students are encouraged to assume more responsibility for reading repeated words, phrases, and sentences.
4. Students have the option of reading the book a third time. At this point the teacher can ask how many would like to hear the story again and how many would like to move on to a new book. The book can be read as many times as students express an interest in doing so. The teacher can also turn over responsibility for leading the Shared Reading to one of the students.
5. Following repeated readings, copies of the book are placed in the class library for independent reading during uninterrupted reading time. One copy is added to the listening center with other predictable books, while the Big Book can be available for small group reading in chorus (*see* Figure 10.15 for the complete Big Book cycle).
6. Shared Reading each day includes time for the introduction of a new predictable book and the rereading of an old favorite selected by students.
7. Shared Reading also includes time for students to extend from the new text in various ways. Teachers can write the extensions in the form of invitations on the board or on large sheets of paper. Invitations should regularly include student as well as teacher ideas: responding to the material through art, using the story pattern to write a personal version of the book, role-playing while parts of the text are read aloud (*see* Appendix A for a Predictable Book Text Set.), etc.

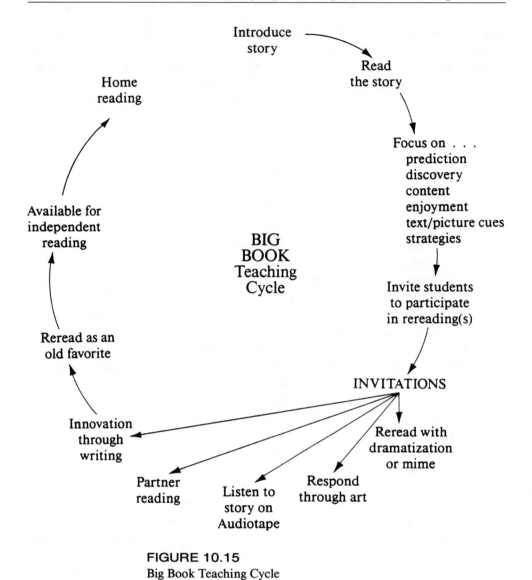

FIGURE 10.15
Big Book Teaching Cycle

Adapted from Andrea Butler.

REFERENCES

Butler, Andrea. *The Shared Book Experience.* Crystal Lake, I.L.: Rigby, 1988.
Holdaway, Don. *The Foundations of Literacy.* Portsmouth, N.H.: Heinemann, 1979.
_____"The Big Book Trend—A Discussion with Don Holdaway." *Language Arts,* 8: 815–821 (1982).

SPELLING EXPLORERS CIRCLE

GENERAL DESCRIPTION

On the way to standard grammar and spelling, learners have to explore the systems with which they are expected to become proficient. The traditional heavy emphasis on drill and rote learning is not supported by current research. Like other language systems, spelling is developmental and learners need time and support to take risks in investigating its complexities and rules within a whole writing context. As with early speech, approximations should be encouraged and valued.

Spelling Explorers gives students an opportunity to consider alternative spelling patterns before conventional spelling is introduced. Students have a chance to think through visual, phonetic, and morphemic (word) relationships. These explorations give them a thorough sense of the complexities and rule-governed nature of the English spelling system. This strategy assumes that students are engaged in all areas of the writing process—self-selection of topics, drafting, conferencing, revision, editing, and publishing—on a regular basis.

BASIC PROCEDURE

1. When writers have completed final drafts and are ready for editing, they should look through the piece to find words they feel are not spelled conventionally. These words are circled.
2. At the beginning of Writing Workshop the teacher asks who is ready for a Spelling Explorers Circle. Those writers bring their drafts with circled words and their Spelling Folders and come together in groups of three. Spelling Folders have several sheets of paper divided into four columns: 1, 2, Peers, Final Spelling.
3. Depending on the age and experience of the spellers, students choose from two to five circled words from their individual drafts.
4. Each speller has a blank form. The original spelling of each selected word (as it appears in the writer's draft) is written in the first column.

5. Each speller considers his or her selected words and writes one alternative spelling for each word in column two.
6. Each speller has the opportunity to introduce the words from their lists, saying what the words are, giving the context from the written piece, and explaining the alternate spellings for each word.
7. Each speller then passes the spelling form to the left, giving other writers in the group a chance to write a different version of the spelling of each word in the "Peers" column.
8. After the spelling form comes back to the owner, peers should explain the spelling decisions they wrote in column 3.
9. Column 4, labeled Final Spelling, is for the standard spelling of each word. Group members should agree on what they think is the conventional spelling of each word and then consult another resource for confirmation. Standard spelling may be confirmed by the teacher, a dictionary, or other print resources such as maps or trade books (*see* Figure 10.16 for an example from a fourth-grade Spelling Circle).
10. Words that are misspelled but do not go through a Spelling Circle can be corrected by the teacher, a parent, or student who is designated Chief Speller for the day or week.

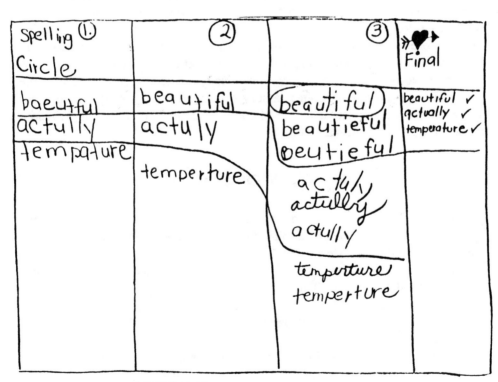

FIGURE 10.16
Example from a Fourth Grade Spelling
Circle

11. Teachers should bring their own invented spellings to Spelling Explorer Circles for group consideration on a regular basis.

PROCESS OBSERVATIONS

Teachers can sit in on Spelling Circles to observe the discussion and make notes about the hypotheses students are trying out as they consider alternative spelling patterns. Process observations can be used to develop specific Mini-lessons* on spelling and to track changes in spelling development.

REFERENCES

Spelling Explorers Circle was developed by Linda Crafton. Pat Miller field tested it and suggested modifications.

Information on spelling development can be found in the following references:

Beers, J. W., C. S. Beers, and K. Grant. "The Logic Behind Children's Spelling." *The Elementary School Journal,* vol. 19, 238–242 (1977).

Bissex, Glenda. GNYS AT WRK: *A Child Learns to Write and Read.* Cambridge, M.A. Harvard University Press, 1980.

Gentry, J. R. "An Analysis of Developmental Spelling in GNYS AT WRK." *The Reading Teacher,* vol. 36, 192–201 (1982).

Zutell, J. "Some Psycholinguistic Perspectives on Children's Spelling." *Language Arts,* vol. 55, 844–851 (1978).

TEXT SETS

GENERAL DESCRIPTION

Learning is primarily a search for connections. When readers read texts that are conceptually related in some way, they are encouraged to engage in an exploration of cognitive and linguistic ties. A reader's comprehension of each text is personalized and extended in qualitatively different ways than if they had read only one text (Crafton, 1980). When readers have the opportunity to read related materials they can come to see reading as a natural knowledge-generating activity in which one reading serves as experience for future engagements.

Text Sets are collections of conceptually related materials. While the name implies the use of only print materials, Text Sets should routinely include related non-print "texts" such as audiotapes, filmstrips, videotapes, and art. Teachers should be careful to include a wide range of reading levels in the Sets. While students always have a chance to discuss their interpretations and responses to one book in the Set, the emphasis here is on discovering commonalities and differences across conceptually related texts.

BASIC PROCEDURE

1. Teachers identify and begin to gather Text Sets that they think will appeal to their students.
   Text Set basic categories include:
   a. Genre Sets (mysteries, fairy tales)
   b. Topic Sets (tornados, U.S.S.R., economics, bears, war)
   c. Theme Sets (feelings, death, problems with parents and siblings)
   d. Content Area Sets (math, science, social studies)
   e. Alternate Versions Sets (same story, different version)
   f. Author Sets (Eric Carle, S. E. Hinton, C. S. Lewis)
   g. Illustrator Sets (Don and Audrey Wood, Tomie de Paola)
   h. Award-winning Sets (Caldecott, Newbery, Coretta Scott King)
   i. Series Sets (The Narnia Chronicles, The Dark Is Rising).
2. Teachers and students can choose any category with which to begin the school year. Author Sets, Series Sets, or Genre Sets work well at all grade levels and multiple copies are easy to obtain from libraries.
3. Book Talks* are given so that students can choose the books they will read (or listen to). Students can list their first and second choices and then groups of three to eight can be formed. Susan Cooper's *The Dark Is Rising* series, for example, has five books.
4. When the books have been read, groups should meet briefly to respond to and discuss interpretations. If books require a period of time to read, groups can meet briefly each day to talk before they continue to read. Reading Journals* can help facilitate discussions; younger students can simply write down one quote or idea from the book on a 3×5 card to bring up for discussion.

   Members of the group can respond or ask questions of one another. Students should have books available during discussion as the exchanges often require readers to go back to the text to reread or read aloud certain sections in order to clarify or underscore a point they are trying to make. Discussions may take one or several days.
5. Following the discussions, groups decide on dimensions from the books that highlight common elements. Charts can be developed which make comparisons across texts. Readers are also encouraged to uncover the differences in the plots, writing style of the author, major characters, and so on. Connections with texts outside of the Set should also be considered.
6. Because Text Sets offer many different directions for readers (exploration of strong themes running through the Set, reading other books in the Set, and others), Extensions from the Set should be offered as Invitations so that students can pursue in greater depth the connections that intrigue them.

Examples of Text Set Invitations can be found in Appendix A along with lists of books in each of the basic categories mentioned.

VARIATION

Carol Porter believes that starting the year with all students reading the same text helps to build a sense of community. She usually begins each year by asking her high school students to read one article and one book related to a topic, author, or genre Text Set. Her initial Text Set selection is based on recommendations from students in the previous year's classes. The Set she used most recently was built around the federal witness protection plan with *Don't Look Behind You* by Lois Duncan as a primary text in the Set.

Carol uses the whole class reading to introduce two process strategies, Say Something* and Written Conversation,* which her students use throughout the school year. Following their reading of the article, students are asked to read a related book as a class. Carol reads the first chapter aloud and then asks students to determine how many subsequent chapters they will read in what length of time. Four or five chapters at a time within two to three days seems to be the standard. After the designated chapters have been completed, students discuss their reading and then determine how many more chapters will be read. The cycle continues until the book is completed.

From the first book, Carol and her students identify themes, issues they have questions about, and lists of other related books (same author, topic, or genre). Carol and her students decide on a direction within the Set, and identify partners or small groups that have the same interests. As Carol and her students complete their extensions and explorations, Carol makes herself ready to help determine new groups and new directions within the Set.

REFERENCES

Creating Classrooms for Authors (Harste and Short with Burke, 1988) describes other Text Sets procedures. Other variations have been developed by Carolyn Burke, Dorothy Watson, and Lynn Rhodes.

TRAVELING JOURNALS

GENERAL DESCRIPTION

Writing is not just, or even primarily, a means of communication. It is a way to discover and explore new meanings and alternative perspectives. The Traveling

Journal is an opportunity for students or teachers to share their thinking and to make new connections through written interaction. The strategy can involve two or more people who have a common interest or experience but who do not have access to one another on a regular basis.

BASIC PROCEDURE I: TRAVELING JOURNAL FOR TEACHERS

1. Anyone can introduce the idea of the Traveling Journal by explaining its purpose: The journal is a place in which people can openly express feelings and ideas in an informal way. It is extremely useful for teachers who are exploring a new model of teaching/learning. It should be a nonthreatening forum for talking about questions, discomforts, breakthroughs, and feelings.
2. The group (self-selected or otherwise) should decide who will write in the journal. The principal and/or consultant may or may not be involved.
3. Some system for moving the journal from person to person should be devised. For example, everyone may decide that by the end of the day the person who has the journal must make an entry (or take a pass) and give it to the next person in line.
4. One person volunteers to write the first entry and then passes it to the next person.
5. No outside person reads the journal unless the entire group agrees.
6. The journal continues until everyone agrees to terminate.

BASIC PROCEDURE II: TRAVELING JOURNAL FOR READERS

This procedure is used with learners who are reading the same book/material but are in different classes.

1. The journal and its purpose are introduced to participating readers. As with the teacher's journal, it is a place to express feelings, explore ideas, ask questions, and make personal connections.
2. A special location in the classroom should be designated in which to keep the journal. It should be a place where all writers have easy access to it so they can comment on their reading or respond to others at various times in the day.
3. Students using the Traveling Journal must write in it at least once daily.
4. Because a long-distance relationship develops between or among the journal writers, each participant must write a final entry when the reading material is completed—some kind of last response, summary feeling, or good-bye to their fellow readers. Readers may want to reread all previous entries as a way of preparing for the final one.
5. Any one journal entry can be used as the beginning of an extended piece of writing to which journal partners can be asked to respond.

VARIATION

Learners in the same class (teachers and/or students) can use the Traveling Journal as a way of exchanging ideas about any experience. Journal writing can be started at the beginning of each time period the group is together with someone reminding the group periodically to keep the journal moving. Again, group members should have a chance to read through all of the journal entries as a culminating experience, with one last opportunity to respond.

REFERENCES

The Traveling Journal was developed by Jerome Harste. Carol Porter developed the version for students.

WORDLESS PICTURE BOOKS

GENERAL DESCRIPTION

Wordless Picture Books tell a whole story through pictures alone. The level of sophistication of these books has increased so significantly in the recent past that they are equally as appropriate for older students as younger ones. These books encourage prediction, writing, awareness of story structure, and use of background information.

BASIC PROCEDURE

1. The teacher gathers together a wide range of wordless picture books.
2. One book is selected and introduced to the entire class. As the teacher guides the class through the book, students are encouraged to predict the content of the book from the title, predict story events from one page or action to the next, and generate a reasonable story line from the pictures and what has come before.
3. The teacher allows time to go through the book several times, inviting students to tell different versions of the story as they go.
4. Students are asked to select one wordless book. This may be done with partners or small groups if there are not enough books to go around.
5. Students may talk through their personal versions of the selected books with a partner or simply review the books silently and then begin to write. The writing may occur on regular-sized paper (unlined for younger students) or on strips of paper taped or paper-clipped directly onto the pages of the book. The teacher circulates during the writing asking simple questions like: "How's your story going?" Or "What are you going to write next?"

Spelling questions should be handled by encouraging students to spell words their own way or by encouraging them to think about what the words *look* like, as well as what sounds they hear. Students should know that they can temporarily leave a line or space to represent a whole word or any part of it as they are writing.

6. After they are completed, stories should be shared and celebrated in whole or small groups.
7. After different students have written alternative versions of the same wordless book, teachers highlight the varied decisions the student authors made.

PROCESS OBSERVATIONS

Teachers can use students' stories of Wordless Picture Books to observe and enhance students' understandings of story structure development.

WRITING FOLDERS

GENERAL DESCRIPTION

When students are immersed in reading and writing, they need organizational tools to keep track of their progress and decision-making. Writing Folders are an efficient, student-centered way of handling the accumulation of writing that occurs when students write on a regular basis.

FIGURE 10.17
Initial Topics List of a Third-grade Writer

BASIC PROCEDURE

1. Writers are given two writing folders at the beginning of the school year. Folders are of different colors: one color for current writing, the other for past writing.

   The folder for current writing includes a Topics List on the inside front cover (*see* Figure 10.17), and a "Strategies I Use" sheet on the inside back cover. The second folder has a sheet on the front indicating the title of each piece, final draft date, and published? yes or no with a place for the date of publication.

2. At the beginning of Writing Workshop students retrieve their current Writing Folders from a box where they are stored during nonwriting time. Folders are returned there at the end of writing time. Final draft pieces are transferred to the second Writing Folder with all drafts stapled together. Students periodically consider the accumulated pieces (usually every three or four) for publication.

3. At the end of each grading period or two to three times a year, students have the opportunity to consider all the writing they have completed and to choose one piece for inclusion in their Portfolios.*

4. Teachers should use Writing Folders during parent conferences and also to consider students' developing strengths when narrative inserts for report cards are written.

PROCESS OBSERVATIONS

Systematically throughout the year Writing Workshop time is used for student evaluation of their writings. Accumulated pieces are spread out so students can consider and try to track changes in their writing processes. To give the evaluation focus, open-ended questions can be developed or forms indicating salient dimensions of writing process can be used to guide the observations (*see* Figure 10.18).

REFERENCES

The two-folder system was developed by Kathleen Visovatti. Other descriptions of the use of Writing Folders can be found in these books:

Calkins, Lucy M. *The Art of Teaching Writing*. Portsmouth, N.H.: Heinemann, 1986.

Graves, Donald. *Writing: Teachers and Children at Work*. Portsmouth, N.H.: Heinemann, 1983.

Harste, Jerome, and Kathy Short and Carolyn Burke. *Creating Classrooms for Authors*. Portsmouth, N.H.: Heinemann, 1988.

WRITTEN CONVERSATION

GENERAL DESCRIPTION

Even very young children bring a strong oral language foundation to early written language experiences. While speech and writing differ, the dialogic nature of oral language can support the move to written language as an interactive exchange between reader and author. Written Conversation is an informal, nonthreatening way to encourage writing and meaning exploration. When it's sometimes difficult

As you look at your writing, consider the following:

	Piece 1	Piece 2	Piece 3	Piece 4

AUDIENCE

Who did I have in mind as I wrote this piece?

To what degree was I aware of an audience for my writing?

REVISION

How often did I revise?

What kinds of revisions did I have in this piece?

INVOLVEMENT

How much of myself did I give to this writing?

DISCOVERIES

What did I discover about myself or my writing process while working on this piece?

TOPIC SELECTION

Where did I get the idea for this piece?

RISK-TAKING

What new things did I try while writing this piece?

COLLABORATION

Did I talk to others as I wrote?

What impact did others have on this piece?

FIGURE 10.18
Areas of Growth to Consider across Pieces
of Writing

to find ways to give all learners a voice, Written Conversation can keep participants actively involved. Written Conversation is valuable in a number of ways:

1. with reluctant and inexperienced writers,
2. as a way of thinking through reading material prior to a whole group discussion,
3. to brainstorm and explore topics before first draft writing,
4. for content area exchanges,
5. as a getting-to-know you procedure at the beginning of school.

BASIC PROCEDURE

1. Teachers introduce the strategy by choosing a student to participate in a public Written Conversation. An overhead projector works well for this first step.
2. The teacher explains to the class that he or she and the student are going to have a conversation in writing. The one rule for the discussion is that neither person can talk during the exchange—everything must be written down.
3. The conversation should start with an open-ended question or statement that calls for more than a "yes" or "no" response. Teachers should be careful to make exchanges genuine, using the same kind of informal tone and content characteristic of speech. Teachers need to plan the opening comments carefully, as students will follow their leads. The initial and follow-up demonstrations can help to show the potential range for the strategy.
4. Following the demonstration students and teacher spend a few minutes reflecting on the conversation. Students can be asked what they noticed during the conversation, what questions and comments they thought were good and why and how they might have steered the conversation in a different direction. Teachers discuss the dead-end problem of many yes and no type of questions. Good open-ended questions can be brainstormed and posted during early use of the strategy.
5. Following the discussion class members pair up to try Written Conversation. Teachers remind them of the rule about no talking (with the exception of very young children or others who may not be able to read the writing). If everyone has a partner, the teacher can move around the room to monitor the progress of the conversations, helping students to think through better quality questions and comments if the conversation has stopped.
6. After five to ten minutes of writing the teacher asks the class to reflect again on the strategy—what happened, what did they learn from it, and when did they think the procedure might be useful.

PROCESS OBSERVATIONS

When teachers observe students using Written Conversation they can watch for a number of things:

■ the reading/writing connection;
■ in-process revision;
■ reading, rereading, and spelling strategies.

If Written Conversation is used to discuss reading material, literature or otherwise, teachers can observe how the participants are extending and elaborating from the text and each others' interpretations.

REFERENCES

Written Conversation was developed by Carolyn Burke.

First Days,
First Weeks

During the first days and weeks of any school year, teachers lay a tenuous foundation that either carries them solidly through the rest of the year or cracks quickly needing repair after repair. In those first critical days together you are learning about your students and they are learning what you value. I asked my co-writers to describe their initial time with students at the beginning of a new academic year. Many of them chose to describe their before-year time, knowing that the energy put into the curriculum before students walk in the door makes a big difference. Even though their descriptions and beginnings are quite different, because they share a whole language perspective you'll see many things in common. Remember, these are not final versions. Most likely, they will change next year and the year after.

PAT RIORDAN: FIRST DAYS IN FIRST GRADE

"Hey, I KNOW this poem! My mom told me it!" Six-year-old Angelica's face lights up as our class shares a favorite Mother Goose rhyme. She eagerly chimes in, happy for the opportunity to connect with a favorite experience and share it with her classmates. This is what our classroom is all about—making those kinds of connections. It is a collaborative effort to create a supportive environment where every child can bring his or her world to our classroom so that together we can create the tools we need to make sense of the world outside of the classroom. We are one of the most culturally diverse classes in the city and my students bring a background that is truly rich in variety and culture. The first weeks of school are especially important in making these connections so that the class gets a sense of

what school is going to be about—learning about, making sense of the world that surrounds them.

GETTING STARTED

Beginning the year with a Mother Goose unit has proved to be a natural and wonderful way for my students to start making connections. The familiarity of the rhymes instantly creates a common bond and encourages a keen interest in hearing the rhymes again and again as we explore them in many different ways.

This particular theme is easily integrated into many different content areas. We read from the many different Mother Goose authors (*see* Appendix A for Mother Goose Text Set), discuss the characters and interpret their role, interview characters, talk about the colorful language, and reflect on the historical significance of the rhymes. We learn new words and their meanings, discuss a rhyme's meaning, act out events, create recipes using math concepts, play charades, change endings, and illustrate some of the rhymes on large pieces of butcher paper that are then hung all around the room for the children to read. I write out some of their favorites in a blank book and have them each illustrate a page. This makes one of our first class books. The illustrated rhymes are a natural tool to help students develop prediction strategies, build sight vocabulary, and learn the conventions of print. The familiarity and predictability of the rhymes support children's very early attempts to read and help them gain confidence as readers and risk-takers. Mother Goose rhymes allow children lots of opportunities to express themselves orally, to be language users. The rhymes helped me see that kids love language! It is language that creates learning, and the more opportunities my students have to use language, the more real learning is going on.

We also start off the year taking a closer look at the environmental print that surrounds us. I bring in many boxes and packages that would be familiar to the children, such as toothpaste cartons, milk, cookies, cereal, and so on, and ask what the labels say, how they know that, and what they expect to find in the packages. They are eager to make predictions, and once again are excited to make connections to their home lives. I encourage them to read all the print in the cabinets and refrigerator at home.

By this time they have begun to get a very strong sense of how print functions in their lives. When we have investigated all the print in our home and school environments, we read *Signs* (Goor and Goor, 1983). We take a walk around our neighborhood with fourth-grade partners and look at all the print. We notice the familiar signs for gas stations, restaurants, and streets. But we also take a look at some that may be unfamiliar: traffic signs, signs for businesses and schools. We talk about what purpose the signs serve, and we take pictures of many of them. When the prints are developed, we come together and make some further connections. These are put on a bulletin board and eventually become part of an environmental print book.

Having a Message Board* in our classroom provides additional opportunities for children to become aware of the conventions of print and get a better sense of the reading/writing connection. I initially use the Board to communicate with the whole class, but then move toward individual messages. I also post newspaper advertisements of neighborhood happenings, exciting shows, and other events, and encourage the children to jot down information and phone numbers if necessary. I also provide "Post-It" notes for them to use to remind themselves to return a forgotten book or other necessary item.

I have learned from my students that they will usually choose to read books they feel connected to in some way (for example, a book that their parents, teacher, or friends have read to them). Our room is filled with good literature, carefully

* All asterisks throughout the book refer the reader to Chapter 10 where full strategy descriptions can be found.

chosen, representing many different genres. I group many of the books in sets and keep them in small plastic baskets around the room with a label on its front indicating what the set is about. Right now, I have sets on Folk Tales, Fairy Tales, Humor, Rhymes, Bears, Animals—Fiction, Animals—Nonfiction, History, and People. In addition, I have sets of magazines—*National Wildlife, Nature,* and *Zoo Books.* Many of the books are predictable, with strong patterns, rhymes, and simple story lines such as *It Looked Like Spilt Milk* (Shaw, 1947) or *The Old Woman Who Swallowed a Fly* (Hawkins, 1987). But many are sophisticated literature such as *Wolf Story* (McCleery, 1947) to which they are first exposed during my daily afternoon read-aloud time. From the beginning they are comfortable with either kind of book because they have some experience to bring to the reading and because they know that I will encourage all of their efforts to read independently.

THE FIRST WEEKS

During these first weeks I give lots of Book Talks* and try to entice them with lots of predictable books, poems, and songs to read. Later, they will use my demonstrations to do their own Book Talks. When there is time for them to choose their books, these are often related to a particular theme we are studying. For example, during a Bears theme, as we begin the day with our language session, we learn poems about bears, sing songs about bears, recite chants and jingles, and create our own poetry and rhyme. The children also see many of these items written on chart paper, but they are especially fond of seeing their own language and stories written and put into books. One of the first writing experiences we have is borrowed from Bill Martin Jr.'s pattern in *Brown Bear, Brown Bear* (1983). We read the story together many times, and the children quickly become familiar with its rhyme and pattern.

After our language session time we begin an hour of Reading Workshop. We usually begin by reading an "old favorite," which we take turns choosing. A new story is introduced to the whole group every few days. This new story may be either a Big Book or be related to a current theme or Text Set* with which we are involved. This part of Reading Workshop provides opportunities for Mini-lessons,* strategy development, and Book Extensions.* The second half of Reading Workshop is a thirty-minute free choice reading time we call "Shared Reading,"* when students read with a partner(s). They might choose to hear a favorite story at the Listening Center, retell a story with either characters they've made or flannelboard characters in the story corner, or they might choose to read a favorite song or poem from a wall chart. They often choose to come together in a small group to discuss a book in a literature circle.

Another popular choice is a song-to-read book. These kinds of books are particularly motivating for learning to read, and the children really feel comfortable with them. Raffi and Tom Glazer have published some of their favorites, and it seems the ones we create as a class never get put down! During the first few weeks of school I carefully introduce their options during Shared Reading.* After about a month students move about the room making choice after choice totally independent from me.

During this Reading Workshop time I usually invite anyone who wants to read with me to do so. I often start with a small group that grows larger and larger as more and more people move from independent reading to community sharing. At this time I try to demonstrate proficient reading strategies. For example, I encourage them to predict at points where I leave off words or phrases. I do think-alouds which include wondering about meanings or miscues I have made. Or I highlight sound-symbol relationships that are salient in a Big Book like *Jump, Frog, Jump* (Kalan, 1981).

Following Reading Workshop is a one-hour Writing Workshop. Each student has a writing folder; and we move toward personal topic selection early in the year. We spend a lot of time brainstorming topics. I demonstrate by thinking of topics I can comfortably share with my students. Sometime I bring in a Me Box* with personal items I can talk about, and then invite them to bring their own collection of treasures. This strategy gives students potential topics for weeks. Borrowing the pattern of another author's book is a wonderful way to get kids writing early. Even the most reticent writers can develop a narrative of their own by borrowing a book's pattern. One of the best I have found is *Oh, Bother!* (Scarffe, 1986)—the children punch holes in their books and create their own pictures and text around the hole; for example, "There's a hole in my nose." Other

books with excellent patterns include the *Jesse Bear* (Carlstrom, 1986) books and Frank Asch books such as *Happy Birthday, Moon* (Asch, 1982).

We have a Writing Center with many different kinds of paper, markers, staples, and other materials children can use to make books and write letters or any other kinds of messages. However, the most important tool I can provide is time. My students count on having a large block of predictable time each day for Writing Workshop. Having an attentive and responsive audience to listen and respond to their writing is critical, so we usually begin and end each Writing Workshop with a group sharing of several pieces, either completed or still in process. This allows me the opportunity to make them aware of appropriate responses and questions that help the author, such as: "I wonder about . . . Why did . . . and I'm a little unsure about . . ."

I am concerned about integrating the language arts with content area learning and have found that one of the best ways to do this is to have some kind of "critter" in the classroom at all times. This year we started with a monarch species of caterpillar that one student, Kate, had been given by her grandmother. We built a whole curriculum around this tiny creature! We explored its world through careful observations, journal entries, books, and magazines. We discovered its life cycle as we crowded around its big glass jar day after day to watch the amazing transformation from caterpillar to butterfly. After reading Eric Carle's *The Very Hungry Caterpillar* (1979) we created our own versions of the book.

One day we were watching the caterpillar eat and eat and eat. Sheldon called out: "Look, Ms. Riordan, it's just like the book— he's *still* hungry!" I asked them where they thought Eric Carle got the idea for his book. The overwhelming response was, "He must have had a caterpillar too!"

We do the things that readers and writers do when they are no longer in a first-grade classroom—or any classroom.

KATHLEEN VISOVATTI: ESTABLISHING A FEELING OF BELONGING IN SECOND GRADE

Very quickly, and for the entire year, I want my students to feel that the classroom, like the learning, belongs to them. In August, before school starts, I send a letter home to my new students and their parents (*see* Figures 11.1 and 11.2). I want to give them a feeling of what to expect; and I want them to begin to think of their contributions to the classroom and the curriculum.

Before students arrive, I spend time arranging the classroom. From the beginning I want it to show that I respect each of them as individuals, while I also value collaborative efforts. The desks are arranged in a large square around a rug that is used as a central meeting area so that all students face one another. The room is organized so that large groups, small groups, and pairs have places to meet. There is a rocking chair and a sofa, a desk in the writing supplies area, a conference table that seats eight, a teepee for individual reading, and a private place with a desk

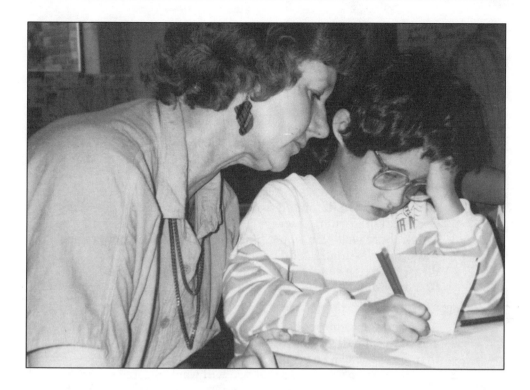

and chair for those times when learning can only happen alone. There is a bulletin board reserved for Special Person of the Week, with a counter close by to display photographs and favorite possessions; the cupboards and shelves are filled with books and art supplies and math manipulatives and science equipment—all easily accessible to the children. The room arrangement encourages independence and self-reliance. Student input is invited by an Interest Table that holds things brought from home, a Message Board* for information of interest to the whole class, and an Interest Clubs* bulletin board.

GETTING STARTED

I meet students outside the building that first day as I do every day of the school year. I want to make eye contact with each one and to greet them as they come in to school. I learn their names within minutes of the start of school (the summer letters give me a head start). When the children enter the room they have three blank name tags on their desks. At my request they write their names on all three and tape one to their new desks—I explain that we will use the others later in the day. I tell them that throughout the day we will do lots of reading, writing, speaking, and listening, and that's why the room is arranged in a certain way. I give them a complete tour of the room, highlighting the rug where we will meet to talk and listen, the inviting places to sit and read, the cardboard post office where

August 1, 19—

Dear <u>Child's Name</u>,

I am so glad you are going to be in my second grade classroom. I am looking forward to seeing you on the first day of school. I have already begun to make plans for our good times together. You can do some things to get ready, too.

Here they are:

1. Think about what you would like to learn about in second grade. We will have a meeting the first day of school to find out what everyone is interested in studying.
2. Think about what you already know how to do that you could help others learn. In our classroom everyone will help everyone else. We will learn together.
3. Think about what you would like to learn how to do better and ways your classmates and I could help you.
4. Please bring the supplies listed on the enclosed sheet the very first day. You will need them.

Here are some of the things I have done:

1. Arranged the room so that you will have your own special space and so that small groups can meet to work on projects and so that the whole class can gather together for meetings.
2. Made the room inviting so that you will want to come in and get involved. There is a lot to look at, a lot to do. You're welcome to brings things for the room, too.
3. Put up my Special Person of the Week display. I will be the first Special Person of the Week to give you an idea of what it's like. Your turn will be in alphabetical order. I have enclosed a list, so you'll know your week. We'll take turns bringing in things that are important to us and drawings or photos of our families. There is a special bulletin board and counter just for this in the room.
4. Thought about what second graders know how to do and what they're interested in and collected some materials that might be useful.

Have a good rest of the summer. I'll meet you outside the front entrance at 8:45 on Tuesday, September _____. Please line up where 116 is painted on the cement. That's our room number. (Be sure to know your bus number too. Maybe you should write it down in your spiral notebook!)

Yours truly,

Mrs. Visovatti

FIGURE 11.1
Teacher Letter Sent to Students Before
School Starts

August 1, 19—

Dear Parents,

I am looking forward to second grade with your child. As I wrote in the letter to your son/daughter (enclosed). I have already begun to make plans for our times together. Please help your child make his/her preparations as specified in the letter.

If you don't know already, you can probably tell from my letter to your child, that I believe in encouraging students to explore topics of interest to them and in the process, they will learn the necessary skills. We will "live" rather than "cover" the curriculum. This kind of learning environment is often called the whole language approach or integrated or literature-based curriculum. Reading, writing, speaking and listening are interconnected and are used as tools of learning in all subject areas.

I have been involved in education for over 20 years and have never been more optimistic about the possibilities for meaningful reform of public schooling as I am now. I travel about the country giving presentations on this approach and spread the word locally by teaching at National College each term. If you would like to learn more, please call me to set a date for a conference. Also, you are most welcome to visit anytime. In fact, you will have an opportunity to sign up as a volunteer to help in the classroom on a weekly basis at the fall Open House. Writing aides are needed Tuesday–Friday from 9:15–10:15, literature circle discussion leaders Monday–Friday from 10:30–11:30, Math helpers Monday–Friday from 1:00–2:00, and Science and Social Studies Interest Clubs facilitators at various times in the afternoons. Some training will be necessary prior to working in the classroom. If you're interested, do call me at school to find out more.

Meanwhile, I am eagerly awaiting the start of school, so that your child and I can get to know one another and begin a year of learning together in joyful, natural ways.

Yours truly,

Kathleen Visovatti

FIGURE 11.2
Teacher Letter Sent to Parents before School
Starts

we will send and receive letters, and the writing area where they can write, get supplies and confer with one another. When I talk about the post office, I ask them to put their second name tags on one of the mail slots.

There is a blank sheet of paper on each desk for a self-portrait. Students spend time drawing themselves, and when they are finished, they go out into the hall, find a coat hook they want to claim as their own for the year, and put the picture underneath. After pictures are completed and displayed, I take a Polaroid picture of each student, which is glued onto a sheet of lined paper. They then write their first impressions of second grade on this sheet.

Throughout the year I take pictures of each child on special occasions that they then write about. At the close of the school year everyone takes home the captioned pictures as a photo album of second grade. A pack of film is one item on the required supplies list sent home with the summer letter.

All this time the students have noticed and wondered about large puzzle pieces —one on each desktop. Each student brings a piece to the rug and when everyone has contributed one part of the whole, the puzzle reads: "We are a group. We cooperate. We learn together." The completed puzzle is put on the back wall of the room and stays there for the rest of the year. It's referred to whenever there is dissension or when we need to be reminded that we are a cooperating group.

On one room door there is a daily schedule. Ideally, I wouldn't want any kind of formal division for the day, and, as the year moves along, the divisions often become blurred as we bring our afternoon science and social studies time into our morning Reading/Writing workshops. I explain our schedule the first day. We start to go through it by showing the big blocks of time we will use for Reading and Writing Workshop. I describe how math time will be spent in a variety of hands-on activities, computer games, collaborative problem-solving (many related to themes or topics we are exploring), and that they will work individually at their own pace—for some, this relieves a lot of anxiety. When we get to science and social studies, I give the definitions we use for the year. Science is defined as the way to learn about the world around us by asking questions; and social studies is defined as finding out the many ways people are alike or different.

After we review the daily schedule I gather them around me for our first day read-aloud, and explain that I will read to them every day, several times a day. To start, I choose the biggest Big Book I can find, *What Do You Do with a Kangaroo?* (Mayer, 1973) and the smallest book, *The Teeny Tiny Woman* (Seuling, 1976). I let students know that sometimes we will read Big Books, sometimes little books, and sometimes books of in between size. Then we talk about the favorites, and I ask them if they have noticed any of these in our room. If not, I ask them to bring in their books. We talk about sustained silent reading, what it is and how they will have time to themselves each day to read anything they choose.

The second day we begin to follow our daily schedule. We go through class business, which includes establishing rules, volunteering for class jobs, such as taking attendance and keeping the bookshelves neat. At 9:00 we start our first Writing Workshop. I ask how many are still working on their first impressions of second grade and let them know that they should finish that first. I remind the whole class of the post office, and tell them that they are free to write letters during this time. I ask them what rules we might need for the post office, and we discuss the importance of signing all correspondence, not hurting feelings, and how many times a day a person should deliver letters. Then I introduce Dialogue Journals.* I explain that this is a special place in which they can write to me, and that I will write back as often as they write but that I would like at least two sentences a week. I walk around with the journals—various colored folders with blank, lined paper inside—and ask them to choose one. I tell them that they may write anything they want in these journals and that I will never, ever grade them. I stress that they needn't worry about spelling or punctuation or anything else except what they want to say to me. If I can't read what they have written, I'll be sure to come and ask them to read to me. When they are ready for a response, they put their journals in the open cardboard file box in the writing area. On this second day of school they already have lots of different writing possibilities from which to choose.

After they start writing, there are still the inevitable questions about spelling. I tell them that I won't ever spell words for them, that spelling is part of the job of writing and they should just spell a word the way it sounds and/or looks. They are convinced very quickly that I'm firm about not taking the responsibility for their spelling. Just as quickly, they start taking risks. But I'm also quick to assure them that those things that will be publicly shared, like the first impressions pieces and published stories, need to be spelled correctly with standard punctuation, and that I will help them when they are at that point. As they are writing, I walk around the room offering words of encouragement and asking questions to help keep them going—these are my first content conferences. When students indicate they are finished with their writing, I ask them to reread the piece, either to me or to themselves or to a neighbor to make sure it makes sense. Then I ask them to reread a second time to pay attention to capitals, punctuation, and spelling—this is my first editing conference. I'm never without my trusty post-its (I don't write directly on their drafts), writing correct spellings when they are at that point and reminding them about missed punctuation. They start their personal spelling folders the second or third week of school.

Toward the end of the first week we begin to talk about more extended writing —stories and exposition. We talk about the possibilities: personal experiences, things they know about, things they wish would happen to them or those that never could. As a class we brainstorm an incredibly long list of topics, and from our collection of narrative and expository ideas they begin an individual topics sheet. I assure them that just because they put a topic on the sheet it doesn't mean they have to write about it. It does mean they will never be stuck for a subject. The topics sheets change all during the year; old ones go into Portfolios* so writers can see the range and change in focus of their writing ideas. The topics sheet goes into a light blue folder reserved for works in progress. On that day I also give each child a dark blue folder for finished work. That folder has a sheet on the inside cover which reads: "Pieces I have Written."

When students start to write their first extended pieces, usually stories, they begin talking to each other spontaneously. I encourage this by doing it myself. At the end of our first uninterrupted block of writing time I ask for volunteers to share what they have written. We celebrate everyone's writing with oohs and aahs and applause. The next day we review the writing choices we now have in place during Writing Workshop time: journals, letters, extended writing. When stories are completed, they go into the dark blue folder until the children have accumulated four. At that time they may choose one to publish. The other stories go into a cumulative folder that's kept in a common file in the Writing Area so they have access to it at any time. Four times a year students go through their writing and arrange it on a scale from what they like best to what they like least. They then choose pieces that will go into their Portfolios.*

Reading Workshop begins with a Reading History (*see* Figure 11.3). I want to get to know them as readers in every way that I can, and I've found that their instructional histories let me know how they view the process of reading and themselves as readers.

We go over the forms together, and then I distribute their Reading Journals.* The reading history is the first entry in these journals. After they finish writing, we share a few pieces and then I explain the primary use of the journal. I tell them

Reading is ⎯⎯⎯⎯⎯⎯⎯⎯⎯
⎯⎯⎯⎯⎯⎯⎯⎯⎯
⎯⎯⎯⎯⎯⎯⎯⎯⎯

I like to read ⎯⎯⎯⎯⎯⎯⎯⎯⎯⎯⎯⎯⎯⎯⎯⎯⎯⎯⎯⎯⎯

The best book I ever read is

⎯⎯⎯⎯⎯⎯⎯⎯⎯⎯⎯⎯⎯⎯⎯⎯⎯⎯⎯⎯⎯⎯⎯⎯⎯⎯

Right now I am reading the book

⎯⎯⎯⎯⎯⎯⎯⎯⎯⎯⎯⎯⎯⎯⎯⎯⎯⎯⎯⎯⎯⎯⎯⎯⎯⎯

The book I loved when I was little is

⎯⎯⎯⎯⎯⎯⎯⎯⎯⎯⎯⎯⎯⎯⎯⎯⎯⎯⎯⎯⎯⎯⎯⎯⎯⎯

My favorite time to read is ⎯⎯⎯⎯⎯⎯⎯⎯⎯⎯⎯⎯⎯⎯⎯⎯

My favorite place to read is ⎯⎯⎯⎯⎯⎯⎯⎯⎯⎯⎯⎯⎯⎯⎯⎯

I learned to read by ⎯⎯⎯⎯⎯⎯⎯⎯⎯⎯⎯⎯⎯⎯⎯⎯⎯⎯

⎯⎯⎯⎯⎯⎯⎯⎯⎯⎯⎯⎯⎯⎯⎯⎯⎯⎯⎯⎯⎯⎯⎯⎯⎯⎯

⎯⎯⎯⎯⎯⎯⎯⎯⎯⎯⎯⎯⎯⎯⎯⎯⎯⎯⎯⎯⎯⎯⎯⎯⎯⎯

⎯⎯⎯⎯⎯⎯⎯⎯⎯⎯⎯⎯⎯⎯⎯⎯⎯⎯⎯⎯⎯⎯⎯⎯⎯⎯

FIGURE 11.3
My Reading History

that for every book they read, I would like a response. The responses can occur before, during, or after reading, or at all three points. When I look at these journals periodically, I can see the kinds of responses they are giving—for example, predicting before, asking questions during, and stating opinions after. If I see any areas that are not represented, I talk to students informally about the extended strategies that readers use, and ask them to try a few new ones. Their experiences with responding to text actually starts with a Text Set* on reading I introduce on the second or third day of school (*see* Appendix A). As I begin to read aloud from one of the books in the set, I encourage predicting from the title, connecting to personal experience, and summarizing and expressing opinions after I finish. We talk about the kinds of reading experiences they've had—what they remember about learning to read, reading with their parents, and so on. All this leads into discussions of favorite books, and I encourage them to bring them to class. The very next day I'm often deluged by books. That kind of sharing goes on all year with a shift in emphasis from their favorites to themes we are exploring and books that support each other's interests or that they simply think a classmate will enjoy. If there is time, I introduce them to my set of predictable books (*see* Appendix A). They can quickly see that these are for independent reading. During our first weeks together I read these aloud and add them to our set from which to choose during Sustained Silent Reading (SSR).

During math time we count out loud to one hundred and write these numbers so I can get a baseline sense of what they know. (I find out about their problem-solving abilities as we actually attempt some simple solutions during the first weeks.) I have a set of math books with numbers and about numbers (*see* Appendix A) and I find that they are a great way to develop, solidify, and extend math concepts. Once introduced, these books are also available during SSR. I encourage certain students to read the books from time to time as a way of strengthening concepts when I have observed they need additional experience. I invite them to bring their own books in which there is anything related to math. We wrap up math for the second day with free exploration of manipulatives patterned after "Mathematics Their Way" (Center for Innovation in Education, 1988).

I started using Interest Clubs* this year as a way of organizing our block of afternoon science time, and making this area of study more student-centered than it had been in the past. Early in the first week we gather on the rug, with science books in our laps, and simply look and talk our way through the texts. Once we have an idea of what is available, even if it isn't a major section represented in the book, we talk about the interest groups we would like to start. I explain that these groups come together during science time to do research, read, write, discuss, and eventually share what they learn about their topics. Once a club has met their goals, they disband and start a new club or join an existing one. Our first Interest Clubs this year were Endangered Species, Doctors, and Sports.

We begin social studies each year with a focus on ourselves. We draw pictures of our families and bring in math by comparing the number of people in each family. These pictures are put up on one of the walls, one on top of the other in a kind of picture graph. This activity kicks off an extended strategy called Family Histories,* which covers many months and includes interviews with parents, grandparents, and siblings. It culminates in a family feast at which families bring favorite ethnic dishes and are presented with precious family albums.

While my basic schedule remains the same throughout the year, my students often bring the afternoon content areas into morning activities. For example, they read and write about science and social studies and math during Reading/Writing workshop. Reading and writing are not items to study in my classroom; they are tools to help my students explore the questions and topics that interest them. Because of my commitment to using language to learn, we begin to think about reading and writing as personal processes the first week of school. As we do this, we develop a sense of community, a sense of confidence, a base for literacy, and a sense of ourselves as individuals.

REFLECTING ON OUR FIRST WEEK TOGETHER

At the end of our first week, usually a Friday, we brainstorm all the things that have happened to us during the week. I announce that each Friday we will spend time reflecting on what we have done, what we have learned, and the activities that were most important to us, so we can capture it all in a class newspaper. I have three purposes for our weekly communication:

1. It encourages students to revisit their learning;
2. It keeps parents in touch with classroom activities;
3. It keeps me in touch with what is important to the kids—how they see the learning that is going on in the classroom.

The parent contact is especially critical in my classroom because student "work" usually stays in the room. Students are always rushing back in to get forgotten newspapers on Friday afternoon because "My mom always looks for it in my backpack."

I have learned to create our Friday newspaper on the spot so that it is written, duplicated, and ready to go home in a couple of hours. First we brainstorm the important events of the week. As they are listed on the board, I put the person's name who mentioned it beside the idea—then I know who to interview for that news item. When everyone is involved in Writing Workshop, I walk around the room and talk to individuals, asking them to expand on what they had said earlier. Fridays are the one day I don't schedule writing conferences or do my own writing, so I can give the newspaper my full attention. Because most of the newspaper is done by hand, I simply design the layout as I go (*see* Chapter 8 for an example of Kathleen's newspaper). I make sure that each child's name is mentioned at least once, commission a few pictures to be drawn, and add my own announcements and highlights. When the students are in gym class, I go down to the office to run the newspaper off and have it waiting when students return.

When I stop and think about our first days and weeks together, I'm amazed at how much is accomplished so quickly—not so much in terms of visible product but with the overall feeling within the group. I want students to feel good about being in school and about being with me. We end our first days comfortable and excited about each other and about learning.

PAT MILLER: EXPERTS IN THE THIRD/FOURTH GRADE

I know what strikes students most strongly that first day of school is the uncommon appearance of the room. The large old desks are not in rows, but are grouped in small clusters of four (referred to as pods). I have a desk at one pod for my participant role and use my teacher desk, which is off to one side, for consulting. I make sure the room is print rich and packed with learning materials at various stations.

My fourth-graders were with me the year before; the third-graders, however, are new. The first days and weeks in my classroom are a great opportunity for me to draw on the older students' strengths and familiarity with the kind of student-directed curriculum I try to set up. My classroom is a place that invites active investigation. In my blueprint for future days and months, students will engage in continual exploration of and reporting on their environment. While I strive for an

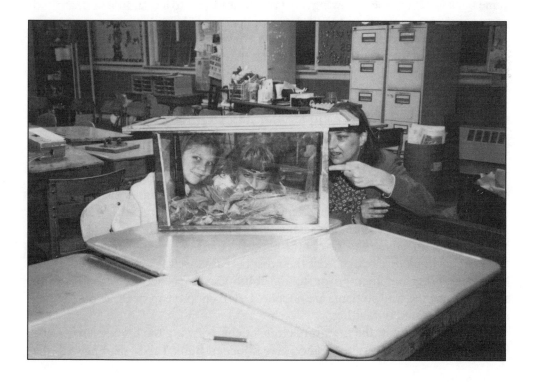

integrated curriculum with content area questions and explorations flowing out of themes and topics, I start with stations so that students can get a sense of the differences in areas of knowledge. I have a science station, art station, library station, and social studies station. Each has an abundant supply of materials and hands-on equipment.

On the first day, I issue written invitations to each student and hand them out as students enter the room. The invitation allows no more than two or three students at each station for fifteen minutes. The basic idea is just to get students familiar with personal and collaborative exploration and the kinds of questions scientists, social scientists, artists, mathmeticians, authors, and others might ask.

I plan for new students to be at stations with returning students. Sergio, for example, shows Michael the writing station. They sit down to look at some of the published work from last year and talk about the process that led to the final products. Harry asks for a new invitation. After watching two veteran students weigh their lunches on the balance scales at the math station, Harry is ready to join two other students at the listening station. (I have to remind one of the lunch weighers that he cannot eat part of his food to change the weight of his lunch!)

Students may ask for new invitations at any time, and I try to monitor their movement. When there is a lot of talk and excitement at any one station, I visit to share the discovery. After a period of time I call the group together for a discussion of what they have noticed and what questions they had at the different stations. I use their questions as a springboard to talk about how our curriculum will be built around their questions and their existing areas of expertise. When we come back to school the following day I introduce them to a schedule built around personal choice, inquiry, and their developing areas of knowledge.

There are three curricular components that are introduced and highlighted during the first weeks of school: Reading Workshop, Writing Workshop, and Expert Demonstrations.

READING WORKSHOP

The forty-five minute Reading Workshop is the first period scheduled each day. The first days at the beginning of the year are centered on the ins and outs of choosing books. We meet in the classroom library corner and begin with the returning students giving new students the grand tour. Returning students are familiar with most of the books, having selected and organized many of the titles housed there. Together they look at the paperback mysteries on the spinning rack; take hardcover picture books from their display case; browse in the poetry and the humor sections; and then go on to the folktales, scary books, and adventure stories. Along the way students are encouraged to choose two or three books they might be interested in reading.

When we regroup in the literature circle of chairs facing the library corner, the fourth-grade returning students and I give informal Book Talks* dealing with the

selections laid before us. Later in the year we will give more formal, creative talks on our favorite stories. We tell personal anecdotes about the books which always include the authors Beverly Cleary, Judy Blume, Laura Ingalls Wilder, William Steig, Roald Dahl, and all the Maurice Sendak selections. Besides our shared experiences with the books, the selection is made easier by referring to our book rating cards. These 3 x 5 index cards are kept in a metal filing box in the library corner. The cards have the titles of most of our library books with the ratings (one to five stars) and opinions of all my past students.

Some students have more trouble making their initial selections than others, and I take extra time to make sure they all make satisfying choices. If needed, we share our personal selection strategies: Toby is only interested in sports and usually looks at the cover and title; Jeff reads the insert description of the plot looking for adventure; Jay jumps right in and reads the first page to see if there is an exciting beginning; I talk about how I look in the front of the book to see what else the author has written that I have enjoyed. My first selection this year was Roald Dahl's *The Magic Finger* (1966) because I love *The BFG* (1982) and *James the Giant Peach* (1961).

The first Reading Workshop culminates in our celebration of books with my reading aloud from one of those titles several students wanted to check out, *Going Hollywood* (1989) by Hudson Talbot. Future reading workshops will focus primarily on silent and buddy reading of initial selections. Uninterrupted reading time begins at ten minutes; we slowly increase to thirty minutes during the first

month and stay at that time frame for the rest of the year. My students insist that this silent reading time is "the nicest way to start the day."

Following the SSR time I give readers pieces of lined stationery and ask them to write me a letter about what they just read. I make sure I respond to each letter before the next Reading Workshop and, after that, the letter writing is more staggered, and readers begin to exchange with one another. I have seen students begin to make more personal connections to a story after just a few days of letter writing. I can also see a difference in their risk-taking and attention to audience through literature dialogues.

Slowly, the letter writing gives way to journaling. I use Reading Journal* entries from my past students to introduce the idea. I respond to journal entries as they come in—I am willing to give over as much time as I need to journal responses because I have found no better way to keep in touch with students' comprehension. All of this responding to literature has fueled my passion for children's books. In order to respond, I have to read or have read whatever my students are reading. I've never spent my professional time in a better way.

When students complete a book they return independently to the library corner to select another. The Book Talks* we give periodically are audiotaped so any one of us can get a quick overview and reader response to a particular selection. Sometimes, when my students "buddy-up" to read together, it's because one has listened to a Book Talk,* gone directly to the reader, asked for a more personal response, and in the excitement of the exchange they have decided to read the book together. I value the rereadings as much as the original experience because of the depth of understanding I can see when readers talk about old favorites they have read more than once. And there are always my personal favorites that I bring in, read one more time, and marvel out loud about the new discoveries I make.

In Reading Workshop I see my big role as connecting the right reader to the right book—it's crucial to connecting that kid to reading. Early school days always concentrate on that responsibility because, once they are hooked, the rest is easy.

WRITING WORKSHOP AND THE EXPERT CONNECTION

Writer's Workshop always follows Reading and is set in motion during the first week of school. Writing begins with students identifying some area of expertise— like things they know more about than others do. I start with their existing areas of expertise but soon the expert connection integrates the curriculum through content areas such as math, music, art, social studies, science, physical education, and even lunch and recess.

The expert strategy begins with a people search (*see* Figure 11.4). Prior to the start of school I have written a list of topics based on what I know about the age group, community, and background of my students—topics that I hope will draw out any experts in the area. The list is narrow, but the activity generates a whole storm of ideas and is a low-risk way to get students thinking about how much they know and how much those around them know. This is important if they are eventually to use each other as resources.

Following the people search, I talk in greater depth about my own areas of expertise. I know about rainbows. I play backgammon and chess. I speak French and pig Latin. And, after last year's class, I know a lot about how caterpillars change into moths. All the other experts in my class then choose their topics of personal knowledge and write them on 3 x 5 cards, which are eventually filed in a metal box and labeled "Experts on File." During the first few weeks of school students take turns drawing from the expert cards and sharing their knowledge and the experiences that helped them learn about the topic. The sharing takes place in whole group and small group sessions and on audiotape. Later, the audiotapes become excellent resources for other students who want to become experts in the same area.

All through the first month these experts talk about, read about, and write about what they know, and their existing areas of expertise expand. Dan's little brother, Chris, on whom he is an expert, comes to visit us on Open House Day, and we all learn more about him (including Dan). Jason brings his pet snakes into class, and his classmates' questions encourage him to read more about snakes. Ann decides that her system for cleaning the cat litter box is better than any other she has heard of or read about.

Find as many classroom experts as you can in the areas listed below. At the first signal bell begin circulating within the room and when you locate an expert in any of the categories, have that person sign his or her name in front of the number. P.S. you may sign yourself in for any topics on which *you* are an expert! Good luck!

_____	1. Has seen a tornado.
_____	2. Knows a Chicago Bear or Bull.
_____	3. Has visited either MGM or Universal Studios.
_____	4. Has written a short story.
_____	5. Speaks a foreign language or "pig Latin."
_____	6. Tells very scary stories.
_____	7. Has more than six brothers or sisters.
_____	8. Plays chess or backgammon.
_____	9. Knows where Iraq is located.
_____	10. Was born in south Chicago.
_____	11. Has read more than one book by Chris Van Allsburg.
_____	12. Witnessed the metamorphosis of a caterpillar.
_____	13. Rides horses.
_____	14. Knows the layout of our school.
_____	15. Can predict the weather.
_____	16. Has made a profit selling something.
_____	17. Can cook a special dish.

FIGURE 11.4
People Search

As students become interested in one another's areas of expertise, I encourage them to write questions about the topic and interview one another. Often the questions are addressed to the expert in front of the whole class, so that everyone has the opportunity to respond and to ask further questions.

In that first portion of the school year the Writing Workshop time is spent in writing on those topics students have firmly under their belts. Topic selection is no problem once they realize how much they already know and how much they would like to know. Sergio's vacation to Puerto Rico is preceded by his study of that island. Syreeta's research and writing about earthquakes comes after a family friend is injured during the 1989 San Francisco earthquake. Tony and Kristian work together caring for tropical fish, and have to do research as they continually raise questions about their care.

Writing Workshop becomes not only a time to write but also a time to talk, do research, read, and question. While most of the workshop time *is* spent drafting and revising their writing about expert topics, that writing is simply an integral part, an extension, of the larger project in which they are engaged. As the year continues, the publication of *Expert Reports* flows throughout the curriculum. I always give an extended, specific block of time on Friday afternoons so students can focus even more intensely on their research and the sharing of what they are learning. Presentations and sharing of what is learned is an important part of the cycle. The presentations often include art; trivia questions from math, social studies, and science (How far is it to San Juan from Miami, Florida?); songs (Therese's Mississippi report includes "Mis-si-ssi-pi" sung to the tune of Handel's "Messiah"); poems (Christopher recites "Little Miss Muffet" as part of his spider report); with occasional bibliographies of fiction and nonfiction on the topic.

"Becoming Experts" has been the most popular part of my curriculum in my years as a whole language teacher. It is not only a solid problem-solving, student-directed component, it is fun for me and the students and the most productive integration of reading, writing, math, social studies, science, music, and art I have used so far. It makes our first days together exciting ones.

PENNY SILVERS: WHOLE LANGUAGE IN A READING RESOURCE PROGRAM

GETTING STARTED

As a resource teacher I often do not see students regularly until a few weeks after school has started. During the first weeks of school, while I am working on my schedule, I try to go into many of the classrooms to read to students. I share favorite, predictable stories like *Q Is for Duck* (Elting, 1980) and *I'm the King of the Mountain* (Cowley, 1984) with the whole class. After I read, I often stay for some follow-up activities. I invite students to write with me, sometimes extending a pattern in a predictable book or making a book of their own or making a class book.

A favorite book Extension* is to use the format of *Q Is for Duck,* having each child in the class think of one special characteristic about themselves, and using that letter in the pattern of the book. For example, "G is for Susan." Why? "Because Susan wears glasses." Each child can write a page of the book in this way, share it with the whole class (and have the class do the guessing as to what the letter stands for), and then the pages can be put together into a class book and left in the class library.

I'm the King of the Mountain also lends itself not only to Shared Reading* but to dramatization, and as a class book as well. Each child can be a character, following the pattern in this book. Many wonderful reading and writing opportunities can develop from this book or other predictable books.

While the whole class is working on a book Extension,* I try to observe and work with the students I know I will be seeing in the reading lab. I watch their

interactions with their peers, their use of oral and written language, and try to get to know them as individuals. After watching for a while I start a page for each student in my Process Notebook, recording such items as selection of books for independent reading, journal entries, things they are interested in, and comments made about print that I have observed from discussions and conversations. I focus my kid-watching on their strengths as learners, how they handle reading and writing, and the kinds of strategies they use to make meaning.

My planning for these students begins a long time before they actually start to work with me. Throughout the summer I evaluate and think about the previous year's experiences. I eliminate themes that weren't interesting, rethink how to get the students more involved in classroom decision-making, and wonder how to get them to take more learning risks.

I am always reading children's books, trying to connect them by theme or with units of study that I know will be going on in the regular classroom. I have often pulled Text Sets* of books together only to discover that students aren't interested in them. I am now keeping a list of possible books and themes and, during the school year, I am always looking for classroom connections to those themes, or students who express interest in a theme or a favorite book. That way, I can make some reading recommendations or have just the right books on hand to nurture and expand that interest.

Another important part of getting ready for my students is to have materials on hand: paper of all kinds for writing or making books, colored construction paper of all sizes, a scrap box of colored paper, pencils, markers, crayons, staplers, tape, masking tape, and other supplies. I also try to have as many books as possible around the room—some grouped in related sets, others by popular demand and general interest, and still others that I have not yet read but am hoping to read with my students as the opportunity presents itself.

There are Big Books, little books, borrowed kids' books that they have written, a tape recorder and tapes, poetry books, songs and plastic baggies (ziplock) so that students can sign out favorite books or their own writing and take them home in book bags. When they have a book and want to share it with their families, they put the book into a bag and sign their names on a library checkout card. If I am really on top of the situation I try to include a book on a similar theme that the parent can read to the child, as well as having the child read the selected book to the parent. Children and parents know that the book must be returned the next day, and the children check their sign-out cards to see who has not returned a book. Sometimes, a child is the "librarian" and does this checking.

I also prepare a parent letter of introduction to the reading lab; a letter about the book bags and checking out procedures; and throughout the year I send a variety of letters home to parents explaining the reading and writing process, favorite bibliographies, and wonderful things their children are reading and writing about in school.

When my classes begin, I usually see small groups of students for thirty minutes twice a week. I can see them in the reading lab or work with them in their classrooms. Often, I continue reading and writing with their classes at different times of the day so I am familiar with all the students in the building.

REVALUING

On the first day of reading lab classes we spend a lot of time talking about what we like to read, favorite books, and all of the other reading that is done outside of classrooms. My students often do not see themselves as readers, and part of my initial responsibility—probably my major one—is to get that image firmly in place. Ken Goodman calls it "revaluing" when students have lost a sense of themselves as readers and need to get it back.

I am always a part of these group discussions—a participant contributing personal information along with the students. I try to establish a comfortable environment in which students are free to express themselves; to try out new ideas; and to experience success in reading, writing, and oral language—all part of valuing themselves as learners. By sharing my own experiences with students, I am able to demonstrate that the learning process is not so different from one person to another. I talk about how I learn, why I read and write, that I make mistakes too, and that I have feelings and insecurities just as they do.

After these initial discussions we start to record some of our experiences in Dialogue Journals.* Students make a folder from construction paper or use a manila folder. They are free to fill up the folder with daily journal entries on notebook paper or plain Xerox paper, which is readily available in the room. These journal entries often turn into a first-draft piece of writing. I respond to their journal entries often and they also begin to write back and forth to each other. I keep samples of writing from the first days and throughout the year. I have a detailed record of their growth and development over time; documents of what they have been doing, thinking, feeling, seeing; and a rich source of information about their interests and needs.

The journal writing usually only takes a few minutes of each class session, and then we often share the entries and spend just a few minutes talking about each others' experiences. The rest of our first session together is spent looking at favorite books, reading, sharing stories, and deciding what everyone wants to read about next time.

In the days that follow, we discuss important issues like spelling—conventional and invented, first drafts versus published pieces, writing the same ways as our favorite authors, and reading as writers. We talk about what each person has expertise in doing—hobbies, lessons, sports, gymnastics, and so on. This leads to the next pieces of writing—a draft of something unique about each of them to be shared with the group. All first drafts are shared. We ask questions, note what we like about what the writer has done (language and content), and everyone is encouraged to go back to their writing to make revisions based on audience response. Along with the writing, students are encouraged to find a book to read in the lab, and time is spent reading a book of their choice each session. When one book is finished, students can share their books by giving a Book Talk,* making a poster, dramatizing a favorite part. From the first book share, interest groups are formed for further reading of the same author.

This year, one second-grade group became interested in reading about pets of all kinds, doing research on a pet of their choice and writing about it, combining facts with what was already known about the pet. There was a lot of group collaboration and the students brought stuffed animals from home, wrote letters to parents inviting them to a pet show, and wrote to the principal requesting permission to do the project. In this group one of the students was unwilling to speak any English, since Chinese was the only language spoken at home. Even though she knew some English, she was unwilling to attempt to speak. When we began to write about pets and animals, Cicely wrote about insects as her contribution, and brought a toy spider for our collection. The group process gave her support and I really learned about her for the first time and was able to communicate with her about something that interested her.

Chris liked fishing and, although he did not have any pet fish, he wrote about fishing and about the different kinds of fish he had caught. This led to Lauren's discussion about her pregnant goldfish—at this point we had to get books out of the library to find out how they lay their eggs and what you have to do with baby fish in an aquarium at home. Meanwhile, the interest and motivation was so high that the classroom teacher was amazed. I have found that my students, who are not known for their involvement, risk-taking, or love of learning anything, look entirely different in my resource classes. When they have a commitment to a project they read and write and learn whatever conventions of language they need. There is ownership and pride in these young learners as they engage in work that is meaningful to them.

A first-grade group discovered Eric Carle's *The Very Hungry Caterpillar* (1979), and after reading and rereading it several times they wrote a pop-up book patterned after Carle's structure. This proud accomplishment went back to their classroom library. We continued the theme by reading a book about real caterpillars, complete with a chart about the life cycle. Then we compared fiction with nonfiction, talked about the differences as well as the similarities, mapped the things that were based on fact about caterpillars from each book, and divided into groups to write reports or fiction based on choice and interest.

These remedial first-graders have not yet mastered the alphabet but not having that narrow piece of knowledge does not keep them from using and developing complex literate behaviors (yes, they do learn the alphabet—easily—in my classroom as they read and write about ideas that are meaningful to them). My students are learning that print conveys personal meaning, that they can construct meaning in reading and writing, that books are different in structure and content, and that people read and write differently for varied purposes. When I asked Brittany to read from Carle's book what the caterpillar ate on Saturday, she said: "I can't read." But, with encouragement, she approximated the print on the page, using the patterns she had heard when we read the book as a group and there was no change in the message. When she finished the page, her wide smile lasted a long, long time.

As I get to know my students during those first days and weeks, record-keeping is always a challenge. I have developed many different ways to take process notes, and rejected most of them. I have devised process-based evaluation forms, and revised most of them. I am interested in capturing behaviors like this: One of my students asked me how to spell "play." I encouraged him to use his own invented spelling, and he seemed satisfied with that. Later in the morning, as he was reading a book, he came across the word and said, "Oh, so that's how you spell play!" Then he went back to his earlier writing and corrected his spelling.

Currently I am using a process checklist (*see* Figure 11.5) that Linda Crafton and I have adapted from Bailey *et al.* (1988). But my most important devices are the daily process notes I keep on each student (*see* Figure 11.6). The observations, written on index cards, help me develop literacy profiles and, when report card time rolls around, they inform my marking of the checklist which I give to classroom teachers and parents.

But my students are also involved in evaluation. Each student records the books he or she has read, and makes a statement about each. We keep folders of drafts and selected journal pages and skills/strategies learned. These are invaluable to

Student _____

Teacher _____

Literacy Development

Grade _____

Year _____

	Beginning	Developing	Independent	Teacher Comments	Parent Comments
Interest in Books					
Selects books independently.					
Samples a variety of genre.					
Chooses books of appropriate difficulty.					
Reads silently for sustained periods.					
Shows pleasure in reading.					
Is becoming an independent reader.					
Reading Strategies					
Before Reading					
Makes predictions about text.					
Uses prior knowledge.					
Generates personal questions.					
During Reading					
Rereads for meaning.					
Processes chunks of language.					
Uses picture clues.					
Considers the impact of miscues on meaning.					
Connects with other texts and experiences.					
Uses context for meaning of unfamiliar words.					
Reads for a variety of purposes.					
Uses phonetic skills when appropriate.					

After Reading

Rereads if meaning isn't clear.				
Retells.				
Summarizes.				
Discusses personal understanding of main idea.				
Understands sequencing, cause/effect, comparisons.				
Recognizes character development.				
Uses information to form opinions.				
Revises interpretations after discussion.				

Writing Strategies

Can choose and develop a topic.				
Is aware of audience.				
Takes risks: Spelling				
Sharing writing				
Length of text				
Form and purpose				
Revision				
Understands and uses punctuation.				
Edits and proofreads writing.				
Responds appropriately to others' writing.				
Has "published" some of the writing.				

FIGURE 11.5
Literacy Checklist

SAM

9-25: Sam asked "I wonder where the center of the world is?" We looked at the globe — then found Egypt and his trip. (Kevin told about his trip to Ireland) — Looked at pictures.

9-27: Lots of predicting — used picture clues; Re-told story about Monet — fits into study of habitats & environments.
      Discussed how to paint with water colors — shared stories.

Rdg. Process: Read "sky" for skunk — knew text didn't make sense — re-read three black skunks instead of the black sky. Discussed how he knew it didn't make sense and the need to re-read.

10-9: Used context clues to figure out words — then looked for beginning sounds to make the best guess.

Read Dinosaur Time — read;
"This dinosaur was a "girl." Then he changed "girl" to "giant." He said, "It ate plates." then he changed it to "plants" — to make sense.

(over-emphasizes graphophonics — but knows to make sense out of the text.)

(Back of card)

FIGURE 11.6
Daily Process Notes

> 10-9 — Talked freely today. Not so reluctant to contribute to discussion. Said winter is his favorite season - Christmas is his favorite holiday - (We were reading a book about Seasons - also mentioned <u>Chicken Soup and Rice</u>).
>
> He reminded me that the group had to practice the "monster" play.
>
> <u>Journal entry</u>: "I like winter and Christmas." Strong invented spelling - Beginning + some middle/end consonants. It helped when I said the words with him. He is beginning to space between his words.
>
> Knows a lot about animals - especially Hermit Crabs, ants, etc. Wants to learn about alligators.

FIGURE 11.6 *(Continued)*

my students as they look through the folders' contents and delight in the changes they have made over the year—and they are invaluable to me when I hold a conference with parents and teachers.

At the beginning of each year I am thrilled at the depth of knowledge the so-called remedial readers exhibit in my resource room; but also saddened that these same strengths are not always seen in regular classrooms. It is painful to note how severely students' anxiety about handling more traditional, skill-based schooling can affect their ability to express what they know and how they learn. When they feel accepted and valued, their learning increases, along with their willingness to explore, express ideas, and make connections from their lives to the topics being studied in school. The curiosity is always there, and it is such a joy to see it emerge and flourish.

DAN POWERS: ENCOURAGING STUDENTS TO OWN THEIR LEARNING IN GRADES SIX, SEVEN, AND EIGHT

I guess the first thing that went through my head when I began to bring changes into my classroom was what to tell the kids. I thought about it for weeks during that summer before, and I decided to tell them as directly as possible what I was going to do and why I was going to try it. I started the school year with a talk about teaching and learning. I opened up to them completely, sharing my beliefs about reading, writing, language, and thinking. I stressed that these topics were inseparable and that the first three were the way we, as a class community, would share our thinking. I told them that a thought trapped in a mind with no ability or opportunity to be communicated was wasted. I let them know up front that I was changing as a teacher and that the curriculum I wanted to try out with them was new to me, too. I said that they would be the ultimate judges of what stayed or was dropped.

I talked about their need to take charge of their education and that my role was to facilitate ways for them to do so. I tried not to get too long-winded, but I felt it important that by sixth grade they learned to control their learning to a great degree. I wrapped it all up by discussing risk-taking—theirs and mine—and that trying out new things was what the year would be about. They left me looking skeptical and more than a little unsure. I felt the same way.

My first year of transition was tough, but it led me to an even stronger conviction about my students' abilities to handle their own learning. It also led me to an organization for my language arts block of time that is established in the early weeks of the school year and works throughout our months together.

WRITING

Schedule

In sixth, seventh, and eighth grade we write two days a week. The days are always consecutive so that the students can have a block of time to carry out their ideas without interruption. I put these on either Monday and Tuesday (to get active and into the week) or Thursday and Friday so students can continue to write into the weekend (which often happens). The rest of the schedule is two consecutive days of reading, and the fifth day is for Sustained Silent Reading and individual conferencing with students. I spend the first full week on writing process before I do anything with reading, and then switch to the 2-2-1 day schedule.

Writing Folders

Each student has two separate Writing Folders.* One they can keep, and it can go home with them; the other stays in the room. In the first they keep all current work "under construction" along with editing sheets and any handouts that deal with writing class or conferencing. In the other they keep finished work or pieces that are put aside. Both folders are valuable evaluation materials. At the end of the year we can all see development over long spans of time. Because I have my students for three years, I can review their folders before the beginning of each year.

Editing Sheets

Incoming sixth-graders receive their first editing sheet at the beginning of the school year. Originally this had a rather large list of items to edit for. Soon I found that it was too much and, anyway, the editing focus for each student and each piece was different. By my second year of teaching I had pared the list down to some essentials focused first of all of meaningfulness—of the piece, individual paragraphs, sentences, vocabulary—and then on mechanics—capitals, spelling, basic punctuation. On the sheet these are followed by a lot of blank lines so students can begin to add other things they want to pay attention to. When I hold conferences with students, we also add new dimensions, as they demonstrate either an interest or need to know how to use other dimensions. The latter is presented in a Mini-lesson* to the individual or, if it seems to effect several people, to a small group or the entire class.

By the second week I present a Mini-lesson* on basic editing markings and how to use them. I present my own writing as a demonstration. At first I focus only on inserting new information into a draft, deletions (crossouts), and how to move material around (with arrows).

Writing Cycle

The concept of a writing process cycle is presented immediately so that students know that the stress is on the process and not on the product. I also want to let them know that thinking about their writing is the main goal, not how fast they can produce a finished product.

I put the words prewriting, writing, revision and editing on the board and begin to draw lines back and forth between the words as I draft a personal story to illustrate the writing process. I ask them to respond to the content of my story and use their ideas to make revisions—it is their first introduction to the importance of audience response to a writer. I always have on hand many other messy drafts, and spend time highlighting in great detail the thinking that the messiness represents. I want students to see that a draft is a thinking copy and is to be used to push them and their thinking forward. They always seem to get a kick out of the idea that making this mess is valued tremendously in my classroom.

Mini-Lessons

I get students started writing as soon as possible on personal topics, and am very careful *not* to use any kind of structured lessons until I have had a chance to observe what is happening to them as writers. Otherwise it's too easy to impose my agenda on theirs—and to unconsciously take control of a curriculum that rightly belongs to them. When I do begin using Mini-lessons, they are simply focused bits of information about the writing process that I think would be helpful: "Ever think about this in your writing?" "Ever run into this problem?" "Listen to the way this author handles poetry (or feeling or detail or transitions)." I am cautious not to turn the brief time into a lecture—Mini-lessons for me are just helpful hints from one writer to another. For that reason my students also share in the development and presentation of Mini-lessons at some point during the year. I do spend time planning lessons that are likely to be profitable based on my experience with writing and with my students from the previous year, but I am careful not to invest too much in these or I might be in danger of missing the all-important "teachable moment" when it comes. Also, if only one or two students need or are ready for a particular topic, I don't waste the entire class' time with it.

Status of the Class Chart

Nancie Atwell (1987) helped me organize my classes when I wasn't sure how I could possibly keep track of so many students doing so many different things. Her status of the class chart has the five school days written across the top and student names written down the left-hand side of the page. I use this for all of my reading and writing classes by simply calling off names at the beginning of each period each day and writing down what each person plans to do. I can fill in the chart for a class of thirty in about three or four minutes. I make many blank charts at the beginning of school and just run off more as I need them. If you try it, work out your own abbreviations or codes ahead of time. Make them simple and natural; within a week they will flow from your pen. And—save them. They are invaluable for keeping track of students, evaluating, and *especially* during a conference with kids and parents if used in conjunction with Writing Folders.*

Topics List

Choosing topics is my first Mini-lesson. Afterward, students keep a running list of ideas in their Writing Folders. Usually I present this lesson the first or second day. I put general topics on the board—such as school, the local park, friends, rockets, book titles, and so on. Then I ask students to think quickly of a specific experience related to the topics. If they can, they have a potential idea to write about. The point I try to bring out is that it's much easier to write about what you know. I then poll the class for other things they feel they know well, and we always cover the board with all the possibilities. They use the brainstormed list to start their "Possible Topics" sheets and then keep adding to it as other ideas occur to them.

Writing Conferences

We are never too long into writing class when I get a draft shoved under my nose with an accompanying: "How's this?" My reply is always: "Well, who in the class (aside from me) do you think would be a good judge of 'how it is'?" That person is asked if he or she would please take a few minutes to listen and talk to the author about the writing. It doesn't take long for this idea of collaboration to catch on, and soon everyone is discussing writing with someone else.

How's it going?

What part do you like best? Why?

Do you have more than one story?

Why is this important to you?

How does this draft sound when you read it out loud?

What problems are you having?

What is the most important thing you are trying to say?

How do you want your reader to feel at the end of the piece?

Does this conclusion do it?

What would you like me to listen for?

FIGURE 11.7
Open-ended Questions Used During
Writing Conferences

(From Atwell and Giacobbe, 1984)

Early in the first week I give my students some strategies for discussing writing. Usually they are in the form of a list of open-ended questions to ask of the author (*see* Figure 11.7). Students keep these written questions in their folders, and pull them out often as they learn to be better and better respondents to one another's writing. During the year we talk about which questions are the most useful and which they rarely use, and the list is modified accordingly.

Physical Environment

Because I want a high level of student interaction in my classes I consider the physical environment carefully at the beginning of each year. I have found that there is no one answer for me, and so I am always changing the seating during the year. But once I paid more attention to this part of my curriculum, new arrangements began to present themselves—and still do. I start by considering what I want students to accomplish, and go on from there. I pay attention to the floor and corner space, as well as how the desks are arranged. I have found that even sophisticated junior-high school students love to work on the floor.

Evaluation

Besides Writing Folders,* individual editing sheets, and status of the class sheets already mentioned, I keep a Process Notebook with a page for each student. Here are brief anecdotal notes I write up after school each day—I put the date and only enough significant information to remind me of the event or behavior. It does take time and effort, but I know my students better now than I ever have before. This notebook feeds my feeling of skill and professionalism as no other evaluative tool I have ever used does.

READING

Sustained Silent Reading

One day a week is given over to uninterrupted reading. Before school starts, I prepare an index card file for each student. Name, grade, and year is recorded, and cards are arranged alphabetically by class. These cards are used by my students to keep track of what they are reading during SSR time. I also make notes to keep track of how often I talk to each student, or when I need to get back to the student. I keep these cards all three years my students are with me.

I read with my students the first part of our SSR day, and then begin to hold conferences with individuals. These book discussions are as honest and as genuine as I can make them. My students realize quickly that I just want to talk to them about their reading, that I really am interested in their opinions and interpretations. I find my honesty is completely returned—right down to being told they haven't read what they had committed to for that day.

Students always choose their own literature (*see* Appendix A for favorites of this age group), and I continue to be amazed at some of the books they bring in—more sophisticated and complex than those I would have chosen for them.

Vocabulary

Vocabulary is simply handled through book discussions. I ask students to keep track of new or interesting words they want to talk about—we then talk about language.

Journals

Each student has a Reading Journal from the first day. I give the students a folder and they insert twelve to fifteen sheets of paper in it. I stress that the Journal is another place to think—this time about their reading. Here I value the messiness of thought about reading in the same way I do with writing. They know they will be graded only on the effort and thought reflected in the writing. I use the Journals for everything from prereading brainstorming, or predicting, to reflections and comments on conferences. I tell them to date everything and ask them how they would like to handle the confidentiality issue. Journals are the major portion of their reading grade—I am satisfied if I can see effort and active engagement and personal understanding on some level.

I introduce the Journals by asking them to reflect on their feeling about reading, favorite books, what they've read lately, and so on. I give them a schedule for collecting and responding, and make sure I am not committed to too many Journal responses per day—otherwise, my responses are limited and my chance to really talk to readers about the literature is decreased.

Book Selection

I read as much children's and young adolescent literature as I can get my hands on, but I also rely on my students to make recommendations. When I started developing my literature-based reading program I talked to other teachers who were already well on their way in such a program. They gave me specific, never-fail titles and themes that had worked well with their students, and I went from there.

I offer two to four books at one time to a class. I prepare a Book Talk* for each at the beginning of the year, and, after that, my students join in with their suggestions. Discussion and reading groups are formed around the books themselves—a common selection is the only criterion for belonging to a group.

Discussion Groups

I find that discussion groups take time, but we start from the first day. I begin with readers who have selected the same book. They just sit together in a circle and begin to read. They can decide if they will read silently or orally and how much. They are free to ask each other questions and make comments about the story as they read. After the initial circle they have to agree on how far to read by the next class. They also have to bring in one idea or question they want to talk to the group about. These are recorded in a separate place in the Journals. The last ten minutes of each class is used for follow-up Journal writing in which students reflect on the exchanges within the group. (Between responding to Journal entries regularly and joining in on group discussions, I find I am quite capable of keeping track of individuals' participation and development.)

While observing the discussion groups in action, I find that not only do they discuss the stories but they help each other comprehend and interpret—the setting is an incredibly rich one for collaborative thinking. If someone is having trouble the group helps by explaining where or how the person has gotten lost. Sometime this is in the form of vocabulary help, explaining a difficult passage, sorting out details, or filling in gaps in a reader's background. All of those teacher things I used to attempt to do happen beautifully within these groups—and there is a power there that wasn't present before. I feel it in my teaching, too.

BARBARA LINDBERG: JUNIOR HIGH BEGINNINGS

I am in a departmentalized junior high school. There are ten periods a day, which means on the first days of school the students are bombarded with a variety

of rules and requirements. Reading gives me delicious time, and my primary wish for my students is that they see reading as a satisfying option all their lives. My reading aloud at the beginning of a school year when all else around them is chaos may help achieve that goal. So, as they get do's and don'ts in a new environment I bring them favorite authors such as Roald Dahl, William Armstrong, Beverly Cleary, perhaps in the new form of her autobiography, *A Girl from Yamhill* (1988). Or, if information about my students precedes them (by reputation or other teachers), I can get action stories or nonfiction ready for them. Eighth graders, many of whom I know, may hear "The Most Dangerous Game" by Connell (1964); it is common in anthologies. If I am sure of my selection/audience, what I choose to read aloud can be long. I do make the choices at this point. Choices for my students begin, however, as soon as I hook them into what I am reading, which always happens if I choose my material well.

Reading aloud takes energy, so I read two, maybe three of the thirty-seven minute periods. The other classes write. Because most students do not know me or my ideas of what writing is, I write a general letter to students. I tell them why I like the school and my classroom in particular. I tell them what I like to read and what I don't like to read, what I like to write and what I am not able to write well, my personal and professional goals for the coming year, what I like and don't like about school. I also share some personal things about myself, like the year I was born, which makes for an authentic math problem and reduces horrifying guesses. (However, I *never* tell how much I weigh.) In my letter I invite students to reply and, while they write to me, I draft another letter to them.

In these ways two things I value—sustained writing and sustained reading—
are where we meet. We do not always meet over rules and assignments, but we
connect in literature or by writing.

Year End

I end each year reflecting on all the things I should have and could have done that
would have moved my students' literacy along faster, deeper, broader. Those reflections lead to ideas about starting the next year differently, about being the
super-teacher next year. This past June, as I reflected and as Linda Crafton and
I talked when she visited my room the last day the students were in attendance, I
decided that establishing more open and helpful Literature Circles and Writing
Groups was the first priority. I wished the students had felt and acted closer to each
other. Linda asked me how I planned to make these changes. "By reading, talking
to you, talking to colleagues, reflecting with my students—whatever it takes."

"Keep a journal on it, will you?" she asked.

"Sure," I promised.

I haven't started it yet, but I will. Maybe tonight. Those are curricular changes I
want to think about and focus on throughout the year, and a journal will be
critical for that; but in the meantime I will keep my beginnings—and hope it is
the beginning of literacy for the great numbers of my students who have not
known literacy before.

CAROL PORTER: LAYING THE FOUNDATION FOR A HIGH SCHOOL COMMUNITY OF READER/WRITERS

GETTING STARTED

On rainy days in August my children, Michelle and Ryan, leave home early with
me so they can help arrange and rearrange my new classroom. Without saying a
word I want my room to carry a message about the class and the teacher. We
decorate the bulletin board to the right of the doorway in red and gray, the school
colors, and display newspaper articles related to school events. In the center of the
room we place several desks in a large circle, others in small groupings, and a few
single ones facing the courtyard window. Past the bulletin board hanging folders
that will hold students' in-process writings, journals, and any messages I might
have for them are set up. On the opposite side of the room Ryan and I plug in the six
computers, while Michelle cleans and arranges two learning centers for special
activities. Paperbacks are put on rotating stands, a rack of newspapers, and a publishing table are prepared. I want my students to see that I value books, writing,
working in groups, and topics that are important to their lives.

I began this school year with an activity, not with the typical lecture of rules and expectations from the front of the room. (As I write this, I realize there is no longer a front of the room in my classroom.) Our first activity on the first day is interviews. Not only does this allow students time to learn about and come to feel comfortable with others in their community, but it also introduces them to a cycle of learning that we will be using as the curricular structure in the classroom (*see* Harste, Short, and Burke, 1988, for an extended description of the authoring cycle).

Day 1

Students are asked to choose a partner to interview and introduce in writing to the rest of the class. We discuss some of the questions they may want to ask, and then they pair up using the rest of the class period to gather information. I also tell them to prepare themselves for pictures on the following day, as some students may want to bring in specific props or wear special clothing to go along with their introductions.

Day 2

On the next day students take their partners' pictures and complete a rough draft of the introduction, moving freely from writing to gathering more information and back to writing again.

Day 3

The third day of class, students bring their rough drafts to a small group meeting where they read their introductions to the rest of the group. I hand out scratch paper to each person and ask that they write comments about what they liked or found particularly memorable in these introductions, and note any questions they still have about the person who was introduced. I have found that the focus in this activity is not just on the writer. The questions asked are focused on really getting to know each person in the class. As the person answers questions about themselves, the writer takes notes to consider later during revision. The writer also receives the slips of paper containing the responses made by each member of the group.

Days 4 and 5

After each author has shared, at least two more class periods are used for revising, editing, and conferencing. Some students may have so many revisions that they may have to share with the group again. My conference with each student focuses on the positive attributes of their pieces. We identify one or two areas to work on in their next writing. These are listed in my gradebook and students also note them on a special sheet of paper that they keep in their Writing Folders. Finally, pictures and introductions are put into a class book, individual book, or displayed on the bulletin board (*see* Figure 11.8).

I feel that our initial activity sends several messages to students. They begin to see that they are important sources of information for writing and that others can support them in their learning. During sharing, the focus is not on the product and what the writer has done wrong. Questions generated are important for revisions and for getting to know each person in the class. By the time the interviews are published, students have experienced the writing process from beginning to end with a piece that has purpose and has evolved through peer support. The social needs of the adolescent during the first few days of class have also been addressed, as this is a time to renew friendships and to get to know new members of the class community.

Week 2

Since many of the students in my classes could be classified as reluctant readers, I like to begin the second week of class with a contemporary fiction unit. One student classified the short stories we read at the beginning of this unit as: "The type you wouldn't find in a reading book." One of my favorite first stories is "Prisilla and the Wimps" (Gallo, 1984), which I read aloud stopping several times during the reading to have students Say Something.* They state reactions, predictions, relate a personal experience, or ask questions. During the general discussion at the end of the story, I ask them to consider topic possibilities for other

American Gymnist Grasps World Title

Today American gymnist, Jimmy Gonzales, won the World Championship Title.

Gonzales grew up in Mundelein, a small town in Illinois. Dismounting his way to the top, in 1989 Gonzales was on the State High School Championship gymnastics team.

The first man to beat Boris Shakhlin (USSR) who held the most individuals titles, Gonzales currently holds the World and American Cup titles along with numerous other titles and trophies, including seven Olympic metals. He's also a dominate force on four different championship games.

When Jimmy Gonzales dismounts for the final time and gives up his uneven bars, he hopes to teach little children how to play sports.

He'd want to be a guest star on the popular television show, Who's The Boss. With Catherine Helmond's humor, he feels it would be "fun". He's sick of hearing the phrase "just do it". After wearing t-shirts with it blasted across the back, people still come up to him and say "just do it" when it's already been done! If the world was in any shape, he'd prefer a triangle because it would be easier to go across.

Although Gonzales prefers *Jason* over the "stupid" *Freddy Krueger,* he's still the number one gymnist in the world today.

FIGURE 11.8
Final Draft of Peer Interview

stories that might be labeled contemporary fiction. The next day we might read a story such as, "Louisa, Please Come Home" (Jackson, 1960), again using the Say Something* strategy at points we determine prior to reading.

On the third and fourth days I set out several stories with themes relating to our first novel. With a partner, students choose two stories to read using the same strategy. By the end of the second week they are beginning to see that stories have been written that relate directly to their lives and that reading is not a solitary activity—together they can consider possibilities that wouldn't have existed in isolation.

Weeks 3, 4, 5, and 6

Although I am a strong advocate of student choice I also have equally strong reasons for starting the whole class with the same book. It gives everyone a common starting point, and students are able to develop a reading community that wouldn't exist if they began making choices too soon.

During the third week we begin reading *The Crazy Horse Electric Game* by Chris Crutcher (1987). I read the first chapter aloud, stopping at natural breaks in the text so we can Say Something.* Together we plan the next few days—when we will have discussions and how many chapters will be included in the discussion. In general, discussions cover five chapters every three to four days, and the novel is completed by the end of the fourth week.

After the first Crutcher book is finished, students chose either *Stotan!* (1986) or *Running Loose* (1983) by the same author. Their third book for the unit is a choice: another book by Crutcher or one that is related to a theme presented in either of the books just read. These are chosen at the beginning of the seventh week. I require that at least two people in the class read the same book, so that discussions can take place.

I bring the class back together at the end of the unit for book Celebrations,* by having students choose their favorite books to do something with in the form of a Book Talk,* skit, illustration, audiotape, talk show, and so on.

We begin our next unit with exposure to another genre or theme, using choices of short stories, poetry, children's books, or any combination of these. Again, we start with the same novel for the whole class, and then branch out in many directions.

In Just a Few Short Weeks . . .

As I observed and listened to my students yesterday I felt that my investment in these early weeks had really paid off. My attention to ideas like ownership and choice and peer support had helped them to see themselves as a community that values and supports others in their learning. So quickly, reading and writing are no longer chores and tasks to complete but activities related to their lives.

Jason announced, "I finished my book everyone. Aren't you guys proud of me? Come on, do something, this is my first book since *Superfudge.*" The class applauded.

Leo told me that he read the last chapter of his novel a second time because he liked the way some of the scenes made him feel.

As we chose books today Doug laid his two choices side-by-side, measuring the thickness, checking the size of print and the number of pages. But after reading the covers, he decided on the longer/larger of the two. He realizes that he will have other members of the class to support him in reading this larger book so he can now make a choice based on interest, not length.

Brian and Corey picked up their books and went to the back of the room to write rough drafts. Jeff took a desk away from everyone and read. Benji and Pat sat at the activity center with a map on Montana, identifying cities and lakes that Crutcher mentioned in the novel they had just finished. Lynette and Doug sat at the discussion circle and started reading their new novels . . .

Getting Started . . .
Moving Forward:
A Personal Change Plan **12**

With its focus on the learner and process, whole language has always felt like a life model to me, and that was one of its original attractions. My early love of it, however, did not protect me from the struggle inherent in any kind of major evolution—once started, I often felt lost and sometimes only moved forward out of sheer determination and commitment to a theory of learning I could see held tremendous potential for kids. (I never dreamed at the time that it had equal promise for me.) Sometimes, however, I didn't move anywhere. I felt immobilized by all of the possibilities connected with this kind of teaching. The opposite happened, too. Sometimes I felt frenzied, and tried to move in too many directions at once. My conversations with my co-authors, and with many other teachers over the years, confirm these difficult experiences as common. But there have always been other, tremendously positive things happening too. Our best intuitions about teaching and learning have been validated. We have felt a joy and satisfaction in teaching we didn't feel before. We share a new respect for students and their capabilities. We are enjoying the journey more and more.

Whether you are getting started or moving forward with whole language, the changes in your classroom will be unique and they will continue as long as you teach. The Personal Change Plan presented in this chapter consists of a series of reflective questions intended to help you focus as you continue to explore and understand more fully different areas of the whole language curriculum. Focusing on one or two curricular dimensions at a time makes change manageable. And, for those times when things seem a bit out of control, selecting one or two areas to think about (or rethink) can help you regain a sense of balance. Theoretically, the dimensions in this plan represent a vision of change for you and your students. Practically, they can't all be accomplished at once. You should keep in mind that most likely, as with a good book, you'll revisit them many times to consider them from a different, more experienced perspective.

Recently I presented at a local whole language conference where the theme was: "Whole Language: One Step at a Time." It was good advice for the audience. In considering your own plan, go over the questions several times. Select a question or area that represents your most pressing curricular concern. Give yourself time with that issue—reread the appropriate chapters in this book, extend your learning with topically related materials, keep a reflective journal, and talk, talk, talk to your colleagues. Then, move personally forward: There has to be something right about a paradigm that focuses on strength and always attempts to bring out the best in all of us.

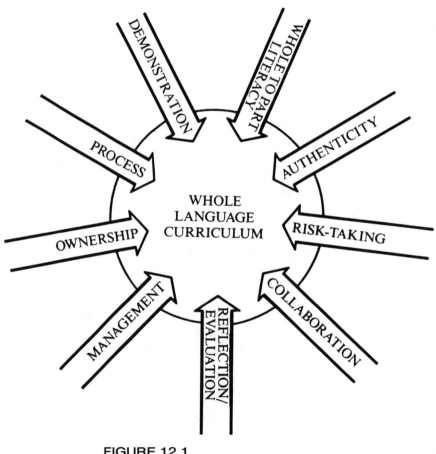

FIGURE 12.1
Critical Dimensions of Whole Language
Curriculum

Diagram adapted from C. Burke, 1990.

A PERSONAL DEVELOPMENT PLAN

WHOLE-TO-PART LITERACY

How can I expand the examination and exploration of many different kinds of whole, intact texts? (do my students have regular access to literature, newspapers, menus, essays, commentaries, letters, environmental print, magazines?)

_____

_____

_____

_____

_____

As I examine my curriculum how do I insure that the parts of reading and writing are examined only in relation to the whole?

_____

_____

_____

_____

_____

AUTHENTICITY

When units are developed and literacy strategies highlighted, how do I consider their relationship to the natural learning that takes place outside the classroom?

_____

_____

_____

_____

_____

What are my students interested in learning about?

_____

_____

_____

_____

What are their existing areas of expertise?

_____

_____

_____

_____

RISK TAKING

How am I encouraging and supporting new explorations related to ideas, genre, strategies, and collaborative efforts?

_____

_____

_____

_____

_____

What more can I do?

_____

_____

_____

_____

_____

DEMONSTRATION

How am I demonstrating my own literacy strategies/proficiencies to my students?

_____

_____

_____

_____

How are my students sharing their strategies and proficiencies with one another?

_____

_____

_____

_____

How can I increase my students' perceptions of me as a person who *uses* reading and writing to learn?

_____

_____

_____

_____

MANAGEMENT

What underlying structure can I use so that students can monitor their own movement through reading/writing activities?

_____

_____

_____

_____

How can I increase time for uninterrupted writing?

_____

_____

_____

_____

How can I increase time for uninterrupted reading?

_____

_____

_____

_____

OWNERSHIP

Where can I encourage more choice and negotiation in the curriculum so students can pursue their own interests, questions, and strategies?

_____

_____

_____

_____

What decisions have I made exclusively in the past that I could share with my students?

_____

_____

_____

_____

_____

Where can I turn over more responsibility for the day-to-day management of the classroom to my students?

_____

_____

_____

_____

_____

How can I increase my understanding of reading/writing processes and the impact of language on learning?

_____

_____

_____

_____

_____

PROCESS

What curricular components do we have in place that highlight reading and writing as thinking processes?

_____

_____

_____

_____

_____

_____

How can I strengthen this area of the curriculum?

_____

_____

_____

_____

REFLECTION/EVALUATION

How am I encouraging students to reflect on their learning—content and process? Independently and socially?

_____

_____

_____

_____

How am I insuring that reflection and student self-evaluation are a built-in, integral part of each school day?

_____

_____

_____

_____

Do I have a satisfactory plan for making systematic observations of my students' reading/writing processes?

_____

_____

_____

_____

_____

COLLABORATION

How can my students and I explore the value of collaborative thought?

_____

_____

_____

_____

How can I increase opportunities for us to read/write/think together?

_____

_____

_____

_____

When students choose collaborative work, how do I encourage them to identify their own purposes and to structure the learning in their own ways?

_____

_____

_____

_____

Do I actively look for ways to adapt strong curricular examples to my students and situation?

_____

_____

_____

_____

_____

BIBLIOGRAPHY

Altwerger, Bess, Carole Edelsky, and Barbara Flores. "Whole Language: What's New?" *Language Arts,* November 1987, pp. 144–154.

Atwell, Nancie. *In the Middle: Writing, Reading, and Learning with Adolescents.* Portsmouth, NH: Heinemann, 1987.

Bailey, Janis, Phyllis Brazee, Sharyn Chiavoroli, Joyce Herbeck, Thomas Lechner, Debra Lewis, Ann McKittrick, Lorraine Redwine, Kris Reid, Betty Robinson and Harry Spear. "Problem Solving Our Way to Alternative Evaluation Procedures." *Language Arts,* 65(4), April 1988, pp. 364–372.

Baratta-Lorton, Mary. *Mathematics Their Way.* Reading, MA: Addison-Wesley, 1976.

Barnes, Douglas. *From Communication to Curriculum.* NY: Penguin, 1975.

Belenky, Mary Field, Blythe McVicker Clinchy, Nancy Rule Goldberger, and Jill Mattuck Tarule. *Women's Ways of Knowing: The Development of Self, Voice, and Mind.* NY: Basic, 1986.

Brown, Margaret. *Goodnight Moon.* NY: Harper, 1947.

Bruner, Jerome. "Play, Thought and Language." *Prospects: Quarterly Review of Education, 16,* 1986, pp. 77–83.

Burke, Carolyn L. "Reading Interview." In Yetta M. Goodman, Dorothy J. Watson, and Carolyn L. Burke. *Reading Miscue Inventory: Alternative Procedures.* NY: Richard C. Owen Publishers, 1987.

Burke, Carolyn L. "Linguistic Data Pool." In Jerome Harste, Virginia A. Woodward and Carolyn L. Burke. *Language Stories and Literacy Lessons.* Portsmouth, NH: Heinemann, 1984.

Calkins, Lucy M. *The Art of Teaching Writing.* Portsmouth, NH: Heinemann, 1986.

Cambourne, Brian. "Language, Learning and Literacy." In Andrea Butler and Jan Turbill. *Towards a Reading-Writing Classroom.* Portsmouth, NH: Heinemann, 1984.

Clark, Eve V. "What's in a Word? On the Child's Acquisition of Semantics in His First Language." In T. E. Moore, ed. *Cognitive Development and the Acquisition of Language.* NY: Academic, 1973.

Clark, M. M. *Young Fluent Readers.* London: Heinemann, 1976.

Clay, Marie. *What Did I Write?* London: Heinemann, 1976.

Cleary, Beverly. *A Girl from Yam Hill: A Memoir.* NY: Bantam Doubleday Dell, 1988.

———. *Dear Mr. Henshaw.* NY: Morrow, 1983.

Cohen, Miriam. *First Grade Takes a Test.* NY: Greenwillow, 1980.

Cole, Michael. "A Socio-Cultural Approach to the Study of Remediation." Paper presented at the New Directions in Studying Children Conference of the Erikson Institute, Chicago, IL, April 1983.

Cooper, Susan. *The Dark Is Rising.* NY: Atheneum, 1973.

_____. *Greenwitch.* NY: Atheneum, 1974.

_____. *The Grey King.* NY: Atheneum, 1975.

_____. *Over Sea, Under Stone.* NY: Harcourt, Brace & World, 1965.

Connell, Richard. "The Most Dangerous Game." *The Study of Literature.* Boston, MA: Ginn, 1964.

Cowley, Joy. *I'm the King of the Mountain.* Ready to Read Series, Department of Education, Wellington, New Zealand. Distributed in the U.S. by Richard C. Owen Publishers, NY, 1984.

_____. *Greedy Cat.* Ready to Read Series, Department of Education, Wellington, New Zealand. Distributed in the U.S. by Richard C. Owen Publishers, NY, 1988.

Crafton, Linda K. "Changing Curriculum: Teachers and Teacher Educators Become a Community of Learners." *Greater Washington Reading Council Journal, XII,* 1987.

_____. "Comprehension: Before, During and After Reading." *The Reading Teacher, 36*(3), December 1982.

_____. "Learning from Reading: What Happens When Students Generate Their Own Background Information." *Journal of Reading, 26*(7), April 1983.

_____. Reading as a Transactional Process. Unpublished doctoral dissertation. Indiana University, 1980.

Crutcher, Chris. *The Crazy Horse Electric Game.* NY: Greenwillow, 1987.

_____. *Running Loose.* NY: Greenwillow, 1983.

_____. *Stotan!* NY: Greenwillow, 1986.

DeFord, Diane E. "Literacy: Reading, Writing and Other Essentials." *Language Arts, 58*(6), 1981, pp. 652–658.

de Paola, Tomie. *Strega Nona: An Old Tale.* Englewood Cliffs, NJ: Prentice-Hall, 1975.

de Regniers, Beatrice. *May I Bring Friend?* NY: Atheneum, 1964.

Donaldson, Margaret. *Children's Minds.* NY: Norton, 1978.

Duncan, Lois. *Don't Look Behind You.* NY: Delacorte, 1989.

Durkin, Dolores. *Children Who Read Early.* NY: Teachers College Press, 1966.

Eckoff, Barbara. "How Reading Affects Children's Writing." *Language Arts, 60,* 1983, pp. 607–616.

Edelsky, Carole. Presentation given at the Annual TAWL in Chicago Conference, Evanston, IL, 1989.

_____, and Karen Smith. "Is that Writing—Or Are Those Marks Just a Figment of Your Curriculum?" *Language Arts, 61,* 1984, pp. 24–32.

Farr, Roger, and Robert Carey. *Reading: What Can Be Measured?* Newark, DE: International Reading Association, 1986.

Ferriero, E. "The Relationships between Oral and Written Langauge: The Children's Viewpoints." In Y. Goodman, M. Haussler, and D. Strickland, eds. *Oral and Written Language Development Research: Impact on the Schools.* Urbana, IL: NCTE, 1981.

Goodlad, John. *A Place Called School.* NY: McGraw-Hill, 1984.

Goodman, Kenneth. *Miscue Analysis: Application to Reading Instruction.* Urbana, IL: NCTE, 1973.

_____. "Reading: A Psycholinguistic Guessing Game." *Journal of the Reading Specialist, 6,* 1967, pp. 126–135.

_____. *What's Whole in Whole Language?* Portsmouth, NH: Heinemann, 1986.

_____, Yetta M. Goodman, and Wendy J. Hood. *The Whole Language Evaluation Book.* Portsmouth, NH: Heinemann, 1989.

_____ and Yetta M. Goodman. "Learning to Read is Natural." In L. B. Resnick and P. A. Weaver, eds. *Theory and Practice of Early Reading.* Lawrence Erlbaum Associates, 1979, pp. 137–155.

Goodman, Yetta. "Kid Watching: An Alternative to Testing." In *Journal of National Elementary School Principals, 57*(4), pp. 22–27.

_____, Dorothy Watson, and Carolyn Burke. *Reading Miscue Inventory: Alternative Procedures.* NY: Richard C. Owen Publishers, 1987.

Goss, Janet L., and Jerome C. Harste. *It Didn't Frighten Me!* Worthington, OH: Willowisp, (1981) 1985.

Graves, Donald H. "Research Currents: When Children Respond to Fiction." *Language Arts, 66*(7), November 1989.

_____. *Writing: Teachers & Children at Work.* Portsmouth, NH: Heinemann, 1983.

Halliday, M.A.K. *Language as Social Semiotic: The Social Interpretation of Language and Meaning.* Baltimore, MD: University Park Press, 1978.

_____. *Learning How to Mean.* NY: Elsevier North Holland, 1975.

Harste, Jerome, and Carolyn Burke. "Examining Instructional Assumptions: The Child as Informant." In Diane DeFord, ed. "Learning to Write: An Expression of Language." *Theory into Practice, 19*(3), 1980, pp. 170–178.

_____. "Understanding the Hypothesis: It's the Teacher that Makes the Difference." In Beverly Farr and Daryl Strickler, eds. *Reading Comprehension: Resource Guide.* Bloomington, IN: Indiana University Reading Programs, 1979, pp. 111–123.

Harste, Jerome C., Kathy G. Short, and Carolyn Burke. *Creating Classrooms for Authors.* Portsmouth, NH: Heinemann, 1988.

Harste, Jerome C., Virginia A. Woodward, and Carolyn L. Burke. *Language Stories & Literacy Lessons.* Portsmouth, NH: Heinemann, 1984.

Heald-Taylor, Gail. *The Administrator's Guide to Whole Language.* NY: Richard C. Owen Publishers, 1989.

Heath, Shirley Brice. *Ways with Words.* Cambridge, England: Cambridge University Press, 1983.

Hinton, S. E. *The Outsiders.* NY: Dell, 1967.

_____. *Rumble Fish.* NY: Delacorte, 1975.

_____. *Tex.* NY: Delacorte, 1979.

Holdaway, Donald. *The Foundations of Literacy.* Portsmouth, NH: Heinemann, 1979.

Hunt, Irene. *Across Five Aprils.* Chicago, IL: Follett, 1964.

Kalen, Robert J. *Jump Frog Jump.* NY: Greenwillow, 1981.

Keller, Holly. *Geraldine's Blanket.* NY: Greenwillow, 1984.

Krahn, Fernando. *The Creepy Thing.* NY: Clarion, 1982.

_____. *The Great Ape.* NY: Clarion, 1982.

Lamorisse, Albert. *The Red Balloon.* Garden City, NY: Doubleday, 1957.

Langstaff, John M. *Soldier, Soldier, Won't You Marry Me?* Garden City, NY: Doubleday, 1972.

MacLachlan, Patricia. *Sarah Plain and Tall.* NY: Harper & Row, 1985.

_____. *Through Grandpa's Eyes.* NY: Harper & Row, 1980.

Maslow, Abraham. *Toward a Psychology of Being.* Princeton, NJ: Van Nostrand, 1968.

Mayer, Mercer. *A Boy, a Dog and a Frog.* NY: Dial, 1967.

_____. *Ah-Choo.* NY: Dial, 1967.

_____. *Hiccup.* NY: Dial, 1976.

Meyers, Jamie. "Making Invitations that Encourage Active Learning." *Journal of Reading, 32*(6), March 1989, pp. 562–565.

Mwenye, Hadithi. *Greedy Zebra.* Boston, MA: Little, Brown, 1984.

Newman, Judith M. "Insights from Recent Reading and Writing Research and Their Implications for Developing Whole Language Curriculum." In Judith M. Newman, ed. *Whole Language: Theory in Use.* Portsmouth, NH: Heinemann, 1985.

_____, ed. *Whole Language: Theory in Use.* Portsmouth, NH: Heinemann, 1985.

Noddings, Nel. *Caring, A Feminine Approach to Ethics & Moral Education.* Berkeley, CA: University of California Press, 1984.

Rhodes, Lynn. "I Can Read! Predictable Books as Resources for Reading and Writing Instruction." *The Reading Teacher, 34*(5), 1981, pp. 511–518.

Rosenblatt, Louise. "Viewpoints: Transaction Versus Interaction—A Terminological Rescue Operation." *Research in the Teaching of English, 19,* 1985, pp. 96–107.

Rylant, Cynthia. *All I See.* NY: Orchard, 1988.

_____. *Waiting to Waltz, A Childhood: Poems.* Scarsdale, NY: Bradbury, 1984.

_____. *When I Was Young in the Mountains.* NY: Dutton, 1982.

Scarffe, Bronwen. *Oh Bother!* NY: Scholastic, 1986.

Shanklin, Nancy. *Relating Reading and Writing: Developing a Transactional Theory of the Writing Process.* Monographs in Language & Reading Studies. Bloomington, IN: School of Education Publications Office, Indiana University, 1981.

Smath, Jerry. *Up Goes Mr. Downs.* NY: Parents Magazine Press, 1984.

Smith, Frank. "Demonstrations, Engagement and Sensitivity: The Choice Between People and Programs." *Language Arts, 58,* 1981, pp. 634–642.

_____. *Insult to Intelligence.* NY: Arbor House, 1986.

_____. *Psycholinguistics and Reading.* NY: Holt, Rinehart and Winston, 1973.

_____. *Reading Without Nonsense.* NY: Teachers College Press, 1978.

_____. *Understanding Reading.* Toronto: Holt, Rinehart and Winston, 1971.

Spencer, Patricia. "YA Novels in the Ap Classroom: Cruthcher Meets Camus." *English Journal,* November 1989, pp. 44–46.

Taylor, Denny. *Family Literacy: Young Children Learning to Read and Write.* Portsmouth, NH: Heinemann, 1983.

Teale, Bill. *Reading Today.* Newark, DE: International Reading Association, March 1989.

Trelease, Jim. *The Read-Aloud Handbook,* rev. ed. NY: Penguin, 1985.

Valencia, Sheila. "A Portfolio Approach to Classroom Reading Assessment: The Whys, Whats and Hows." *The Reading Teacher, 43*(4), January 1990, pp. 338–340.

———, and David Pearson. "Reading Assessment: Time for a Change." *The Reading Teacher, 40*(8), April 1987.

Vygotsky, Lev S. *Thought and Language.* Cambridge, MA: MIT Press, (1934) 1962.

Waber, Bernard. *Ira Sleeps Over.* Boston: Houghton Mifflin, 1972.

Watson, Dorothy J. "Reader Selected Miscues: Getting More from Sustained Silent Reading." *English Education, 10*(1), 1978, pp. 75–85.

———, Carolyn Burke, and Jerome Harste. *Whole Language: Inquiring Voices.* Ontario, Canada: Scholastic, 1989.

Wells, Gordon. *The Meaning Makers: Children Learning Language and Using Language to Learn.* Portsmouth, NH: Heinemann, 1986.

Young, Ed. *Lon Po Po: A Red-Riding Hood Story from China.* NY: Philomel, 1989.

Zemach, Harve. *Mommy Buy Me a China Doll.* Chicago, IL: Follett, 1966.

Zemelman, Steven, and Harvey Daniels. *A Community of Writers.* Portsmouth, NH: Heinemann, 1988.

APPENDIX A

TEXT SETS

ALTERNATE VERSIONS SETS

CINDERELLA SET

(Includes Multicultural Variants)

Adams, Edward, ed. *Koren Cinderella*. Seoul, Korea. Seoul International Tourist Publishing, 1982.

Berger, Terry, reteller. *Black Fairy Tales*. "The Moss-Green Princess" (Swazi). N.Y.: Atheneum, 1975, pp. 3–14.

Climo, Shirley. *The Egyptian Cinderella*. N.Y.: Crowell, 1989.

Cole, Babette. *Prince Cinders*. N.Y.: Putnam, 1987.

Dowling, Colette. *The Cinderella Complex: Women's Hidden Fear of Independence*. N.Y.: Summit, 1981.

Elmer, Belle L. *Cinderella Rockefeller*. N.Y.: Freundlich, 1986.

Grimm, Jakob. *Cinderella*. N.Y.: Larousse, 1978.

Haviland, Virginia, ed. *Favorite Fairy Tales Told in England*. "Cap O'Rushes." Boston: Little, Brown, 1959, pp. 76–88.

_____. *Favorite Fairy Tales Told in Italy*. "Cenerentola." Boston: Little, Brown, 1965, pp. 3–18.

_____. *Favorite Fairy Tales Told in Norway*. "Princess on the Glass Hill." Boston: Little, Brown, 1961, pp. 3–29.

Hillert, Margaret. *Cinderella at the Ball*. Chicago: Follett, 1970.

Knight, Hilary. *Cinderella*. N.Y.: Random House, 1978.

Louie, Ai-Ling, reteller. *Yeh-Shen: A Cinderella Story from China*. N.Y.: Philomel, 1982.

Razzi, Jim. *Cinderella's Magic Adventure*. N.Y.: Bantam, 1985.

Steel, Flora Annie, reteller. *Tattercoats: An Old English Tale*. Scarsdale, N.Y.: Bradbury, 1976.

Yolen, Jane. *The Moon Ribbon and Other Tales*. "The Moon Ribbon." N.Y.: Cromwell, 1976, pp. 1–15.

Invitations

1. Compare the Cinderella variants from different cultures. How can you tell the stories are from different countries?

2. Compare and contrast the male version of Cinderella (*Prince Cinders*) to any female version. Make a chart that highlights the important dimensions of the stories.
3. See how many cultural variants of Cinderella you can find.
4. Keep a journal of personal connections to any Cinderella version and her experiences/feelings.

JACK AND THE BEANSTALK SET

Cauley, Lorinda Bryan. *Jack and the Beanstalk.* N.Y.: Putnam, 1983.

De la Mare, Walter. *Jack and the Beanstalk.* N.Y.: Knopf, 1959.

Galdone, Paul. *The History of Mother Twaddle and the Marvelous Achievements of Her Son Jack.* N.Y.: Seabury, 1974.

Howe, John. *Jack and the Beanstalk.* Boston: Little, Brown, 1989.

Jacobs, Joseph. *Jack and the Beanstalk.* N.Y.: H.Z. Walck, 1975.

Pearson, Susan. *Jack and the Beanstalk.* N.Y.: Simon & Schuster Books for Young Readers, 1989.

Ross, Tony. *Jack and the Beanstalk.* N.Y.: Delacorte, 1980.

Invitations

1. Rewrite one version of *Jack and the Beanstalk* into a script for a play.
2. Dramatize the story for other classes, teaching them the "Fe Fi Fo Fum" refrain so that they can join in at the appropriate times. Make copies of the refrain so each person can read from their copy.
3. Compare and contrast the different versions of the story. Include comparisons related to Jack's age, the size of the giant, the role of his wife in the story, and so on.
4. In most of the versions the giant says, "I'll grind your bones to make my bread." Explore what *really* gets ground during breadmaking and what all of the ingredients are.
5. One version of *Jack and the Beanstalk* talks about exactly how much food the giant eats for breakfast. Speculate about how much the giant might eat at other meals and compare it to your own meals.

SLEEPING BEAUTY SET

Grimm, Jacob. *The Sleeping Beauty.* N.Y.: Scroll, 1967.

Hutton, Warwick. *The Sleeping Beauty.* N.Y.: Atheneum, 1979.

MacDonald, Ross. *Sleeping Beauty.* N.Y.: Knopf, 1973.

Perrault, Charles. *The Sleeping Beauty.* N.Y.: Knopf, 1961.

Taylor, Elizabeth. *The Sleeping Beauty.* N.Y.: Viking, 1953.
Yolen, Jane. *Sleeping Ugly.* N.Y.: Coward, McCann & Geoghegan, 1981.

Invitations

1. Talk about the differences between being beautiful on the inside and beautiful on the outside.
2. Compare and contrast *Sleeping Ugly* and any version of *Sleeping Beauty.*
3. Compare and contrast the original Grimm classic with a more modern retelling.

AUTHOR SETS

Author studies are a rich way of engaging in exploration of literature and encouraging an understanding of authorship. Student sets of published stories/books should be used as well as commercially published trade books for author studies. Students can build personal and professional profiles of authors by attempting to get inside their heads and considering the kinds of decisions they had to make while writing and the kinds of research they may have had to do to understand and write about their topics (for example, E.B. White kept a spider on his desk and observed it for long periods of time while he was writing *Charlotte's Web* (1952).

Students and teachers can develop questions they would like to ask the authors being studied—local authors are wonderful for this but letters and conference calls can be used as well. There are a number of good resources available that provide biographical information on authors and illustrators.

Commire, Anne. *Something about the Author* (series). Detroit: Gale, 1971.
Kingman, Lee. *Illustrators of Children's Books.* Boston: Horn Book, 1968, 1977.
———. *The Illustrator's Notebook.* Boston: Horn Book, 1978.

ERIC CARLE SET

All about Arthur. N.Y.: Franklin Watts, 1974.
A House for Hermit Crab. N.Y.: Scholastic, 1987.
I See a Song. N.Y.: Crowell, 1973.
The Very Busy Spider. N.Y.: Philomel, 1984.
The Very Grouchy Ladybug. N.Y.: Crowell, 1977.
The Very Hungry Caterpillar. N.Y.: Collins, 1979.
Watch Out! A Giant. N.Y.: Collins-World, 1978.
The Tiny Seed. N.Y.: Scholastic, 1987.

ROBERT CORMIER SET

Novels

After the First Death. N.Y.: Pantheon, 1979.
Beyond the Chocolate War. N.Y.: Knopf (distributed by Random House), 1985.
Bumblebee Flies Anyway, The. N.Y.: Pantheon, 1983.
Chocolate War, The. Boston: G.K. Hall, 1974.
Fade. N.Y.: Delacorte, 1988.
I Am the Cheese. N.Y.: Pantheon, 1977.

Short Stories

Eight Plus One: Stories. N.Y.: Pantheon, 1980.

Invitations

1. Explore alternative story structures as Cormier used them in *I Am the Cheese.* Suggested books include:

   • Childress, Alice. *A Hero Ain't Nothin' But a Sandwich.* N.Y.: Avon, 1973.
   • _____. *Rainbow Jordan.* N.Y.: Coward, McCann & Geoghegan, 1981.
   • Zindel, Paul. *The Pigman.* N.Y.: Harper & Row, 1968.
   • _____. *The Pigman's Legacy.* N.Y.: Harper & Row, 1980.

2. Compare and contrast Cormier's and S.E. Hinton's messages about gangs.
3. Read *Downtown* by Norma Mazer (N.Y.: Avon, 1984), another book about a boy living through a change in identity as Adam does in *I Am the Cheese.*
Compiled by Carol Porter

TOMIE DE PAOLA SET

Retold Stories

Big Anthony and the Magic Ring. N.Y.: Harcourt Brace Jovanovich, 1979.
Fin M'Coul: The Giant of Knockmany Hill. N.Y.: Holiday House, 1981.
Legend of Old Befana: An Italian Christmas Story. N.Y.: Harcourt Brace Jovanovich, 1980.
Strega Nona: An Old Tale. Englewood Cliffs, N.J.: Prentice-Hall, 1975.
Strega Nona's Magic Lessons. N.Y.: Harcourt Brace Jovanovich, 1982.

Factuals

Charlie Needs a Cloak. Englewood Cliffs, N.J.: Prentice-Hall, 1973.
The Cloud Book. N.Y.: Holiday House, 1975.
Quicksand Book. N.Y.: Holiday House, 1977.

Grandparents

Nana Upstairs, Nana Downstairs. N.Y.: Putnam, 1973.
Now One Foot, Now the Other. N.Y.: Putnam, 1981.

Childhood Problems

Andy (That's My Name). Englewood Cliffs, N.J.: Prentice-Hall, 1973.
Oliver Button Is a Sissy. N.Y.: Harcourt Brace Jovanovich, 1979.

Wordless Picture Books

Flicks. N.Y.: Harcourt Brace Jovanovich, 1979.
The Hunter and the Animals. N.Y.: Holiday House, 1981.
The Knight and the Dragon. N.Y.: Putnam, 1980.
Pancakes for Breakfast. N.Y.: Harcourt Brace Jovanovich, 1978.

Period Pieces

Clown of God. N.Y.: Harcourt Brace Jovanovich, 1978.
Helga's Dowry: A Troll Love Story. N.Y.: Harcourt Brace Jovanovich, 1977.
The Legend of Bluebonnet: An Old Tale of Texas. N.Y.: Putnam, 1983.
Marianna May and Nursey. N.Y.: Holiday House, 1983.
Compiled by Kathleen Visovatti

LEO LIONNI SET

Books are listed by themes determined by second-grade readers during literature discussion groups.

Friendship Is Important

Alexander and the Wind-up Mouse. N.Y.: Pantheon, 1969.
Fish Is Fish. N.Y.: Pantheon, 1970.
Little Blue and Little Yellow. N.Y.: McDowell Obolensky, 1959.

There Are Many Ways to Solve Problems

Alphabet Tree. N.Y.: Pantheon, 1968.
Six Crows. N.Y.: Knopf, 1988.

Believe in Yourself

Geraldine, The Music Mouse. N.Y.: Pantheon, 1979.

Share

Tico and the Golden Wings. N.Y.: Pantheon, 1964.

Stick Together

Swimmy. N.Y.: Pantheon, 1963.
Compiled by Kathleen Visovatti

CONTENT AREA SETS

ART SET

Ames, Lee J. *Draw Draw Draw.* N.Y.: Doubleday, 1962.
Benjamin, Carol. *Cartooning for Kids.* N.Y.: Harper & Row, 1982.
de Paola, Tomie. *The Art Lesson.* N.Y.: Putnam, 1989.
Emberly, Ed. *Ed Emberly's Drawing Book: Make a World.* Boston: Little, Brown, 1972.
_____. *Ed Emberly's Drawing Book of Animals.* Boston: Little, Brown, 1970.
_____. *Ed Emberly's Great Thumbprint Drawing Book.* Boston: Little, Brown, 1977.
Shepard, E.H. *The Pooh Sketchbook.* N.Y.: Dutton, 1982.
Compiled by Pat Riordan

MATH SET

Anno, Masaichiro, and Mitsumasa Anno. *Anno's Mysterious Multiplying Jar.* N.Y.: Philomel, 1983.
Anno, Mitsumasa. *Anno's Counting Book.* N.Y.: Crowell, 1975.
_____. *Anno's Counting House.* N.Y.: Philomel, 1982.
_____. *Socrates and the Three Little Pigs.* N.Y.: Philomel, 1986.
Brandley, Franklyn M. *How Little and How Much: A Book about Scales.* N.Y.: Crowell, 1976.
Brown, Marcia. *Listen to a Shape.* N.Y.: Franklin Watts, 1979.
Burningham, John. *Just Cats.* N.Y.: Viking, 1983.
Charosh, Mannis. *Number Ideas through Pictures.* N.Y.: Crowell, 1974.
Froman, Robert. *Angles Are Easy as Pie.* N.Y.: Crowell, 1975.
_____. *The Greatest Guessing Game.* N.Y.: Crowell, 1978.
Gersting, Judith L., and Joseph E. Kuczkowski. *Yes—No; Stop—Go: Some Patterns in Mathematical Logic.* N.Y.: Crowell, 1977.
Hoban, Tana. *Circles, Triangles and Squares.* N.Y.: Macmillan, 1974.
_____. *Count and See.* N.Y.: Macmillan, 1974.

Lewin, Betsy. *Cat Count.* N.Y.: Dodd, Mead, 1981.
Lionni, Leo. *Inch by Inch.* N.Y.: Obolensky, 1960.
Matthews, Louise. *Bunches and Bunches of Bunnies.* N.Y.: Dodd, Mead, 1978.
Myller, Rolf. *How Big Is a Foot?* Bloomfield, Conn.: Connecticut Printers, 1962.
Schwartz, David. *How Much Is a Million?* N.Y.: Lothrop, Lee & Shepard, 1985.
_____. *If You Made a Million.* N.Y.: Lothrop, Lee & Shepard, 1989.
Sitomer, Mindel, and Harry Sitomer. *Circles.* N.Y.: Crowell, 1971.
Srivastava, Jane Jonas. *Number Families.* N.Y.: Crowell, 1979.
_____. *Spaces, Shapes, and Sizes.* N.Y.: Crowell, 1980.
Ziefert, Harriet. *How Big Is Big.* N.Y.: Viking Kestrel, 1989.

GENRE SETS

ADVENTURE SET

Novels

Cole, Brock. *The Goats.* N.Y.: Farrar, Straus & Giroux, 1987.
George, Jean Craighead. *Julie of the Wolves.* N.Y.: Harper & Row, 1972.
_____. *My Side of the Mountain.* N.Y.: Dutton, 1959.
Mazer, Harry. *The Island Keeper.* N.Y.: Delacorte, 1981.
_____. *Snow Bound.* N.Y.: Delacorte, 1973.
Mowat, Farley. *Never Cry Wolf.* N.Y.: Franklin Watts, 1963.
O'Dell, Scott. *Island of the Blue Dolphins.* Boston: Houghton Mifflin, 1960.
Paulsen, Gary. *Hatchet.* N.Y.: Bradbury, 1987.
Richter, Conrad. *The Light in the Forest.* N.Y.: Knopf (distributed by Random House), 1953.
Speare, Elizabeth George. *The Sign of the Beaver.* Boston: Houghton Mifflin, 1983.

Picture Books

Carle, Eric. *The Tiny Seed.* N.Y.: Crowell, 1970.
Cole, Joanna. *Bony-Legs.* N.Y.: Four Winds, 1983.
Howe, John. *Jack and the Beanstalk.* Boston: Little, Brown, 1989.
Mayer, Mercer. *Just Me and My Dad.* N.Y.: Golden, 1977.
Sendak, Maurice. *Where the Wild Things Are.* N.Y.: Harper & Row, 1963.
Yolen, Jane. *Owl Moon.* N.Y.: Philomel, 1987.

Invitations

1. Explore the emotional changes characters undergo as a result of surviving on their own.

2. Develop a survival handbook based on the experiences of the characters in the books you have read in the Adventure Set.
3. Compare and contrast the survival of Brian in *Hatchet* to Cleo in *The Island Keeper.*
4. Read adventure books with similar settings: for example: Alaska: *Julie of the Wolves* and *Never Cry Wolf;* contemporary setting: *The Goats, Hatchet, The Island Keeper, Snow Bound.*
Compiled by Carol Porter

JOKES AND RIDDLES SET

Bishop. Ann. *Noah Riddle?* Chicago: Albert Whitman, 1977.
Cerf, Bennett. *Bennett Cerf's Book of Animal Riddles.* N.Y.: Random House, 1964.
Hall, Katy. *Snakey Riddles.* N.Y.: Dial, 1990.
Kessler, Leonard. *Old Turtles Riddle and Joke Book.* N.Y.: Greenwillow, 1986.
McKie, Roy. *The Riddle Book.* N.Y.: Random House, 1978.
Phillips, Louis. *The Upside Down Riddle Book.* N.Y.: Lathrop, Lee & Shepard, 1982.
Sarnoff, J., and R. Ruffins. *Giants!: A Riddle Book.* N.Y.: Scribner, 1977.
Sterne, Noelle. *Tyrannasauraus Wrecks: A Book of Dinosaur Riddles.* N.Y.: Harper & Row, 1979.

Invitations

1. Consider why jokes make you laugh.
2. Think about the similarities and differences between jokes and riddles.
3. Write your own jokes and riddles book. Where did you get your ideas? How did you know how to write the jokes and riddles?
Compiled by Pat Riordan

POETRY SET

This set includes books appropriate for upper and lower grades and professional books on teaching poetry.

Dunning, Stephen, Edward Lueders, and Hugh Smith, eds. *Reflections on a Gift of Watermelon Pickle and Other Modern Verse.* Glenview, IL: Scott Foresman, 1966.
Fleischman, Paul. *Joyful Noise: Poems for Two Voices.* N.Y.: Harper & Row, 1988.

Heard, Georgia. *For the Good of the Earth and Sun: Teaching Poetry.* Portsmouth, N.H.: Heinemann, 1989.

Hopkins, Lee Bennett. *Still as a Star.* Boston: Little, Brown, 1989.

Hughes, Langston. *The Dream Keeper and Other Poems.* N.Y.: Knopf, 1932.

Koch, Kenneth. *Rose, Where Did You Get that Red? Teaching Great Poetry to Children.* N.Y.: Random House, 1973.

Koch, Kenneth, and Kate Farrell, eds. *Talking to the Sun.* N.Y.: Holt, Rinehart & Winston, 1985.

Margokis, Richard. *Secrets of a Small Brother.* N.Y.: Macmillan, 1984.

Moore, Lilian. *I Feel the Same Way.* N.Y.: Atheneum, 1967.

Prelutsky, Jack. *Random House Book of Poetry.* N.Y.: Random House, 1983.

———. *Read Aloud Rhymes for the Very Young.* N.Y.: Knopf, 1986.

Silverstein, Shel. *Giraffe and a Half.* N.Y.: Harper & Row, 1964.

Weiss, Renee Karol. *A Paper Zoo.* N.Y.: Macmillan, 1968.

Zolotow, Charlotte. *All that Sunlight.* N.Y.: Harper & Row, 1967.

PREDICTABLE SET

Reading materials are predictable for young readers when they reflect life experiences or contain particular text structures. Lynn Rhodes (1981) discusses predictability in terms of elements such as the match between text and illustrations, the rhythm of the language, familiar sequences, rhymes, and cumulative patterns. Such books (and those that children have heard repeatedly either at home or at school) make learning to read by reading an immediate reality for even the youngest, least experienced beginning reader. A good collection of such books can be used as the core component of a kindergarten and first-grade reading program. Shared Reading* is a strategy that uses predictable materials to support beginning readers. These materials are also uniquely suited for extending reading into writing by borrowing the author's patterns while communicating a personal message.

Shared Reading* is a strategy that uses predictable materials to support beginning readers. It involves introducing the story through oral reading and discussion, and repeated readings, during which students assume more and more responsibility, and independent reading.

Asch, Frank. *Happy Birthday, Moon.* N.Y.: Scholastic, 1982.

Bonn, Rose. *I Know an Old Lady.* N.Y.: Scholastic, 1961.

Brown, Margaret Wise. *Goodnight Moon.* N.Y.: Harper & Row, 1947.

———. *The Runaway Bunny.* N.Y.: Harper & Row, 1942.

---

* All asterisks throughout the book refer the reader to Chapter 10 where full strategy descriptions can be found.

Butler, Andrea (project editor) and a Year One Class. *The Bean Bag that Mom Made.* Crystal Lake, I.L.: Rigby (distributor), 1984. (Same pattern as *This Is the House that Jack Built.*)

Carle, Eric. *The Grouchy Ladybug.* N.Y.: Crowell, 1977.

_____. *The Very Busy Spider.* N.Y.: Philomel, 1984.

_____. *The Very Hungry Caterpillar.* N.Y.: Collins, 1979.

Cowley, Joy. *Greedy Cat.* Wellington, New Zealand. N.Y.: Richard C. Owen (distributor), 1986.

_____. *Greedy Cat Is Hungry.* Wellington, New Zealand. N.Y.: Richard C. Owen (distributor), 1988.

de Regniers, Beatrice Schenk. *The Day Everybody Cried.* N.Y.: Viking, 1967.

_____. *May I Bring a Friend?* N.Y.: Atheneum, 1972.

_____. *Willy O'Dwyer Jumped in the Fire.* N.Y.: Atheneum, 1968.

Ecker, John. *Seven Little Rabbits.* N.Y.: Scholastic, 1973.

Elting, Mary, and Michael Folsom. *Q Is for Duck.* N.Y.: Clarion, 1980.

Flack, Marjorie. *Ask Mr. Bear.* N.Y.: Macmillan, 1932.

Galdone, Paul. *The Gingerbread Boy.* N.Y.: Seabury, 1975.

_____. *Henny Penny.* N.Y.: Scholastic, 1968.

_____. *Little Red Hen.* N.Y.: Scholastic, 1973.

_____. *Little Red Riding Hood.* N.Y.: McGraw-Hill, 1974.

_____. *The Three Bears.* N.Y.: Scholastic, 1972.

_____. *The Three Billy Goats Gruff.* N.Y.: Seabury, 1973.

_____. *The Three Little Pigs.* N.Y.: Seabury, 1970.

Goss, Janet L., and Jerome C. Harste. *It Didn't Frighten Me.* School Book Fairs, 1981.

Guarino, Deborah. *Is Your Mama a Llama?* N.Y.: Scholastic, 1989.

Hale, Sarah Josepha, ed. *Mary Had a Little Lamb.* Tomie De Paola, illus. N.Y.: Holiday House, 1984.

Hoboran, Mary Ann. *A House Is a House for Me.* N.Y.: Scholastic, 1978.

Hutchins, Pat. *Rosie's Walk.* N.Y.: Macmillan, 1968.

Kasza, Keiko. *The Wolf's Chicken Stew.* N.Y.: Putnam, 1987.

Martin, Bill, Jr. *Brown Bear, Brown Bear, What Do You See?* N.Y.: Holt, Rinehart & Winston, 1983.

Neitzel, Shirley. *The Jacket I Wear in the Snow.* N.Y.: Greenwillow, 1989. (Same pattern as *This Is the House that Jack Built.*)

Polushkin, Maria. *Mother, Mother, I Want Another.* N.Y.: Crown, 1978.

Rosen, Michael. *We're Going on a Bear Hunt.* N.Y.: McElderry, 1989.

Scarffe, Bronwen. *Oh Bother!* N.Y.: Scholastic, 1986.

Scheer, Jullian, and Bileck, Marvin. *Rain Makes Applesauce.* N.Y.: Holiday House, 1964.

Slobodkina, Esphyr. *Caps for Sale.* N.Y.: Scholastic, 1940.

Tolstoy, Alexi. *The Great Big Enormous Turnip.* N.Y.: Franklin Watts, 1968.

Shaw, Charles. *It Looked Like Spilt Milk.* N.Y.: Harper & Row, 1947.

Stevens, Janet. *The House that Jack Built*. N.Y.: Holiday House, 1985.

Wildsmith, Brian. *The Twelve Days of Christmas*. N.Y.: Franklin Watts, 1972.

Wood, Audrey. *The Napping House*. San Diego: Harcourt Brace Jovanovich, 1984.

Zemach, Margot. *The Teeny Tiny Woman*. N.Y.: Scholastic, 1965.

Invitations

1. Choose one of your favorite predictable books. Borrow the author's pattern to make your own book. Whole class books can be made with individuals or partners writing and drawing their own pages.

2. Dramatize a predictable story using Readers' Theater. Adapt the selected literature to make a simple script—use a narrator for transitions and shorten long or complicated parts. Don't worry about props or costumes, just focus on bringing the story to life. (For more on Readers' Theater, *see* Harste, Short and Burke, 1988; or write to Readers' Theater Script Service, P.O. Box 178333, San Diego, CA 92117.)

3. Map the structure of a predictable story. For example, when the main character in the story starts out and ends up in the same place (for example, Max in his room in *Where the Wild Things Are,* or the bunny with her mother in *The Runaway Bunny*), use a circular frame divided into pie sections to track the character's movements from the beginning of the story to the end. Other story structures can look like stairsteps, extending step-by-step toward the top (the story's climax) and then gradually descending. *The Napping House* is an example of this kind of structure and can be diagrammed on the chalkboard, on an overhead transparency, or on chart paper. Once readers see the form of a story they should be involved in the mapping and encouraged to create their own representative diagrams.

4. Use an oral cloze to vary significant words or phrases in a predictable story. For example, *The Great Big Enormous Turnip* can become *The Great Big Stupendous Tomato;* or *We're Going on a Bear Hunt* can become *We're Going on a Treasure Hunt*.

5. Make a class Big Book following a predictable pattern, such as *Brown Bear, Brown Bear*. Have one or two students write and illustrate individual pages, and then decide as a class on the order.

6. Make stick or finger puppets using tagboard or tongue depressors, and dramatize a predictable story. Perform for other classes.

7. Using *I Know an Old Lady* write different verses by choosing other animals the old lady could swallow and other people who could do the swallowing (old man, old teacher, old farmer); create a lift-the-flap book that shows the animals in the old lady's stomach when her apron is raised.

Compiled by Pat Riordan

SCIENCE-FICTION/FANTASY SET

Fantasy Novels

Alexander, Lloyd. *Westmark.* N.Y.: Dutton, 1981.
Babbitt, Natalie. *The Search for Delicious.* N.Y.: Farrar, Straus & Giroux, 1969.
———. *Tuck Everlasting.* N.Y.: Farrar, Straus & Giroux, 1975.
Kaye, M.M. *The Ordinary Princess.* Harmondsworth, Middlesex, England: Kestral Books, 1980.
Lewis, C.S. *The Lion, the Witch, and the Wardrobe.* N.Y.: Macmillan, 1983, 1981.
McKinley, Robin. *The Hero and the Crown.* N.Y.: Greenwillow, 1985.
Sleator, William. *Interstellar Pig.* N.Y.: Dutton, 1984.
Voigt, Cynthia. *Building Blocks.* N.Y.: Atheneum, 1984.

Fantasy Picture Books and Short Stories

Barrett, Judi. *Cloudy with a Chance of Meatballs.* N.Y.: Atheneum, 1978.
Gackenbach, Dick. *Harry and the Terrible Whatzit.* N.Y.: Seabury, 1977.
Rand McNally. *The Princess Book.* Chicago: Rand McNally, 1974.
Small, David. *Imogene's Antlers.* N.Y.: Crown, 1985.

Science-Fiction Novels

Bradbury, Ray. *The Martian Chronicles.* Garden City, N.Y.: Doubleday, 1958.
Danziger, Paula. *This Place Has No Atmosphere.* N.Y.: Delacorte, 1986.
Heinlein, Robert. *Have Space Suit — Will Travel.* N.Y.: Scribner, 1958.
L'Engle, Madeleine. *A Wrinkle in Time.* N.Y.: Farrar, Straus & Giroux, 1962.

Science-Fiction Short Stories

Bradbury, Ray. *The Illustrated Man.* Garden City, N.Y.: Doubleday, 1951.
———. *R Is for Rocket.* Garden City, N.Y.: Doubleday, 1962.
Lipsyte, Robert. "Future Tense," *Sixteen Short Stories by Outstanding Writers for Young Adults.* Donald R. Gallo, ed. N.Y.: Dell, 1984.
Slesar, Henry. "Good Morning! This Is the Future." *Read Magazine.* Middleton, Conn.: Division of *Weekly Reader,* November 26, 1976.

Invitations

1. Using several of Bradbury's short stories, explore his predictions regarding changes in the structure of families.
2. Read books and short stories in which a woman is the major character.
3. Develop generalizations for or characteristics of the fantasy and science-fiction genres. Compare and contrast the two.

4. Read a sequel to one of the books.
5. Read another book and/or short story with similar settings (for example, medieval) or characters (for example, animals talking).

Compiled by Carol Porter

SONGS TO READ SET

Glazer, Tom. *On Top of Spaghetti.* N.Y.: Doubleday, 1982.

Raffi. *Down by the Bay.* N.Y.: Crown, 1987.

_____. *One Light, One Sun.* N.Y.: Crown, 1988.

_____. *Wheels on the Bus.* N.Y.: Crown, 1987.

Sendak, Maurice. *Chicken Soup with Rice.* N.Y.: Harper & Row, 1962.

_____. *Pierre.* N.Y.: Harper & Row, 1962.

Westcott, Nadine Bernard. *Skip to My Lou.* Boston: Little, Brown, 1989.

Compiled by Pat Riordan

THEME SETS

DEATH SET

This set was developed by Barbara Lindberg for a workshop given to elementary and junior high school teachers on using literature in the classroom. To begin the workshop Barbara filled the room with materials on the topic. Desks and chairs were placed so that they formed small groups. Felt pens and paper were provided. This was the way members of the workshop could issue invitations to others to join them in Literature Discussions (the idea was adapted from Carolyn Burke). Multiple copies of books were placed together on one or two tables. Single copies of books, topically related, were on other tables, and collections of materials were set out. These included books of poetry and individual poems, plays, a collection of short stories and a list of appropriate stories in the basal. There were also newspapers that contained articles on legal issues and court decisions, local newspaper obituaries, and a newspaper published in northern Wisconsin that had information on causes of Native-American deaths. There were art books that had the works of painters like Munch and Delacroix, and a few songs. Periodicals were found that had articles on different aspects of the main topic.

Teachers were asked to form their own Literature Discussion groups. They were to participate in two circles: one in which everyone read the same book; the other where participants selected a topic and each person read a different book on that topic. Some of the topics of interest to teachers were euthanasia, the right to die, the life cycle in nature, suicide, anorexia, Alzheimer's disease, and cystic fibrosis.

Barbara read *Come Again in the Spring* aloud and led a discussion on predestination. She also wrote a piece on the death of her mother and read that aloud, asking for responses. Time at the end of each workshop was reserved for reflection and writing in journals. Barbara was careful to give personal responses to each entry. She says of the workshop:

> Teachers are still borrowing books from me and we talk books when we meet. They appreciated being pulled away from manuals and into wonderful reading materials. Our brainstorming produced ideas like journaling, learning from demonstrations or by doing, reading, writing, sharing; but the most powerful thing that got them started doing those things was an environment in which reading was made exciting because of the many choices and the openness with which discussions took place.

Following are selected materials Barbara used in her thematic unit on death.

Fiction

Babbitt, Natalie. *Tuck Everlasting.* N.Y.: Farrar, Straus & Giroux, 1975.
Brown, Margaret Wise. *The Dead Bird.* Reading, Mass.: Addison-Wesley, 1938.
Clifton, Lucille. *Everett Anderson's Goodbye.* N.Y.: Holt, Rinehart & Winston, 1983.
Coatsworth, Elizabeth. *The Cat Who Went to Heaven.* N.Y.: Scholastic, 1958.
Cormier, Robert. *The Bumblebee Flies Anyway.* N.Y.: Pantheon, 1980.
Duncan, Lois. *Killing Mr. Griffin.* N.Y.: Dell, 1978.
Gipson, Fred. *Old Yeller.* N.Y.: Scholastic, 1956.
Gunther, John. *Death Be Not Proud.* N.Y.: Harper & Row, 1949.
Henry, O. *The Last Leaf.* Mankato, Minnesota: Creative Education, 1980.
Hinton, S.E. *Rumble Fish.* N.Y.: Dell, 1975.
Kennedy, Richard. *Come Again in the Spring.* N.Y.: Harper & Row, 1976.
Lowry, Lois. *A Summer to Die.* N.Y.: Bantam, 1977.
Mazer, Norma Fox. *After the Rain.* N.Y.: Avon, 1987.
Miller, Robyn. *Robyn's Book.* N.Y.: Scholastic, 1986.
Paterson, Katherine. *Bridge to Terabithia.* N.Y.: Avon, 1977.
Peck, Robert Newton. *A Day No Pigs Would Die.* N.Y.: Dell, 1972.
Smith, Doris Buchanan. *A Taste of Blackberries.* N.Y.: Scholastic, 1973.
Terris, Susan. *Nell's Quilt.* N.Y.: Scholastic, 1987.
Walker, Alice. *To Hell with Dying.* San Diego: Harcourt Brace Jovanovich, 1967.
Woolf, Virginia. *The Widow and the Parrot.* San Diego: Harcourt Brace Jovanovich, 1982.

Nonfiction

Deford, Frank. *Alex: The Life of a Child.* New American Library, 1983.
Dolan, Edward F. *Matters of Life and Death.* N.Y.: Franklin Watts, 1982.

Hazen, Barbara Shook. *Why Did Grandpa Die?* N.Y.: Golden, 1985.

Hermes, Patricia. *A Time to Listen: Preventing Youth Suicide.* San Diego: Harcourt Brace Jovanovich, 1987.

Kübler-Ross, Elisabeth. *To Live Until We Say Good-Bye.* Englewood Cliffs, N.J.: Prentice Hall, 1978.

LeShan, Eda. *Learning to Say Good-by.* N.Y.: Macmillan, 1977.

Pringle, Laurence P. *Death Is Natural.* N.Y.: Four Winds, 1977.

Rofes, Eric E., ed. *The Kid's Book about Death and Dying.* Boston: Little, Brown, 1985.

Rogers, Fred. *When a Pet Dies.* N.Y.: Putnam, 1988.

Schleifer, Jay. *Everything You Need to Know about Teen Suicide.* N.Y.: Rosen Publishing, 1988.

Compiled by Barbara Lindberg

FEELINGS SET

Aliki. *Feelings.* N.Y.: Mulberry, 1984.

Cleary, Beverly. *Dear Mr. Henshaw.* N.Y.: Dell, 1983.

Cowley, Joy. *A Walk with Grandpa.* New Zealand: Shortland Publications, 1988.

Demers, Jan. *On Sunday I Lost My Cat.* Worthington, Ohio: Willowisp, 1986.

de Paola, Tomie. *Now One Foot, Now the Other.* N.Y.: Putnam, 1980.

Fox, Mem. *Wilfrid Gordon McDonald Partridge.* N.Y.: Kane/Miller, 1985.

Graham, Margaret. *Benjy's Dog House.* N.Y.: Scholastic, 1983.

O'huigin, Sean. *Scary Poems for Rotten Kids.* Windsor, Ontario: Black Moss, 1988.

Rylant, Cynthia. *All I See.* N.Y.: Orchard, 1988.

_____. *Birthday Presents.* N.Y.: Orchard, 1987.

_____. *Miss Maggie.* N.Y.: Dutton, 1983.

_____. *Night in the Country.* N.Y.: Bradbury, 1986.

_____. *The Relatives Came.* N.Y.: Bradbury, 1985.

_____. *When I Was Young in the Mountains.* N.Y.: Dutton, 1982.

Sendak, Maurice. *Where the Wild Things Are.* N.Y.: Harper & Row, 1963.

Shreve, Susan. *The Flunking of Joshua T. Bates.* N.Y.: Scholastic, 1984.

Viorst, Judith. *The Tenth Good Thing about Barney.* N.Y.: Macmillan, 1971.

Zion, Gene. *No Roses for Harry!* N.Y.: Scholastic, 1958.

Zolotow, Charlotte. *William's Doll.* N.Y.: Harper & Row, 1972.

Compiled by Penny Silvers

FEMALE PROTAGONIST SET

Bauer, Carolyn Feller. *My Mom Travels a Lot.* N.Y.: Puffin, 1981.

Brink, Carol. *Caddie Woodlawn.* N.Y.: Macmillan, 1935.

Cooney, Barbara. *Miss Rumphius.* N.Y.: Puffin, 1982.

Frank, Anne. *Anne Frank: The Diary of a Young Girl.* N.Y.: Doubleday, 1967.

George, Jean Craighead. *Julie of the Wolves.* N.Y.: Harper & Row, 1972.

Greene, Bette. *Summer of My German Soldier.* N.Y.: Dial, 1973.

Kerr, M.E. *Dinky Hocker Shoots Smack.* N.Y.: Harper & Row, 1972.

Klein, Norma. *Girls Can Be Anything.* N.Y.: Dutton, 1973.

Komaiko, Leah. *Annie Bananie.* N.Y.: Scholastic, 1987.

L'Engle, Madeleine. *A Wrinkle in Time.* N.Y.: Farrar, Straus & Giroux, 1962.

Lindgren, Astrid. *Pippi Longstocking.* N.Y.: Viking, (c 1950) 1969, 1976.

Lowry, Lois. *Anastasia Again!* Boston: Houghton Mifflin, 1981.

———. *Anastasia Has the Answers.* Boston: Houghton Mifflin, 1986.

———. *Anastasia Krupnik.* Boston: Houghton Mifflin, 1979.

———. *Anastasia on Her Own.* Boston: Houghton Mifflin, 1985.

Montgomery, L.M. *Anne of Green Gables.* N.Y.: Grosset & Dunlap, 1935.

Munsch, Robert. *The Paper Bag Princess.* Toronto, Canada: Annick, 1980.

O'Dell, Scott. *Island of the Blue Dolphins.* Boston: Houghton Mifflin, 1960.

Paterson, Katherine. *The Great Gilly Hopkins.* N.Y.: Crowell, 1978.

———. *Jacob Have I Loved.* N.Y.: Crowell, 1980.

Speare, Elizabeth George. *The Witch of Blackbird Pond.* Boston: Houghton Mifflin, 1958.

Steig, William. *Brave Irene.* N.Y.: Farrar, Straus & Giroux, 1986.

Voigt, Cynthia. *Dicey's Song.* N.Y.: Atheneum, 1982.

———. *Tree by Leaf.* N.Y.: Atheneum, 1988.

LIFE CYCLES SET

Back, Christine. *Chicken and Egg.* Morristown, N.J.: Silver Burdett, 1986.

———. *Tadpole and Frog.* Morristown, N.J.: Silver Burdett, 1986.

Brooks, Robert B. *So That's How I Was Born!* N.Y.: Little, Simon, 1983.

Cole, Joanna. *A Fish Hatches.* N.Y.: Morrow, 1978.

———. *A Frog's Body.* N.Y.: Morrow, 1980.

Fischer-Nagel, Heiderose, and Andreas Fischer-Nagel. *Life of the Honeybee.* Minneapolis, MN: Carolrhoda, 1986.

Freschet, Berniece. *The Web in the Grass.* N.Y.: Scribner, 1972.

Hogan, Paula. *The Life Cycle of the Honeybee.* Milwaukee, WI.: Raintree, 1987.

Newton, James. *A Forest Is Reborn.* N.Y.: Crowell, 1982.

Oxford Scientific Films. *The Butterfly Cycle.* N.Y.: Putnam, 1976.

Parker, Nancy Winslow, and Joan Richards Wright. *Frogs, Toads, Lizards, and Salamanders.* N.Y.: Greenwillow, 1990.

Terry, Trevor, and Margaret Linton. *Ant: The Life Cycle.* N.Y.: Bookwright, 1988.

Thompson, Susan L. *Diary of a Monarch Butterfly.* Riverside, CT.: Magic Circle; N.Y.: distributed by Walker, 1976.

Williams, John. *The Life Cycle of a Frog.* N.Y.: Bookwright, 1988.

MOTHER GOOSE SET

Chambless-Rigie, Jane, illustrator. *The Real Mother Goose Clock Book.* N.Y.: Checkerboard, 1984.

Delfiner, Gary. *Mother Goose Car Rhyme Book.* Philadelphia, PA.: Running Press, 1988.

Lucas, Barbara. *Little People's Mother Goose.* N.Y.: Derrydale, 1988.

Marzollo, Jean. *The Rebus Treasury.* N.Y.: Dial, 1986.

_____. *Three Little Kittens.* N.Y.: Scholastic, 1985.

Piper, Watty. *Mother Goose: A Treasury of Best Loved Rhymes.* N.Y.: Platt, 1972.

Provensen, Alice, and Martin Provensen. *Old Mother Hubbard.* N.Y.: Random House, 1977.

Reid, Barbara. *Sing a Song of Mother Goose.* N.Y.: Scholastic, 1987.

Wyndham, Robert. *Chinese Mother Goose Rhymes.* N.Y.: Philomel, 1968.

Invitations

1. Choose and dramatize selected rhymes.
2. Interview Mother Goose characters.
3. Use some of the nursery rhyme language for math concepts, such as time, numbers.
4. Write rhymes on butcher block paper, then illustrate and use them for Shared Reading.*

Compiled by Pat Riordan

PEACE SET

Adler, David A. *Martin Luther King, Jr.: Free at Last.* N.Y.: Holiday House, 1986.

Alexander, Martha. *I Sure Am Glad to See You, Blackboard Bear.* N.Y.: Dial, 1979.

Anno, Mitsumasa. *All in a Day.* N.Y.: Philomel, 1986.

Baumann, Kurt. *The Prince and the Lute.* N.Y.: North-South Books (distributed by Holt, Rinehart & Winston), 1986.

Blaine, Marge. *The Terrible Thing that Happened at Our House.* N.Y.: Parents Magazine, 1975.

Burningham, John. *Mr. Gumpy's Motor Car.* N.Y.: Crowell, 1976.

Carle, Eric. *The Grouchy Ladybug.* N.Y.: Crowell, 1977.

Carrick, Donald. *Harold and the Giant Knight.* N.Y.: Clarion, 1982.

Charters, Janet. *The General.* N.Y.: Dutton, 1961.

Clymer, Eleanor. *The Big Pile of Dirt.* N.Y.: Holt, Rinehart & Winston, 1968.

de Paola, Tomie. *The Hunter and the Animals.* N.Y.: Holiday House, 1981.

———. *The Knight and the Dragon.* N.Y.: Putnam, 1980.

———. *The Mysterious Giant of Barletta.* Harcourt Brace Jovanovich, 1984.

Emberly, Barbara. *Dummer Hoff.* Englewood Cliffs, N.J.: Prentice-Hall, 1967.

Erickson, Russell. *Warton and Morton.* N.Y.: Lothrop, Lee & Shepard, 1976.

Ernst, Lisa Campbell. *Sam Johnson and the Blue Ribbon Quilt.* N.Y.: Lothrop, Lee & Shepard, 1983.

Fitzhugh, Louise, and Santa Scoppettone. *Bang, Bang, You're Dead.* N.Y.: Harper & Row, 1969.

Gauch, Patricia. *Once Upon a Dinkelsbuhe.* N.Y.: Putnam, 1977.

Hamanda, Kirusuke. *The Tears of the Dragon.* N.Y.: Parents Magazine, 1967.

Hoban, Russell. *A Bargain for Frances.* N.Y.: Harper & Row, 1987.

Hutchins, Pat. *Changes, Changes.* N.Y.: Macmillan, 1971.

Kellogg, Steven. *Island of the Skog.* N.Y.: Dial, 1973.

Larrick, Nancy. *When the Dark Comes Dancing: A Bedtime Poetry Book.* N.Y.: Putnam/Philomel, 1983.

Leaf, Munro. *The Story of Ferdinand.* N.Y.: Viking, 1977.

Lionni, Leo. *Swimmy.* N.Y.: Pantheon, 1963.

Lobel, Anita. *Potatoes, Potatoes.* N.Y.: Harper & Row, 1967.

Minarik, Else Holmelund. *No Fighting, No Biting.* N.Y.: Harper & Row, 1978.

Piatti, CeLestino. *The Happy Owls.* N.Y.: Atheneum, 1964.

Pinkwater, Manus. *Bear's Picture.* N.Y.: Holt Rinehart & Winston, 1972.

Provensen, Alice, and Martin Provensen. *A Peaceable Kingdom: The Shaker Abecedarius.* N.Y.: Viking, 1978.

Seuss, Dr. *The Butter Battle Book.* N.Y.: Random House, 1984.

———. *The Lorax.* N.Y.: Random House, 1971.

Steadman, Ralph. *The Bridge.* London: Collins, 1972.

Udry, Janice. *Let's Be Enemies.* N.Y.: Harper & Row, 1961.

Wildsmith, Brian. *The Lazy Bear.* N.Y.: Franklin Watts, 1973.

———. *The Lion and the Rat.* N.Y.: Franklin Watts, 1963.

———. *Owl and the Woodpecker.* N.Y.: Franklin Watts, 1971.

Williams, Vera. *Music, Music for Everyone.* N.Y.: Greenwillow, 1985.

Invitations

1. Watch for peaceful behaviors/gestures in your family and friends. Write them on a classroom chart or keep a Peace Journal.
2. Explore the idea of peace from the different perspectives taken in some of the books.
3. After reading several books on peace chart the various dimensions of peace.
4. Map the times in history when our nation has been at peace. Find out what countries in the world have had the longest periods of peaceful existence.

Compiled by Kathleen Visovatti

READING SET

Allington, Richard, and Kathleen Krull. *Beginning to Learn about Reading.* Milwaukee, WI.: Raintree, 1980.

Armstrong, William H. *Sounder.* N.Y.: Harper & Row, 1969.

Bunting, Eve. *The Wednesday Surprise.* N.Y.: Clarion, 1989.

Cohen, Miriam. *When Will I Read?* N.Y.: Greenwillow, 1977.

Duvoisin, Roger. *Petunia.* N.Y.: Knopf, 1950.

Martin, Bill, Jr. "The Making of a Reader: A Personal Narrative." In *Children's Literature in the Reading Program.* Bernice E. Cullinan, ed. Newark, Del.: International Reading Association, 1987.

Seuss, Dr. *I Can Read with My Eyes Shut!* N.Y.: Random House Beginner Books, 1978.

Compiled by Kathleen Visovatti

TRANSFORMATION SET

Transformation is a common literary tool used in many old and modern tales. It is usually taken to mean a physical change of some kind (for example, when Sylvester, the donkey, turns into a stone in William Steig's *Sylvester and the Magic Pebble,* 1969). This Text Set expands the concept to include personality and attitudinal transformations.

Transformation is also an idea that cuts across content areas (for example, see the Life Cycle Set for transformation ideas in science) and so makes for a strong, natural integration of literature and content material. This set includes multi-age texts. (For a detailed description of a focus unit developed around the idea of transformation in literature, see Moss, Joy F. *Focus on Literature: A Context for Literacy Learning.* N.Y.: Richard C. Owen Publishers, 1990.)

Andersen, Hans Christian. *The Ugly Duckling,* R.P. Keigwin, trans., Joyannes Larsen, illus. N.Y.: Macmillan, 1967.

———. *The Wild Swans.* Marcia Brown, illus. Scribner's 1963.

Cleary, Beverly. *Dear Mr. Henshaw.* N.Y.: Morrow, 1983.

Craig, M. Jean, reteller. *The Donkey Prince* (Grimm tale). Garden City, N.Y.: Doubleday, 1977.

Crutcher, Chris. *The Crazy Horse Electric Game.* N.Y.: Greenwillow, 1987.

———. *Running Loose.* N.Y.: Greenwillow, 1983.

———. *Stotan!* N.Y.: Greenwillow, 1986.

Gerstein, Mordicai. *Prince Sparrow.* N.Y.: Four Winds, 1984.

Grant, Joan. *The Monster that Grew Small.* N.Y.: Lothrop, Lee & Shepard, 1987.

Grimm, Jacob, and Wilhelm Grimm. *The Frog Prince.* Paul Galdone, adaptor and illus. N.Y.: McGraw-Hill, 1975.

———. *King Grisly-Beard.* Edgar Taylor, trans., Maurice Sendak, illus. N.Y.: Farrar, Straus & Giroux, 1973.

———. *The Seven Ravens.* Elizabeth D. Crawford, Lisbeth Zwerger, illus. N.Y.: Morrow, 1981.

Hayden, Torey. *One Child.* N.Y.: Putnam, 1980.

MacLachlan, Patricia. *Sarah, Plain and Tall.* N.Y.: Harper & Row, 1985.

Mayer, Marianna, reteller. *Beauty and the Beast.* Mercer Mayer, illus. N.Y.: Four Winds, 1978.

Paterson, Katherine. *Bridge to Terabithia.* N.Y.: Crowell, 1977.

———. *The Great Gilly Hopkins.* N.Y.: Crowell, 1977.

Pearce, Phillipa, reteller. *Beauty and the Beast.* Alan Barrett, illus. N.Y.: Crowell, 1972.

Saint Exupery, Antoine de. *The Little Prince.* N.Y.: Harcourt Brace Jovanovich, 1943.

Steig, William. *Caleb and Kate.* N.Y.: Farrar, Straus & Giroux, 1977.

———. *Solomon the Rusty Nail.* N.Y.: Farrar, Straus & Giroux, 1985.

———. *Sylvester and the Magic Pebble.* N.Y.: Simon & Schuster, 1969.

Turnbull, Ann. *The Sand Horse.* N.Y.: Atheneum, 1989.

Yashima, Taro. *Crow Boy.* N.Y.: Viking, 1955.

Yolen, Jane. *The Simple Prince.* N.Y.: Parents' Magazine, 1978.

White, E.B. *Charlotte's Web.* N.Y.: Harper & Row, 1952.

Invitations

1. What are your own life transformations (physical and psychological)? Why did they occur? Did you welcome them? How did other people react to them?
2. Compare the nature of transformations in at least three books.
3. Find other transformation tales and create one of your own.
4. Discuss the similarities and differences between internal and external transformations (outside/inside, physical/psychological).
5. Choose one transformation story and represent it through dance, art, or mime.

For other sets of thematically related texts see Lima, C.W. *A to Zoo: Subject Access to Children's Picture Books.* N.Y.: Bowker, 1982.

TOPIC SETS

AFRICA SET

Aardema, Verna. *Bimwili & the Zimwi.* N.Y.: Dial, 1985.

———. *Bringing the Rain to Kapiti Plain.* N.Y.: Dial, 1981.

———. *Oh KoJo! How Could You?* N.Y.: Dial, 1984.

_____. *Why Mosquitos Buzz in People's Ears.* N.Y.: Dial, 1975.

Dayrell, Elphinstone. *Why the Sun and the Moon Live in the Sky.* N.Y.: Houghton Mifflin, 1968.

Feeling, Muriel. *Moja Means One: Swahili Counting Book.* N.Y.: Dial, 1971.

Lewin, Hugh. *Jafta's Father.* Minneapolis, Minnesota: First Ave. Editions, 1983.

Musgrove, Margaret. *Ashanti to Zulu: African Traditions.* N.Y.: Dial, 1976.

Seeger, Pete. *Abiyoyo.* N.Y.: Macmillan, 1986.

Invitations

1. Collect travel brochures to see how they are organized and what content is included. Make your own brochure for a trip to Africa.
2. Find out what African animals are endangered and what you could do to help.

Celebration

Have a safari. Dress in native costume and prepare African stories for story-telling.

Compiled by Pat Riordan

ALPHABET SET

Archambault, John, and Bill Martin, Jr. *Chicka Chicka Boom Boom!* N.Y.: Simon & Schuster, 1989.

Barrett, Judi. *Animals Should Definitely Not Wear Clothing.* N.Y.: Macmillan, 1970.

Base, Graeme. *Animalia.* N.Y.: Abrams, 1987.

Bayer, Jane, and Steven Kellogg. *A My Name Is Alice.* N.Y.: Dial, 1984.

Beller, Janet. *A-B-C-ing: An Action Alphabet.* N.Y.: Crown, 1984.

Carle, Eric. *All About Arthur.* N.Y.: Franklin Watts, 1974.

Duke, Kate. *The Guinea Pig ABC.* N.Y.: Dutton, 1983.

Feelings, Muriel. *Jambo Means Hello: Swahili Alphabet Book.* N.Y.: Dial, 1974.

Folsom, Michael and Mary Elting. *Q Is for Ducks.* N.Y.: Clarion, 1980.

Hoban, Tana. *A, B, See!* N.Y.: Greenwillow, 1982.

Lobel, Arnold, and Anita Lobel. *On Market Street.* N.Y.: Greenwillow, 1981.

MacDonald, Suse. *Alphabatics.* N.Y.: Bradbury, 1986.

McPhail, David. *Animals A to Z.* N.Y.: Scholastic, 1988.

Merriam, Eve. *Where Is Everybody?: An Animal Alphabet.* N.Y.: Simon & Schuster, 1989.

Miles, Miska. *Apricot ABC.* Boston: Little, Brown, 1969.

Provensen, Alice, and Martin Provensen. *A Peaceable Kingdom: The Shaker Abecedarius.* N.Y.: Viking, 1978.

Ryden, Hope. *Wild Animals of America ABC.* N.Y.: Dutton, 1988.

Sendak, Maurice. *Alligators All Around.* N.Y.: Harper & Row, 1962.
Sloat, Teri. *From Letter to Letter.* N.Y.: Dutton, 1989.
Van Allsburg, Chris. *The Z Was Zapped.* Boston: Houghton Mifflin, 1987.

Invitations

1. Using *Animalia,* keep a "What's New?" list to add new discoveries each time children find something else in the incredibly rich illustrations for each letter of the alphabet.
2. Using *Q Is for Duck,* write new variations using children's names; for example:

   F is for Stefanie.
   Why?
   Because Stefanie is Freaky, Fine, Foxy.
   S is for Amie.
   Why?
   Because Amie is Sweet, Smart, Super.

3. Discuss how and why the author uses such strong, definite language in *Animals Should Definitely Not Wear Clothing.*
4. Using *A My Name Is Alice,* repeat the rhymes as you are bouncing a ball or jumping rope. Make up your own rhymes.
5. Audiotape the whole class reading *The Very Hungry Caterpillar.* Make the tape available for free choice reading time.

Compiled by Pat Riordan

BEARS SET

Asch, Frank. *Goodbye House.* N.Y.: Prentice-Hall, 1986.
_____. *Happy Birthday, Moon.* N.Y.: Prentice-Hall, 1982.
_____. *Mooncake.* N.Y.: Prentice-Hall, 1983.
Bucknall, Caroline. *One Bear All Alone: A Counting Book.* N.Y.: Macmillan, 1985.
Freeman, Don. *A Pocket for Corduroy.* N.Y.: Viking Penguin, 1978.
_____. *A Rainbow of My Own.* N.Y.: Viking Penguin, 1966.
_____. *Beady Bear.* N.Y.: Viking Penguin, 1954.
_____. *Corduroy.* N.Y.: Viking Penguin, 1968.
Galdone, Paul. *The Three Bears.* N.Y.: Scholastic, 1972.
Gretz, Susanna. *Teddy Bear's ABC.* N.Y.: Macmillan, 1986.
Hofmann, Ginnie. *Who Wants an Old Teddy Bear?* N.Y.: Random House, 1978.
Kaufman, Elizabeth E. *Bears: An Animal Information Book.* Los Angeles: Price/Stern/Sloan, 1987.
Kennedy, Jimmy. *The Teddy Bears' Picnic.* Hong Kong: Green Tiger, 1983.

Mack, Stan. *10 Bears in My Bed.* N.Y.: Pantheon, 1974.

Martin, Bill, Jr. *Brown Bear, Brown Bear, What Do You See?* N.Y.: Holt, Rinehart & Winston, 1983.

McLeod, Emilio. *The Bear's Bicycle.* Boston: Little, Brown, 1975.

Minarik, Else Holmelund. *Little Bear.* N.Y.: Harper & Row, 1957.

————. *Little Bear's Friend.* N.Y.: Harper & Row, 1960.

Invitations

1. Do bear research on questions such as Why do bears hibernate? How is bear fur used? Where do different bears live?

Celebration

1. Using *Teddy Bears' Picnic,* have a classroom picnic—make posters and invitations, have students bring their teddy bears. Entertain guests by dramatizing the story or dancing to the audiotape. Make props (trees, tables, masks).

Related Themes

Similar research can be done on such topics as Eskimos, migration, whales, and environmental issues such as oil spills and how animals are affected.

Compiled by Pat Riordan

CHICKS SET

Heller, Ruth. *Chickens Aren't the Only Ones.* N.Y.: Scholastic, 1981.

Hutchins, Pat. *Rosie's Walk.* N.Y.: Macmillan, 1968.

Kwitz, Mary DeBall. *Little Chick's Big Day.* N.Y.: Scholastic, 1981.

————. *Little Chick's Story.* N.Y.: Scholastic, 1978.

Luton, Mildred. *Chicks Mothers and All the Others.* N.Y.: Viking Penguin, 1983.

Prelutsky, Jack. *The Baby Uggs Are Hatching.* N.Y.: Mulberry, 1982.

Snowball, Diane. *Chickens.* N.Y.: Scholastic, 1986.

Invitations

1. Keep an observation journal on the rapid changes in newborn chicks.
2. With a partner, talk about the changes you think might take place inside the eggs as chicks develop. Make sketches of the different stages and then compare your drawings to those in one of the books.
3. Measure the chicks when they are born, and then keep a chart of their growth.

Compiled by Pat Riordan

DINOSAURS SET

Brandenberg, Aliki. *Digging Up Dinosaurs*. N.Y.: Crowell, 1981.

———. *Dinosaurs Are Different*. N.Y.: Crowell, 1985.

———. *Dinosaur Bones*. N.Y.: Crowell, 1988.

———. *My Visit to the Dinosaurs*. N.Y.: Harper & Row, 1969.

Davidson, Rosalie. *Dinosaurs—The Terrible Lizards*. Golden Gate, 1969.

Halstead, Beverly. *A Closer Look at Prehistoric Reptiles*. N.Y.: Gloucester, 1978.

Sandell, Elizabeth J. *Triceratops: The Last Dinosaur*. Mancato, MN.: Bancroft-Sage, 1988.

Sheehan, Angela. *Stegosaurus*. Windmere, FLA.: Ray Rourke, 1978.

———. *Tyrannosaurus*. Windmere, FLA.: Ray Rourke, 1978.

Schick, Alice. *Just This Once*. Philadelphia: Lippincott, 1978.

Seymour, Peter. *Baby Dino's Busy Day*. Los Angeles: Price Stern Sloan, 1988.

Simon, Seymour. *New Questions and Answers about Dinosaurs*. N.Y.: Crown, 1990.

———. *The Smallest Dinosaurs*. N.Y.: Crown, 1982.

Zallinger, Peter. *Dinosaurs*. N.Y.: Random House, 1977.

Invitations

1. Do research on your favorite dinosaur. Using what you have learned, prepare a brief presentation to give in front of the dinosaur when your class visits the museum.
2. Compare and contrast two dinosaurs you think were the most interesting.
3. Create a dinosaur rummy or other card game based on the facts you have learned.
4. With a small group of interested peers, create a diorama showing the dinosaurs in their natural habitat.

EARLY AMERICA—PIONEERS SET

Fiction

Anderson, Joan. *Joshua's Westward Journal*. N.Y.: Morrow, 1987.

Brink, Carol. *Caddie Woodlawn*. N.Y.: Macmillan, 1935.

Dalgliesh, Alice. *The Courage of Sarah Noble*. N.Y.: Scribner, 1954.

Fritz, Jean. *The Cabin Faced West*. N.Y.: Coward-McCann, 1958.

———. *Early Thunder*. N.Y.: Coward-McCann, 1967.

Howard, Ellen. *Edith Herself*. N.Y.: Atheneum, 1987.

Kirby, Susan. *Ike and Porker*. Boston: Houghton Mifflin, 1983.

Lawler, Laurie. *Addie across the Prairie*. Niles, Il.: Whitman, 1985.

MacLachlan, Patricia. *Sarah, Plain and Tall.* N.Y.: Harper & Row, 1985.

Naylor, Phyllis, and Laura Reynolds. *Maudie in the Middle.* N.Y.: Atheneum, 1988.

Roop, Connie, and Peter Roop. *Keep the Lights Burning, Abbie.* Minneapolis, Minn.: Carolrhoda, 1985.

Speare, Elizabeth. *The Sign of the Beaver.* Boston: Houghton Mifflin, 1983.

Turner, Ann. *Nettie's Trip South.* N.Y.: Macmillan, 1987.

Wilder, Laura Ingalls. *By the Shores of Silver Lake.* N.Y.: Harper & Row, 1953.

———. *The First Four Years.* N.Y.: Harper & Row, 1971.

———. *The Laura Ingalls Wilder Song Book.* N.Y.: Harper & Row, 1968.

———. *Little House in the Big Woods.* N.Y.: Harper & Row, 1953.

———. *Little House on the Prairie.* N.Y.: Harper & Row, 1953.

———. *A Little House Sampler.* Lincoln, Neb.: University of Nebraska Press, 1988.

———. *Little House Sound Record.* Newbery Award Records, 1977.

———. *The Long Winter.* N.Y.: Harper & Row, 1953.

———. *On the Banks of Plum Creek.* N.Y.: Harper & Row, 1953.

———. *On the Way Home—The Diary of a Trip from South Dakota to Mansfield, Missouri, in 1894.* N.Y.: Harper & Row, 1962.

Nonfiction

Burton, William. *Illinois—A Student's History of the Prairie State.* Louisiana: Panoramic Teaching Aids, 1969.

Carpenter, Alan. *Illinois, Land of Lincoln.* Chicago: Children's Press, 1968.

Clark, Allen. *Growing Up in Colonial America.* N.Y.: Sterling, 1961.

Fritz, Jean. *Homesick, My Own Story.* N.Y.: Putnam, 1982.

Kalman, Bobbie. *Early Settler Children.* N.Y.: Crabtree, 1982.

Palmer, Ann. *Growing Up in Colonial America.* Hove, England: Wayland Publishing, 1978.

Rounds, Glen. *The Prairie Schooners.* N.Y.: Holiday House, 1968.

Sabin, Francene. *Pioneers.* N.J.: Troll Associates, 1985.

Tunis, Edwin. *Frontier Living.* N.Y.: Crowell, 1961.

Woodin, G. Bruce. *Pioneers (1797–1850).* N.Y.: Sterling, 1971.

Content Integration

Social Studies

- Explore early American heroes.
- Compare historical fiction with true stories.
- Compare family life then and now.
- Form interest groups to do research on Indians, survival, history of America, and so on.

Science

- Compare living conditions then and now.
- Do research on herbal remedies versus contemporary medicine.
- Compare diets then and now.
- Consider changes in the environment.

Invitations

1. Do research on quilt-making. Locate a local quilter and invite him or her to class.
2. Make a hornbook.
3. Make a "Little House" scrapbook. Include photos, drawings, maps, recipes, character sketches, interviews, and so forth.
4. Write directions to some of the games mentioned in the books (for example, cat's cradle).

Celebration

1. Have an early America-Pioneer party. Make invitations and food; create entertainment and displays.

Compiled by Penny Silvers

FAMILY HISTORIES SET

For Teachers

Brooke, Pamela. "Exploring Family Folklore." *Instructor,* November–December, 1986.

Davis, Dullom, Kathryn Back, and Kay Maclean. *Oral History: from Tape to Type.* American Library Association, 1977.

Ginns, Patsy Moore. *Rough Weather Makes Good Timber.* Chapel Hill, N.C.: University of North Carolina Press, 1977.

Gundlack, Susan. "Putting the Story Back into History." *Curriculum Review.* January–February, 1986.

Herman, Gail, and Claire Krause. "A Trunkful of Family Stories." *National Storytelling Journal,* Summer, 1987.

Hoopes, James. *Oral History: An Introduction for Students.* Chapel Hill, N.C.: University of North Carolina Press, 1979.

Keillor, Garrison. *Lake Wobegon Days.* N.Y.: Viking, 1985.

Kyvig, David E., and Myron A. Marty. *Nearby History.* Nashville, TN.: The American Association for State and Local History, 1982.

Livo, Norman. "Preserving Family History." *National Storytelling Journal,* Fall, 1984.

Middleworth-Kohn, Vicky. "Family Folklore." *Cobblestone,* July, 1983.

Page, Linda Garland, and Eliot Wigginton, eds. *Aunt Arie.* N.Y.: Dutton, 1983.

Rolvaag, O.E. *Giants in the Earth.* N.Y.: Harper & Row, 1927.

Sitton, Mehaffey, and Cullom Davis. *Oral History: A Guide for Teachers (and Others).* Austin, TX: University of Texas Press, 1983.

Stratton, Joanna. *Pioneer Women.* N.Y.: Simon & Schuster, 1982.

Thompson, Paul. *The Voice of the Past: Oral History.* N.Y.: Oxford University Press, 1978.

Weitzman, David. *My Backyard History Book.* Boston: Little, Brown, 1975.

Welty, Eudora. *One Writer's Beginnings.* Warner, 1983.

Wigginton, Eliot. *Moments: The Foxfire Experience.* Kennebunk, ME: Foxfire Fund, 1975.

Zeitlin, Steven J., Amy J. Kotkin, and Holly Cutting Baker. *A Celebration of American Family Folklore.* N.Y.: Pantheon, 1982.

Zimmerman, William. *Instant Oral Biographies.* N.Y.: Guarionex Press, 1981. (Available through *Teachers and Writers Collaborative,* 5 Union Square West, New York, N.Y. 10003.)

Children's Books

Adoff, Arnold. *Black Is Brown Is Tan.* N.Y.: Harper & Row, 1973.

_____. *Make a Circle, Keep Us In: Poems for a Good Day.* N.Y.: Delacorte, 1975.

Bond, Felicia. *Poinsettia and Her Family.* N.Y.: Crowell, 1981.

Clifton, Lucille. *Amifika.* N.Y.: Dutton, 1977.

Cole, Babette. *The Trouble with Dad.* N.Y.: Putnam, 1985.

Greenfield, Eloise. *First Pink Light.* N.Y.: Crowell, 1976.

Hoopes, Lyn Littlefield. *Mommy, Daddy, Me.* N.Y.: Harper & Row, 1988.

Johnson, Angela. *Tell Me a Story, Mama.* N.Y.: Orchard, 1988.

Johnston, Tony. *Yonder.* N.Y.: Dial Books for Young Readers, 1988.

Kraus, Robert. *Another Mouse to Feed.* N.Y.: Windmill/Wanderer, 1980.

_____. *Whose Mouse Are You?* N.Y.: Macmillan, 1970.

Levinson, Riki. *I Go with My Family to Grandma's House.* N.Y.: Dutton, 1986.

_____. *Watch the Stars Come Out.* N.Y.: Dutton, 1985.

Loh, Marag Jennette. *Tucking Mommy In.* N.Y.: Orchard, 1988.

Meeks, Esther. *Families Live Together.* Chicago: Follett, 1969.

Moore, Elaine. *Grandma's House.* N.Y.: Lothrop, Lee & Shepard, 1985.

Newton, Laura. *Me and My Aunts.* Niles, IL: A. Whitman, 1986.

Oxenbury, Helen. *Family.* N.Y.: Wanderer, 1981.

Pearson, Susan. *Happy Birthday, Grampie.* N.Y.: Dial Books for Young Readers, 1987.

Rylant, Cynthia. *The Relatives Came.* N.Y.: Bradbury, 1985.

Sandin, Joan. *The Long Way to a New Land.* N.Y.: Harper & Row, 1981.

Sharmat, Marjorie Weinman. *Sometimes Mama and Papa Fight.* N.Y.: Harper & Row, 1980.

Simon, Norma. *All Kinds of Families.* Chicago: A. Whitman, 1976.

Tax, Meredith. *Families.* Boston: Little, Brown, 1981.

Note: See Family Histories* in Chapter 10 for Invitation ideas.

Compiled by Kathleen Visovatti

ETHNIC SET

Belpre, Pura. *Santiago.* N.Y.: Warne, 1969.

Binzen, Bill. *Miguel's Mountain.* N.Y.: Coward-McCann, 1968.

Greenfield, Eloise, and Lessie Jones Little. *Childtimes: A Three-generation Memoir.* N.Y.: Crowell, 1979.

Hamilton, Virginia. *Anthony Burns: The Defeat and Triumph of a Fugitive Slave.* N.Y.: Knopf, 1989.

_____. *The People Could Fly, American Black Folktales.* N.Y.: Knopf, 1985.

_____. *Sweet Whispers, Brother Rush.* N.Y.: Philomel, 1982.

Hopkins, Lee Bennett, ed. *Don't You Turn Back: Poems by Langston Hughes.* N.Y.: Knopf, 1969.

Lester, Julius. *This Strange New Feeling.* N.Y.: Dial, 1982.

_____. *To Be a Slave.* N.Y.: Dell, 1968.

Lord, Betty Bao. *The Year of the Boar and Jackie Robinson.* N.Y.: Harper & Row, 1984.

Meltzer, Milton. *The Chinese Americans.* N.Y.: Crowell, 1980.

_____. *The Hispanic Americans.* N.Y.: Crowell, 1982.

_____. *The Jewish Americans: A History in Their Own Words.* N.Y.: Crowell, 1982.

Myers, Walter Dean. *Fallen Angels.* N.Y.: Scholastic, 1989.

Walter, Mildred Pitts. *Because We Are.* N.Y.: Lothrop, Lee & Shepard, 1983.

Yashima, Taro, and Mitsui Yashima. *Momo's Kitten.* N.Y.: Viking, 1955.

PETS SET

Fiction

Bridwell, Norman. *Clifford, the Big Red Dog.* N.Y.: Scholastic, 1963.

_____. *Clifford at the Circus.* N.Y.: Scholastic, 1977.

Cowley, Joy. *Greedy Cat.* N.Y.: Richard C. Owen, Publishers, 1988.

Craig, Jean. *Puss in Boots.* N.Y.: Scholastic, 1966.

Hurst, Marjorie-Mary. *I Love Cats.* N.Y.: Scholastic, 1986.

Hoban, Lillian. *Arthur's Honey Bear.* N.Y.: Scholastic, 1974.

Keats, Ezra Jack. *Pet Show.* N.Y.: Collier, 1972.

Lobel, Arnold. *Frog and Toad Are Friends.* N.Y.: Scholastic, 1970.

Mahy, Margaret. *The Bubbling Crocodile.* Wellington, New Zealand (distributed by Richard C. Owen, Publishers, New York), 1983.

————. *A Crocodile in the Library.* Wellington, New Zealand (distributed by Richard C. Owen, Publishers), 1983.

————. *Shopping with a Crocodile.* Wellington, New Zealand (distributed by Richard C. Owen, Publishers), 1983.

Marshall, James. *A Frog and Her Dog.* Boston: Houghton Mifflin, 1977.

Mayer, Mercer. *What Do You Do with A Kangaroo?* N.Y.: Scholastic, 1973.

Roy, Ron. *What Has Ten Legs and Eats Corn Flakes?* N.Y.: Clarion, 1982.

Nonfiction

Bolton, Faye. *Animal Shelters.* N.Y.: Scholastic, 1987.

Gregor, Arthur. *Animal Babies.* N.Y.: Scholastic, 1959.

Patterson, Dr. Francine. *Koko's Story.* N.Y.: Scholastic, 1987.

Selsam, Millicent. *How Puppies Grow.* N.Y.: Scholastic, 1981.

Tyler, Michael. *Frogs.* N.Y.: Scholastic, 1987.

Simon, Seymour. *Animal Fact/Animal Fable.* N.Y.: Crown, 1979.

Invitations

1. Using *What Has Ten Legs and Eats Corn Flakes?* as a pattern, do research on different animals and write questions that include unusual facts.
2. Write specific guidelines for caring for pets. Publish a class series of "How to Care for Pets" books.
3. Imagine you have an unusual pet like the crocodile in Margaret Mahy's books. What kinds of problems could you run into?
4. Make a scrapbook of famous pets.
5. Find someone in your community who has a seeing eye dog. Ask the person for an interview to find out how the dog helps, how it was trained, how it is different from other animals, and so on.

Compiled by Penny Silvers

ROYALTY SET

Andersen, Hans Christian. *The Emperor's New Clothes,* Erik Blegvad, illus. N.Y.: Harcourt Brace Jovanovich, 1959.

————. *The Emperor's New Clothes,* Jack Delano and Irene Delano, illus. N.Y.: Random House, 1971.

————. *The Emperor's New Clothes.* Anthea Bell, adapt., Dorothee Duntze, illus. N.Y.: Holt, Rinehart & Winston, 1986.

Bell, Anthea. *The Wise Queen: A Traditional European Folktale.* Natick, MA: Picture Book Studio U.S.A. (distributed by Alphabet Press), 1986.

Brunhoff, Jean de. *Babar the King.* N.Y.: Random House, 1935.

Canfield, Jane White. *The Frog Prince: A True Story.* N.Y.: Harper & Row, 1970.

Cole, Babette. *Prince Cinders.* N.Y.: Putnam, 1988.

Darling, David J. *Diana, the People's Princess.* Minneapolis, Minn.: Dillon, 1984.

de Regniers, Beatrice Schenk. *May I Bring a Friend?.* N.Y.: Atheneum, 1964.

Grimm, Jacob. *The Twelve Dancing Princesses.* N.Y.: Scribner, 1966.

Isele, Elizabeth. *The Frog Princess: A Russian Tale Retold.* N.Y.: Crowell, 1984.

Levite, Christine. *Princesses.* N.Y.: Watts, 1989.

Lobel, Arnold. *Prince Bertram the Bad.* N.Y.: Harper & Row, 1963.

Mayer, Mercer. *The Queen Always Wanted to Dance.* N.Y.: Simon & Schuster, 1971.

Munsch, Robert. *The Paper Bag Princess.* Toronto: Annick Press; (distributed by Firefly Books), 1988.

Oppenheim, Joanne. *The Story Book Prince.* San Diego: Harcourt Brace Jovanovich, 1987.

Seuss Dr. *The King's Stilts.* N.Y.: Random House, 1939.

Stephenson, Dorothy. *The Night It Rained Toys.* Chicago, Follett, 1963.

Vesey, A. *The Princess and the Frog.* Boston: Atlanta Monthly, 1985.

Waddell, Martin. *The Tough Princess.* N.Y.: Philomel, 1986.

Wersba, Barbara. *Do Tigers Ever Bite Kings?.* N.Y.: Atheneum, 1966.

Wood, Audrey. *King Bidgood's in the Bathtub.* San Diego: Harcourt Brace Jovanovich, 1985.

SUMMER SET

Byars, Betsy. *The Summer of the Swans.* N.Y.: Viking, 1970.

Dixon, Paige. *Summer of the White Goat.* N.Y.: Atheneum, 1977.

Enright, Elizabeth. *Thimble Summer.* N.Y.: Holt, Rinehart & Winston, 1938.

Ferris, Jean. *Invincible Summer.* N.Y.: Farrar, Straus & Giroux, 1987.

Fine, Anne. *The Summer-House Loon.* N.Y.: Crowell, 1978.

Florian, Douglas. *A Summer Day.* N.Y.: Greenwillow, 1988.

George, Jean Craighead. *The Summer of the Falcon.* N.Y.: Crowell, 1962.

Lipstyle, Robert. *The Summerboy.* N.Y.: Harper & Row, 1982.

Lowry, Lois. *A Summer to Die.* Boston: Houghton Mifflin, 1977.

Toye, William. *How Summer Came to Canada.* N.Y.: H.Z. Walck, 1969.

Invitation

In summer keep a journal of important changes, events, or just how you spend lazy summer days. Compare your summer to the ones in the summer books you read.

TRANSPORTATION SET

Fiction

Burningham, John. *Come Away from the Water, Shirley.* N.Y.: Crowell, 1977.
_____. *Mr. Gumpy's Motor Car.* N.Y.: Crowell, 1973.
_____. *Mr. Gumpy's Outing.* N.Y.: Holt, Rinehart & Winston, 1970.
Burton, Virginia Lee. *Mike Mulligan and His Steam Shovel.* Boston: Houghton Mifflin, 1967.
Crews, Donald. *Freight Train.* N.Y.: Greenwillow, 1978.
_____. *School Bus.* N.Y.: Greenwillow, 1984.
_____. *Truck.* N.Y.: Greenwillow, 1980.
Graham, Thomas. *Mr. Bear's Boat.* N.Y.: Dutton, 1988.
Hutchins, Pat. *Rosie's Walk.* N.Y.: Macmillan, 1968.
Keats, Ezra Jack. *The Trip.* N.Y.: Greenwillow, 1978.
Kovalski, Maryann. *The Wheels on the Bus.* Boston: Joy Street Books, 1987.
Lenski, Lois. *The Little Airplane.* Walck, 1966.

Nonfiction

Provensen, Alice, and Martin Provensen. *The Glorious Flight.* N.Y.: Viking, 1983.
Pierce, Jack. *The Freight Train Book.* Minneapolis: Carolrhoda, 1980.
Robbins, Ken. *Trucks of Every Sort.* Crown, 1981.
Scarry, Huck. *Life on a Barge (a sketchbook).* N.J.: Prentice-Hall, 1981.
Zaffo, George. *Airplanes and Trucks and Trains, Fire Engines, Boats and Ships and Building and Wrecking Machines.* N.Y.: Grosset & Dunlap, 1966.

Invitations

1. Using *The Train* make a giant wall mural. Small groups can choose a different medium (paper, watercolor, and so on) and be responsible for recreating one of the pages in the book. Toothpicks can be used for bridge supports.
2. Write different versions of *The Wheels on the Bus.* For example, the horn on the truck, train, ship, and bus. Make big and little books of these extensions. Whole series of books can be created for the class library.
3. Pair up with a junior high school partner and make graphs of the number of cars, trucks, and buses on different streets around both of your schools. Compare and contrast the numbers.
4. Take a trip to a museum that highlights different modes of transportation.
5. Interview a bus or truck driver. Invite them into the class to talk about what they do.
6. Help set up a classroom dramatic play center. Include train and bus schedules, conductors' hats, suitcases, notepads (to plan trips and write tickets), and so on.

7. Make a fact book for all the things you have learned about transportation. Categorize your information or choose a favorite vehicle and write a book around that topic. Junior high school partners are helpful for this project, especially for final drafts.
8. Bring in transportation toys. Categorize and graph them. Compare their different characteristics.

Celebration

1. Take a mass transit ride to the library to find more books on transportation. Phone for a route schedule in advance so you can plan your trip.
Compiled by Sue Smeaton

WAR SET

These books are listed in the chronological order of the war portrayed in each text.

Forbes, Esther. *Johnny Tremain.* N.Y.: Dell, 1943.
Set in Boston in 1773, the book follows a young apprentice from a tragic accident in the silversmith's shop to his dramatic involvement as a patriot in the exciting days just before the American Revolution.

Collier, James Lincoln, and Christopher Collier. *My Brother Sam Is Dead.* N.Y.: Four Winds, 1974.
When Tim's brother Sam brings home news of how the Minutemen defeated the British, there are mixed emotions from the people, especially Tim's family, in their small Connecticut town. An argument breaks out between Sam and his father. Days later, Sam steals his father's gun and Tim fears the worst. What happens later to Sam and Tim and their mother and father, who are caught up in the bitter turmoil of war, is a suspenseful and moving tale.

O'Dell, Scott. *Sarah Bishop.* Boston: Houghton Mifflin, 1980.
Left alone after the deaths of her father and brother, who have taken opposite sides in the War for Independence, and fleeing from the British who seek to arrest her, Sarah Bishop struggles to shape a new life for herself in the wilderness.

Hunt, Irene. *Across Five Aprils.* Berkley, 1964.
The story of young Jethro Creighton, who comes of age during the turbulent years of the Civil War. As the war divides the country, so too does it divide the Creighton family. Based on history, this is a sensitive and intriguing novel of life, liberty, and the pursuit of happiness during war.

O'Dell, Scott. *Sing Down the Moon.* N.Y.: Dell, 1970.

Bright Morning's people, the Navahos, are forced from their homeland in Arizona to Fort Sumner, New Mexico. Told from Bright Morning's point of view, the story centers on the struggle of a young woman and her people to survive life in the 1860s, in a new place, against all odds. This is historical fiction.

Magorian, Michelle. *Good Night, Mr. Tom.* N.Y.: Harper & Row, 1981.

Willie is evacuated from his home right before the outbreak of World War II. He is timid at first, but with the help of Mr. Tom, the man with whom he is staying, he learns about wonderful things such as friendship and affection, things which the abused boy had never known. Later, Willie is summoned to return home to London, and when Mr. Tom hasn't heard from him, he sets out in search of the boy he now regards as a son.

Mazer, Harry. *The Last Mission.* N.Y.: Dell, 1979.

In 1944, while WW II is going on, 15-year-old Jack Raab dreams of being a hero. He lies his way into the Air Force where he experiences all that he dreamed of and all the stuff that nightmares are made of too. Jack learns that war is hell.

Frank, Anne. *Anne Frank: The Diary of a Young Girl.* N.Y.: Doubleday, 1967.

A powerful memorial to all who died in the Holocaust. After hiding in a secret attic for two and one-half years, Anne Frank and her family are sent to Nazi concentration camps. This is Anne's diary, which she left behind.

READ Magazine. Field, Vol. 39, #3, October 6, 1989.

An issue devoted to views on racism, particularly against Jews and minorities. Of special interest for this set are "She Would Have Been 60," an article about Anne Frank; and "Reunion," a story about two young men who befriend one another during the turbulence of WW II.

Stathi Zidovské Museum. *I Never Saw Another Butterfly.* N.Y.: McGraw-Hill, 1976.

A book of children's drawings and poems from Terezin Concentration Camp, 1942–1944.

Tsuchuyo, Yukio. *Faithful Elephants.* Boston: Houghton Mifflin, 1988.

When Tokyo was bombed by the Allies, the Japanese army decided all the animals in the Tokyo zoo should be killed to eliminate the possibility of them running wild in the city, should the zoo be hit by a bomb. This is the true story of how all these zoo animals were put to death because of the war. The author highlights three elephants who did not want to die.

Noell, Chuck, and Gary Wood. *We Are All POWs.* Fortress, 1975.

The authors discuss the "Vietnam generation's" war experiences and its effect on people who served in the war and those who resisted.

Dear America: Letters Home from Vietnam. N.Y.: Norton, 1985.
   A compelling collection of letters and poems written to families and friends by those who served in the war.

Audiovisual Aids

The Vietnam Conflict. Chicago, IL.: Society for Visual Education, 1986. Cassette
   tape with one filmstrip.
   The reasons for the Vietnam conflict are explained and the U.S. history and involvement in the conflict are outlined. Shows political and social consequences of U.S. involvement.

America Divided: The Civil War. Encyclopedia Britannica, 1985.
   Set of four filmstrips with cassettes. Shows the progression, reasons, and consequences of the war.

Invitations

 1. Maintain a journal of your personal thoughts and feelings while reading a novel about war. Use the journal in comparison discussion groups.
 2. Invite a war veteran to come and talk to the class.
 3. After reading *Dear America* write a letter to one of the Vietnam War veterans.
 4. Write a letter to a government official asking what is being done about POWs.
 5. Find current newspaper and magazine articles on wars of the present. Make a collage.
 6. Imagine that you had to live in an attic for two and a half years and could only move about at night. What would you do to keep yourself busy? Write your own diary entries as if this were happening to you.
 7. You are familiar with the "Uncle Sam Wants You" slogan and poster. Create your own poster/jingle to recruit people for the military—or make the same to deter people from joining.
 8. Pretend that you are a newspaper reporter. Write a book review recommending or criticizing the book you are reading. Give specific examples of characters, setting, and a summary of the plot.
 9. Build model airplanes, ships, cannons from toothpicks that resemble those used in one of the wars.
10. Play a game of "Family Feud" using questions based on stories everyone has read. Have the North versus the South, the Patriots versus the Tories, Hitler versus Jack Raab, and so on.
11. Interview one person from the family of someone who fought in a war. How did it effect them?
12. Will there be a World War III? If so, when and why? What weapons will be used? Write your own short story and/or draw pictures of the weaponry.

Compiled by Barbara Lindberg

WOLF SET

Fiction

Allard, Harry. *It's So Nice to Have a Wolf around the House.* Garden City, N.Y.: Doubleday, 1977.

Corcoran, Barbara. *Sasha, My Friend.* N.Y.: Atheneum, 1969.

de Regniers, Beatrice. *Little Red Riding Hood.* N.Y.: Atheneum, 1972.

Dixon, Paige. *Silver Wolf.* N.Y.: Atheneum, 1973.

Gable, Paul. *Dream Wolf.* N.Y.: Bradbury, 1990.

Galdone, Paul. *Little Red Riding Hood.* N.Y.: McGraw-Hill, 1974.

Gay, Michel. *The Christmas Wolf.* N.Y.: Greenwillow, 1983.

George, Jean Craighead. *Julie of the Wolves.* N.Y.: Harper & Row, 1972.

Hunia, Fran. *Peter and the Wolf.* Laughborough, England: Ladybird, 1978.

Kasza, Keiko. *The Wolf's Chicken Stew.* N.Y.: Putnam, 1987.

McCleery, William. *Wolf Story.* Hamden, CT.: Linnet, 1947.

Nolan, Dennis. *Wolf Child.* N.Y.: Macmillan, 1989.

Rose, Elizabeth. *Wolf! Wolf!* London: Faber & Faber, 1974.

Scieszka, Jan. *The True Story of the 3 Little Pigs by A. Wolf.* N.Y.: Viking Kestrel, 1989.

Willis, Kristine. *The Long-Legged, Long-Nosed, Long-Maned Wolf.* Austin, TX., Steck-Vaughn, 1968.

Young, Ed. *Lon Po Po: A Red-Riding Hood Story from China.* N.Y.: Philomel, 1989.

Behavior

Crisler, Lois. *Captive Wild.* N.Y.: Harper & Row, 1968.

Lawrence, R.D. *In Praise of Wolves.* N.Y.: Holt, 1986.

Mowat, Farley. *Never Cry Wolf.* N.Y.: Watts, 1963.

Young, Stanley Paul. *The Wolves of North America.* N.Y.: Dover, 1944.

Folklore

Delaney, A. *The Gunnywolf.* N.Y.: Harper & Row, 1988.

Legends and Stories

Hellmuth, Jerome. *A Wolf in the Family.* N.Y.: New American Library, 1964.

Leslie, Robert Franklin. *In the Shadow of a Rainbow: The True Story of a Friendship between Man and Wolf.* N.Y.: Norton, 1974.

Lumi, Marika. *Wolf . . . Kill! The Wilderness Called Shunka.* N.Y.: Van Nostrand Reinhold, 1976.

Invitations

1. Consider the stereotypical profile of the wolf in children's literature. Find out if this character is based on fact.
2. Compare and contrast the wolf in *The Wolf's Chicken Stew* to the one in *Little Red Riding Hood.*
3. Compare the transformation of the wolf in *The Wolf's Chicken Stew* to other animals that are "transformed." (*See* Transformation Set.)
4. Compare the ancient Chinese panel art in *Lon Po Po* to the watercolor illustrations in *The Wolf's Chicken Stew.*
5. With a partner, place five or six wolf illustrations side by side. Talk about what you see—differences, similarities, feelings from the pictures, characteristics the illustrators are trying to communicate and how they do that, and so on.
6. Do research on wolves' habitats, eating habits, appearance, parenting behaviors, and so on. Look at the books under "Behavior" and consider how the authors organized their information. Write your own "wolf behavior" book to add to the set.
7. Compare and contrast the perspectives found in one version of *The Three Little Pigs* and *The True Story of the 3 Pigs by A. Wolf.*

APPENDIX B

PORTFOLIOS

Two portfolios are included, one from Abbey, Grade 2, the other from Tracey, Grade 11. Both represent final, end-of-the-year selections and reflections regarding reading and writing processes. This is the first time Abbey and Tracey and their teachers, Kathleen Visovatti and Carol Porter, were involved in portfolio assessment. While complete artifacts were too lengthy to include here, a few representative samples in reading and writing are given in each document.

Key Ideas Related to Portfolio Evaluation

1. *Portfolios are part of a larger, reflective curriculum.*
   Portfolio development, a reflective learning experience in and of itself, is enhanced when students see reflection as an integral part of all learning and are involved in it daily. Initially, students may have a difficult time selecting items for their portfolios and reflecting on the changes these represent. Reflective experiences of all kinds will strengthen portfolio assessment.

2. *Portfolios belong to the learner.*
   This is the learner's chance to assess himself or herself. What students select to include in their portfolios may or may not match teachers' judgments; the purpose is to encourage the learner's thoughtful judgment of their own work, processes, and development.

3. *Portfolios highlight process.*
   Portfolios are personal change histories. They give students an opportunity to consider where they have been, how they got there, and where they might go as learners. While portfolios certainly include products like final drafts, their major intent is to highlight significant learning processes from the learner's perspective. Products, then, become part of a larger learning process.

TRACEY'S PORTFOLIO

Classroom Context

Carol Porter and Janell Cleland, colleagues in the same high school, worked together on their first portfolio assessment. Prior to the implementation of the portfolio strategy at the end of the first semester, students had been reflecting regularly on their learning after literature discussions and after final written drafts. Carol and Janell also held Process Share* discussions on a regular basis, during which students talked about major changes they observed in themselves as readers/writers during each six-week grading period. Personal conferences were held with each student every six weeks so that collaborative observations (teacher and student) could be made regarding areas of growth in reading and writing and to set goals for future experiences. Letters summarizing these conferences were sent home to parents.

Students engaged in portfolio development at the end of the first and second semesters. Each student was given a letter that described portfolios as "a way of displaying what a person *can* do"—their growth as readers and writers. Students were asked to include their first piece of writing and all related drafts, and some of their early reading journal entries. Beyond that, the decisions were up to them.

Carol and Janell provided a few reflective questions to get them going:

1. What frustrations did you have with reading (writing) earlier in the year, and how has that changed?
2. What was your favorite piece of reading (writing)?
3. What was different about that experience that made it so memorable?
4. How did you choose what you read (wrote) at the beginning of the year? How do you do that now?

After students reviewed their reading and writing over the year and selected artifacts for their portfolios, Carol and Janell asked them to organize the items: "We would like for you to decide how to put your portfolios together. Last semester we glued everything to construction paper which was ok, but maybe you have some unused scrapbooks or photo albums at home that you could use—or a better idea." Students were also asked to present their observations and insights in a summative way: "Possibly a letter or question/answer format might be interesting. A personal narrative may be more appropriate. Any other ideas?" Tracey listed the items she chose on a Summary Sheet and noted the reasons she had selected each as a contribution to her learning profile. Finally, she consolidated her reflections by writing a personal narrative.

PORTFOLIO SUMMARY SHEET
Tracey Vos Burgh

Date	Item	Why I Included It
September	*Writing* "Jimmy"	My "Jimmy" piece was the first piece I wrote for the Reading/Writing Lab. I wrote it in a newspaper style—something I never tried before—by using the excerpts from an interview I conducted with Jimmy. After

---

* All asterisks throughout the book refer the reader to Chapter 10 where full strategy descriptions can be found.

Date	Item	Why I Included It
		reading this piece and reading "Lennie" or the play (also included), I can see how much I've grown as a writer, how much more real and effective my descriptions are.
September	*Reflective Evaluation Form*	This shows that I was just beginning to think about revising my thinking in reading and writing. Before I could care less what other people thought—no way would I consider what anyone else said about my reading and writing. Now I listen and I see the value of rethinking to how I understand and how good my writing is.
February–March	*Reading Wizard of Oz* Journal Entries	I included these entries because I put more thought into the comparisons of the movie (which I loved) and the book (which I hated) than any other thing I read. I compared and contrasted the two in every way I was aware of—that sharpened my thinking a great deal.
March	*Writing* "Make-Believe Miracle" A Children's Play	This is a collaborative play. Through a lot of frustrations we created this piece and brought it to a performance, starring a kindergarten class. I will never forget the experience of both collaboration and the performance. The play is in a format that is extremely flexible to fit the needs of any particular class—we experimented with that for a long time.
March	*Reading After the First Death* Journal Entries	My entries I conducted with Brian for this book frustrated me. Everyday he would find some great and significant symbolism I had never picked up on. His comments made me think and out of complete frustration I would pick up on every detail I could to make a point he couldn't argue with. Unfortunately, the book ended and I never actually pinned him down but now I believe I pick up on some of the smallest details when I'm reading and I didn't do that before.

Date	Item	Why I Included It
October– May	*Writing* "Lennie" (also known as "The Biggest Buck I Ever Saw")	Included because of the amount of time I spent and the personal feelings I have towards it. For several months consecutive I worked on this piece and then for several months I worked off and on with it. It took me 26 revisions to get where I am—and I'm still working on it. If I was not so concerned about this piece being 'perfect'— the detail, capturing the exact feelings—I wouldn't have spent so much time on it, I didn't on any other piece and I learned a lot about revision. The subjects, Lennie and Minnesota, are something I hold very dear to me. I am very proud of this piece and feel I should show it off a bit.

I have always re-read my writing to make it comprehendable but now I try to answer any questions my peers have even before I read it allowed. I think I began to change my ideas during my *Lennie* piece! I wanted it perfect not only for me but also for anyone else reading it so maybe they could understand my desire to be in MN!

PORTFOLIO NARRATIVE
Tracey

Once upon a time, there was a girl named Tracey (that's me). Tracey was sitting in study hall one day when Mrs. Porter (her eight grade English teacher) entered. Mrs. Porter called off several names, one of which was Tracey's, and began to talk about a reading writing class she had that she felt would benefit Tracey and several students. Mrs. Porter explained it would be very similar to the class Tracey had with Mrs. Porter in eight grade. Remembering how much fun the class was Tracey accepted the invitation.

The following day Tracey entered her new third hour classroom. Only a few students occupied the dozen or so desks that made a circle in the middle of the room. Mrs. Cleland (Tracey's freshman year English teacher) was the instructor for this hour.

After several days of reading short stories, the students were given the assignment of interviewing another student. It was Tracey's job to interview Jimmy Gonzales. With knowing very little about Jimmy and his life, Tracey thought up some very interesting questions. She did know that Jimmy was a vidal person in

MHS's state-championship gymnastics team. So, one day Tracey was reading an article about Boris Shakhliln and Tracey got the idea of Jimmy beating Boris and winning the championship.

The hardest part of writing the article was getting the first few words, in the correct order, down on paper. Later Tracey found there was no "correct" or "wrong" way about the order of her words. After pulling her piece out of the computer printer Tracey brought it to author's circle. There she read her piece out-loud to the class and they offered suggestions and asked questions about unclear sentences or paragraphs. Tracey left the circle and revised her piece.

After the semester was over Tracey switched to a different hour class and ended up having Mrs. Porter for her teacher. During the fantasy unit, Mrs. Porter introduced the idea of several students getting together and writing a play for a kindergarten class. Accepting the challenge, Tracey met with three other students and entered into the kindergarten room to met the teacher and see the costumes. Tracey wrote down notes as Mrs. Prezell explained to the collaborative writing team exactly what she was looking for in the play. That was when the students had the opportunity to look at the costumes. One of the students went right over to the kids' toys and began playing around with them, the next students sat right in her seat and just looked around the room admiring the art work on the wall. It was Tracey and last student, Corey, who went to the costumes and began getting ideas.

After several attempts to get together and begin writing after school, Tracey, Corey and the two other "writers" met at Mrs. Porters' house to discuss the play. As soon as Tracey arrived she found the two "writers" playing with Ryan's (C.P.'s little boy) and Corey rushing out the door. Mrs. Porter and Tracey began talking about what had been discussed before Tracey had arrived. CP got out several of her children's books and Tracey began to read through them for ideas. Remembering her all-time favorite book, Wizard of Oz, Tracey got the idea of having the kids go on a journey. Wendy and Kim (the two "writers) were too preoccupied with the Ghost Busters' gun then what CP and Tracey were discussing. The next day they had a meeting for the writing team and only Tracey and Corey attended. Tracey sat down at the computer and began typing while Corey wrote out his homework for some class. Tracey remembers the hardest part of writing the Play was not strangling her writing team! It was becoming to look more like it would be Tracey alone coming up with the ideas for the play.

But, she was wrong. Draft after draft Corey and Tracey began working as a team and sharing ideas. One would read the play outloud to the other and the listener would stop the reader when something was read that she/he disliked. After they were satisfied with a very rough draft they sent it to Mrs. Prezell. She seemed to like the basic idea but shot down half of the text. Starting just about over again Tracey and Corey met and revised one evening.

When they were finally satisfied with the Play Tracey and Corey sent Mrs. Prezell another draft. She liked it but still there were things that needed to be changed. So once again Tracey and Corey met and met and met until they were FINISHED!

After starting the practices for the performance they decided there would be invitations to be made and sent out to the parents. Corey wrote the initial draft and handed it over to Tracey to read and revise. Tracey took over the invitation until it was complete with the kindergarteners' drawings and all.

Tracey's favorite piece was a piece she began when she was still in Mrs. Cleland's class. Tracey needed a quick piece to read to the class and she didn't have any ideas. One night when she was laying in bed Tracey got her idea. With only the dim light her desk lamp gave off, Tracey began writing about her vacation. She couldn't find any paper so she searched under her bed and found her progress reports to use.

Tracey's best piece ended up being her most revised piece with 26 revisions (and still going.) Beginning it in late October Tracey feels she is just about ready to resubmit it to a magazine, it's now early June! Considering this is her best piece, Tracey put forth a lot of effort, emotion, and time to make this piece be just perfect. Several teachers and friends read her "Lennie" piece and added comments and suggestions to make it even better.

Currently as a writer Tracey still gets frustrated at getting the ideas and getting the initial words down on paper. She gets her ideas for sitting looking at a old tree to watching her little cousin run in the yard. When she begins her revision process, Tracey no longer just tears it out of the printer and rushes to the author's circle, she tears it out and reads it. By the time the author's circle hears it, it is usually her fourth or firth draft! Her best piece differs from her first piece because of the effort she puts forth and the time she spent revising. One last observation Tracey wants to share is the she no longer feels her writing is always correct as it is. She is open more to suggestiongs. She has grown as a writer because she is much more willing to listens to people as critics.

Her first journal enteries were in the form of book marks. Tracey was given a small piece of paper and told she was to write her feelings and comments about the book. Her first enteries were frustrating because Tracey was use to picking up a book, reading it, and find another book. Now Tracey was expected to share her thoughts. What would she say?

After several books and keeping journals Tracey read the Wizard of Oz. It was the fantasy unit and Tracey didn't want to read a book with anyone in her class so she chose a book she knew no one would have thought of. Because the libraries didn't have a copy on hand of the Oz Tracey went out and bought the last copy in a local book store. Tracey is a Wizard of Oz movie freak! Every year Tracey would have her TV turned on to the Oz. As she began to read the book she noted the severe differences from the book and the movie. Tracey was very disappointed in the book!

As a reader the only frustrations Tracey has is stopping in the middle of the book to write down her feelings. Tracey had always been the type of person who reads and that's it. She'll use her own experiences to understand a character, or she'll put a face with a character but she still has a problem with writing down her feelings at the end of each chapter. Before the lab, Tracey would read anything with a neat cover or anything by V.C. Andrews. She is still an fan of V.C. Andrews but she no

Conference Time __10 — 19 — 89__

REFLECTIVE EVALUATION

Name _____
Date __10-19-89__

+ = Quite A Bit
√ = A Fair Amount
— = Not Very Much

	Reading		Writing		READING COMMENTS
	Self	Teacher	Self	Teacher	
INDEPENDENT LEARNING					
Draws On Personal Experience	+	+	√	√	Good — I now think that I have to get because after the first few chapters it
Takes Risks By Trying Out New Ideas	+	√	√	√	got good so I didn't want to stop anyway.
And/Or Process Strategies	—	√	√	√	Right now it depends on how
Sets Goals For Growth In Learning	—	√	+	√	determined I am w/ what I
Strives To Meet Goals		√			am doing.
Pushes Thinking So That Pieces Make Sense	+	+	+	+	
SOCIAL LEARNING					WRITING COMMENTS
Shares Thinking With Others	√	+	√	√	Goals — to get & clearly say
Asks Others Genuine Questions	√	+	√	+	I usually do some naturally after
Supports Peers	√	√	√	+	I've been told one.
Revises Thinking	√	√	+	+	It's easier for me to write my thoughts down instead of verbally speaking.

One thing that I'm doing better.

Acknowledging that there are skills I'm good at.

One thing I'm having trouble with.

telling others my ideas — in vocal communication!

√ can't express my self vocally as well as written

One thing that I would like to work on in the future.

more interesting ideas.

TM = Tin man
SC = Scarecrow

2~23

In the movie, Dorothy and
the Scarecrow (SC) never spent
the night in a cabin, yet in
the book SC + Dorothy stayed
in "Tin-Woodman's" cabin.

Through-out the book, Dorothy
has been worried about food.

In the movie, ~~Dorothy~~ Tin
man never told the story
about why he was a tin person
and also why he so desperately
dreams of ~~a~~ having a heart!

Meeting the cowardly lion
was slightly different. At least
I don't remember the lion
hitting SC +/or TM!

There was a scene where they
had to jump over a ravene, which
I don't remember from the movie
& I don't remember Dorothy ever
riding on lion's back!

Reading Journal Entry

Scene I   "In the Classroom"

By Tracey VosBurgh and Corey McVey

SETTING: The teacher is sitting on a chair in a typical kindergarten classroom with students sitting on the floor in a semi-circle around him/her. The children are dressed in school clothing.

Teacher: Boys and girls, what would you like to be when you grow up?

The children raise their hands but shout out their answers all at once.

(Jason N.   ) Child: Football player.
(Maggie   ) Child: Princess.
(Sarah   ) Child: Nurse.
(Mena   ) Child: Singer. (long dress and mink)
(John   ) Child: Fireman.
(Kevin G.   ) Child: Brave knight.
(Chris   ) Child: Dave Crocket.
(Timmy   ) Child: Astronaut.
(Kate   ) Child: Dancer. (flapper)
(Mike M.   ) Child: Cowboy.
(Katrina   ) Child: Actress. (hoop dress)
(Pat   ) Child: Magician.
(Michael C.) Child: Ghostbuster.
(Rachelle   ) Child: Mother.
(Rebecca   ) Child: President.

Teacher: SHHH! One at a time. Raise your hands children and wait to be called on.

The children settle down and the teacher calls on one student.

(Jason N.) Child: I want to be a football player.

Teacher: Kate?

(Kate) Child: I want to be a dancer.

Teacher: Mena?

(Mena) Child: I want to be a singer.

Teacher: John?

(John) Child: I want to be a fireman.

Teacher: Kevin?

First Page of Collaboratively Written
Children's Play.

It Was the Biggest Buck I Ever Saw

After a ten-hour car ride, the last thing any 16 year old girl, especially

me, would want to do is go to a bar. But, after a short series of "I don't

know's" and "doesn't matter to me's," ~~from my father, cousin Jerry, his~~ *my father, cousin Jerry,*

~~son Skyler, and myself~~ *his son Skyler & I*, we climbed into the old clunking "Bingo Mobile."

This Tank-turned-car should have been junked after World War I! It

rattled all the way down the dirt and gravel road to our destination.

Climbing out of the depths of the back seat (after what appeared to be a

never ending ride), we entered Jackson's Hole. Definitely not Minnesota's

finest!

This badly ~~lighted~~ *lite* bar had a ten-point Buck head ~~and~~ antlers ~~hanging~~ *with* *hung*

over the door ~~as a~~ welcome*d me*. The usual drunks were slumped over the

bar ~~vomiting last week's~~ *smelling like last week's* *gray* alcohol. Through the smoke and crowd we

fought our way to a table *in a far back corner*. Immediately I began to ~~chip away with~~ *use* my

short fingernails *to flake away* what appeared ~~to be hardened chocolate pudding that~~

~~some considerate customer left behind from who knows when!~~

Searching the room through the thick *haze of* cigarette smoke, I ~~could tell~~ *noticed*

nothing had changed ~~from~~ *since* my last vacation, ~~only~~ 3 months before. The

~~same~~ corners contained the same *large, spread out* cob-webs with most likely the same

flies stuck to them. An old-fashioned horse harness hung beside an ax, *gathering dust,*

on the wall directly behind us. The jukebox

First Page of First Draft of "The Biggest
Buck I Ever Saw"

longer judges a book by it's cover. In the beginning if she didn't understand something she was reading she would just reread it but now, if she still doesn't understand it, there is usually someone she can discuss it with.

Well, it's now time for Tracey to do her portfolio. The year is over but as a reader and writer Tracey knows she will carry what she has learned with her throughout the summer and her life.

ABBEY'S PORTFOLIO

Classroom Context

Four times a year Kathleen Visovatti asks second graders to go through their cumulative writing folders and rank order their writing from the most important to the least important. Prior to the ranking the class brainstorms reasons writers might consider one piece of writing more valuable than another: the amount of time and energy that went into the writing; the degree of personal importance; the way readers have responded to the writing; the representation of a genre never tried before, a new style of writing, or a different kind of structure; the illustration of experimentation; the inspiration by a special piece of literature; the capture of an experience in just the right way; and so on. Students label their writing as they decide what each piece represents about them as a writer. Writers talk about their decisions to each other and to the teacher. Reflection in reading occurs daily in Reading Journals* and Reading Discussion Groups.* Students also reflect at the end of each week about significant events. These reflections go into a class newspaper that is sent home each Friday.

Portfolio Development

Two major questions are considered:

1. What did you notice about yourself as a reader/writer?
2. Was there anything different about reading this book (or writing this piece) when you compare it to other things you've read (or written)?

At the end of the year portfolios were described to Abbey in this way:

Do your parents keep picture albums of you and your family that show important events? It's fun to see how much you change from one year to the next, isn't it? And maybe they also keep scrapbooks that have special things in them that you have made or done? Well, we're going to do something like that with your reading and writing. It's called a portfolio and it will have the special changes that have happened to you this year because you were reading and writing all year long.

Writing: Let's spread out all the writing you did this year so you can get familiar with it again. After you've read through it, would you start choosing the pieces that are really special to you—even if you didn't finish or publish them. Then we'll start looking at those and see what you notice about yourself as a writer—how your pieces are different, maybe how you tried out new things or discovered something wonderful about writing. I'm going to do the same thing and we can talk about mine, too.

Reading: First look at the list of all the books you read this year! You read mysteries and chapter books. You read about frogs and bears and rabbits and lots about families. Spend some time looking through your Reading Journal so you can remember all the wonderful books you read. If any of your journal entries seem *really* special in some way, pencil a little star in the corner of the page so we can talk about this later.

PORTFOLIO SUMMARY SHEET
Abbey Eusebio

Date	Item	Why I Chose It
September	*Writing* *The Sunny Day*	(Transcribed Interview) It was a long story and I like it and maybe it wasn't so interesting as some of my others. I though a lot about the ending and I read it over a lot and after I wrote it I thought I should not have written. That was the first time I thought I should change the ending. And I noticed I acted like an author at the end—I put a note to my readers.
November	*Mystery*	Because it was my first mystery *and* it is a chapter book—two things at once. I wrote my first chapter book at the beginning of school and that was just some straight stuff about going to the park. I wasn't sure I could do it but I tried to make all the things fit it and make them make sense.
December	"Cousins"	It's a chapter in my family book but I noticed that it's different than anything else I wrote—I remember that day really well and I wanted to write it just like that. Everybody in the class really liked it.

Date	Item	Why I Chose It
January	*Fortunately/ Unfortunately*	I wrote this after I read the book—at home on my computer. I really want to be a writer when I grow up.
February	Sign made for school hallway about littering and polluting.	Because it was my idea, I never did this kind of writing before and I thought if I would just write something people would think: "That's a point" and they might do it.
May	*Me and My Grandma*	This is really true—it's non-fiction and I was trying it out to see if people would really care about her the way I do—and they might think that I cared about her because I kept saying: "She's old but I love her." I thought more about readers really.
September	*Reading Happy Birthday Molly*	This book reminded me of myself and my friend Diana— we are a lot like the girls in the book.
January	*Prince Cinders*	I noticed that it was like Cinderella except it was boys. Now I sometimes think about how some books are like other books.
March	*Mystery of the Blue Rings*	I noticed that I started reading longer books and I could figure out words better. In the beginning when I read mysteries I thought it was hard, but after reading a lot, it got easier.
May	*Reading/Writing Research* *Horses Sally Stallion & Teddy Thoroughbred*	I learned how to do research. I read a lot of books on horses—fiction and non-fiction—and I talked about my research and I wrote my own book.

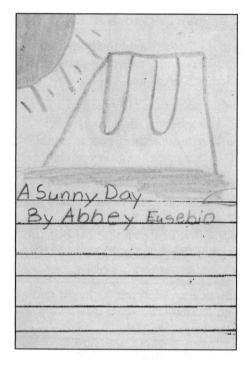

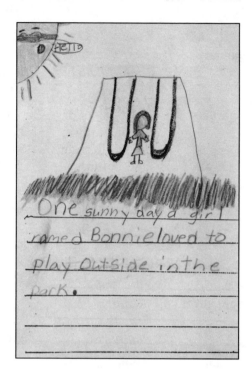

First three pages of *The Sunny Day*

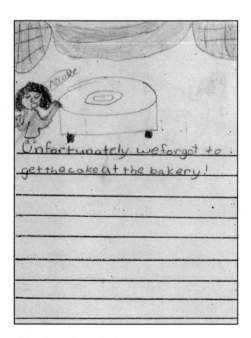

Title Page and First Two Pages of
Fortunately, Unfortunately

I dedicate this story to my grandma who I really love! MY mom's mom   is my grandma and I really love her!

Dedication Page from *Me and My Grandma*

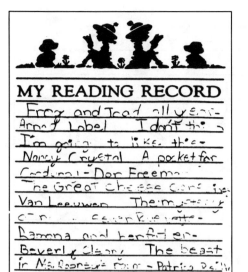

MY READING RECORD

Frog and Toad all year-
Arnold Lobel I don't thi...
I'm going to like the-
Nancy Crystal A pocket for
Cordina-Don Freeman
The Great cheese ...
Van Leeuwen The mystery
...
Ramona and her father-
Beverly Cleary The beast
in Ms. Rooney's room - Patricia Reilly
Giff   The case of the cool ...
Kid- Patricia Reilly ...

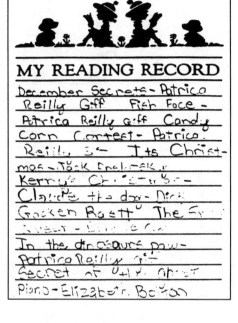

MY READING RECORD

December Secrets- Patricia
Reilly Giff Fish Face-
Patrica Reilly giff Candy
Corn Contest- Patrica
Reill... ... Its Christ-
mos - Jack Prelutsky
Kerry's Christmas -
Claude the dog- Dick
Gacken Roett The ...
... - ...
In the dinosaurs paw-
Patrica Reilly ...
Secret of ...
Piano- Elizabeth Bolton

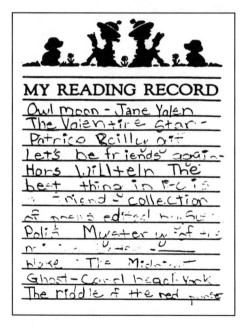

MY READING RECORD

Owl moon - Jane Yolen
The Valentine Star-
Patrica Reilly gif
Let's be friends again-
Hans Willteln The
best thing in F-c i s
... friend- collection
of poems edited by Sue
Polis Muster ... of the
... ...
... The Midnight
Ghost - Carol beach york
The riddle of the red ...

Three of Seven Pages of Abbey's Reading
Record for Second Grade

PRINCE CINDERS
By Babette Cole
It's Just like Cind-
crella. But it's funny
and good. The FARTY
MADE All kinds of
mustakes. And he wore
a bathing suit to the
ball. But he was too
big to go to the ball.
HE LOST HE'S Pants too.

Page from Abbey's Reader Response
Journal

Chapter 1

Horses live all over the world. Their first ancestor was 20 inches, it was called Eohippus. It lived 55 million year ago. They looked like racing dogs.

The next ancestor was Mesohippus, it lived 35 million years ago. Horses were around when dinosaurs were alive. At one time there were no horses in America. Spainards brought them to Mexico.

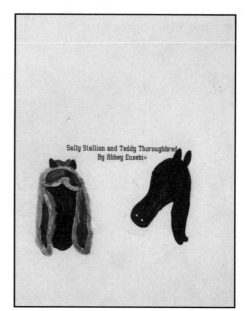

Sally Stallion and Teddy Thoroughbred
By Abbey Eusebio

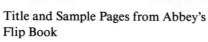

Title and Sample Pages from Abbey's
Flip Book

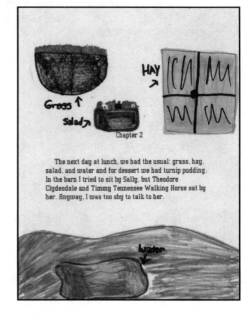

One day in Horse School, when the bell rang, I heard "Ekk! Ekk!" The door opened. There was a beautiful stallion. "Excuse me, but I'm sorry I'm late." Everyone stared at her. Everyone was whispering. "I'm Sally Stallion. I'm new here." I began to stare at her wherever she went.

The next day at lunch, we had the usual: grass, hay, salad, and water and for dessert we had turnip pudding. In the barn I tried to sit by Sally, but Theodore Clydesdale and Timmy Tennessee Walking Horse sat by her. Anyway, I was too shy to talk to her.

Title and Sample Pages from Abbey's Flip Book *(Continued)*

APPENDIX C

LITERATURE DISCUSSIONS

I. What kind of talk can you expect in a literature discussion?[1]
    Comprehension
    Reading processes
    Literary elements (even with young audiences)
    Illustrations
    Content beyond the book
    Personal stories
II. What is the role of the teacher?
    Make genuine reader contributions
    Validate different responses/interpretations
    Occasionally pose open-ended questions
III. How do you keep the discussion going? Open-ended responses/questions that work.[2]
    Open-ended questions/responses that teachers and students have used during literature discussions to help keep a rich, continuous dialogue going:

1. What do you want to talk about? *Wait and listen.*
2. What's one thing the author did that you wish he or she had *not* done?
3. Does this remind you of anything else you've ever read, seen, done?
4. What do you make of this story?
5. Who *will* start the discussion (compared to: Who *wants* to start)?
6. Who will share from your log? Response Journal?
7. Comment on something important to you (teacher).
8. Before the group meets, quietly ask one member if he or she will start the discussion.
9. At the end of one session agree on a topic for the next.
10. What is this story *really* about?
11. Ask one real question as a reader (teacher).
12. Outside of our group have you talked to anyone else about the book?
13. What do you think about the author's writing and language?
14. Did you know he or she (character) was going to die?
15. What was your strongest feeling when you read this part?
16. Do you feel changed by this book? How?
17. Who else should read this book and why?

[1] Hanssen, Evelyn. "Planning for Literature Circles." In *Talking about Books.* Kathy Gnagey Short and Kathryn Mitchell Pierce, eds. Portsmouth, N.H.: Heinemann, 1990.
[2] Watson, Dorothy. Whole Language Umbrella Conference. St. Louis, MO., 1990.

18. What's one thing you are going to remember?
19. Who did you get to know in the book today?

IV. How can teachers and students evaluate literature discussions?

Self-evaluation:

Ask students to use the last two or three minutes of each literature discussion to self-evaluate and to evaluate the group discussion:

> How did I contribute to the discussion today?
>
> How did the group do today? What should I (we) think about to make the discussion more effective next time?

Process observations:

Teachers and students need some tool to assist with their observations of literature discussions. The following grid is one possibility. See Short and Pierce, 1990, for others.

Book _____   Date _____

Group Names _____

Connections   Names

  Connects to personal experience   _____

    _____

    _____

  Connects to other texts   _____

    _____

    _____

  Connects ideas with others in group _____

    _____

    _____

Comprehension
  Asks for clarification   _____

    _____

    _____

  Helps others think through
  questions/confusions   _____

    _____

    _____

  Revises/extends interpretations   _____

    _____

    _____

    Uses text for confirmation/exploration   _____

                                                     _____

                                                     _____

Participation
    Initiates discussion   _____

                                                     _____

                                                     _____

    Considers differences in thinking   _____

                                                     _____

                                                     _____

APPENDIX D

REFLECTIONS AND LEARNING

When learners have a chance to reflect on their reading/writing/language experiences, they can assume an altered stance on their learning and see it in a new way. They also become aware of and learn to value the strategies they are developing.

Teacher Demonstrations of Reflection

1. Maintain a personal learning log outside of the classroom for a short time. Notice what you learn in some activity that is important to you. Include process and content information. Put the entries on an overhead and share them with your students.
2. Capture your literate thought by trying the "Last Night When I Was Reading . . ." strategy. During and after reading any self-selected material, write the ideas you thought about, the responses you made to the author and his or her decisions, the connections that you made, and so on. Use language like:

   - When I was reading, I wondered . . .
   - I went back to reread and thought about . . .
   - I remember the same thing happening to me . . .
   - I hated it (or loved it) when the author . . .
   - I spent a long time rewriting that section in my head . . .

   Share your thoughts first thing the next morning with your students. Continue for a week or so before encouraging students to bring in their own "Last Night When I Was Reading . . ." Not only does it encourage reflection and the sharing of literate thought, it sets up the expectation that students will read (or be read to) outside of school.

   Nancy Casserly has her fourth-graders write their musings on a large posterboard every morning. She has found that whatever is written becomes the beginning of the literature discussion that follows in her daily schedule.
3. Sit in on a Literature Discussion group (or any discussion) just to observe the kinds of exchanges and thinking going on in the group. Make notes as you listen and share your reflections immediately following the discussion.

REFLECTIVE QUESTIONS

1. What is one new thing that I learned (in school today, from the book that I just read, the discussion I just had, and so on)?
2. What did I understand about the work I did in class today? What didn't I understand?

3. What did I think about that I've never thought about before?
4. Did my thinking go off in a surprising direction when I was reading/writing? What did that look like?
5. What did I wonder about when I was reading/writing?
6. What connections did I make when I was reading/writing?
7. Did I run into any problems? How did I solve them?
8. How was this day different for me as a learner?
9. What do I know now that I didn't know before I got to school today? Before we read this book? Before we discussed this article?
10. How did I make this decision?
11. How did I decide that this piece needed revision? Was finished? Was worth publishing?

REFERENCES

Graves, Donald. Evaluation presentation given in Rosemont, IL, October, 1990.
Harste, Jerome, Kathy Short, and Carolyn Burke. *Creating Classrooms for Authors*. Portsmouth, NH: Heinemann, 1988.

Index